Music in American Life

*A list of books in the series appears
at the end of this book.*

Blue Rhythms

Blue Rhythms

═══ SIX LIVES ═══
IN RHYTHM AND BLUES

Chip Deffaa

University of Illinois Press
Urbana and Chicago

© 1996 by the Board of Trustees of the University of Illinois
Manufactured in the United States of America
C 5 4 3 2 1

Library of Congress Cataloging-in-Publication Data

Deffaa, Chip, 1951–
   Blue rhythms: six lives in rhythm and blues / Chip Deffaa.
      p.   cm. — (Music in American life)
   Includes bibliographical references (p.   ) and index.
   ISBN 0-252-02203-3
   1. Blues musicians—United States—Biography. 2. Rhythm and blues
music—History and criticism. I. Title. II. Series.
ML400.D4   1996
781.643'092'273—dc20
[B]   95-4414
                                                                        CIP
                                                                        MN

For Ferris Professor of Journalism Emeritus
Irving Dilliard
—one of the two best memories I have of Princeton

Contents

Acknowledgments

I am deeply grateful to Dan Morgenstern (whom I think of as my spiritual father among music historians), director of the Institute of Jazz Studies at Rutgers University, and to his associates, Ed Berger, Vincent Pelote, and Don Luck. They have always been ready and able to give whatever assistance was desired. I have drawn upon the institute's collection of recordings, clippings, books, oral histories, and photographs. My gratitude, too, to Howell Begle and Suzan Jenkins, executive directors of the Rhythm and Blues Foundation, and to Joan Myers and Jill Richmond of Myers Media, who were public relations representatives for the foundation while this book was in preparation, and to the staff of the Library of the Performing Arts at Lincoln Center.

Many thanks to the editors (present and past) at various publications for which, over the years, I've written articles about (or reviews of) musicians in this book: V. A. Musetto (I've never worked for a better editor, and he's an R&B fan, besides), Steve Cuozzo, Matt Diebel, and Sue Byrom of the New York *Post;* Peter Lee of *Living Blues;* Mike Joyce and W. Royal Stokes of *JazzTimes;* Bill Smith and John Norris of *Coda* (Canada); Dennis Matthews of *Crescendo* (England); and David Hajdu, Mary Kaye Schilling, Melissa Rawlins, Dulcy Israel, and David Browne of *Entertainment Weekly.*

I appreciate the insightful critiques provided by three people who read this book in manuscript form: Frank Reuter, who has been the invaluable first reader of all of my books; Nathan Pearson, whose comments on this book, as on *Voices of the Jazz Age,* strengthened the text; and especially Robert Pruter, who alerted me to pertinent articles and recordings, shared generously of his considerable expertise on rhythm and blues, and forced me to think more deeply about the material.

The following performers have in one way or another helped me better understand the subjects of this book: comedian Nipsey Russell, singers Carrie Smith, Dakota Staton, Nellie Lutcher, Hadda Brooks, and Linda Hopkins, master showman Cab Calloway, vibes king Lionel Hampton, dancers Harold Cromer and Tarik Winston, bandleader Panama Francis, saxist Bill Easeley, pianist Bross Townsend, bassist Carline Ray, guitarist Rodney Jones, and organist (and musical director for Ruth Brown) Bobby Forrester. I'm grateful to Jimmy McDonough, an exceptional music journalist (and now a budding record producer), whose writings initially piqued my interest in Jimmy Scott, and to Alan Eichler, who's helped in guiding the career revivals of Ruth Brown, LaVern Baker, Johnnie Ray, and other worthy veterans.

I appreciate the assistance in various ways provided by Jerry Wexler and Herb Abramson, who helped produce so many classic Atlantic R&B recordings; Ralph Jungheim, who's produced some more recent recordings of Ruth Brown, Jimmy Witherspoon, and others I've admired; Bob Porter, who's produced reissues of recordings of Ruth Brown, Jimmy Scott, and other greats; Kathleen Barlow of Right-Time Productions, manager of Floyd Dixon; Joe Fields of Muse and Savoy Records, whose artists have included Jimmy Witherspoon, Jimmy Scott, and Charles Brown; Didier Deutsch, who worked for Atlantic Records when this book was in preparation and now works for Columbia; Terri Hinte of Fantasy Records; Ron Levy of Rounder Records; Hugh Fordin of DRG Records; Marilyn Lipsius of BMG Records; Michael Bloom of GRP Records; Sandra Miller of Laserlight Digital; Phil Schaap of WKCR-FM; Marilynn LeVine of P.R. Partners; Don Lucoff of D.L. Media; Susan Pontillo of V.I.E.W. Video; Rebecca Reitz (and family) of the New York Swing Dance Society, who's aided in my appreciation of R&B as well as swing music; Abby Hoffer, booking agent for Jimmy Witherspoon; George Wein and Charles Bourgeois of Festival Productions; Gil Wiest, proprietor of Michael's Pub and his press representatives, Terry Lilly, David Gersten, and the late Henry Luhrman; John Condon, Mary Condon, and the late Dwain Tedford, proprietors of Condon's, and their press representative, Deborah Cohen; Phil Romeo and Lenny Triola of Tavern on the Green; Jack Kleinsinger, producer of New York's Highlights in Jazz concert series, and his press representative Harriet Wasser; and Helene Greece of Third Floor Media. I am also grateful to Joe Franklin, Lanny Jones, Leslie Johnson, Frank Driggs, Roy Hemming, Gary Giddins, C. A. Tripp, Rich Conaty, Andy Rowan, Russ Dantzler, Stanley Dance, Ed Castleberry, Marlys Mullen, Ian Whitcomb, George T. Simon, Phil

Leshin, Lloyd Rauch, Billy Vera, Howard Cruse, Delilah Jackson, Peter Grendysa, Eric Orseck, Bill Maguire, Wil Wheaton, Gene Santoro, Karen Kelly, Leslie Gourse, Virginia Wicks, Frank Jolliffe, Maybonne Mullen, Danny Scott, Peter Watrous, David Cassidy, David Hinckley, Enid Farber, Brian Gari, Will Friedwald, R. J. Capak, Berenice Doyle, Chris Burchfield, and Nancy Miller Elliot.

I owe thanks to the writers of *Living Blues* who've helped shape my thoughts about blues through the years (notably Tom Mazzolini). And, like so many music historians, I owe a debt to Joel Whitburn, whose painstaking compilations of the data from the various R&B and pop music charts published over the years in *Billboard* magazine I have relied on throughout this book. My thanks to Andreas Johnsen for many helpful deeds and some superb photos. Even if she weren't into this kind of music, Sister Lynda Barry would also rate thanks for the uplift she's provided at the right time (and thanks for that Chinese lunch, too).

I'm grateful for the help of my literary agent, Kevin McShane, and to ever-supportive Judith McCulloh, the executive editor at the University of Illinois Press, who for several years has gently but firmly kept this project moving in the right direction. I appreciate the assistance of proofreader Gary Westby-Gibson. I am particularly indebted to Mary Giles for her subtle, sensitive, and conscientious copyediting of this book. I'm lucky to have a copy editor who remembers the words to "Tweedlee Dee." And, of course, my deep thanks to my family, who've always been there for me, and to the subjects of this book, who've enriched my life.

Note on the
Rhythm and Blues Foundation

The Rhythm and Blues Foundation grew out of Ruth Brown's struggle to obtain royalties she felt were owed to her and other R&B recording artists. In 1988 attorney Howell Begle, with the moral support of sympathetic entertainers and politicians, succeeded in getting Atlantic Records (by then a part of Warner Communications) to provide $1.5 million in seed money for the foundation and to pledge $150,000 a year for three years toward the foundation's operating expenses. Since then, the foundation has also received a contribution of $150,000 from EMI, a major label that owns the masters of some now-defunct early R&B independent record companies, and additional corporate support.

One reason that Begle was able to deal more successfully with Atlantic than with other companies was that by the 1980s only Atlantic was still being run by one of its original founders, Ahmet Ertegun, who knew—and could empathize with—the R&B artists involved. It was harder for Begle to convince younger executives at other record companies—which may have acquired rights to R&B records from now-dead owners of former independent record companies that they had a responsibility to right all the wrongs others committed earlier. Begle believes that today's prosperous, mature recording industry should (and can afford to) set aside funds to help ensure that veteran performers who came up in harder times—and who may not have health insurance or pensions—can age with dignity. The foundation has sought to encourage record companies unwilling to contribute funds to reexamine their royalty payment practices. Some older R&B performers do not even collect Social Security benefits, having been paid in cash for their work on the road.

From Begle's viewpoint, there were two problems concerning the payments of royalties to R&B artists. First, companies often charged so many expenses to their artists' accounts that the companies could deny being able to recoup all that they had invested in the artists and thus were relieved of any obligation to pay royalties. Companies in many cases were able to—and, in some cases, are still able to—reissue recordings (presumably making money for themselves) without their artists reaping any financial benefits. Second, the contracts often promised such small royalties (none in some cases) that potential financial rewards for artists were slight even if expenses were not charged to them unfairly.

The following information is drawn primarily from Howell Begle's "I Smell a Rat: Royalty Practices of Classic R&B Recording Companies" in the *Rhythm and Blues Foundation News* (October 1994), as well as from remarks by Brown and Begle (both of whom, as of 1995, continue to serve as trustees of the foundation) and Suzan Jenkins, executive director of the foundation.

Begle's first success at obtaining hoped-for industrywide reform occurred in May 1988, when Atlantic agreed to forgive "unrecouped balances," retroactively to 1970, for thirty-five pioneering R&B artists. In 1988 and 1989, those artists (or their estates) received payments for royalties on all sales of their recordings since 1970. Those payments, of course, were based on royalty rates specified in the original contracts, which are below current industry norms. Since 1988 discussions have been held with Atlantic (now a part of Time/Warner) about both applying the forgiveness of "unrecouped balances" to other artists beyond the original thirty-five and possibly raising the royalty rates so that artists may receive a greater share of the profits if their recordings continue to be reissued.

Other companies have attempted to address the problem in different ways. In 1989 MCA, which had acquired the Chess and Checker record labels in 1985, agreed to increase royalty rates to 10 percent (retroactively to 1985) for all Chess and Checker artists whose recordings had been reissued by MCA. The company has not yet instituted comparable reforms relating to R&B recordings they control originally released by labels other than Chess or Checker.

In April 1992 Capitol/EMI forgave unrecouped balances for a great number of recording artists (of various musical genres, not just R&B) who had recorded for them or for labels (such as Imperial, Aladdin, Modern, and Flair) that Capitol/EMI had acquired. In addition, Capitol/EMI raised royalty rates for reissues to 10 percent of retail list price.

In 1994 Denon/The Nippon Columbia Company, which owns re-cordings originally released on the Savoy, Royal Roost, and National labels, began considering reforms, examining the contracts of artists one at a time. For example, the company agreed to pay Little Jimmy Scott a royalty of 10 percent of retail sales for all Denon reissues of his Savoy recordings, and he is finally sharing fairly in the profits.

In February 1995 Sony instituted a royalty reform program affect-ing sixty artists. Sony has agreed to forgive all unrecouped balances. In addition, artists who had previously been receiving royalties of less than 10 percent (or no royalties at all) were raised to royalty rates of 10 percent. That same month, Rhino Records agreed to comparable royalty terms for its reissues.

Polygram, which controls such labels as Motown, Phillips, and Mercury, has not yet instituted any reform. In 1989-90, its manage-ment considered forgiving unrecouped balances for many artists but decided not to do so. (At least one artist has been able to get her unrecouped balance eliminated through litigation, however; she now receives royalties for reissues of her 1960s hits at the miserly rate spec-ified in her original contract: 2 percent of retail list price.)

Fantasy has not yet undertaken any royalty reforms, nor have the current owners of assorted other catalogs, including King, Federal, Deluxe, and Vee-Jay. Recordings made for those labels by such prom-inent R&B artists as Roy Brown, Wynonie Harris, Jimmy Reed, Jerry Butler, and the Five Royales continue to be reissued without those artists (or their estates) receiving royalties. Clearly, more work remains to be done.

Interest from the Rhythm and Blues Foundation's endowment is used to pay for the Pioneer Awards (as the Career Achievement Awards have been renamed) and to provide aid to needy artists, where possible, in cases of crises via the Doc Pomus Emergency As-sistance Program. Through award programs and special grants the foundation provides more than $200,000 annually to R&B artists. It has also, from time to time, presented rhythm and blues semi-nars and concerts. Based in the Smithsonian Institution's National Museum of American History, the foundation is working jointly with the museum's Division of Musical History, Division of Com-munity Life, the Archives Center, and the Department of Public Pro-grams to develop the History of Rhythm and Blues Collection. It also hopes to be able to reissue classic rhythm and blues recordings from assorted labels and to obtain funding so oral histories of rhythm and blues pioneers can be collected, made available for re-searchers, and perhaps published.

The tremendous growth of the Rhythm and Blues Foundation in the last few years has not only been gratifying for Ruth Brown, but also a source of some concern. She's seen a music that appeared all but forgotten by the seventies now, happily, being celebrated in lavish annual awards galas that draw record business bigwigs and young, contemporary pop artists, as well as veterans. She hopes, she told me in 1994, that all the money spent on such gala affairs and on running the foundation throughout the year is being spent prudently. She knows well that there are aging rhythm and blues performers who have serious, pressing financial needs. Jenkins says that, as of June 1995, the foundation has given away approximately a million and a quarter dollars through its awards and emergency assistance programs. She continues to urge record companies to "do the right thing." These R&B veterans, she says, are "our grandparents."

Those who would like to learn more about, or make contributions to, the Rhythm and Blues Foundation may contact the foundation at Fourteenth and Constitution Avenue N.W., Room 4603, Washington, DC 20560.

Blue Rhythms

Introduction

November 10, 1989. I'm sitting in the Smithsonian Institution's Carmichael Auditorium, but today it feels more like a church. The recently established Rhythm and Blues Foundation is presenting its first annual Career Achievement Awards. Those being honored are Ruth Brown, Charles Brown, Little Jimmy Scott, LaVern Baker, the Clovers, Etta James, Percy Sledge, and Mary Wells. Most of the artists either are present or represented by family members. Other veteran rhythm and blues stars, assorted friends, fans, and well-wishers pack the auditorium.

Accepting her award, Ruth Brown, the "Queen of Rhythm and Blues," struggles to hold back tears. "Today is really, really special," she tells us. "And I made a very special effort to try to look my best." Laughter, applause, and calls of "all right" and "you succeeded" interrupt her remarks; it's a very warm audience. She continues, "But you are about to get a look at the real Ruth Brown—because my eyelashes are getting ready to fall off." There's much laughter and applause. "Just to be in this room, just to look in back of me on this stage at these faces, brings memories that I will never be able to explain to you. Charles Brown—he nearly went to jail in Mississippi for me, because they wouldn't let me use the restaurant. They wanted to take us to jail. Remember that, Charles?"

Charles Brown affirms, "That's right."

From the audience comes more applause and a call of, "Yes indeed, that's the South."

"How many buses we rode together," Ruth Brown recalls. "How many back doors did we go through together?"

A man's voice responds, "A lot of them, baby." A woman in the audience calls out, "No other way."

Brown takes time to comment in turn on each of the principals who are present, from singer Little Jimmy Scott ("I was sixteen years old when I first met this man in Virginia") to attorney Howell Begle, who has spearheaded the drive to create the Rhythm and Blues Foundation and whose mother had taken him to see Brown perform when he was a boy during the mid-fifties ("I'm glad his mama had good taste"). The foundation, housed at the Smithsonian's National Museum of American History, aims to honor rhythm and blues pioneers, document and preserve their contributions, and provide financial assistance to needy but deserving artists. Brown discusses the importance of the foundation, finally reflecting in wonder, "To stand here on the stage of the Smithsonian, realizing that something of quality has come to a *place* of quality." Her next words are lost in applause.

Each individual being honored receives not just a plaque from the foundation, but also a check for $15,000. (A group receiving the annual award divides one payment of $20,000.) The funds are intended to help make up for the exploitation of performers—including underpayment or nonpayment of royalties—that so frequently marked the field of rhythm and blues. Brown adds, only half-kidding, "This check means quite a bit for me. I'm going to pay my rent. Maybe I don't have to answer the telephone with a strange voice and say, 'She went to Europe.' Whatever is done with this little award, that is left entirely to the artist—and I think that's what's so very wonderful about this. It is a key to re-open the door to your dignity."

"That's right," calls out a woman in audience. And in the applause that follows you sense an appreciation for Brown not just as a longtime performer of great impact, but as a survivor who has endured injustices and prevailed.

Others being honored reinforce Brown's remarks. Charles Brown uses his words sparingly, "We went through a lot of things together. We went through the one-nighters when things were kind of tough down south." With grace, he recalls periods when the gigs he got weren't paying enough for him to cover the bills: "You have to do something to make a living. I can say that I had the chance to wash some movie stars' windows." If you've followed rhythm and blues at all, you know that, like Ruth Brown, Charles Brown (no relation) has been a giant in the field. As Dick Shurman and Jim O'Neal once noted in *Living Blues*, "From the 1946 success of 'Driftin' Blues' until after B. B. King was established as a star, almost every blues vocalist in Texas and California was a Charles Brown man."[1] (Some early Ray Charles records, for example, reveal an intentional imitation of Charles Brown's style.) But Brown, at sixty-seven, has no "star ego" problems. He comments simply, honestly, and gratefully, "It's such a pleasure to be able to have good health and still perform."

Little Jimmy Scott chooses the occasion to recall some good memories of the old days. "There was a time, when I came into the business," he begins, when performers didn't need agents or record companies to promote them "because we had a friendship—with sincerity—in the business." Yes, R&B performers may have faced difficulties due to racial prejudice during the forties and fifties, but they supported each other in a way he suspects many of their successors now do not. And despite whatever obstacles they encountered, he remembers, "We grinded our way through, seeking out the advantages."

Looking around the room, I can see black entertainers of varied ages, including Rufus and Carla Thomas, Isaac Hayes, Lou Rawls, and Sam Moore (from the sixties' soul duo Sam and Dave), as well as one-time members of fifties' doowop groups like the Swallows. Never before have I been in an audience with such a concentration of rhythm and blues artists. Among younger performers present, who attend out of respect for the contributions of these pioneers, I note in particular Bonnie Raitt, who, as a champion of R&B music, has periodically had veterans tour with her, helping expose them to her younger fans. Soon she is joining the honorees and some of the other singers in the room on a wailing, impromptu performance of the 1969 Sam and Dave hit "Soul Man." I savor the contrasting sounds and styles, as one voice after another picks up the refrain. Charles Brown intones the words in a dignified baritone. Scott (after protesting to no avail that he doesn't know the song, it's from a later era) crouches low, turns shyly away from the audience, and yields up a high-pitched, oddly affecting wail: "I'm *soul* man."

Ruth Brown hugs me before leaving. She must hurry back to New York, where she's appearing on Broadway in *Black and Blue*. I have to get back myself, to my usual routine as a critic for the New York *Post* and various magazines. During the train ride north, it's clear to me that I'd like to do a book of profiles of rhythm and blues performers. I realize I may not be able to write it promptly—I'm currently in the midst of writing a book on jazz—but I know I'll do it, I feel I've seen the nucleus of the book onstage that afternoon. My most difficult task will be limiting the book to a select group of performers. Many are worthy of inclusion, but I'd rather cover a representative handful of performers in some depth than try to provide superficial coverage of a larger number.

The dynamic Ruth Brown, I knew, would have to be in this book. No other woman now living had more R&B hits on the *Billboard* charts during the fifties and early sixties than Brown. She's also one of my favorite entertainers—an extremely giving performer who has

a rare gift for reaching an audience and involving them in her performances. (She's more vivid live than on most of her records; an
extra energy seems to come into play.) I've been very happy for her,
witnessing her tremendous comeback in recent years—particularly
since opening in *Black and Blue* in January 1989. I've interviewed her
before and like the idea of talking further with her about her life.

If I wanted to write about Ruth Brown, Chicago-born LaVern Baker would be a logical inclusion, too, because they were often compared to one another during the fifties. Brown was, I felt, the stronger talent, but Baker, who broke through a bit later than Brown and
supplanted her on the R&B charts, made some truly thrilling sides;
"Soul on Fire," for example, was unforgettable. She had also shown
further range with an album saluting Bessie Smith; a rough-and-ready
version of "Gimme a Pigfoot" stuck in my memory. I had also liked
her "See See Rider" when I was a boy and didn't care for many of
the Top 40 sides I heard on the radio. Baker became a rock 'n' roll
star. She was too good for some of the slight, commercial material
she was asked to record, but she brought to whatever she recorded a
gutsy, spicy, sly energy. She was for real, even if some of the songs
she was given were not—which is why her old recordings are generally more pleasureable to listen to than those of more plastic pop singers who sang the same type of material during the fifties. For the past
twenty or so years Baker had lived in the Philippines, not even returning to the United States to receive her Rhythm and Blues Foundation award. I wondered whether I'd have to journey to the Philippines to seek her out, but, to my pleasant surprise, fate intervened,
returning her before long to the United States.

Little Jimmy Scott seemed another natural for the book. His importance to rhythm and blues should be obvious from the fact that
he was in the very first group of artists selected to receive the Rhythm
and Blues Foundation's Career Achievement Award (since renamed
the Pioneer Award). Those awards are selected by a committee composed of R&B performers, music critics, and other authorities in the
field. Scott's style is so unique, though, that some people have had
trouble pigeonholing him. On my desk, there's a flyer announcing a
club appearance by Scott, with a quote from the *New York Times* calling him "one of the most strikingly original singers in jazz." Is he a
jazz singer? An R&B singer? Disc jockey and record producer Joel Dorn
says Scott is neither, but rather "a category unto himself." No matter. I love truly original talents in any field—people unafraid to express their individuality fully, whether in dress, speech, or performance. Scott's singing style is so radically different and can be so

emotionally challenging as to almost preclude his ever winning and sustaining mass popularity. Every time he performs, he seems to be on a tightrope, blindfolded and without a net. You don't know where he's going to take a song. I've sometimes seen him head off in strange tangents and lose virtually everyone in the audience—an uncomfortable experience. At other times I've seen him pushing listeners' emotional buttons completely—as on a night when he upstaged even as masterly, if more conventional, a singer as Tony Bennett.

Charles Brown also seemed a wise choice. He doesn't have to do any more than ease into an original of his like "Driftin' Blues" or "Please Come Home for Christmas" to get to me. As the veteran R&B record producer Jerry Wexler said of him a few years back, "Master Charles—how I dearly love him—is still playing and singing his heart out today around L.A. and in occasional forays into places like Tramps in the Apple. He is the ineffable master of the style he invented, but he's been done in by fashion, slow horses, backbiters and syndicators, and rock 'n' roll in general."[2] Brown is not a dynamic performer like Ruth Brown or LaVern Baker; he's temperamentally more subdued but always capable of reaching listeners with his polished, after-hours "club blues." Judging from recordings, he is also a more affecting singer now than he was in early years, when he sometimes seemed overly mannered. Now he sings in a simpler, more natural style that allows the audience to feel the gentleness and strength of his spirit. I particularly like it when he dismisses his sidemen and lets us hear in stark relief his voice and piano on something like "Nobody Knows the Trouble I've Seen."

Floyd Dixon, like Charles Brown, his long-time friend and early inspiration, is considered a representative of a relaxed "West Coast style" of R&B. Dixon and Brown, both Texans, were transplanted to southern California. I wanted to include both men as reminders of the thriving R&B scene that flourished in Los Angeles's black community. Dixon has often done numbers in a low-key manner reminiscent of Charles Brown, but he's also shone on more ebullient numbers never associated with Brown, such as his original "Hey Bartender," which the Blues Brothers revived a generation later, or Jerry Leiber and Mike Stoller's "Too Much Jelly Roll." A performer of considerable warmth and heart, Dixon can move unexpectedly from a happy jump-blues—he's one of the best living practitoners of that idiom—to something revealing and tinged with pathos like "Hard Living Alone." I knew that if I wanted to interview Dixon I'd have to make a trip to the West Coast; although he's still active as a performer he rarely comes east.

Arkansas-born Jimmy Witherspoon was a "must-include," too, not just because his 1949 recording of "Ain't Nobody's Business" stayed on the *Billboard* R&B charts for a whopping thirty-four weeks—fully thirty-four *years* would pass before another record would enjoy as long a run on the R&B charts—but because, in a club, Witherspoon can be as moving as any singer I've heard. Many of his records don't do him justice. It's not technique that marks his live performances as special, for many singers have far better voices; it's emotional honesty, which he offers in highly distilled form. Witherspoon can sing "Nobody Knows You When You're Down and Out" with such conviction that from the very first line—"Once I lived the life of a millionaire"—you don't feel that he's singing lyrics written decades earlier. It's as if someone you know intimately is sharing something personal. Witherspoon reaches way back in his repertoire, carrying on a long blues tradition; I don't see younger stars carrying on that legacy.

Once I knew which performers I wanted to include in the book, I got to work. Eleven days after the awards presentation in Washington, I was conducting my first interview with Little Jimmy Scott. Other interviews took place, as opportunities permitted, over the next several years. (As with my previous books, I tape-recorded the interviews and transcribed them myself.) The six profiles that make up this book are all written in the present tense, reflecting conditions at the time I wrote each one. In some instances, to form a continuous narrative, I've woven together recollections that a subject may have shared during the course of two or more interviews. Ruth Brown's profile is drawn from five interviews between 1988 and 1990 (specific dates are indicated in the notes); Little Jimmy Scott's from three interviews in 1989; Charles Brown's from two interviews in 1990 and 1991; Floyd Dixon's from an interview in 1991; LaVern Baker's from two interviews in 1990; and Jimmy Witherspoon's from an interview in 1989. I have also had opportunities to have followup chats with the artists and their representatives. In all instances, I've augmented what I have learned from the interviews—and from watching performances by the artists over the years—with findings from additional research. Although most of the performers have not received much attention in books, they have all been covered in newspaper and magazine articles, which I have consulted. I've also benefited from the generously offered comments of other performers and authorities in the field.

Because this is a collection of profiles, readers should not expect to find a narrative running throughout this book. The careers of the performers, all of whom came up shortly after World War II, have at times connected and overlapped, however. Collectively, they have something to tell us not just about themselves, but about the forties' and fifties' rhythm and blues scene generally. The six performers represent a much larger group of artists.

All of the subjects were in their sixties when I spoke with them, an age when people in most careers are thinking of retirement. However, I found that all six were not only eager to keep on working but also generally believed—and with good reason—that their careers were moving forward. In recent years they had all found more public interest in their work and in rhythm and blues generally than they found throughout much of the sixties, seventies, and eighties.

* * *

Rhythm and blues—I'm talking about popular music that arose in black communities after the swing era and before the arrival of the Beatles, roughly between 1945 and 1960—hasn't received its due. It's far easier to find books about music that came before it or emerged after it. George T. Simon, Stanley Dance, and others (myself included) have written assorted books dealing with musicians of the swing era, roughly from 1935 to 1945. Paul Oliver, Samuel Charters, and Albert Murray have written superbly about the contributions of vintage bluesmen. Peter Guralnick and Robert Pruter, among others, have made valuable contributions to the documentation of soul music. Any number of writers have retold the history of rock 'n' roll. *Rock of Ages* by Ed Ward, Geoffrey Stokes, and Ken Tucker is a standout; the first one-fifth or so of the book also contains good coverage of R&B.

The best book thus far about rhythm and blues, Arnold Shaw's *Honkers and Shouters* (1978), is also very nearly the only comprehensive book that's been written about the topic. Shaw provides a broad overview, offering sketches and recollections not only of many singers, including a few profiled in this book, but also of instrumentalists, record producers and promoters, disc jockeys, and others. In seeking to provide as big a picture as possible, he discusses everyone from vaudevillian Mamie Smith (whose "Crazy Blues" was a hit in 1920) to the "King of Rock 'n' Roll," Elvis Presley.

In this book, I've concerned myself more with depth than breadth. In all six profiles I've aimed to tell the performers' stories more thoroughly than they've been told elsewhere, for I believe a writer's obligation is to bring some new information to light, not merely rehash what's been in other books.

The term *rhythm and blues* was popularized during the late forties by the music trade publication *Billboard*. It replaced the term *race music,* which had fallen out of favor, and referred to music of considerable stylistic variety being created by black artists and being marketed primarily—at least initially—to black listeners. It was popular music with a black sensibility that had roots in blues and church music. Whether they were black or white themselves, disc jockeys who began using "rhythm and blues" had shows clearly aimed at black listeners. For example, Birmingham's Ed Castleberry and Los Angeles's Hunter Hancock (who promised KFVD listeners in the late forties "the latest and greatest Negro performers and entertainers") found that with each passing year more and more whites were tuning in and discovering the music. Emotionally R&B was more potent than the over-refined pop being played on so many stations across the dial.

American society was more divided along racial lines during the late forties than it is now. Shortly after World War II, a number of small, independent record companies sprang up and specialized in recording black artists for sales in black communities. Such companies had little hope of having their records played on most mainstream pop radio stations, whose orientations were largely white. Instead, they hoped to place their records in black homes and in jukeboxes played primarily in black ghettos. But with each passing year, more whites—particularly younger whites—seemed to be discovering their music and buying their records. They were inadvertently laying the groundwork for the emergence of rock 'n' roll, and more mainstream radio stations were—at least occasionally—playing their records.

Those independent record companies thought that R&B had achieved tremendous radio penetration by 1953, and it had made great progress since the late forties, when a *Billboard* survey had indicated that only 25 percent of radio stations programmed R&B, on average just two and a half hours a week. By contrast, pop programming filled thirty-one hours a week, country music programming eleven and a half hours a week, and news, sports, and dramas divided the rest of the time. In the early fifties, an R&B performer could become a success in the field—known to many or most black Americans—and still remain unknown to most whites. If R&B performers of the late forties and early fifties toured in package shows, all artists on the bill would customarily be black, as would most of their audiences.

Elements from various traditions— commercial pop music, blues, swingin' jazz, boogie-woogie, gospel—went into R&B. The American music scene was in a state of flux at the end of World War II. Big bands, which had held a spell over the public for a decade, were declining in popularity. In 1946 eight "name" big band leaders announced that they were throwing in the towel. And if bookers were able to sell as many tickets to a dance or a theater date with Louis Jordan's five musicians as with Count Basie's sixteen—and such was the case in the late forties—they'd go with the smaller group. Modern jazz, meanwhile, was busily exploring new directions. The bebop innovators who most impressed critics, other musicians, and hardcore jazz devotees were producing sounds that often weren't easy for average listeners to follow, much less dance to, and jazz was becoming more esoteric.

Singers and instrumentalists who were top draws on the R&B circuit—black theaters, clubs, and dancehalls (even warehouses that could be used, at times, for dances)—had to produce music that was more accessible to average listeners than modern jazz. R&B bands, sometimes made up of big band alumni, were apt to be small—a couple of gutsy, bluesy saxes favoring the extroverted "honking" approach popularized by Illinois Jacquet, maybe a trumpet or two, and a rhythm section. Singers expressed themselves through pop songs and blues songs, both old and new. The independent but undercapitalized R&B-oriented record labels of the late forties and early fifties didn't always last long, and other companies weren't always interested in acquiring their libraries when they folded. Some small labels changed hands repeatedly. All of which helps explain why reissues of many fine early R&B sides are now hard to come by, making the music less familiar to listeners than the repeatedly reissued recordings, of all different styles, produced by major record companies. Under these very difficult conditions, some strong talents emerged on the R&B circuit.

In order to set the stories told in this book in a historical context, it's worth keeping in mind the evolving status of race relations in this country during the forties and fifties. The six performers started singing professionally during, or shortly after, World War II, when the American armed forces were still segregated. (By the Korean War they would be integrated.) Blacks in the South were still routinely denied the right to vote.

The civil rights movement began to gain a little momentum after World War II. When black soldiers returned home, they felt entitled to fair treatment. When the Democratic Party put a pioneering civil rights plank into its platform in 1948, the resultant controversy caused some southern Democrats to bolt the party. In 1954 the Supreme Court ruled that school segregation was unconstitutional; the integration of school systems in subsequent years spurred calls for integration in other areas. In 1956 Martin Luther King was organizing boycotts of city buses in Montgomery, Alabama, in order to protest the practice of seating blacks at the back of the vehicles. In 1957 President Dwight D. Eisenhower ordered federal troops to enforce the desegregation of Central High School in Little Rock, Arkansas. In 1960 sit-ins to protest segregated southern restaurants made news. In 1962 James Meredith, defying taunts of racist crowds, became the first black student to enroll at the University of Mississippi.

As in American society generally, racial barriers were falling in the music business, too. The performers in this book, who initially toured in all-black package shows that played to largely black audiences, saw more and more white Americans picking up on their music, and in some cases they helped to pioneer racially integrated touring package shows.

When *Billboard,* in the late forties and fifties, ran separate charts for R&B and pop, it did so for a good reason. There were clearly— and to a greater degree than now exists—two audiences in America. Initially, *Billboard* kept track of which records were most popular in the black marketplace as indicated on R&B charts and in the white marketplace on pop charts. During the forties and early fifties, only rarely did a hit on the R&B charts cross over and also show up as a hit on the pop charts. Black performers of the late forties knew how hard it was, and how rare it was, for any of them to break through to great commercial success. As late as 1955, eighteen out of twenty of the year's most commercially successful recording artists, based on the *Billboard* pop charts, were white. No blacks were among the top three.

Now, of course, it's not unusual for black artists to be very well represented on the pop charts in any given year and also the most commercially successful recording artists overall. For example, two of the top three commercially most successful recording artists during 1989 happened to be black. As the fifties wore on, according to the *Billboard* charts, black artists began to cross over more readily. By the end of the decade, far more were achieving some pop success than had done so at the start of the decade. By 1963 black artists were breaking through with great regularity on the pop charts as well as the R&B charts, so much so that some people thought the charts were growing redundant and *Billboard* suspended its R&B charts for a while.

In the profiles that follow, references to how high a record rose in the charts, unless otherwise specified, refer to its highest position in

Billboard R&B charts, which continued without interruption—but with various names—from the forties into the sixties. For simplicity's sake, I have used the term *R&B charts,* even though at a given time *Billboard* may have actually used any of a number of variant headings: "Best Selling Retail Race Records," "Best Selling Retail Rhythm & Blues Records," "R&B Best Sellers in Stores," "Hot R&B Sides," "Hot R&B Singles," and so on. In some periods *Billboard* simply listed which R&B records were most popular overall; in other periods *Billboard* ran separate charts indicating which records were getting the most play in jukeboxes, which were getting the most play on radio, and which were selling best in stores. To avoid minutiae, I've indicated the maximum height a record may have attained in any of *Billboard's* R&B charts (whether dealing with retail sales, jukebox, or radio play). Readers seeking more detailed and specific chart information should consult Joel Whitburn's standard reference works *Top R&B Singles: 1942–1988* and *Top Pop Singles: 1955–1986,* which I've also relied upon.

* * *

The profiles that follow are of varying lengths. It should not be inferred that the length of a profile correlates with the importance of the artist; some profiles may be longer partly because the artist had more to say or perhaps has a better memory. Ruth Brown's recall is particularly sharp. LaVern Baker warned me she was apt to be a bit fuzzy about details, which proved to be the case.

My jazz-buff friends have inquired why, after having written five books profiling jazz artists and cowritten one about a pop artist, I was writing about rhythm and blues artists. For me, jazz, blues, and rhythm and blues are all connected. (At one time or another, most of the R&B performers in this book have been invited to appear at jazz as well as blues festivals.) I get pleasure from both genres. A good artist is simply a good artist, and all of these artists have made valuable contributions.

* * *

In all but one case, the performers I've chosen to write about are still going strong as this book goes to press, doing pretty much what they were doing when we last spoke. But some significant changes have occurred in their lives between the time I finished doing the primary interviews and completed writing text.

Since her interviews with me, LaVern Baker has, unfortunately, been forced to restrict her activities because of assorted health problems, including a stroke (from which she has essentially recovered), and the amputation of both legs below the knees. During her comeback following her return to the United States in 1990, she recorded two impressive CDs and gave a number of acclaimed performances in the United States and Europe. A show-stealing Chicago Blues Festival appearance in the summer of 1992 made it clear she was still capable of greatness. She was inducted into the Rock 'n' Roll Hall of Fame and was looking forward to a heavy touring and recording schedule when her health problems began snowballing in 1993. After a hiatus of more than two years, she resumed public performances with a successful September 1995 engagement at the Hollywood Roosevelt Cinegrill—performing from a wheelchair.

Her spirit remains remarkably resilient. In a voice as wonderfully vibrant and sensual as ever, she vowed to me in early 1995 that she would work clubs and concert halls again. She soon reentered the recording studios to do a song for a proposed album. I hope that she may be able to resume all the activities she desires. She is, along with Brown, a master of classic R&B.

Since I finished writing my profile of Little Jimmy Scott, his career has blossomed in a way that has happily surprised him. Scott has played the prestigious Hollywood Roosevelt Cinegrill, where he was seen by David Lynch, who subsequently had Scott make an appearance on his television series "Twin Peaks" (portraying a singing ghost). Scott has sung on the soundtracks of the films *Rage in Harlem* and *Street of Dreams*. He's also set up a little office in Newark, where he's helping coach and manage young artists—a project dear to his heart. And, after years of neglect from record companies, he has been signed to a recording contract, with options for five albums, by a major label, Sire Records, a part of Warner Brothers. Two albums are out, bringing him to the attention of a new generation of fans.

He received the record contract through an odd twist of fate. For years, songwriter Doc Pomus ("This Magic Moment," "Save the Last Dance for Me," etc.)—a long-time Scott admirer—had tried without success to stir interest in him and wrote an open letter to the industry in *Billboard*. Pomus even requested that Scott sing at his funeral. Scott did so—giving a peak performance of "Someone to Watch Over Me," accompanied by Dr. John on organ, before an audience that included countless record company executives. Sire Records president Seymour Stein signed Scott as a result of what he heard at the funeral.

Scott has also done some touring and appeared on television, mostly singing backup, with the androgynous rock star Lou Reed. Alec Baldwin asked Scott to sing at his wedding to Kim Basinger (Scott sang "All of Me"). And when Scott played the tony Tavern on the Green—now his base in Manhattan—in February 1994, Madonna came out to see him two nights in a row. She told photographer Andreas Johnsen that Scott was the only singer who'd ever really made her cry.

Although his voice is no longer as dependable an instrument as it once was—his pitch control is much less certain—he's enjoying the greatest commercial success of his career—success that has prompted the issuing of recordings from the early seventies and even before, capturing his voice at its peak, that would otherwise have remained in the vaults.

The ever-laid-back Charles Brown, who in the early eighties couldn't find a company interested in recording him, now records prolifically. He is accepted as a much-loved, masterly elder statesman of his field. As *Living Blues*'s John Anthony Brisbane has observed, "Wifeless and childless in old age and exceedingly sweet in spirit, Charles Brown is perhaps an unlikely father figure. But . . . Brown is all a father figure should be: patient, kind, wise, and self-critical."[3] In the 1991 *Down Beat* critics' poll, his Grammy-nominated album *All My Life* was voted the best blues album of the year.

Floyd Dixon (performing mostly on the West Coast) and Jimmy Witherspoon (still touring nationally, his voice markedly better some nights than others) received the Rhythm and Blues Foundation's Pioneer Awards in 1993, which means that all of the artists discussed in this book have been so honored. Dixon keeps the jump-blues tradition vibrantly alive. His signing with Alligator Records should raise his visibility considerably, and he hopes to do more touring, nationally and internationally. Witherspoon's major New York appearances in 1994 included a Carnegie Hall concert in which his voice was in painfully bad shape and a week-long, year-end booking at Fat Tuesday's in which he sounded strong and self-assured.

Since I profiled Ruth Brown, she has been inducted into the Rock 'n' Roll Hall of Fame and has performed at major jazz festivals, including the JVC Festival in New York. She has had knee-joint replacement surgery on both knees, made a full recovery from a mild heart attack, and continues to maintain a heavy touring schedule. She enjoys recognition by fellow singers as an outstanding performer. At the 1994 Society of Singers awards presentation to Peggy Lee, for example, Brown was chosen to sing "Fever" in tribute to Lee. Brown's renewed success enabled her to move from her Harlem apartment to Hollywood Hills, where her splendid new home was totally demolished in the January 1994 earthquake. The barking of her dog, who died in the quake, prompted her to get safely out of her bedroom just before it hit. She has now relocated to Las Vegas. The Rhythm and Blues Foundation she helped bring into being has grown mightily. Its annual awards ceremonies, which were held in 1994 at New York's Roseland Ballroom, have become star-studded gala celebrations with high-priced tickets.

The performers discussed in this book have further contributions to make and, by and large, haven't received the financial rewards or general public recognition that their successors—younger black entertainers of comparable abilities—are reaping. But, as Baker told me, "Somebody has to pay the dues." She also noted, wisely, that black performers of the generation before hers endured even harder times. The artists had many stories to share, some of which surprised me. Their memories, which in some cases might otherwise go unrecorded, are well worth preserving—not just for what they tell us about these individual performers but for what they tell us about our culture.

1

"Nobody knows you. . . ."

"We're going to do 'St. Louis Blues.' There's no arrangement. I want everybody's input for what they think is best," Ruth Brown tells the musicians gathered around her in the studio. Guitarist Rodney Jones asks if he might switch to banjo for this number; she nods. She tells trumpeter Spanky Davis he is to start it out, specifying: "I want an intro that won't give away what I'm going to sing—not the melody." She directs the other musicians to hold off until she reaches a certain point in the lyrics. Davis experiments with possible introductions.

In the control room, producer Ralph Jungheim says to engineer John Eargle: "Let's roll tape." They don't inform the musicians they're rolling. Davis settles on an intro, and Brown intones, "I hate to see."

I watch the unfolding of this song in fascination, marveling at the expressiveness she can bring to a line like "if I'm feeling tomorrow like I feel today"—a line that takes on added meaning because I know that in recent days, due to the flare-up of an injury, her legs have been giving her much pain. In fact, yesterday, the first day of the recording session, she had been in a wheelchair. Now she repeats the line, coming in just a bit later than you'd expect and thereby building anticipation; she's calling out now, testifying with an unexpected urgency: *"If I'm feeling tomorrow."* This timeless blues is a perfect song for Brown. Not every song is big enough, sturdy enough to suit her majestic, often highly dramatic style.

She extends a hand toward Rodney Jones, summoning him to take a banjo solo. Finally, she begins to wrap it all up—or so we think. But Davis plunges forward on trumpet, former Ellingtonian Britt Woodman opens up on trombone, and Brown returns to take one final pass at the lyrics, ending—as she sometimes will—with a note that has a hint of sadness in it. Jungheim looks at the clock: "Nine and a half minutes of pure heaven," he remarks. Some disc jockeys will be afraid to play a song that long. But that will be their loss, because this is a magnificent performance. There is no need for a re-take. And that's much the way this whole 1989 session for Fantasy Records goes; most songs are recorded in single takes.

But Ruth Brown has been preparing for these performances all her life. As she puts it during a break in the taping, "You got to live 'em a little to sing 'em." And Lord knows, she's had her ups and downs in her career. After making so many hit records for Atlantic in the 1950s that industry wags referred to the company as "the house that Ruth built," Brown's career gradually went into an eclipse that by the 1970s seemed total.

She sings "Nobody Knows You When You're Down and Out" to-day with a conviction, a sense of authority she couldn't have pro-jected in the early years of her career when she and Dinah Washing-ton vied for the title of the nation's top female rhythm and blues singer. "I try to pick a lyric I can relate to," she explains as we listen to the playback. "And I can relate to this, baby! You can't find 'em when you need 'em."

In recent years, she's made a striking comeback, scoring successes on records, in clubs, on screen, and on stage, and in the process reaching many who are too young to remember her first period of fame. When she's inspired and performs the right material, Brown can pack about as great an emotional wallop as any performer I've seen.

In 1989 she won the Tony Award for best female starring perfor-mance in a musical for her galvanic work in Broadway's *Black and Blue*. She made her way to the stage of the Lunt-Fontanne Theatre to accept that award, saying, "It took me forty-two years to climb those eight steps." When we got together for the first of our inter-views for this book, I asked Ruth Brown to begin by telling me of the earliest steps she took in her career as a singer.

*   *   *

"I sang for practically as long as I can remember, whether it was some-thing that I just wanted to do or whether it was required," recalls Brown, who was born Ruth Weston on January 30, 1928, in Ports-mouth, Virginia. "In the very beginning, it was like required because Sunday was the day that we went to church and participated in Sun-day school, and after Sunday school, the morning service, and after the morning service, a little bit of break and then you come back for youth counsel, and after youth counsel, you would go to the night service. Those things occurred actually after I was old enough to have friends that we would go to Sunday school or whatnot together. But in the very beginning, it was a case of the children being taken to church by their parents. If my mother was not able to take us—which on many Sundays she was not able to, due to the fact that she was a domestic and some Sundays she was required to be at her job—I had an aunt who acted in mother's place. But there was always somebody to see to it that we got to church. You didn't plan to do anything on Sunday."

You can hear a good bit of soulful southern church feeling in Brown's singing today. The church, not surprisingly, plays a strong role in her early memories. "As a child, I was christened as a Methodist in the Emanuel A.M.E. [African Methodist Episcopal] church, and that was the church I mostly grew up in. That was my father's people's religious persuasion. But my mother's people, who were North Carolinians, were Baptists, and when I got to be a little older, I was torn between those two. In the summertime, when we went to North Carolina to work in the fields, my grandmother there was a Baptist. And she indeed did believe that unless you had been submerged, you had not been truly baptized. And baptizing came about after you had heard the word. At some point or other, the word had a spiritual effect on you—you took it upon yourself to make a decision that you wanted to be submerged, which signifies that you will be washed clean. I was baptized when I was about twelve.

"Every true southerner knows that the third week in August is revival, all around. And Revival Week meant being in the churches from sunup to nearly sundown, with a break for lunch and dinner. And you usually didn't have to stray far from the church for that, because when you came to the church in the morning, with the wagon or whatever you drove to the church, you brought your food with you, and the mothers and grandmothers would spread the tables out under the trees at the church. And once the service broke, everybody would come out to eat, and you would go from one table to the next. So you didn't have to leave the grounds of the church at all. There was a well there for drawing the water, and the graveyards of parents and loved ones was right on the grounds, so it was all very closely connected.

"First, we had to sit on a mourners' bench. That's when you had not received the spirit, so to speak; you sat on those benches, listening to the preaching and confessions, sometimes for days on end; for me, I think it was at least sixteen, seventeen days maybe. Not only myself, my other sisters and brothers—we were all here together—and it's only after you find that you feel you want to stand up and confess that the spirit has touched you, then you become a candidate for baptism. My sisters and brothers and I became a little restless, we got tired of sitting there, so we had a scheme we planned at night. We talked about it and by the time we got back to the church for probably the tail-end of the revival, we already had choreographed what we were going to do." She chuckles at the reminiscence.

"So after a while, one of the deacons started marching around—and one of the songs I remember yet was 'Sit Down, Sinner, You Can't Sit Down'—you ain't going to heaven so you can't sit down. And I had given the cue that when I got up, everybody else was sort of timed to get up shortly after that. So eventually I stood up and I went into my 'holiness dance' and my sister Goldie followed. We almost followed in age group—my sister Goldie, my brother Leonard, and then Benny and then Leroy, in succession. But my grandmother was very wise. She knew. She knew that we had done this, and nothing had touched us deep, nothing had touched us except restlessness. And she had a way of just looking at you—she didn't have to open her mouth—and you knew that when you got home, the best thing for you to do was to go out and select your switch for your whipping, because you were going to get it, baby. And she gave us one look, and I'll never forget it, as we were coming out of the church, she said, 'Oh, you're going to play with God, right?' And that's all she said. But we knew that without a doubt, punishment time would be coming.

"I have fond memories of my singing beginning. I started singing like that, just sitting in the church as a listener to the minister, because my grandmother was sitting there, requiring that everybody at least be able to sing a children's song, 'Jesus Loves Me, This I Know.'" It's hardly surprising that there's much of the church feeling in Brown's singing today. "It was there then," she acknowledges, "because that was all I'd ever heard." She sang spirituals throughout her formative years, first in a soprano that eventually ripened into a contralto. "You are familiar with what you hear constantly. And I grew up in that. In the Methodist church, the spirit and feeling was a little more laid-back and a little more reserved, because they indeed had the big organ and the piano and everything. But when we went to North Carolina, to the rural church that my mother grew up in, which was Lovely Hill Baptist Church, there were none of these things. Someone in the back just started the tune, and the hands went together, and the feeling just took over, and you sang. And we had no thought of drums and instruments and everything else—not at that particular church. It was all done a capella and just being improvised as the spirit touched. And somebody would just pick up a song and start singing it, somebody else would join in."

Brown mentions, as an aside that at today's matinee of *Black and Blue,* drummer Grady Tate was not able to get to the theater in time to play for her first number. Although some performers backstage voiced concern about having to go on without a drummer setting the beat, Brown says she recalled how many times she'd sung in church without any instrumental support whatsoever; she knew she didn't have to hear a drum to have a sense of rhythm. She sang without drums until Tate got to the theater and doubts if anyone in the audience noticed.

When did Brown first know she wanted to sing for a career?

"First time I got paid," she says with a laugh. "I sang for a wedding once and I got paid. I think I made $5 or $10, and that was a lot of money. I was seven or eight. Yeah, by that time I had a little bit of a reputation—the little Weston girl (Weston was my family name) could sing. And my dad was a singer, so he introduced me to a lot of those things. He played piano by ear. And I was sort of like his little prize. He would stand me up on the piano because I was small, and he would play and I would sing. And I could sing 'Oh Promise Me,' 'I Love You Truly,' 'The Lord's Prayer,' and 'Ave Maria,' all those strong things. And I had gotten to be a little familiar at the Tom Thumb weddings in the church. And all the children of the church, their parents would make them little tuxedos and little gowns, like the bride, and they'd have a Tom Thumb wedding. And they'd sell like little raffles, to earn money for the children, for picnics or whatever. They always had little Tom Thumb weddings, with the little bride with the veil, the cutest things. All children. Wonderful, wonderful. I used to love those Tom Thumb weddings, which you never see any more, when I was a child. And I was always a part of that, always had to be the one that did the singing. I never got to be the bride. All of that is the foundation upon which Ruth Weston Brown has grown."

Did her family feel good about her going on to become a professional singer? Did they encourage that?

"Well, I think my father was very proud once I really got a foothold. I'm sure he was, but it went against everything that he had stood for, because he had said, 'No, no, no—you're not going to sing outside the church.' You see? And then there were these awful untrue thoughts about people involved in show business. That everybody involved in show business, as the movies and radio and everything else depicted them—you know, you have visions of the ballroom girl or the 'hostess with the mostess'—and *no, I will not have my child be a part of that.* If you sang anything outside the church, it was truly the devil's music. So, his standing in the church and the fact that he only sang gospel kind of went against the grain for me. But I think that secretly, outside of the confines of Portsmouth and when he really was with his real friends and could let his hair down and just tell the truth about it, he was probably the most proud. He was probably *the* most proud because I've gone home and heard people say, 'Oh your father told me you was making a movie.' I wasn't even making no movie, because he could exaggerate a little bit. So I think indeed he was proud, and mostly because everybody would say to him, 'Well, she got that voice from you.' And indeed I did. It was passed down." The baritone voice of her father, Leonard Weston, rang out strong when he sang in the church choir. He was also active in the all-male Hiram Simmons Glee Club. And he'd sing with his family at home—not the blues, of course, for the blues, with their often frank dealings with sexuality, were considered profane—but some favorite older pop songs and novelties.

"We had an old raggedy upright piano, and when he was in a good mood, he would sit down and we'd all sit around and he would sing some of his little things. 'Down by the Old Mill Stream.' It's interesting—'Am I Blue' [which Brown recorded on her album *Blues on Broadway*] was one of the old things he used to do. And 'I Ain't Got Nobody.' Oh, my Daddy used to sing it. Someday I'd like to record that song. And there was a little novelty thing he used to do, like, 'Saturday night in the pale moonlight . . . the vegetables was having a stew. Even the turnip top was dancing with Miss Turnip Top.' Yeah, he always had some cute little things he would do to keep us entertained." Brown says that someday she'd like to do a whole album of songs her father taught her.

When she began singing, Brown did not really feel comfortable singing the blues. That was something she'd do out of earshot of her parents—out with the boys who were sneaking smokes.

"Well, I had been given this understanding that blues was just *not* the proper thing to sing. The people who had made these decisions, of course, probably were listening to the blues with the doors closed," she notes. "Because as I have become a woman and experienced life, I know that at one time or the other, the best Christian in the world has had the blues about something. And it's not until you get the blues that you go to Christ for help—believe me. You understand? When they get so low down they can't deal with it, *then* everybody jumps on the other side and says 'Lord have mercy.' Even when they sing the blues, people say, 'Lord have mercy, have mercy on me.' Even within the song itself. So it all has to do with the interpretation, what you give it. You can make it as filthy as you want—depending on where your head is, it can be as nasty and as filthy as you want. And then again, it can be sarcastic. But it can be warm [and her remarkably expressive voice abruptly turns soft and comforting as she says the word *warm*]. You can speak for a lot of people, depending on what you do with it. It is all about that old saying 'it ain't what you do, it's the way that you do it.'"

Her father chastised her when he first heard she was singing some blues, but in time, she recalls, he came around. "I know he was proud of me. And in later years, when he was able to come to New York and visit, he got to see me at the Apollo and in a number of instances that made him really, really proud.

"He was a laborer. He worked on the docks, unloading trains and boats, and then he did day work at a hardware store, maintenance, custodian, whatever. And my mother worked in private homes, as a cook and a cleaning person, took care of other people's children. But, even though they had to do those menial things, I—being the oldest child—have fond memories. I can never remember being hungry. That is, while dad and mama were taking care of us. I've come kind of close to it a number of times when Ruth Brown took over. And as a mother who has had to struggle at times to survive with only two children, I am in awe of how they took care of eight of us. One died, but seven living children fortunately are standing on their own two feet. And I'm sure it had to be very hard. I don't know that my father ever made over $50 a week, if he made that. But we were kept together as a family. My mama and daddy took care of us, the best they could. I became the rebel when I realized that I could do something to help. I found out that I could sing and make some money."

But when she began taking gigs and bringing money into the house, it seemed to rankle her father's pride—as if she were implying he needed help from her to earn the money the family needed. "My father was reluctant [to approve of my singing professionally]. The father at that time was the head of the household, regardless of what he brought in. And in my home, that was indeed the rule, and my mother and father worked," she recalls. Her singing professionally "was a no-no, up until at least I could get through high school. Of course, I had some little menial jobs while I was still in school."

The school system, Brown notes, was segregated, which she simply accepted as a fact of life when she was growing up. She doesn't recall being bothered by racial prejudice in her youth; in her hometown of Portsmouth she didn't experience the gross indignities of bigotry that she later found during some of her performing tours throughout the South. "I'm sure that as a child there probably were some incidents that had I come closer to them would have probably bruised me emotionally, but I can't remember any. I cannot remember any," she remarks. "I remember *living* next door—I had white neighbors, we played in the streets together—I didn't realize until I went on the road the magnitude of this thing called segregation. I never really felt it that much in Portsmouth. True, we went to different schools. But it wasn't really the issue. There was not much that I could see going up on Woodrow Wilson [the high school for whites] that we didn't have at I. C. Norcum [the high school for blacks]. I thought I. C. Norcum was the school of all schools. We had good football teams, I was on the cheerleading squad. And Woodrow Wilson—we were proud when they won. If they beat Craddock, we were glad. We were indeed happy when each other won.

"Three or four years ago I went home, when my hometown gave an affair called 'A Notable Occasion.' And they honored twenty-nine people from Portsmouth who had made worldwide names for themselves," Brown recalls. She was amazed to discover that many successful people in various fields had grown up in Portsmouth around the same time she had—including many whom, due to racial segregation, she had never known. Saxist Tommy Newsom, assistant conductor of the Tonight Show Orchestra, for example, had grown up less than four blocks up the street from her, and the current U.S. ambassador to Kuwait had grown up just two blocks from her, but because they had gone to white schools and she to black schools their paths had never crossed. She learned that fashion designer Perry Ellis, jazz clarinetist Mahlon Clark, and figures active in the space program and politics had all grown up in Portsmouth. "I sat there that night with my mouth wide open, saying, 'I can't believe this. These people went to Woodrow Wilson High School; I went to I. C. Norcum—walking distance apart.' These people are world-known figures. We were in the same town at the same time. That was one of the most mind-boggling affairs that I've ever attended. To sit there and hear these names called, of the people whose names I knew—but I had no idea that they had come from the same place I did. And we were the same age-group." She was proud to be part of such company and pleased to see people who had been educated separately, due to race, now being honored together. To show her gratitude, she made a video for Portsmouth schoolchildren in the hope that the success she has achieved, despite obstacles of poverty and racial segregation, might inspire and bolster their self-images.

Which singers inspired Brown when she was a teenager? Who did she want to emulate?

"Billie Holiday. Ella Fitzgerald, naturally. Oh, these are the first records that I heard, " she recalls. But she makes it clear that she did not hear many records when she was young. Her family didn't have the money for them. "I heard mostly country and western singers. How? Because my mama worked in a restaurant, over on Fourth Street, where all the things on the jukebox were country and western. Most of the radio stations at that time tuned in country and western. And I used to hear that quite a bit."

Just as many streams will contribute to the flow of a mighty river, diverse musical traditions contributed to the development of Ruth Brown as a singer. In the church, she developed her sense of rhythm and emotional expressiveness; the fervent eruptions in her singing hearken back to church singers in her youth suddenly "feeling the spirit." Her fondness for having an organ, rather than a piano, back her as she sings—and even as she speaks, in her club appearances—likewise stems from her church background. Less obvious is what she may have picked up from country and western (or "hillbilly," as the music was called) traditions, but traces can be found. The "hoo-ee" vocalizing she'll do when she closes "Mama, He Treats Your Daughter Mean" seems derived from country and western, along with, perhaps, a certain feeling she has for melodrama. Brown listened to, and learned from, leading pop singers on the radio, both white and black. Although her singing now, with its great strength and sense of authority, might seem inspired at least in part by such classic blues singers of the twenties as Bessie Smith (1894–1937) and Ma Rainey (1886–1939), she never heard their records in her youth. They had been the singers of her parents' generation and no doubt influenced her indirectly by influencing some of the older singers she heard.

"I didn't hear many professional singers until I heard records by Ella Fitzgerald: her 'Have Mercy' and 'I'm Up a Tree' [from 1938] were the first records ever played in our home. We didn't own a record player. My uncle bought one, and brought this record of Ella's from New York City.

"The first woman that I really tried to emulate was Billie Holiday. But of course, locally now, there were some little clubs when I was sneaking out. There was a singer called Honey Brown. And Betty Roche [who had been Duke Ellington's vocalist] was probably one of the first that I heard in person. There was a club in Norfolk called the Big Track Diner. And these New York stars used to come down—well for us they were stars—and I heard Betty Roche there.

"But there was this woman I used to listen to who had such strength: Maude Thomas. Now I realize, she was probably a cross between a Bessie Smith and a Ma Rainey. I didn't hear Bessie Smith myself until I became older. (Growing up at home, I heard country and western.) I'm sure my father and them were probably aware of who she was, but I wasn't until later. But this woman that I admired, Maude Thomas, very possibly had listened a lot to Bessie. She was older. She was sort of a celebrity. I don't know if she was from Baltimore or Chicago or where—but she wasn't local. During the war years, because this was a navy area, there were a lot of little small places that had entertainment. I saw Redd Foxx down there in Newport News, before I saw him up here. All of them used to come down there. I was sneaking out to see them because I didn't have no business in there. But this place called the Big Track Diner, then there was a place in Newport News called the TWA, the Tidewater Athletic Club. And there was George Page's Offbeat."

She listened, on radio, to everything. "I heard Bing Crosby and the Andrews Sisters and the Mills Brothers. The Charioteers, Red Foley, Hank Williams, Glenn Miller, Tex Beneke. Those were things that I heard and those were the songs that I sang in the USO shows. 'Chattanooga Choo-Choo' and Vaughn Monroe; I was hearing all those things. So I was learning to sing all of their things, mostly. And there was a show called 'The Mail Bag' [on which] I started to hear really the first real records by black singers, and that was like the groups—the Ink Spots, the Charioteers, and I heard Sonny Til and the Orioles. Those are the first vocal groups I heard. But then on Sunday I heard 'Wings over Jordan' and the Southernaires and the Golden Gate Quartet. That's all I heard. That wasn't bad company, though, was it? [She laughs.] Yeah. A lot of different influences."

The fact that Brown listened to so many different types of performers, white as well as black, undoubtedly contributed to her ability to later communicate successfully with a broad audience. According to Atlantic Records head Ahmet Ertegun, it was an important element in her commercial success. Her singing, although soulful, was more accessible to white audiences than the rougher, more wholly black style of itinerant blues singers. She wanted to sing not only with rich emotion but also with polish, the words sung in tune and with clear articulation. For example, the song she chose for her first New York appearance—as a contestant in the famed amateur show of the Apollo

Theatre, which had launched the careers of Ella Fitzgerald and many others—was "It Could Happen to You." She learned it from a recording by Bing Crosby.

* * *

It was the summer of 1944. Brown at sixteen did not feel that she could reveal to her parents her dreams of show business glory. When she got on the bus for New York, she didn't tell them that she was going to enter the Apollo contest. "I told them that I was riding up here to visit my uncle who lived at 153d Street. That was the truth. But it was the sneaky way to come up here and get on the amateur show.

"I'll never forget walking on that stage. I passed the tree of hope; I didn't touch it.[1] And the emcee that night, Doc Wheeler, said, 'Oh, little girl, go back, go back, and touch that tree.' And I went back and touched the tree and I came back and he said, 'And where are you from?' I said, 'Portsmouth, Virginia.' 'Portsmouth, Virginia? Where in the world is Portsmouth, Virginia?' I said, 'Near Norfolk.' He said, 'Oh, all right. That's right. Name the big cities.' And when I started to sing, I think I got right into it and the audience started to applaud. At that time, they at least gave you a chance. It's a little different now, from the way I've seen it on television—they're really unfair to the contestants. It's all done for the benefit of the camera. And I feel so sorry for some of the contestants who are not getting a fair shake. But at that time you had people like Doc Wheeler and Leonard Reed and Ralph Cooper and Willie Bryant to kind of keep the crowd in control.

"I sang, 'It Could Happen to You,' and when I got through the house just screamed. When you first start singing, you're only working with the pianist. And the band—Tiny Bradshaw's was there that week—heard that I was going to actually do well, and they started filling in. And by the time I got to the end of the song, the whole Tiny Bradshaw Orchestra was improvising behind me. When I got through and I walked off, he said, 'Oh no, come back, come back. We have never done this before, but let us sing that again.' I sang it a second time.

"And I won first prize! But it didn't change things overnight. No. I had to go back home to Portsmouth and I was scared to tell my family I had won the amateur contest. I had to go home, back to school. I never did get my week in the Apollo—the prize for winning the contest—until later when I had a record contract."

Against her parents' wishes and sometimes without them know-

ing where she was—they'd think she was going to choir practice—
Brown would sing in little clubs and USO shows, playing at places
like Langley Field Air Force Base and Camp Lejeune. She added songs
of Hadda Brooks and Una Mae Carlisle to her repertoire. Good local
musicians influenced her style of singing as well. Sometimes she'd
sing just with piano backing, but at other times she'd sing with five-
piece combos—rhythm and blues combos featuring a heavy beat and
hot-blooded tenor sax solos that foreshadowed rock 'n' roll. While
working at the Big Track Diner in Norfolk, she met a trumpeter named
Jimmy Brown, then still in the navy, who would eventually became
her first husband.

Brown was finding herself as a singer. She had a rather commanding presence and a lush, full voice. What sort of songs did she most
like singing then? "Torch," she answers without hesitation. "I always
was interested in singing something that I could really get a hold
of. . . . I was doing like 'Happiness Is a Thing Called Joe,' 'Good for
Nothing Joe,' 'Where Can I Go?' 'Stormy Weather.' These are the great
songs—strong songs, songs with a beginning and a middle and an
ending, songs that told something. And I still am like that."

After graduating from high school, Brown was free to take gigs out
of the area. A 1947 appearance at the Frolic Show Bar in Detroit
brought her to the attention of Lucky Millinder, whose bluesy, big,
swing band was playing at Detroit's Paradise Theater. Although Millinder's band never reached the very top rung occupied by such bands
as Duke Ellington's, Count Basie's, and Jimmie Lunceford's, it had
always been quite good, and, by moving in a rhythm and blues direction, it was maintaining its popularity after many other big bands
had lost theirs. Brown was thrilled when Millinder offered her a job
singing with the band; she could hardly imagine having a better
showcase. The only problem was that Millinder already had two well-
liked vocalists, Bullmoose Jackson and Anisteen Allen, and Brown
would not be singing much—at least at first. For now, Millinder wanted her to observe and learn the ropes; her time would come. Allen,
Brown recalls, "was like my mama when I got on that bus; she took
care of me. And Lucky had great musicians in the band at that time,
like Jimmy Nottingham, Clark Terry, Billy Mitchell, Al Grey, Al Cobbs,
Frank Galveston. I traveled with that band for almost a month and I
never got to sing anything. Finally, the first time I was going to get
a chance to sing was in Washington, D.C.—Turner's Arena—and I got
all prepared.

"I had two songs. One was Dinah Washington's 'Evil Gal Blues'
and the other one was 'Tomorrow Night.' These were my two debut

tunes. So I went up, I did the first set—oh, I was delighted. So I did these two, and I came down and people were going [she claps and says, "Raayyy,' suggesting an enthusiastic crowd]. I guess it was about the first time I had anybody ask me for my autograph. So I'm just standing there by the side of the stage. And I think that originally it was Billy Mitchell, the saxophone player, who said, 'Hey Ruth, would you go up there and get us some sodas?' Billy Mitchell, Al Grey, Al Cobbs. So I pushed my way through the crowd, went up to the refreshment stand, came back with this cardboard carrying the sodas; I had about seven or eight of them. I set these paper cups and thing down on the side of the stage, and the musicians were reaching down, getting them, and passing them. And Lucky Millinder looked over at me, came to the edge of the stage, and said, 'I hired a singer not a waitress. You're fired! And besides, you don't sing too good anyway.' Oh God. Every time I see Billy Mitchell and Al Grey up until this day, I tell them, 'You guys owe me!'"

* * *

Brown can laugh at the memory today, but it was far from funny at the time. Millinder refused to pay her anything. When she said he owed him, he countered she owed *him* because he'd been providing room and board for a month. She was stranded, two hundred miles from home with no money—and little enthusiasm for returning home a "failure" even if she had money. An acquaintance got her an audition with singer and former big band leader Blanche Calloway, Cab's older sister, who was then running the Crystal Caverns in Washington. Brown sang "It Could Happen to You." Calloway told her the club didn't need any more performers, but she'd let Brown work until Brown had earned enough money to get back home.

That temporary gig at the Crystal Caverns proved to be the real start of Brown's career. Calloway was impressed enough by Brown's talent to offer to become her manager and helped manage Brown for about ten years, until declining health eventually forced her to withdraw completely. Brown credits the extroverted Blanche Calloway, who reportedly had been an influence on Cab's singing style when he was starting out, with also being an influence on her singing style.

The Crystal Caverns was an important venue in Washington at that time; the fact that Brown clicked there did not go unnoticed. She recalls that "Willis Conover of Voice of America radio came in the club one night, along with Duke Ellington and Sonny Til and the Orioles; they were all sitting there together. Willis got up and went to the pay phone, right there in the check room, called Ahmet Ertegun and Herb Abramson, who were just forming Atlantic Records, and said, 'You better get down here and hear this young girl that's singing at the Crystal Caverns!' Ahmet had been around Washington because his father was Turkish ambassador to the United States. Ahmet, Herb Abramson, and a fellow named Blackie Sales came down from New York to Washington to hear me. And they talked to Blanche about offering me a record contract. And as far as I knew, they were the only people that were trying to get me. I never knew until a few years ago that Capitol Records was one of the record companies that was fighting to get me. I never, ever knew that. Because we went with Atlantic Records." Herb Abramson recalls:

> Before she came to us, she had been on the road; she had sung with the USO. It had helped, I'm sure, to sharpen her up. The first time we heard her, when she was at the Crystal Caverns, where Ahmet and I went at the invitation of Willis Conover— she was at that time, as good as she ever was. I mean, she was a finished performer, one of the best that we had seen. And Blanche Calloway was her "manager" in quotes—she had gotten her the job singing as a single at the Crystal Caverns and became quasi-manager. Ahmet and I wanted to not only sign her up, which we did, but also to have control of her career and try to build her. We had great faith in her, because she was great. And Blanche Calloway diplomatically agreed to become co-manager—we were the co-managers. So Ahmet and I were managers of Ruth Brown for a period of time. However, before the hits started to come in, I would say that our function as managers really consisted of laying out money for gowns, arrangements, and transportation—everything to try to build her. But we never took a cent in commission.
>
> Ruth Brown has been one of the few artists that has been genuinely appreciative of the work that I did. And I'm not denigrating Ahmet's contribution; he and I worked as a team for six years, very, very well. She's just always been very appreciative. So, like for example, as recently as her "live" recording session at the Hotel Roosevelt for another label, she introduced me from the stage, saying, "This is the man, without this man, there'd be no Ruth Brown." I'm a modest person and sort of embarrassed for that. But anyway, I'm happy for her, that she's on the brink of a big revival.[2]

Technically, Brown did not sign with Atlantic while she was in Washington. She agreed verbally to go with the fledgling label; they planned to go through the formality of signing contracts when she got to New York. Blanche Calloway telephoned Apollo Theatre owner Frank Schiffman, whom she had known for years; her recommendation was enough to get Brown a booking right away. Brown was set to make her New York debut at the famed Apollo. The headline attraction was to be Dizzy Gillespie and his big band. Brown was looking forward to singing with Gillespie's band, which was then riding high.

"Every time I see Dizzy, he talks about how they waited for this young singer that was supposed to be coming that was so good. And I never got there," she recalls. "You see, it was while I was coming here for that, that I had an automobile accident that put me in the hospital for months. I was in Chester, Pennsylvania. And so Ahmet and them came down to the hospital, and they signed me to Atlantic Records in the hospital room. On my birthday [in January 1949], they came down and they offered me a pitch pipe and a music book; I'll never forget it because I had told them I wanted to learn how to read music, and they brought me a pitch pipe and a music book and a scratch pad so I could write songs. I was trying to do a little writing to pass the time away in the hospital. And my love of Ahmet Ertegun and Herb Abramson began right there in that hospital. Because they had never even known what I would sound like in the studio. They had heard me at the Crystal Caverns. But they cared enough about me that they signed me anyway. And they waited. And they paid my hospital bills—I don't know until today what it was—because I didn't have anything. Of course I had gotten a couple of dollars out of the insurance company. But the insurance company people had come to the hospital while I was really sick. Nobody was there but me. They talked to me and I signed papers, and I think I got a thousand dollars if it was that, which is nothing."

She spent ten and a half months recuperating from the accident, most of the time in the hospital, and then in Cab Calloway's Westchester County, New York, home. The damage to her left leg was extensive; the injury still bothers her. "The accident was in October 1948, and I didn't get to make my first record until [May 25th] 1949," she recalls. She was on crutches and in leg braces when she recorded "So Long." It became a hit, reaching the number six spot on the *Billboard* R&B charts. It was only Atlantic's second record hit, but over the next dozen years Brown would give them many more successful recordings, including twenty-three more *Billboard* chart hits. Ironically, "So Long" was not originally recorded with the idea of releasing it; Atlantic was just interested in making a test of how Brown

would sound on record when she had a chance to sing with some
top-flight musicians. Abramson recalls the story behind the making
of "So Long":

> The "March of Time" wanted to show how a record was made.
> So they contacted Ernie Anderson, who was a well-connected
> publicist and a good friend of Eddie Condon, and he arranged
> to have Eddie Condon's band be the one. Ernie then contacted
> us and said, "How would you like to do the other side of this
> record?" We jumped at the chance because we were planning
> to record Ruth Brown anyway, and Eddie Condon's band had
> all good studio musicians—Ernie Caceres on baritone sax, Dick
> Cary, trumpet and piano—these were very fine men who not
> only played Dixieland but they were also skilled musicians from
> the big swing bands. So yeah, we'll have Eddie Condon's band
> back up Ruth Brown, and Dick Cary will make the arrangements.
> We especially wanted to record "So Long" because that was Ruth
> Brown's killer number. It had previously been recorded by Lit-
> tle Miss Cornshucks [Mildred Cummings]; this was her big num-
> ber and Ruth Brown did it even better—she really had a tear in
> her voice. So this "So Long" record had this young rhythm and
> blues singer who was giving her all and being backed up by a
> smooth, Tommy Dorsey-type of big band sound, which is love-
> ly—in other words, it put Ruth Brown into a better category.[3]

According to Brown, the musicians, after spending a long time recording their own number, initially did not seem too pleased about
having to back an unknown singer, but after she began singing, drummer Big Sid Catlett said something to the effect that this girl could
really sing and encouraged the other eight musicians (including such
lyrical pros as cornetist Bobby Hackett and trombonist Will Bradley)
to give it their best. Abramson recalls, "'So Long' was a hit record
that helped establish Atlantic and it helped establish Ruth Brown."
Atlantic's only previous hit was Stick McGhee's "Drinking Wine Spo-
Dee-O-Dee." The success of those two numbers helped make Atlantic viable.

In the meantime, she was appearing around town in venues ranging from Harlem's Baby Grand Club (where she became friends with
a then-unknown comedian who would have a great future, Nipsey
Russell) to the Apollo Theatre (where she made her debut as a featured attraction, singing with Louis Jordan's band). She was paired
on gigs with artists including Charles Brown, Roy Brown (neither a
relative), Paul "Hucklebuck" Williams, and Amos Milburn. She was

particularly thrilled with a booking at Barney Josephson's prestigious Cafe Society Downtown (where Brown was billed second to folk singer Josh White), because the club had long been the base for one of Brown's idols, Billie Holiday. "She was quite something," Brown says of Holiday, some of whose songs she still sings. "When I think of her, there's a real warm feeling." One night, Holiday came into Cafe Society to catch the show. Brown recalls: "When they told me she was there ohhhhh!—I pulled out all the stops; I pulled out every Billie Holiday song I could think of. She got up from the table—I could just see her kind of moving off, in the light—and she kind of stormed off, went over to the dressing room area. I couldn't imagine what was happening. It hurt me. I had thought that she would be so proud. I was just working to get this Billie Holiday ovation here.

"Well, she said to me: 'Every time you do what you did, it makes it better for me. Now I know who I am; it's for you to find out who you are.' I didn't understand. And she said, 'You are too good to copy me. Because there's only one me. I am already me. Every time you copy me, it's just better for me. And until you get to the point that somebody wants to copy you, you don't matter.' That's what she told me, and God knows, that was probably the best advice, the most constructive criticism that I ever got. I didn't understand it then, but I understood it later." Holiday discouraged Brown from simply emulating her style. Brown adds, "I saw her again just before she died [in 1959]. She was working in Philadelphia at Pep's Show Bar and I went. As she was coming down, I stopped her and I said, 'Lady, do you remember me? I'm Ruth Brown.' And she looked at me and she said, 'I remember you. See, they're copying you now, aren't they?'"

But in 1949 Brown was still in the process of finding herself as a singer. She had married trumpeter Jimmy Brown a few years earlier and did some touring with his rhythm and blues group. Billed as Brown and Brown, they sang vocals together, such as "Sentimental Journey" and "Hey Pretty Baby" (a thinly disguised reworking of "Caldonia," a song she liked because of the way Little Jimmy Scott used to sing it). The two recordings they made, neither of which was released at the time, show more youthful high spirits than polish. ("Hey Pretty Baby" was included—for its historic value—in Atlantic's 1989 double compact disc set *Ruth Brown: Miss Rhythm, Greatest Hits and More*.) Jimmy Brown also tried, without much success, to make it as a vocalist on his own. Abramson remembers, "We recorded, perhaps like as a favor to Ruth Brown, Jimmy Brown's band, and the song was called 'Climbing up to Heaven Blues.'" It didn't go anywhere, nor did a couple other sides Jimmy Brown made for Atlantic, all of which were released under the pseudonym Jimmy Earle. He later re-corded as vocalist with Paul "Hucklebuck" Williams's popular band, but he never attained the success that Ruth Brown did. The marriage did not last long.

* * *

Between 1949 and 1961, Ruth Brown cut nearly one hundred sides for Atlantic. To be sure, not all of them are R&B classics. In the quest for records that would sell, producers had Brown record material of varying styles and quality, including ballads, blues, gospel-inflected pop tunes, and even some mambos when mambos were in vogue. Indeed, as we listened to tapes in her Broadway dressing room, she sang along with some numbers but admitted she had forgotten re-cording some others. But her big records, trend-setters in the field of R&B, evoke memories for anyone who listened to that music during those years, and her best recordings should interest anyone getting into rhythm and blues now.

She scored a success with "I'll Get Along Somehow," which she recorded in 1949. Nipsey Russell, who toured with Brown in the ear-ly fifties and remains a great admirer of her talent, remembers that number as proving for the first time—via the lines Brown declaimed in numerous live appearances—that she was an actress, not just a singer. Backed by the smoothly harmonizing Delta Rhythm Boys, she gave "Sentimental Journey" a forthright approach. She sounded wist-ful on "I Can Dream, Can't I?" and sultry and sensuous on a laid-back "Rockin' Blues." Brown still believed—a carryover from her church upbringing—that ballads, which she sang in a lush style, were purer and "more respectable" than blues, but she recorded what Abramson recommended. Abramson knew she handled blues effec-tively. He sensed that she had just enough refinement (without los-ing soulfulness) to appeal to a broader audience than pure "down-home" blues singers could have. That blend of the finesse associated with the white pop singing tradition and the stronger emotional qual-ity of the black gospel and blues traditions would help Atlantic sell a lot of records by Brown and others working in a somewhat similar vein throughout the fifties.

The recording that really took off for Brown, and to a consider-able extent determined the direction she would pursue, was "Tear-drops from My Eyes," which landed in the number one spot on *Bill-board*'s R&B charts in October 1950 and stayed in that spot for eleven weeks. It was on the charts, in total, an incredible twenty-five weeks. This was Brown's first rhythm number—a comfortably chugging band arranged and conducted by Budd Johnson (whom Abramson had known and admired from his arranging work for Billy Eckstine's big band) set Brown off effectively. The song's great popularity encouraged Atlantic to have her record more numbers with an easy-rockin' tempo and feel—a feel that foreshadowed rock 'n' roll. "Teardrops," which Brown says she never imagined would be a hit, was written by Rudy Toombs, a dancer turned songwriter who was to create many hits for Brown, Joe Turner, the Clovers, and other R&B notables before being beaten to death by muggers in front of his New York apartment in 1962. It was also the first record Atlantic released as a 45, the new speed for singles, rather than as a 78. After the record took off, Brown went on tour, backed by saxist Willis "Gator Tail" Jackson's band.

In 1951 Brown hit the charts again with a moderately up-tempo number "I'll Wait for You" (piping out the song's final notes in a voice evocative of young Ella Fitzgerald's) and "I Know." The flip side of "I'll Wait for You"—which was not as well received at the time but has become one of her most frequently requested specialties—was the intense "Standing on the Corner," known now as "Miss Brown's Blues." That same year she recorded a gutsy, driving, life-filled version of "Shine On (Big Bright Moon)," a number created by old-time bluesman Tampa Red and arranged and conducted by jazz trombonist Slide Hampton. With all of those up-tempo successes to her credit, it's no wonder that Frankie Laine nicknamed Brown "Miss Rhythm" that year. The billing caught on. Brown was also billed as "The Girl with the Tear in Her Voice," a reference to her distinctive way of sometimes cracking a note at the conclusion of a phrase, producing a kind of squeak or squeal. The first time that happened during a recording session, she thought that she had made a mistake and wanted to do a retake, but Abramson wisely told her to keep it in. The squeal—or "tear in her voice" as Abramson named it—became one of her identifying marks.

Brown made the charts again in 1952 with a light mambo "Daddy Daddy," which was backed by the unforgettable "Have a Good Time" (a number Tony Bennett also recorded). On the latter, she was given a sentimental backing reminiscent of any number of old Pied Pipers' hits while she sang lyrics more sophisticated than ever sung by the Pied Pipers—encouraging her man, if he must, to have a good time having a fling with another. Her "Three Letters" was successful enough for Kay Starr to cover it. And then came "Five-Ten-Fifteen Hours," a monster hit that stayed seven weeks at number one on the R&B charts and remains among her most-requested numbers. Abramson, who played a key role in guiding Brown's career during the period, recalls that Rudy Toombs originally wrote the song as "Five-Ten-Fifteen Minutes": "He came in and sang, 'Give me five-ten-fifteen minutes of your love.' I said that 'minutes' wasn't enough in this era of 'The 60 Minute Man'—we better make it 'fifteen *hours* of your love.'" As Brown and I listen to this recording in her Broadway dressing room, she scats along with every sax lick—she hasn't forgotten a single nuance. "That was Willis 'Gator Tail' Jackson," she explains to me; they were lovers then. "He used to talk to me through his horn." And then, listening to the sax interjections of Jackson, who became her second husband, she begins singing what she hears him saying to her with his sax: "Baby, baby," and, "You know I love you, baby." The rhythmic piano work of Vann "Piano Man" Walls contributed to the success of the record as well. "Five-Ten-Fifteen Hours" was the third-best-selling R&B record of 1952; Brown was the sole female among the top ten R&B artists of that year.

Like all black performers in the era, Brown suffered her share of indignities on tour. "Ruth's Cadillacs Cause Unpleasantness in South," *Ebony* magazine headlined in May 1952. The story told of an FBI agent in Atlanta stopping Brown and asking to see proof that the Cadillac she was driving was really hers; he claimed that he was on the lookout for stolen Cadillacs. On another occasion, when she drew up to a roadside fruit juice stand in Opallacka, Florida, the proprietor objected, "We don't allow niggers to park that close to us down here, particularly Yankee niggers in expensive cars." *Ebony* reported, "An incident developed during which Nick Zal, her road manager, was denounced by local citizens as 'a damned nigger lover.' Ruth broke down and cried."

Other sorts of difficulties also cropped up from time to time on tour. Brown played a dance in Philadelphia with bandleader Sonny Stitt, for instance, in which a fight broke out between two teenage boys over a girl. A riot developed, with guns and knives drawn, and a thousand patrons scrambled for safety. One sixteen-year-old was shot to death, and several other youths were seriously injured. Two bullets hit the wall inches from Brown, *Ebony* reported. *Ebony* also said that singer Arthur Prysock escorted Brown away from the turmoil—the one part of the account that she doesn't confirm. Her memory is that he was scrambling to safety like everyone else.

In 1953 Brown reached the number three spot on the R&B charts with the infectious "Wild, Wild Young Men," a great favorite of Jerry Wexler, who produced or coproduced a number of Brown's recordings, including this one. Wexler sees this number as containing the

essence of funk; it was written by Atlantic's president Ahmet Ertegun under his songwriting pseudonym, A. Nugetre—Ertegun spelled
backward. After making the record, she played some New York–area
dates, took time off to have her tonsils removed, and then toured in
the summer in a package with the Clovers, Louis Jordan, and Wynonie Harris.

That same year yielded a number with which Brown is still identified—her biggest hit, "Mama, He Treats Your Daughter Mean." It
was number one on the R&B charts for five weeks (staying on the
charts sixteen weeks in total) and reached as high as number twenty-three on the pop charts in a period when it was exceptionally rare
for an R&B hit to also become a pop hit. (Not until 1957 would Brown
again show up on the pop charts.) *Down Beat* readers voted it the
number one R&B record of 1953. The song was written by Johnny
Wallace and Herb Lance, although, like some other notable R&B successes, it's actually based on older material. Abramson recalls that the
number has an interesting history: "They said they'd heard a blind
blues singer sitting on the curb in downtown Atlanta with his hat
out for coins, singing a mournful song that included the line, 'Mama,
don't treat your daughter mean.' They made a song out of that, and
they switched it around to, 'Mama, he treats your daughter mean.'
When they brought it to me, it was a slow, mournful ballad. And I,
working with Ruth Brown, decided to put it into tempo."[4] Abramson adds that in 1949 Atlantic had made a recording (unreleased until
1972) of Blind Willie McTell singing "Last Dime Blues" that included the line "mama, don't treat your daughter mean." But exactly how
far back that line may go is unknown. "Last Dime Blues" dates back
at least to the 1920s, when it was sung by Blind Lemon Jefferson.

Of "Mama, He Treats Your Daughter Mean," Brown says, "That
tune I didn't want to do. I thought, when I first heard it, 'That's the
silliest mess that I have ever heard.' At that time, I wasn't having
too much of a problem [with men], so I felt like: 'What is she talking about, *Mama he treats your daughter mean . . . mama, the man is
lazy, almost drives me crazy.* I wasn't dealing with that kind of a life-
style, so that didn't make sense to me. But when they got in the studio with it, I think I really paid attention to it because the two guys
that had written it were friends of mine—Herb Lance, who was a singer, he had a hit in the fifties called 'Close Your Eyes,' and Johnny
Wallace, who was a friend of mine, who was a brother to Coley Wallace, the fighter. And they said, 'Ruth, do this song.' And so my outlook at that moment was, 'Well, if I do it, they're going to make a
buck.' And we went in the studio, and I think that tune was proba-

bly done in two takes at the most. They just sat around and talked about the idea, and I think there were some lead lines written." Brown's recording contains repeated examples of her trademark way of cracking a note. Listen for the suggestion of a squeal with which she ends such key words as "mama," "man," and "understand."[5]

The tambourine heard on the record was played by disc jockey Hal Jackson, who happened to be in the studio when the musicians were running the number down and—caught up in the rhythm—picked up a tambourine and began hitting it. The musicians decided to keep his playing in, so the record opens with four bars by Jackson on tambourine, setting the beat, and his tambourine is heard throughout. Brown notes, "When I started to do that tune in public, I used to play the tambourine on it. I got away with that for quite a while 'til I got down to Washington. And the [musicians' union] representative down there showed up one day at the Howard Theater, and I was with Basie, and he said, 'You can't play that.' I said, 'I beg your pardon?' He said, 'Well, that's an instrument, a percussion instrument.' And I'll never forget, for that show, [tenor saxist] Eddie 'Lockjaw' Davis played it, the introduction. They wouldn't let me play it. I finally had to join the musicians' union just to play those four bars on tambourine. So I belong to every union, now. I'm *bad* on the tambourine."

Brown shared bills with both jazz and R&B musicians in those years. "You see, not only did I work with Jackie Wilson and Sam Cooke and Charles Brown, I also worked with Charlie Parker, and Lester Young, and Bud Powell. Oh! And John Coltrane went through the South in the band with me. You understand? Also, I toured with Joe Louis, the heavyweight champion of the world, and I toured with Sugar Ray Robinson. You know? I toured with the Basie band all through the Deep South [circa 1953–54]—with Count Basie, George Shearing, and Billy Eckstine."

Nipsey Russell, emcee of that headline package tour (Brown insisted he be hired—he went from making $125 a week at the Baby Grand to $500 and more a week, on tour), recalls: "She was a superstar by then. She would have at that time, I would guess, maybe four hit records on the charts. At that point she was bigger than Dinah [Washington] or anybody. She was *the* thing."[6] Those hits were all on the R&B—not the pop—charts, however. When I asked Jerry Wexler whether it was difficult to get R&B records played on the general-audience radio stations during the early fifties, he answered, *"Difficult would have been easy—it was impossible."*[7] Atlantic was recording black artists, and their records originally got played primarily on stations aimed at black listeners—although comparatively small but growing numbers of whites were tuning in. Most whites in the early fifties, Wexler suggests, would have been unaware of this music. The real crossover, when black R&B artists often made it big on white pop charts, would not occur until the 1960s.

Russell points out, "Ruth Brown appealed to anybody that heard her—she didn't just appeal to black listeners. The limitation of her appeal at that time would just be the limitation of the exposure. Many of the records that they called rhythm and blues—which is a euphemism for race and black—were not played on some general stations. It would mean she would be big in a city like Detroit where there's a mass black population and therefore two or three radio stations that played black records. In a city where there's not much of a black population and no black station, she wouldn't be as well known."[8] But on tours, whether playing theaters, tobacco warehouses, or intimate clubs, Russell recalls, she tore the audiences up.[9] Her following during the early fifties, Herb Abramson says,

> definitely was mostly black people. This was like the so-called chitlin' circuit. However, stations like Randy's Record Shop in Nashville began to play the hit rhythm and blues songs, and they began to attract the white youth. Even before the birth of rock 'n' roll, we had rhythm and blues crossing over and becoming the music that the youth preferred. In other words, R&B was on its way to becoming what it is today, the music of young Americans. The records were played not only on black stations but also on some very powerful clear-channel stations like WGN in Chicago, but mostly I'm talking about Randy's Record Shop in Nashville, on a fifty thousand-watt clear channel that could be heard all the way to Chicago. And Randy sold records by mail, so he would play a Ruth Brown record and say, "Get this record and two others—send two dollars plus postage to the address of Randy's Record Shop." It was an important way for companies like Atlantic to promote records. For example, we made every effort to cultivate Randy, to put our records on his rhythm and blues program. So Randy was responsible—there was a black jockey who was playing the records at the station, but I can't remember his name right now, and there were three or four or five others. And we would make calls on these disc jockeys, make sure that they were supplied with the records. The distributor used to promote records, too. The distributor had a territory, to handle Coral Records, Atlantic Records, Savoy

Records, et cetera. And he had promotion, he would go around
to the jockeys. Later that developed into payola.[10]

Based on chart hits, Brown was almost certainly the top-selling
black female recording artist from 1951 to 1954. (Dinah Washington had more hits than she in 1950 and in the later fifties and early
sixties.) But exactly how big were the big R&B hits of the early fifties? What were the actual sales figures? Abramson comments: "To tell
you the truth, I don't know that myself. In those days, a selling record
was 50,000, and a minor hit was 150,000. Didn't sell no million
records until 'Sh-Boom' [a record by the Chords, which was a hit for
Atlantic in the summer of 1954]."[11] Abramson doubts that any of
Brown's records sold a million copies; in R&B, he says, a strong sell-
er sold maybe two or three hundred thousand copies. Very few R&B
records ever sold a million copies—*maybe,* Abramson guesses, Louis
Jordan's record of "Caldonia" and a few others actually sold a million. He stresses that the record sales figures touted to—and printed
uncritically by—the press were often inflated. And Abramson should
know—he was helping to put out such hype for Atlantic. Atlantic's
Ruth Brown bio flatly claimed that her record hits included many
"million-copy sellers." It lists "Teardrops from My Eyes," "Five-Ten-
Fifteen Hours," "Daddy Daddy," "I'll Get Along Somehow," "Three
Letters," and a "string of others." But in reality, an independent like
Atlantic was not getting nearly the sales for its R&B artists that a
major label like RCA was getting for such mainstream pop artists as
Perry Como or Eddie Fisher.

While newspaper and magazine write-ups about Brown repeatedly suggested that she was earning a fortune—one account estimated
she could make as much as $200,000 in a year—Brown says she nev-
er became rich. She got about $69 for each tune she recorded, she
recalls, against a promised royalty of 5 percent. But she actually received little in royalties, because costs of hiring musicians and arrangers, renting recording studios, and so on were billed to her account, and—at least on paper—her records did not appear to be
making much money for Atlantic. Nipsey Russell says Brown gave
away a lot of what she earned anyway; it was her nature to share
her blessings generously with others who weren't so well off. But he
also observes that black performers of Brown's generation had more
limited money-making opportunities than black performers now
have. The independent record companies had limited funds for pro-
motion, and live appearances by the artists were usually in comparatively small venues. Today, Janet Jackson, for example, will play are-

nas and stadiums that hold many times more people than did the theaters of Brown's era, and even accounting for inflation, admission prices are much higher. When Michael Jackson releases an album or goes on tour an international marketing campaign of proportions inconceivable in the 1950s goes into effect. Brown and her contemporaries didn't have the chance to earn anywhere near the sums that the most popular black recording artists of subsequent generations could.

Brown would typically do two twelve-week tours a year. Abramson recalls, "Booked by Shaw Artists agency, she toured the country with a package show—they made shows with two or three rhythm and blues headliners and the band—doing one-nighters. And so she toured up and down the South—including some venues that are surprising to people that don't know the South. I think in the fall season, the spring season, the tobacco sheds are empty—they use them for dances, and she played many a tobacco warehouse in the Carolinas and like that."[12]

Brown explains: "When you toured through the South, there were no big auditoriums. We worked in warehouses where they stacked the tobacco and the cotton on work nights. And on the one night off for the dance, they just pushed all that stuff in one corner. Trucks and stuff was put together to make the stage. And that's what we worked on. That's what the stages were. Yes. And there'd be a clothesline down the center, with a piece of cardboard or paper folded over it, and somebody would take a pencil and write 'white' on one side of it and 'colored' on the other, hang it over the rope, and staple it. Believe it, my darling. It was real. I tell you." She halts to regain control, the memories getting to her. For her, rhythm and blues is linked inextricably with that time when blacks had not yet won the battle against segregation. In a low voice, she continues, "Yeah, it was real. I remember it *well*. I think that's why I want so much, so much for them not to just throw away this music. It's lasted. And it's something that is now surfacing all over again. And it hurts me to see it come out of Europe and everywhere else, and have our young people think that that's where it started. It did not come from there [she is near tears now]—it came from here. People paid heavy dues to perform the music, you understand? People paid heavy dues to perform this. And the people who remember that music paid heavy dues to pay to hear the music. Because they came on the nights that they were not working in the fields, you understand? The nights that they were not marching and being sprayed with water hoses—whatever that quiet night was, that's where this music was. And it just kind of gets underneath. I turn on the radio sometimes and I hear new versions of things that I have done or songs that I know who did them. I *know* where the song came from, I know where the whole arrangement came from. And all of a sudden—this is new?" There is a militant edge to her voice. Then she adds softly, sounding for a moment almost like a little girl, "It's not fair."

Probably no booking meant more to Brown than one she got in 1953 in Norfolk, Virginia, near Portsmouth, where she had grown up. Family and hometown friends would be seeing her return as the most popular female artist in her field. But a half hour before showtime, she received word that her father had just died. The promoters insisted she perform. After a few numbers, she struggled to sing "Have a Good Time," which begins with the words, "Good-bye, I hate to see you go." But Brown broke down and was unable to continue. That number would henceforth be so strongly associated with the day her father died that for many years afterward she refused all requests to sing it.

Later that year, Brown was presented by the *Pittsburgh Courier,* a leading black newspaper, with the Bessie Smith Award for being the best female blues singer. Brown had won the *Courier's* readers' poll by an unprecedented margin. She responded, "I am overcome, both with humility and gratitude. Bessie Smith was the very greatest of blues singers. For me to receive an award in her name and honor is the biggest honor I could have ever dreamed of."

Billboard reported on October 24, 1953, that Atlantic had emerged as the clearly dominant company in the rhythm and blues field—and a lot of the credit was due to Brown. *Billboard* noted that in the first nine months of the year, using their National Best-Seller list as a measuring standard, Atlantic recordings had by far the largest total number of weeks on the R&B charts—fifty-six in all, twenty-seven of them due to just two Ruth Brown records, "Mama, He Treats Your Daughter Mean" and "Wild, Wild Young Men." The other record labels with the most weeks on the R&B charts were: Apollo (thirty-eight weeks), Chess (twenty-seven), Imperial (twenty-four), RPM (twenty-three), Duke (twenty-three), Federal (twenty-two), Aladdin (twenty), RCA Victor (twenty), OKeh (nineteen), Peacock (fourteen), Prestige (twelve), Savoy (twelve), and Specialty (twelve). In 1953, six-year-old Atlantic's roster of R&B artists included—in addition to sales leader Brown—the Clovers, Joe Turner, Clyde McPhatter and the Drifters, LaVern Baker, and Ray Charles.

Brown ended the year by making the most uninhibited-sounding recording of her career, "Hello Little Boy." She remembers that everyone was exhausted when they cut the number at an after-midnight session in a little studio above Patsy's Restaurant in New York, but the results were exhilarating. Although "Hello Little Boy" would later become a collector's item and remain in her working repertoire for many years, it failed to make the charts, probably because its frenzied, high-speed style—anticipating by a couple of years the direction some rock 'n' rollers would take—was ahead of its time.

It was never easy for anyone to predict which records would prove popular. Brown was often surprised. "The way they gave tunes to me at that time, they used to say, 'Ruth, I've got some demos, pick 'em up,' and they'd have a stack of things, and I would take them home and listen to them. Jesse Stone and Rudy Toombs were writing, and people were sending in things. Jesse Stone was probably the busiest, he and Rudy Toombs. Jesse was *the* writer over at Atlantic. He was quietly 'Mr. Atlantic' for the music. He's in his late eighties now, living in Florida. He came to see me since I've been doing *Black and Blue*." Others who contributed numbers included Leroy Kirkland, the team of Charles Singleton and Rose Marie McCoy, Budd Johnson, Doc Pomus, and Otis Blackwell. And there was give-and-take in the studios among the singers, musicians, arrangers, and producers. "At the recording sessions, you had great musicians," Brown remembers, "and everybody was allowed to give input. Usually, we would know the key. And sometimes the guy who wrote the song was there, would go to the piano, plunk it out, and everybody would come up with an idea. Maybe eventually it would go down on paper, but most times it was just right there: 'The horns, we're going to play so and so and so. And you play eight bars of this and then so and so you take that note, and then—bop.' A lot of times it was like that, you see, because a lot of your great musicians didn't read.

"It was probably one of the better musical periods—ever. You understand? The music was *very* honest. The difference from the way they make records today—and it was quite a difference—was that music then was done purely on the spot, with everybody present in the studio, everybody looking at one another. And if a musician hit a bad note, you could stop and say, 'What the heck was that you played?' Or if I sang out of tune, they would stop and say, 'Hold it, Ruth, just a minute now, this is ridiculous. Let's go back.' But now, you go in and more than likely you sing with the rhythm track, and you go home, and you don't hear it again. And when you do, you have to really say, 'My God, is that what I did?' Because in the room where they do all of the engineering wonders of this new age, they overdub [other instruments] and they double track, and singers double up—you work with five singers and when you hear it you sound like you've got twenty-five. Life moves on and technology is here and it's good in one respect. But it's not the best thing to happen in another way, because it does not allow the singer to think and improvise at all."

The big guns at Atlantic—Ahmet Ertegun, Herb Abramson, Jesse Stone, and (a little later) Jerry Wexler—all loved jazz and blues, and they strove to give their singers the best instrumental backing they could provide. They wanted records that discerning adults could appreciate, not just teenagers. Some other labels might cut corners by backing singers with fewer musicians—often playing sloppily at that— but Atlantic's R&B records had a greater polish to them.

Atlantic used the best available musicians, veterans from the greatest of the big swing bands and small jazz groups. Jesse Stone often served as musical director, contracting the musicians, arranging and conducting the band, and, in the early years, playing piano on sessions. Howard Biggs and Budd Johnson also turned in memorable arranging-conducting jobs on Brown recording sessions. Seven or eight musicians were the average: a trumpet (once in a while a trombone would be added), a tenor sax (perhaps featured in a honking solo) and a baritone sax (once in a while an alto would be added), and full rhythm section. Personnel varied from session to session, but among the personnel of four Ruth Brown sessions in 1953–54, all of which were directed by Jesse Stone, were trumpeters Taft Jordan (from the old Chick Webb band) and Ed Lewis (from the Count Basie Band); reedmen Arnett Cobb (from the Lionel Hampton band), Heywood Henry (from the Erskine Hawkins band), Sam "The Man" Taylor (from the Cab Calloway band), and Paul "Hucklebuck" Williams; and the rhythm section players (besides electric guitarist Mickey Baker and Vann "Piano Man" Walls, both Atlantic regulars) included some of the most respected players in modern jazz: pianist Hank Jones, drummer Connie Kay, and bassist George DuVivier.

Brown's hits in 1954 included two that reached the number one spot on the R&B charts: the topical "Mambo Baby," which enjoyed a twelve-week run on the charts in total (one week at number one) and the sentiment-drenched, era-evoking "Oh, What a Dream," which enjoyed a seventeen-week run (eight weeks at number one). Chuck Willis wrote "Oh, What a Dream" especially for Brown, and it remains one of her favorites. She had matured considerably as an artist and was phrasing with better taste. Her voice had more grace; there is a particular tonal beauty on such sides as "Oh, What a Dream," the following year's poignant "I Can See Everybody's Baby," and 1959's "Don't Deceive Me" that was not in evidence on her earliest recordings. (The removal of her tonsils in 1954 lowered her voice, too, she notes.)

Ruth Brown's career received a setback when Herb Abramson was inducted into the service. She had always felt that he took a special interest in her career and trusted his ability to come up with the right songs for her and guide her generally. "'Oh, What a Dream' was the last record that I rehearsed with Ruth before I went into the service," Abramson recalls. "I think that the actual session occurred just after I left for overseas. [Atlantic recording engineer] Tom Dowd sent me the tape, to approve the takes and to select the song to promote. He sent me the tape—I still have that box—and next to 'Oh, What a Dream,' I wrote: 'Hit!'"[13] Abramson's instinct, in this case as in many others, was right on the money. The popularity of Brown's recording prompted Patti Page and Mary Dell to cut cover versions. After serving for two years in Germany, Abramson, on his return, was put in charge of a new Atlantic subsidiary, Atco. Others handled Ruth Brown's career. Although she continued to do well, her career was beginning to slow down. She continued to have hits all through the 1950s, but 1954's "Mambo Baby" and "Oh, What a Dream" would be her last recordings to reach the number one spot.

By now she and Willis Jackson had gotten married, and she took some time off to start a family. Her first public appearance after giving birth to a son in January 1955 was when she went to Birdland with LaVern Baker and others from Atlantic to see Count Basie and his orchestra. On March 8, 1955, Brown made her network television debut on NBC-TV's "Tonight!" starring Steve Allen. Several days later, during one of Brown's frequent appearances at the Apollo, Ahmet Ertegun and Jerry Wexler presented her with a special gold disc in honor of, they said, having sold a total of five million records. On April 30 Atlantic released a new Ruth Brown single that turned out to be a double-sided hit. The soulful "I Can See Everybody's Baby" (a pop song with substance by Leroy Kirkland and Mamie Thomas that, Wexler notes, was a swipe from an older gospel song, "I Can See Everybody's Mother"), which reached number seven on the R&B charts, was coupled with "As Long as I'm Moving," which reached number four. "As Long as I'm Moving" was written by "Charles Calhoun" (whose "Shake, Rattle and Roll" was a big hit the year before), the pen name of veteran Kansas City pianist-bandleader-composer Jesse Stone. Stone notes that, as a songwriter, he's always thought of the rhythm first, aiming to make listeners want to dance. "As Long as I'm Moving" is, like so much of Stone's work, infectiously rhyth-

Whether belting the blues or talking to the audience between numbers while her band continues playing softly, no performer is better at connecting with a club audience than Ruth Brown, captured in performance at the Downbeat Club in New York, 1994, by Danish photographer Andreas Johnsen. (Author's collection)

THANKS DOWN BEAT READERS

↓

For voting "Mama, He Treats Your Daughter Mean" the TOP Rhythm and Blues record of 1953.

Ruth Brown

Atlantic placed this ad in *Down Beat* magazine (January 13, 1954), celebrating Brown's winning of the *Down Beat* readers' poll for best rhythm and blues performance of 1953. (Author's collection)

Ruth Brown in the 1960s. (Author's collection; courtesy of Jerry Ohlinger's
Movie Materials)

Brown sings the show-stopping double-entendre number "If I Can't Sell It, I'll Keep Sitting on It," which has remained a staple of her repertoire ever since, in the Broadway production of *Black and Blue* in 1988. (Photo by Martha Swope; author's collection; courtesy of Marilynn LeVine)

Brown enjoys a get-together with old friend Nipsey Russell at Sam's, a New York theater-district restaurant, July 5, 1989. In the early fifties, Brown gave the comic's career a jump start by insisting that he be hired as emcee for the package show in which she was touring. (Photo by Chip Deffaa)

Member of Congress John Conyers presents Brown with her Career Achievement Award at the Rhythm and Blues Foundation's first awards ceremony, Washington, D.C., November 10, 1989. (Author's collection; courtesy of Joan Myers)

Brown in a celebratory mood with attorney Howell Begle (who helped her and other R&B stars get back royalties), Little Jimmy Scott, and an unidentified friend. (Author's collection; courtesy of Jimmy Scott)

mic, and Brown gave it a knock-out performance. Stone has only good memories of her ("just a very tiny little thing when we first saw her") but adds, "She was kind of temperamental—not as difficult as Joe Turner, but some certain songs she wouldn't like, and didn't want to do."[14]

She recorded a couple of duets ("I Gotta Have You" and "Love Will Join Us Together") with Clyde McPhatter; they had worked together during a Christmas R&B show hosted by disc jockey Dr. Jive at the Brooklyn Paramount Theater. But the records did not sell as well as Atlantic had hoped. "Love Has Joined Us Together" reached number eight on the R&B charts; "I Gotta Have You" didn't make the charts at all. (It's a pity Brown did not get to record duets with any of the other greats with whom she worked live during the fifties, from Billy Eckstine to Ray Charles.) She did a tour of West Coast clubs and sang songs by some of the newer writers, such as Bobby Darin and Neil Sedaka. "All these young kids were bringing in material," she says.

Atlantic didn't seem to have a clear idea of where her career should be headed. Some sides she recorded were thoughtful and somewhat sophisticated; others were so slight and commercial that Atlantic appeared to be reaching down toward the bubblegum set. As she listens to the old recordings now, she's amazed at all of the different musical attitudes she was asked to express. Atlantic would back her with a doo-wop-type vocal group on one record, give prominence to a rock 'n' roll guitar on another, and put her in a jazz setting on the next. On "When I Get You, Baby" she was given a brisk, marching band kind of backing; on "Don't Deceive Me," with its wonderfully sweet sadness (Brown's voice was often so revelatory of her feelings), she was supported, quite effectively, by a dozen strings.

Composers Jerry Leiber and Mike Stoller, who had emerged as important forces in rock 'n' roll via such hits as "Kansas City," "Hound Dog," and "Jailhouse Rock," concocted a flimsy song called "Lucky Lips" for Brown. Released in March 1957, it reached the number six spot on the R&B charts and, as an early example of crossover, reached the number twenty-five spot on the pop charts. Gale Storm did a cover version—white artists were forever copying the hits of black artists—which reached only seventy-seven. Brown also turned up on European charts with this number.

Leiber and Stoller produced some of Brown's records in this period, too, including her 1958 hit "This Little Girl's Gone Rockin'" (written for her by Bobby Darin), which reached the number seven spot on the R&B charts and the number twenty-four spot on the pop charts. Like "Lucky Lips," "This Little Girl's Gone Rockin'" is a reminder that the greatest commercial successses aren't always the high-est quality songs. But both catchy numbers, promoted to the best of Atlantic's limited abilities, went over big with teenagers. Wexler re-calls that Atlantic, unlike the biggest companies, had no staff for pro-motion in the fifties. He had to go to stations himself to get the records played. In Georgia, he succeeded in getting one DJ to play "Lucky Lips"—which the DJ introduced as "Lucky Tips."

Television exposure would have helped Brown's career, but televi-sion was still a white domain; opportunities for black artists—partic-ularly black R&B artists—were restricted. The only black performer to get a network show during the 1950s was smooth balladeer Nat King Cole (who was on NBC in 1956–57), and when he appeared, some affiliates refused to carry his show. Big variety shows were much more likely to give exposure to Georgia Gibbs or Gale Storm than to Ruth Brown or LaVern Baker. The power of television to sell records and make careers, of course, was enormous. As a case in point, Ricky Nelson, just shy of his seventeenth birthday, recorded a cover ver-sion of Fats Domino's "I'm Walking." Then, on television's popular "Adventures of Ozzie and Harriet," Ozzie Nelson mentioned that his son had just recorded a "rhythm and blues tune." Ricky sang "I'm Walking," and within weeks that record—his first—had made it into the top twenty on the pop charts, launching his career as a top-sell-ing singing star.

By the late fifties rock 'n' roll was the music of American teenag-ers. New stars were rapidly coming up or being manufactured. Cal-low singers of the Fabian-Frankie Avalon sort were becoming house-hold words, their records selling far better than those of many more talented and creative older R&B performers who had helped lay a musical foundation for them. Ruth Brown was aware—and under-standably resentful—of the way institutionalized racial prejudice had affected her career. Yes, she had made it big and was certainly earn-ing a lot of money "according to my standards," as she expresses it, but she knows she could have been better known were it not for prej-udice. An undercurrent of bitterness, and of a grim determination born of overcoming hardships, still informs much of her work and gives it guts. She put her emotions into her singing.

"I wasn't so upset about other singers copying my songs because that was their privilege, and they had to pay the writers of the song," Brown says. "But what did hurt me was the fact that I had originat-ed the song, and I never got the opportunities to be on the top tele-vision shows and the talk shows. I didn't get the exposure. And oth-er people were copying the style, the whole idea." Generally speaking, she wasn't impressed with those who tried copying what she and her R&B colleagues created. "There is no way that I would mistake a duplicate for the people that I knew and watched from the curtains doing these things. There's nobody, as far as I'm concerned, that could duplicate what it was that Jackie Wilson had. There's nobody that had the charisma that Sam Cooke had. To be backstage at the Apollo and see the Clovers just rehearsing what they're going to do, or the Cadillacs, the Five Keys—it was wonderful."

Meanwhile, there were personal as well as professional changes in her life. She and Willis Jackson divorced, and she married another sax player, Earl Swanson, who became the father of her second son. A strongly sung "Why Me," effectively mixing lamentation with assertiveness, returned Brown to the R&B charts (peaking at number seventeen) in 1958. She had a chart hit a year later as well with the breezy "Jack o' Diamonds," which was written for her by Lloyd Price and reached number twenty-three on the R&B charts and ninety-six on the pop charts. "I Don't Know" reached number five on the R&B charts (and number sixty-four on the pop charts) in 1959, and "Don't Deceive Me" reached number ten on the R&B charts (and number sixty-two on the pop charts) in 1960.

Brook Benton wrote a couple of songs for Brown, too, and she toured with him. After years of recording nothing but singles, she recorded her first album, *Late Date;* she also sang on all-star rock 'n' roll stage shows. But she was in her early thirties now, not old by most standards but getting old in the eyes of an army of teenage record buyers who favored young singers, preferably teens, as spokespersons for their generation. Atlantic was still coming up with some intriguing songs for Brown, although the overall quality of the songs they gave her was declining. Wexler liked such distinctive numbers as "I Can't Hear a Word You Say" (1959) and "Takin' Care of Business" (1960), but the hoped-for sales didn't come. Abramson comments, "An artist's popularity gains and wanes. It fluctuates. Inevitably, a hot artist cools down."[15] "'Takin' Care of Business' didn't do squat," Wexler says. "By then, entropy had set in. Her career had slowed down, the way every career does eventually, from the Coasters to Joe Turner. We couldn't get a hit anymore. It had nothing to do with the quality of her voice; it was just a shift in trends, in tastes. It's a miracle when someone becomes a hit."[16]

"I stayed with Atlantic until in the sixties," Brown recalls, "when the music changed, a lot of things changed. The company got bigger, and I didn't get the kind of material that I used to get because there were too many people to spread it around among. Of course, by that time they had like Ray Charles—the label was very big." In 1961 Brown switched from Atlantic to the Phillips label, making the charts once again—just barely—with "Shake a Hand" (ninety-seven on the pop charts) and a remake of "Mama, He Treats Your Daughter Mean" (ninety-nine on the pop charts), the last chart appearances of her career. "And for an album *Along Comes Ruth,* I did tunes done by everybody else; I did LaVern Baker's material, I did Clyde McPhatter's, I did Bobby "Blue" Bland, the Clovers, and a couple of original things," she recalls. She sang on the Playboy Club circuit for awhile and then went into semiretirement.

* * *

From late 1962 through late 1972 Ruth Brown largely withdrew from the business. She never got out completely—she still made occasional albums and sang in local clubs when opportunities came up—but her desire to be home with her two young sons, Ronald and Earl, ruled out extensive touring. She had tried taking her sons on the road with her, handing them to friends standing in the wings when she performed, but she didn't believe that was fair to them; children deserved "roots." And when her marriage to Swanson ended in divorce, she was more determined than ever to be home with her boys.

Then in the mid-sixties, the pop music scene underwent so complete a transformation that she wondered if her time as a performer had indeed passed. Beginning in 1964–65, British groups dominated American pop charts: the Beatles, the Rolling Stones, Herman's Hermits, the Dave Clark Five, the Kinks, Gerry and the Pacemakers, and others. To Brown, that "British invasion" seemed to sound a death knell for R&B. "The music got pushed out of the way. And I just didn't fit into that new mold," she says. "I could not travel. And the clubs around the New York area where I could have worked—all these eventually became discos and went for a different kind of music. All that changed." She made some attempts to win a jazz audience, playing an Apollo Theatre bill, for example, headlined by Miles Davis, but without much success.

In the fifties, when she had been making all those hit records, she admits, "I was comfortable; I wasn't rich—never was, that's by any stretch of the imagination; just comfortable," she says. But in the sixties, as a singer working but sporadically, her earnings were meager. "It got down to little things that I needed for my children, money for education, a decent house to live in. And what I could earn, I couldn't do that—I just couldn't do that," she says.

Accountants always seemed to have ways of showing that her new recordings weren't making money and neither were reissues of her old ones, so no royalties could be paid to her. Although Atlantic continued selling albums compiled from her old singles, she had not received a dime in royalties since leaving the company. Like a number of other artists, she received quarterly royalty statements that indicated that she *owed* Atlantic money. After 1969 she stopped receiving royalty statements from Atlantic altogether. Bootleggers put out Ruth Brown albums as well. "After a while," she notes, "I looked up and saw records coming from everywhere. Go in the stores and records cost so much—and I said, 'Well, my God, I'm not being paid for this!'" She wrote to Atlantic a few times but says that she got no reply. She also consulted with several lawyers, all of whom told her that there was nothing they could do.

Occasionally, Brown would resurface to do a new album, winning admiration from other singers and musicians, if not sizable record sales. Several albums from those years of semiretirement remain favorites of hers. Mainstream's *Ruth Brown '65* (later retitled *Softly* and rereleased as *Help a Good Girl Go Bad*) was an attempt to position her as a superior pop singer who recorded for mature listeners. With lush orchestral backing, she sang such quality songs as Johnny Burke and Jimmy Van Heusen's "Here's That Rainy Day" and Jimmy McHugh and Dorothy Fields's "Porgy." (It's a pity she'd never been given a chance to record material like this before.) Perhaps the standout track was a languorous, wistful, pure rendition of "On the Good Ship Lollipop." "I liked that album, very, very much," Brown comments. "And I would love to hear again the album that I did with Thad Jones and Mel Lewis [and their jazz orchestra]. I can't even find it."

She married for a fourth time, "to a police officer from Long Island named Bill Blunt. Well, it didn't last because we were totally in two opposite worlds. But in the short time we were together, he gave my boys a wonderful outlook on life—the need for sports and keeping themselves clean. And I'm very sure that if there was anybody in the world that was good for them, it was he. In that relationship, I tried to be a suburban housewife, but music called more often." She sang in a church choir and occasionally at Sonny's Place, a club in Seaford, Long Island.

It was not easy for Brown, a single mother trying to raise two sons in Deer Park, Long Island, to make ends meet. "I have no other background except music. I can't type, I don't know shorthand," she points out. She took what jobs she could. At times she worked as a domestic, cleaning homes; her employers had no idea she was a singer. "When I did the jobs in the big homes in the hills up there, I was using my marriage name: Ruth Blunt," she notes. When her boys saw her in her white uniform, she told them she was going to beauty school. (She wanted them to go to college someday.) At times, she couldn't pay her bills. She can now joke about answering her phone in a different voice to tell bill collectors something like "Miss Brown is in Switzerland this month," but it wasn't funny at the time. Nor was it funny when, while she was signing autographs after a club performance one night, her car was towed because she hadn't been able to keep up the payments.

Some friends from the early days remained steadfast. For example, she notes, "Nipsey [Russell] has always been there. If I needed help or someone to cry to when I was struggling with my children by myself, many times he helped me then." And she feels a deep debt of gratitude to her family. "Those brothers and sisters of mine, ain't nothing like 'em in the world—no place," she tells me, struggling to hold back tears as she remembers their aid when times were hard. "I get full, because there have been times I couldn't pay the rent, and they have always gotten together, and without asking me, 'Why can't you pay it?'—they paid it. If I was ill, if it was just a matter of coming and spending one hour, they got there and went back [to Portsmouth]. They're still punching time clocks, they're all nine-to-five people. No rich people in my family. The only thing that they're rich in is respect and love for one another. And all of that comes from the strong lady that my mama was. She made us that way. And the strong man that my father was gave my brothers a strong identity. My mother gave me a strong strength of a strong woman. My father made me respect myself, irregardless to what. It was like, 'If you get whipped, I'll whip you. And you cannot let it beat you, you understand? You cannot let it beat you. If you can't do one thing, do another. It doesn't matter, so long as you pay the rent. And as you're doing that, thank God for giving you the strength to pay the rent, no matter how you have to pay it, so long as it's not in a manner that will shame you.' And when you can maintain that kind of an understanding, then you can move.

"It wasn't too long ago that I did those other jobs. In Long Island, I rode and I tended the school bus, and I worked in preschool as an aide, a playground counselor. I worked with retarded children. I worked as a domestic. Did everything to pay the rent. And sang at night, whenever I could. But the only thing that kept me alive musically in those lean years was a group in Long Island called the International Art of Jazz led by Anne Sneed. They did school programs, where they'd go into the schools, and she included me; I was the singer with a lot of those instructional programs, I dealt with rhythm. Somebody dealt with harmony and melody. I would take whatever song that they had done, basically, and then change the tempo, with my tambourine, and show them how it could be turned into a rhythm and blues tune." Her powers as a performer still continued to mature. She had time to reflect on what songs she most wanted to sing; she dropped from her repertoire many of the numbers she had recorded for Atlantic, reaching back in many cases for older numbers she felt had more substance.

When Brown made her first major New York appearance in about a decade at the popular club Folk City (renamed Jazz City during her engagement), John S. Wilson noted in *The New York Times* on July 1, 1972:

> She is a polished and commanding performer who delivers her songs with a crisp urgency that often erupts into shouting statements—a manner that is frequently reminiscent of Dinah Washington. But Miss Brown has her own positive and assured way of using this approach and she also has her own rather unusual choice of material. Along with a traditional blues, "Trouble in Mind," and a Ray Charles song, both of which one would expect from her, she comes up with the unexpected, "Sonny Boy," for instance, and "Yes Sir, That's My Baby," both done with a marvelously slinky beat. Nellie Lutcher's audience rouser of thirty years ago, "Hurry on Down to My House, Baby," was sung surprisingly slowly and extremely effectively with a pair of saxophonists riffing behind her.

In a review on December 17, 1972, of a performance by Brown at New York's Village Gate, Wilson noted he had never seen the legendary Ma Rainey perform, but when he watched Brown's commanding, declamatory way of putting over numbers, he felt he was "seeing and hearing something of what Ma Rainey projected." She hadn't gotten that kind of praise in her youth.

Such reviews were not enough to launch a true comeback for Ruth Brown—the timing simply wasn't right yet. But she did begin working a little more frequently, using (among others) the great Don Pullen on organ and Charles C. I. Williams, who still works with her, on alto sax. Brown has always taken care to hire the best musicians she could find to accompany her, even if it meant reducing her own earnings. Her sons were old enough now for her to focus more on performing. (The older son entered Howard University in 1973; the younger one would enter U.S.C. four years later.) In 1973 she also recorded another album for a minor label but recalls that "the check that I got for it bounced. I've been trying to catch the guy. There's so much floating around that's not out there with my consent." Several years later, she began recording an album for another company, but midway through the project the producer told her they had run out of money and the project was put on hold.

In the meantime, she had come up with a young organ player whom she has used as her music director ever since. "When Don Pullen went off with Charles Mingus [around 1973], Bobby Forrester was recommended to me by someone to take his place. At that time, we were rehearsing out at George Benson's house in the Bronx; George had a basement with all the set-ups and everything. So when I walked in the first day with my music and saw this little bushy-haired kid sitting there I thought, 'This white kid don't know my music.' I said, 'Well, sweetheart, I think we're going to need more than one day to rehearse this music, you and I.' I was just so sure he couldn't play it. He said, 'Oh no, Miss Brown'—he was very polite—'I know everything you do.' I said, 'What?!' And do you know, I don't think that from that day until this we have had a really stretched-out rehearsal. Because Bobby's fantastic. I told him, 'You're a smart dude, because you know all my music. You never even open the book. So I can't hire nobody if the music gets lost, because you've got it here in your head.' But he's fantastic in that he hears me, he anticipates."

Opportunities for work were still spotty, and things got so bad in 1975 that Brown's telephone was disconnected. She had to make calls from the pay telephone of a Texaco station across the street from her home. The head mechanic, Mike Balducci, would whistle for her when she'd get a call.

One night in September 1975 Brown noted that two of her friends from the old days, comedian Redd Foxx and Billy Eckstine, were appearing at the Westbury Music Fair. She tried to go backstage to see them, but a security guard stopped her. Foxx, standing in the hallway in his underwear, spotted her and hollered, "Let her in!" Eckstine came out, too. After the hugging and kissing and reminiscing, Foxx—distraught that Brown had fallen upon hard times—said he was going to send for her when he got back to California. She protested, but he reminded her that years before, when he had been without funds for food or rent, he had sought help from her. She had pointed to her money, lying on her dresser, and told him to take whatever he wanted, no questions asked. He hadn't forgotten her generosity.

Several weeks later, Brown heard Mike Balducci's whistle from the Texaco station. She looked out and he yelled that Redd Foxx was calling her—*from Hollywood.* All the mechanics were gathered around the pay telephone. She had everyone at the gas station say hello to Foxx, who told her that he was sending her plane tickets to Los Angeles, along with $500. He was rehearsing *Selma,* a musical based on the work of Martin Luther King, and he had had the role of Mahalia Jackson written into the script for Brown. That role started a new career for her in the theater.

For several years she lived in Las Vegas, where she played General Cartwright in an all-black production of *Guys and Dolls* and eighty-three-year-old Big Mama Cooper in *Livin' Fat.* She also sang at Circus Circus and other venues as her schedule permitted. She adds, "I took Bobby Forrester to Vegas, the first time he'd ever left here [New York]. The only reason that his mother wanted him to go was because I agreed that he was going to live in my place. He shared a room with my son. So he sort of just grew up with us."

Although Brown has always considered herself first and foremost a singer not an actress, she was glad for the heightened visibility that acting on television gave her. Norman Lear cast her in a supporting role in a short-lived television situation comedy, "Hello Larry," starring McLean Stevenson. Following that, she got parts in the film *Under the Rainbow* (which starred Chevy Chase) and a series, "Checkin' In" (starring Marla Gibbs). To Brown's surprise, acting became a means of survival. "I've had to learn how to act," she says. "But that hasn't come too hard to do. Because the whole thing is not that far from what I was doing all my life: running up onstage grinning, pretending everything was all right, while the finance company was outside taking my car. So I've been acting a long time."

She traveled to Japan as singer in an all-star group that included Dizzy Gillespie and Mel Lewis in 1979. Mayor Marion Barry proclaimed a Ruth Brown Day in Washington, D.C., in 1980, an event tied to the fact that her career began at the Crystal Caverns. She also received word that year that funds had been found to complete an album begun in 1976 but put on hold. She went into a New York recording studio to sing with an orchestra arranged and conducted by Manny Albam.

Meanwhile, Barney Josephson, who had run the famed Cafe Society nightclubs during the 1940s, had returned to the entertainment business, running a popular Greenwich Village club called the Cookery. He was looking for a replacement for his summer 1981 booking, Helen Humes, who had taken ill. Albam sent word that Brown was back in town and sounded better than ever. Josephson went to the recording studio and signed her for eight weeks in his club after hearing her belt out just eight bars of one song. The Brown's Cookery engagement—her first Manhattan club appearance in nine years—left no doubt that she had become a more powerful performer than she had been in her heyday. In *The New York Times*, John S. Wilson suggested that her experience acting on stage and television had enhanced her abilities as a singer. But there was more to it than that. The hardships that she had endured had added character to her work. Wilson noted, "Her voice is, if anything, stronger than ever when she is shouting the blues or rising to a gospel urgency in an inspirational song such as 'You'll Never Walk Alone.'"

But Brown's run of bad luck hadn't quite ended. She still couldn't get a major-label record deal. She recorded a critically acclaimed album in 1982, but the company for which she did it, Flair, soon went out of business. "That was the story of my life," she says. That same year, she got what appeared to be her biggest break in ages. Brown was to make her Broadway debut in a show with Leslie Uggams called *Blues in the Night*, which would include classic blues songs associated with Bessie Smith, Alberta Hunter, and others. However, Brown's elation soon turned to sorrow when the producers replaced her with Jean DuShon, a much less distinguished—but much younger—singer from the cast of *Sophisticated Ladies*. The *Daily News* reported on June 2, 1982, that a source close to the production of *Blues in the Night* had said that Brown "had arthritis and couldn't cut it. She got through the rehearsals but never made the first preview."

The show—an attempt to cover some of the same sort of musical territory *Black and Blue* would cover so successfully a few years later—flopped, and Brown was soon disproving the notion that she didn't have the strength to carry a stage show. She appeared in the 1983 production of James Baldwin's *The Amen Corner*. "My mama saw me in that show—she died five days after it closed," Brown remembers, adding, "I would have given anything for her to have seen me in *Black and Blue*—she wanted me to make Broadway." When she had another starring role in Vernel Bagneris's acclaimed off-Broadway R&B musical *Staggerlee* (in 1987), she could feel momentum building.

Her success in *Staggerlee* led to her being cast as Motormouth Maybelle in the 1988 John Waters film *Hairspray*, with a cast including Deborah Harry, Ricki Lake, and, in a dual role, the transvestite actor Divine, who had appeared in other of Waters's offbeat productions. "I didn't know much about the character when I agreed to do *Hairspray*," Brown says. "I was just so excited and happy about being called to do a movie: 'Are you serious? I'm going to do a movie!' And—to show you how naive I was—I had not heard of John Waters before. Well, I went to the theater where I was doing *Staggerlee* and all of the kids backstage—the tech crew, they used to all talk with me, because I became like the mother hen backstage—they said, 'Miss Brown, I hear you're going to do a movie. Who's the director? Who's the producer?' I said, 'What's that man's name? Oh, John Waters.' And they screamed: 'What?! John Waters? Have you ever seen one of his films? What are you going to do in a John Waters film?' Because he already was this cult figure and had this reputation for the so-called, as the press says, trashy movies. So I said, 'I don't know who he is.' They said, 'You've never seen a John Waters film? Well, you better be careful.' So I said, 'I'll be careful.'

"*Hairspray* is a spoof of the early sixties. It has to do with dance programs—like Dick Clark kind of things—dance programs in Maryland where the white kids were dancing to black music but the black kids were not allowed to attend. And I have my own record shop and dance program in the ghetto, where the black kids dance. So the white kids eventually find their way over to my record shop, and the black kids are having such a good time, and we teach them dances called the Bird and the Roach and the Itch. And I decide that no longer are we going to take this—if they can dance to our music, then we can dance to the music with them. The whole scene is about integrating the dance program. The character I played in the film acts like she's kind of insane most of the time but she makes her point. As John Waters says, 'It's a funny movie about a very serious situation.' I grew to be very fond of John Waters although the first time we met wasn't the happiest of times because I refused to put that blond wig on my head. And he had to sit down and remind me that the character on the screen was Motormouth Maybelle and not Ruth Brown. That wig! I don't want my people walking with signs in protest, after all these years—because I've usually been walking with them, with the signs. But it's a good movie. People come out laughing. The dances are good, the music is good. Divine was wonderful to work with. The name was perfect because he was divine. I knew him for a short time, but I feel a lot of fulfillment from just having met the man, for the perfectionism and what he gave to it. And he was a very, very warm human being. Whenever I was in his presence, he made me feel so welcome. One day I looked at one of the stills from the movie, where I was wearing this wig and this crazy costume, and I said, 'Oh my God, Divine—my children, my family, everybody's going to put me up for adoption when they see this film!' He said, 'Well, darling, don't worry about it. For every one that you lose, I got one of mine that you will gain. So put your wig on and march on to the bank!' Yeah, he was a nice person. Everybody was very nice in the film."

Hairspray gave Brown more visibility than she'd had in a long while. At the time, she was living rather anonymously in Harlem. The people in her neighborhood, she felt, were kind. Many of them had no idea who she was, other than someone with whom they'd chat if they'd run into each other when she was out walking her dog or buying groceries. But after *Hairspray* people recognized her: "I went in the supermarket, and this little kid said [she gasps], 'You're that lady I saw in *Hairspray*.' Incredible! I had on a blond wig in that movie; I'd hoped I looked better than that," Brown says. But she knows that doing the film was good for her career: "I owe a lot to Motormouth Maybelle."

Brown gained further exposure when she got a weekly show on National Public Radio, "Harlem Hit Parade," on which she played classic R&B records, offered recollections, and interviewed the artists who had made the records. "One of the nicer things that happened was the mail that I got from listeners to the show, all around the country. People wrote to me about how long they had been Ruth Brown fans. And I think some of the good luck that started came because there was many a person praying around this country for Ruth Brown to surface again. Every other letter that I received would say, 'I'm going to remember you in my prayers. I'm praying that I will soon see you being received the way you should be.' And I've got mail I wouldn't get rid of for the world. That's my inspiration. When I'm really feeling low down, I open my scrapbooks and read some of these letters. I've kept every letter because I hope at some time to be able to answer each one," Brown says.

"And I received a lot of mail from young people who were in prisons. A lot of the people were listening to the music for the first time as adults. They had heard it in their homes because their parents were my age. But they were so glad to be able to find out something about the people who performed the music. And I think what was special about my interviews was that most of the people I spoke with on the show I had at one time or another worked with. So we talked about a lot of personal things and we had good laughs." Doing the series prompted her to reflect upon her career. "It's only after I started doing the radio show that I really started listening to my own records; I never really listened to my own music that much other than when I was performing it."

She often sang at Harlem's Baby Grand Club, even when she began receiving offers from clubs in midtown that could pay much bet-

ter. She felt that she had gotten her start in New York at the Baby
Grand, and she also liked the idea of giving something back to her
own community.

In the meantime, she had met a fan named Howell Begle, who
became her lawyer. She recalls, "I did an appearance and he showed
up with all these albums of mine to get them signed. I said to him,
'Where'd you get all these records?' He said, 'I paid dearly for them.'
He's a collector. I said, 'Well, somebody's making money because I'm
not.' And he said, 'What?'" When she told him she hadn't received
royalties in many years, Begle vowed to do what he could—on a pro
bono basis—to right that wrong. From 1983 to 1988 he devoted legal time worth an estimated $60,000 to settle the issue of whether
Brown and others had been compensated fairly. Brown introduced
him to Big Joe Turner, Sam and Dave, and other R&B artists whose
stories echoed her own. In the end, Begle investigated the cases of
some thirty-five R&B artists. He found that their royalty records often appeared to have been maintained poorly, and in some cases were
no longer maintained at all. When records did appear accurate, royalties were being calculated according to original contract terms,
tightfisted by contemporary standards.

Begle found that the pioneers of R&B, recording for various labels
from the late 1940s through the mid-sixties, typically signed contracts
promising just 1 to 4 percent of retail price, a fraction of what would
be offered now. They typically received advances per song recorded
that ranged from a low of $50 to a high of $350, and some artists
recorded for one-time-only payments of $200 or less per song; they
were promised no royalties whatsoever. What was worse, the record
companies that did offer royalty contracts often billed artists for so
many diverse costs (recording sessions, fees paid to arrangers, producers, managers, and choreographers, and even, in some instances,
lessons in charm, fashion, and other forms of "personal enhance-
ment") that companies claimed they owed no royalties at all. They
said that they had never recouped what they had so generously invested in the artists. Popular R&B artists thus often received little or
no payment beyond the initial advance on royalties, even for hit recordings that might be endlessly reissued.[17]

Brown recalls that Atlantic's royalty accounts in the mid-eighties
indicated that she *owed* Atlantic some $30,000. After scrutinizing At-
lantic's bookkeeping practices, Begle was certain that the negative
balance in Brown's account—and those of many other artists recording for Atlantic and other labels following similar practices—was radically wrong. Begle found other artists who had been told that they

had negative balances ranging from \$20,000 to \$60,000, which meant that they were being paid no royalties whatsoever for reissues of their recordings.[18]

He eventually hoped to effect industrywide reforms but Atlantic was his first target, and he pressured Atlantic by generating publicity. For example, Begle got CBS to do a segment on its newsmagazine "West 57th" on the problem, and Brown and Joe Turner appeared. Turner, dying of kidney disease and without health insurance, described being too ill to be out working in clubs but said that he had no choice financially. He had to try to pay for dialysis treatments. He and Brown thought it grossly unfair that their accounts had recently been billed for the remastering of some reissued recordings made a quarter of a century or more before. That seemed unfair to a lot of viewers as well. Ahmet Ertegun, chair of Atlantic Records, which had by then become a part of the Warner Communications empire, canceled the remastering bills. The larger question of what, if anything, Atlantic really owed to artists such as Brown and Turner was still being looked into when Turner died. Ertegun paid Turner's funeral expenses.

Begle obtained further publicity for the issue when he got Ruth Brown to take the stand at a congressional hearing on consumer fraud. Atlantic saw that the question of whether Brown and other R&B recording stars had been exploited was somehow becoming a federal issue, and the company didn't need that kind of negative PR, especially while gearing up for a heavily promoted fortieth anniversary celebration. Brown was surprised—and delighted—to discover how many people she met in Washington still remembered her from the years she turned out one R&B hit after another; to her, those years seemed long past. She remarks, "I had the privilege of being at a hearing with the Reverend Jesse Jackson. And he came from Greenville, South Carolina—I played there so many times, at a place called Textile Hall. When they said, 'Do you remember Ruth Brown?' he said, 'Ruth Brown!? "Mama, He Treats Your Daughter Mean."' And then there was Congressman John Conyers, who was chairing the meeting, and he said, 'Ruth Brown—"Every Time It Rains, I Think of You."' He sang 'Teardrops.' And then there was a white senator—I can't recall his name—I think he was from North Carolina, who said, 'Well, I won't be outdone, because I also heard Ruth Brown, even though I had to be in the spectators' gallery.' And he said, '"Five-Ten-Fifteen Hours" was my favorite song,' which just killed me."

Many others also assured her that they had been fans. "Alex Haley said he went AWOL to listen to me perform. Katie Hall, the wom-

an who placed the nomination up for Dr. Martin Luther King's birthday, brought her daughter to see me and said, 'I want you to meet
the Aretha of my day'—talking about me. And recently Aretha made
a statement that there were a lot of singers when she was coming
up, but for her it was Ruth Brown. Etta James said the same thing.
Ray Charles, in his book *Brother Ray,* makes mention of the fact that
the first person he went out with, with his band, was Ruth Brown.
Little Richard said, 'I heard Ruth Brown's voice and I loved Ruth
Brown.' There there are so many people who are now saying, 'Hey,
I've been a Ruth Brown fan all these years,' that that makes up for
some of the time I felt left out of things."

Jesse Jackson helped Begle get access to top brass at Warner Communications. And, after five years of wrangling, Begle received a settlement from Atlantic, which made no admission of any intentional
wrongdoing, that was better than Brown had hoped for. In 1988 she
received her first royalty check from Atlantic in twenty-eight years—
$21,000 after deductions. "It was all settled amicably," Brown says.
"It was a little late coming, but it did come. And my friendship is
intact with Ahmet, which I'm very glad of." Many of Brown's R&B
colleagues also received royalty checks. She notes, "A lot of people
benefited. That's one of the reasons *U.S. News* and *Newsweek* and all
picked the story up. When I started it was only me, but I drew in
other R&B artists who had the same problem so it ended up being
about thirty people that are getting royalties now. The settlement is
going to be a long-range benefit for everybody concerned, because
they've erased the debts. A lot of us were supposed to be in the red
[with Atlantic], and one of the things in the agreement was—all of
that was erased."

The royalty payments that Brown and the others received in 1988,
however, were calculated solely from sales of post-1970 reissues. Atlantic's bookkeeping records before that date were incomplete, and
there was no longer any way of accurately determining what additional royalties might have been due individual artists for sales from
earlier years. Yet Begle and Atlantic worked out an imaginative and
equitable solution to the problem. A nonprofit foundation was established—Brown likes to think of it as "her" foundation because it
came about as a direct result of her struggle to get the back royalties
she was owed, but its formal name is the Rhythm and Blues Foundation—that could help channel funds to deserving older R&B performers.

"Atlantic has given the foundation almost a million and a half
dollars," Brown notes. "And from that, we are setting it up so that

there will be death benefits, pension, welfare, health benefits—you won't be turned away from a hospital because you can't pay—and career development for people like myself who want to remain in the business, who cannot afford a press agent. These benefits are coming from my Rhythm and Blues Foundation. Plus, every year, we get together and there's a Board of Directors, including Jesse Jackson, Dan Ackroyd, and Bonnie Raitt." Brown hopes other record companies will follow Atlantic's lead in making donations to the Rhythm and Blues Foundation. She has sung in benefit shows to help raise additional funds for it, and Begle has sought to get other labels to reform their royalty accounting practices.[19]

For Brown, the struggle to get a settlement from Atlantic was about more than just money; it was about recognition, about feeling that the contributions she and other early R&B stars had made had been appreciated. Too often, she had felt slighted, had felt her role in music history was being forgotten. It bothered her, for example, that she was never asked to appear on television shows dealing with the roots of rock 'n' roll, or at jazz and blues festivals, or even at award ceremonies. Why couldn't she be given a chance to present a Grammy Award to a current R&B star? As she comments, "It's a little heart-rending to watch the years pass by and then, when your music starts to surface again, to see it being done by everybody but you." She recalls, for example, the day her sons told her how much they liked a "new" song that the Honeydrippers sang called "Sea of Love." They were unaware that "Sea of Love" had been recorded years before by a number of other singers, including their mother.

Brown feels that one of the best things that came out of her struggle for back royalties is her friendship with Howell Begle, who "stood by me when nobody else did, and he's remained a friend. He looks at all the contracts I'm offered and lets me know if they're good contracts. I don't have an agent. The work I get all comes by word-of-mouth."

Brown loves performing for audiences. She likes to draw listeners close to her, establish a one-to-one feeling so they'll feel comfortable requesting songs, which, unlike many performers, she sings. With that rapport established, she can then build up steam to the big, house-rockin', powerhouse numbers. As she describes her club act, "The very first thing that I do is try to get the audience to understand how grateful I am that they came. I feel very fortunate that after forty-two years of being in this profession, there are still those people who would come to see me if I worked in an outhouse. And I always try to set the songs up. I'm sort of a story-teller. I do some things and then I tell what year it was. And then I'll remember something about that period, some town in the South where I played and how wonderful the people were. They would come and bring food to the dances in the warehouses and spread a table, and then invite you to their table. And you had to get in town early so you could meet some of these people. And sometimes you had to stay in their homes, because there were not always hotels available. And the good times that we had on the buses. The buses were like home for us, when we were doing the big shows.

"I sing according to what I feel. Sometimes I don't feel the lyrics the way I sang it the night before. I'm just human. And I come into a job with the same kind of problems the average woman would come into. I have children who sometimes concern my heart. And sometimes I will have cried before I got to my job. But thank God for the Max Factor and the pancake and the makeup, you can sort of do something about that. You can put the smile on your face. You can't always wipe it out from inside your heart." She adds with a laugh, "And it's a good thing I wear long gowns—so they won't see the knee braces, or the surgical stockings, right? You've got to look cute on the stage. But I've got to go to the doctor about these legs. The dampness gets in this leg, after all these years, when it gets cold. And it's been playing tricks on me, so I've been walking with the knee brace on.

"A singer has to deal with the emotions of the people that they're performing for," she emphasizes. "You may go in some night, and a woman or a man sitting in front of you will take your attention. And you focus your whole evening on them, because either they are giving you something good, or you're concerned about this negative attitude that's coming up—they're not smiling. So you just may want to stop and say, 'Hey, what's wrong? Would you like me to do another number?' You have got to deal with your audience and why they're there. If they need their spirits lifted, you've got to realize that's what they came for; they don't want to deal with your troubles. Not at the prices they're paying to sit down at a table—when nowadays a person could really stay at home where you feel safer and have all the conveniences—videos, cable TV, everything.

"Outside of being a rhythm and blues singer, I'm a stylist. I can sing anything that is needed. There are pockets [in my club act] where I will do show tunes, pockets where I'll do strong torch materials, yeah, and ballads. I have a rhythm and blues band behind me. Charles C. I. Williams and Bill Easely are on saxes, Clarence "Tootsie" Bean's on drums, Bobby Forrester's on Hammond B-3 organ, Bill Williams out of New Orleans is on guitar. I would go lacking in my funds just to have my musicians because they give me a sense of being at ease. Bobby Forrester, on organ, is incredible. I like the organ because it substitutes for a lot of the lacking instruments—but basically I like it because it gives me the spiritual undertone. That's my beginning. Rhythm and blues, jazz—everything you listen to is built on that spiritual basis. And there's nothing that will send a cold chill up you like a Hammond organ, which is possibly the one strong sound in the world. And so, when I do the laid-back and sentimental things that I really need to talk about and feel myself, when I need energizing myself, then I give it to Bobby and myself, because he's got a special thing with me." Indeed, Forrester continues playing the organ softly while Brown talks with the audience between numbers, much the way organists in some churches continue playing softly while the preachers speak. "When we do our show, we never let up; I just go from one thing into the other, and the music lays under," Brown notes. "And I think we make a cozy feeling. I try to get everybody in the club to feel like they're in my living room."

* * *

You'll often hear jazz and blues artists say that foreigners appreciate our music more than Americans do. Whether that is generally true or not, the fact remains that the two men who were to play the biggest roles in bringing about the comeback of Ruth Brown were Argentinians. After making names for themselves with the internationally successful musical spectaculars *Tango Argentino* and *Flamenco Puro* (creating the overall concepts; designing the sets, costumes, and lighting; and directing the shows as well), Claudio Segovia and Hector Orezzoli decided to create a revue, to be presented in Paris, that would evoke the world of old-time black show business. They hired veteran choreographers Fayard Nicholas (of the Nicholas Brothers), Cholly Atkins (of the song-and-dance team Coles and Atkins), Frankie Manning (of the original Whitey's Lindy Hoppers), and Broadway pro Henry LeTang, along with such eminent older hoofers as Bunny Briggs, Jimmy Slyde, and Ralph Brown, as well as a teenaged wonder named Savion Glover. They assembled an orchestra richly laden with jazz talent. And as the focal points of their show, they chose three singers: gospel and blues shouter Linda Hopkins (best known for her one-woman tribute to Bessie Smith, *Me and Bessie*), Sandra Reaves-Philips (best known for her one-woman show, *The Late, Great Ladies of the Blues*), and Ruth Brown.

In the fall of 1985, *Black and Blue* opened for what was announced as an eight-week limited engagement at the three thousand-seat Chatelet Theatre in Paris. The show ran for eight months. Brown and her costars received ten to twelve curtain calls nightly. Plans to revise and open the show in New York within a few months of its Paris closing faltered, however, because raising the needed funds for so lavish a production in New York was difficult. Although news of Brown's triumphant reception in Paris did not reach the general public in the United States, it spread within show business circles, helping her land better club bookings here. From *Staggerlee* and *Hairspray* to her radio series and the Paris production of *Black and Blue,* her career picked up speed throughout the eighties. And a documentary featuring Brown, "That Rhythm, Those Blues," which was televised on PBS in January 1988 after being presented at several prominent film festivals, no doubt introduced her to many new listeners.

In the spring of 1988 she played top rooms in New York (Michael's Pub) and Los Angeles (the Cinegrill at the Hollywood Roosevelt Hotel), scoring successes on both coasts that surprised even her. She recalls, "I played the Hollywood Roosevelt and I couldn't believe it; when I came downstairs at night, people were standing three-deep in line. I broke everybody's house record that had ever played that room—including Michael Feinstein. And it was incredible because people like Richard Gere came, Mrs. Mancini—Henry Mancini's wife—Hank Ballard, B. B. King, Bobby Womack, just so many people that I was in awe of. When I came down through the lobby of the hotel at night, I said, 'Are you sure you're in the right place? Ruth Brown is singing here, not Tina Turner.' And everybody laughed. I made so many friends and I tell you, the reviewers in Los Angeles were just wonderful to me. One reviewer's first line was, 'We should get some buses and go down to—and he named about six clubs, discos and things where the young people are—and load everybody in these buses that think that they know how to entertain, and take them up to the Hollywood Roosevelt to see Ruth Brown.' And one morning my son calls on the phone, 'Mama, Mama, turn on the TV!' And there's this man on 'Good Morning, Los Angeles' saying, 'Last night I went to the Hollywood Roosevelt, and I heard rhythm and blues being done the way rhythm and blues is supposed to be done. I saw a woman; they tell me she's sixty years old—I don't believe it—but I heard the name Ruth Brown when I was a young kid, and I had to go for myself to see. And I'm telling you, don't you walk—you run to the Hollywood Roosevelt to see Ruth Brown. Because I feel better for having seen her this morning.' That was probably the greatest compliment that I got. It was just one of the most incredible stays that I have had."

The producers of *Black and Blue* were still hoping to mount their production in the United States and were still encountering difficulties. Plans to stage the show in Los Angeles during the summer of 1988, before moving it to Broadway, fell through. The producers decided to preview the show in New York in the fall, skipping out-of-town tryouts, with the official opening night scheduled for December. In the meantime, Fantasy Records, an important jazz/blues label, had released an album by Brown, *Have a Good Time*, recorded live at the Hollywood Roosevelt—her first album by a record company with strong financial resources and good distribution since the 1960s. The album—which included several of her biggest numbers such as "Teardrops from My Eyes," "Mama, He Treats Your Daughter Mean," and "Five-Ten-Fifteen Hours," along with such newer songs as "You Won't Let Me Go" and a tenderly sung "Always on My Mind"—sold well enough for Fantasy to tell Brown that they wanted more recordings by her. She also received good offers to play Las Vegas and Atlantic City, but with *Black and Blue* being readied for Broadway she had no time to think about anything else.

How did she feel about the renewal of public interest in her in the late 1980s? "Sort of amazed—and very fortunate," she says. "These last seven or eight years have been very good for me. Sometimes it scares me. I say, 'What's happening?' In my heart I feel like, 'Well, I've been around this long, they're coming back around to me. Yes, I deserve this, I worked for it.' And then on the other hand, I say, 'Oh, my goodness! If I get this good job, am I physically able to stand up under it?' After all, I'm not twenty-one any more."

That reality was brought sharply home to her when *Black and Blue* began rehearsing and then previewing in New York in late 1988. She found the stage floor hard on her legs and the theater chilly. She had trouble shaking a cold. Her health collapsed and she was hospitalized, forcing postponement of the opening. The *Daily News* reported January 11, 1989, that she had suffered "an angina attack complicated by pneumonia." Singer Dakota Staton was rushed in to take her place temporarily, while Broadway insiders feared that Brown might not have the stamina to do the show.

But she was not going to let this opportunity pass her by. When the show finally opened on January 26, 1989, it was Brown who commanded the most attention—no small feat considering she was in the company of such talents as Linda Hopkins, Carrie Smith, and Bunny Briggs. She brought to her performance more than the skills of singing and showmanship she had acquired over four decades as a professional. She brought attitudes forged from her experiences in

life: intimations, at times, of resentment, of feeling put-upon combined with an unshakable determination not to be beaten down, to
laugh despite hardships. When she sang that she was "a woman . . . a
ball of fire," she smoldered with a bitter-edged pride. When she asked
what had she done "to be so black and blue," she drew upon remembered injustices. While maintaining an air of bruised dignity, she ex-
tracted all of the exuberant, bawdy comedy contained in the old-time
number "If I Can't Sell It, I'll Keep Sittin' on It." She found the simple majesty in "St. Louis Blues" and turned "T'aint Nobody's Bizness
if I Do" into a potent battle of one-upsmanship with Linda Hopkins
that the audience assumed was just a stage routine but that actually
reflected their offstage rivalry. (Both are strong women, musical de-
scendants of Ma Rainey and Bessie Smith; both were nominated for
Tony Awards as best actress in a musical for their work in *Black and
Blue*. It is hardly surprising that friction developed between the two.
Each struggled to outshine the other; ironically, the audience was the
beneficiary.) The only number that didn't really suit Brown's broad
style was "Body and Soul." But she was a pillar of strength in that
show, her star turns—along with those of Hopkins and Briggs—being far more important to its success than the big but impersonal
production numbers such as "I Can't Give You Anything but Love."
Bedecked in striking gowns and tiaras; backed by an orchestra including such distinguished jazz musicians as Sir Roland Hanna, Claude
"Fiddler" Williams, Jerome Richardson, and Grady Tate; and socking
home first-rate songs, Brown was every inch a star. Never before had
she been showcased so well.[20]

It's a pity no one had presented Brown on Broadway before. Her
larger-than-life performing style is perfectly suited to the theater. In
her singing she can be heavily dramatic in a way that would seem
overly dramatic in a close-up on screen but works terrifically onstage.
The most powerful of musical theater personalities, from Al Jolson
to Ethel Merman, have never achieved the same degree of success
on film as in person. The brassy dynamism that can leave theater
audiences feeling supercharged tends to register differently on screen.

Audiences enjoying Brown in *Black and Blue* never imagined, however, the degree of pain she often felt in her legs—pain that became
so severe that she had to move out of her apartment uptown and
into a hotel across the street from the theater. From the hotel, she
was taken to the theater by wheelchair. With grim perseverance she
would get out of that wheelchair long enough to sing her numbers
and say her few lines onstage; afterward she'd get back into the chair.
A doctor advised her that if she were willing to take some months

off to recuperate, an operation to replace her knee joints could afford her considerable relief. But taking time off now—when she was in demand she had thought she would never again experience—was out of the question. She endured the pain, letting it, perhaps, add intensity to her singing, and postponed the much-needed operation for several years.

Success on Broadway brought her greater attention than she had enjoyed in many years, particularly after she won the Tony Award: countless newspaper and magazine interviews and offers of bookings. She recorded a new album for Fantasy, *Ruth Brown: Blues on Broadway* (arriving at the studio in a wheelchair made her think of her first recording session, forty-one years earlier, while on crutches), as well as the original cast album of *Black and Blue* for DRG Records. She was asked to do a pilot for a television sitcom, "Uptown at Sylvia's." National Public Radio signed her to host—and occasionally sing on—a new weekly series, "Blues Stage," featuring blues and R&B singers and taped during actual performances in clubs around the country. She got booked onto talk shows, including Johnny Carson's.

How did Brown feel about winning the Tony Award? "I like to say Tony is the one man that came in my life that had a lot to say. He spoke *loudly* for me. It's just kind of mind-boggling." She adds, "The Tony got inside my spirit because it's an award for doing a Broadway show in which I am singing; I'm not acting. I've been singing all my life—[her voice takes on a coloration of sadness, as if she's bearing a burden; she has an unusually expressive, even musical, speaking voice]—and I never got nothing. This award is like saying, 'We know you're here. We know that you exist.'"

She accepted every outside engagement she could—maybe more than she should have, taxing her strength. It was as if, after so many lean years, she were afraid to forego any opportunities to work, as if she were worried such opportunities wouldn't come again. She might fly to Martha's Vineyard to sing for a night or two one week, then down to Chattanooga to be honored at a festival another week. She'd almost always be working someplace on Monday (*Black and Blue's* night off), sometimes other nights as well. In fact, her standby in *Black and Blue*, Melba Joyce, got to cover for her a good bit. Brown was living up to the wording sometimes used to introduce her club act: "the hardest-working woman in show business."

It wasn't money that impelled her to take so many jobs. She headlined, for example, a benefit concert for the International Art of Jazz, Inc., the outfit that had once hired her to participate in school assembly programs, "because they were there when I needed them. I have to pay debts. I survived, but it wasn't all by myself. Many nice people along the way reached out to help me, and there are those out there that, no matter, if they call I go. Anne Sneed [head of the International Art of Jazz] was one of those persons."

Her billing was always "Ruth Brown and Friends"—"*and friends*— that's really my thing." If she got work, it also meant work for her backup band directed by Bobby Forrester (which, as her prices rose, she enlarged from a quintet to a sextet and then a septet) and also, quite often, for singers and musicians of her generation whom she would have open for her. If she was enjoying good fortune, she wanted to share it with her friends. She also used "Blues Stage," her NPR radio program, as a venue for helping revive interest in them, fighting with her producer if he would try to book too many younger R&B singers rather than talented veterans who could use the work. (I've heard her argue with him, "Where are all my R&B people? I've been working hard with R&B to keep that floating.") "When the music changed and the British influence came in," she comments, "a lot of rhythm and blues artists got pushed back. Believe me, some of the good singers and groups are still around. A lot of us had to do other things—you had to raise families and some had to go out of the country to live." Bringing some of the R&B pioneers back into the spotlight as guests on her radio show or at her club gigs, she says, "is just my way to help them to smell their own flowers."

Brown began working every Monday night when she was in town at the Lonestar Roadhouse on Fifty-second Street; they would put up a sign announcing that it was "Ruth's Place" whenever she was there. Although her name was packing the club, she would have old friends open the show each week, performing from perhaps 9:30 to 11 P.M. before she would come on to sing for as long as she felt like singing. The nights I caught her at the Lonestar her opening acts included Al Cobbs's eighteen-piece swing band (Cobbs had played trombone in Lucky Millinder's band when Brown was with the band), Panama Francis and his Savoy Sultans (Francis had drummed on some recordings with Brown during the fifties), and unique song stylist Little Jimmy Scott, whom she had known since the late forties. (For awhile, she got Scott a weekend gig of his own at another club, using her backup band.) She got Charles Brown, Lowell Fulson, Chuck Jackson, and LaVern Baker to appear at the Lonestar, too, and Carl Fisher served as her regular announcer and between-the-acts singer. "The whole purpose of Monday night at Ruth's Place is to re-open some faded scrapbooks," she'd tell the audience.

I've sat in the Lonestar until one in the morning, marveling at the way Brown can fill the room with her energy. With the band rockin' behind her, she'll take chorus after chorus—building excitement for ten minutes—on "Mama, He Treats Your Daughter Mean" and then hit the audience with a fervent "Miss Brown's Blues," which she sings now with much more impact and authority than in her youth.

"WELL," Brown calls out electrically, testifying to the whole world, "I'M STANDING ON A CORNER." Now her voice abruptly drops down, sounding as vulnerable as a little girl's, "and I don't know which way to turn." She wrings every ounce of drama possible out of her blues, breaking the rhythm of one phrase by repeating words urgently, over and over, to build tension then cutting the pathos with a hint of humor, "He said, 'You know I love you baby, better than I love myself.' He was crazy about himself."

With Forrester noodling softly at the organ, she talks directly to the audience between numbers. "There have been many highs and lows in the career of Ruth Brown," she says, and someone calls out: "I hear you." She reminisces about doing gigs down south, early in her career, when she was paid only "in buns and pies," recalls singing ballads and watching young couples pressed closely to each other on the dance floor "grinding coffee. . . . I watched a whole lot of coffee get ground."

She belts out "Teardrops from My Eyes," the saxes shimmering wonderfully, and a couple of youths at a table in the front get up and begin dancing, which she appreciates. She introduces celebrities in the audience, too, such as Bernie Wayne, composer of "Blue Velvet"; Rolanda Watts of WABC-TV Eyewitness News; and jazz singer Betty Carter. She kids another singer in the house good-naturedly, "Look at that Julia Steele—dressed in red, the color of Jezebel!" She introduces, too, her astrologer, whom she says predicted her comeback; she won't make a move without consulting her. She also offers tributes to Dinah Washington, Ella Johnson, and Billie Holiday, which are effective in evoking memories but risky in the sense that it's particularly hard to compete with the memory of Holiday. Brown's rendition of "Lover Man" seems exaggerated; she's hasn't Holiday's subtlety although there are moments when her pronunciation of words conjures up Holiday.

It's when she does her own rhythmic specialties in her no-holds-barred style, however, that Brown overwhelms us. "All right, children," she calls out first to get our attention—and the energy level up—as she prepares to set up the next song. In this room, the audience and the band are all her children. She digs into "Five-Ten-Fifteen Hours" with a ferocious drive. "Sing the song!" someone in the audience calls out in affirmation.

Brown's voice is lower than it was in her youth and has more of an edge. It's not as smooth as it once was; it's had years of heavy-duty use. She never had voice lessons; the way she'll rise to a near shout is exciting to hear but hard on the vocal cords. It is, however, a much more commanding voice than it was in her youth. In her wordless, "whoo-ee," yodel-like vocalizing at the end of the song she expresses ecstatic power; you feel the force.

What strikes me, as I catch several of Brown's performances at the Lonestar, is that she is singing more powerfully than she was just a few years earlier, more powerfully than on her *Have a Good Time* album. (Someone ought to be making new live recordings of her club performances.) It's as if feeling wanted and appreciated again—hearing the cheers from audiences at *Black and Blue,* getting the Tony, and so on—have fortified her. One night I bring to the club a musician who had worked with Brown a few years earlier; she was always strong, he reflects, but there's a whole "'nother dimension to her work now."

Brown, too, is aware that—for whatever reasons—there is more to her singing these days than in her youth. "It takes you many years sometimes to really find out and accept who you are," she says; perhaps that is why she sings now with more conviction. She also reflects, "I don't know what it is, but lately I have really started to have very close relationship to the lyrics that I do. Things I've been singing a long time—all of a sudden I'm hearing them, they're coming out different or something. Maybe it's the turns that my life has taken. Maybe it's that. People are helping me to celebrate something that I've been working on a long time. This whole thing is kind of mind-boggling." There is definitely something more in her singing these days. "Yes," she acknowledges, her voice suddenly becoming hushed and tender. "Yes. It took all those years to get to this point. I think now I'm a soul singer. I wasn't. But I think I am, about now.

"I can still sing everything—depending on what you want to hear. And I'm listening to singers closer than I ever did before, because the lyrics are becoming very important. I think that that's the saving grace right now. Otherwise we're going to look up and not have no singers left. You understand? We're just going to have people who do words and music. But unless we get some people who are sensitive enough to look inside the lyric, we ain't going to have no more Dinahs and no more Lady's and no more Ellas to interpret that lyric. I don't care how many years ago it was Billie Holiday sang 'Lover Man,' I don't care who starts to sing it, people say, 'That's Billie Holiday's song.' Because it was her interpretation of it, and what she felt.

Why was it her song? She sang about what life was giving her. And we don't do that much any more. Because we're too covered up. It's all blanketed, and electronics and the engineer in the booth and the producer. And there's not room for any imagination. We have ceased to be creative. . . . It's sad in a way. There really have been no places for young performers to apply their crafts. If anything happens that their tapes break down, there's no show."

Eventually, the producers of *Black and Blue* made Brown stop her weekly appearances at the Lonestar. She was stretching herself too thin. There was no point in her working so hard she couldn't give her all on Broadway—and no point in her club act competing for customers with her Broadway show. At times, her relationship with the producers of *Black and Blue* was strained. The show, she acknowledges, "has paid me in dividends because it has brought me to the attention—and I feel very strongly that I have been just as good for the show as the show has been for me. That has been an even trade-off. I don't know how long I'll stay in *Black and Blue*. Because I just have to move on. And indeed, it does not pay enough for me to sit down the rest of my life and do this. I am a singer. And there's a song that goes, 'So little time and so much to do.' There's still a lot I want to do. I want to do a jazz festival. I want to go to Europe. And I want to have a good album. I want to record 'My Man.' I want to do 'God Bless America' which Kate Smith did. I'd like to sing 'The Star Spangled Banner' once in my life. Because I can sing it. And I'll give it some feeling, too. I can sing 'The Battle Hymn of the Republic' like you wouldn't believe. These are things I have not had the opportunity to do, because right away people put you in a pocket. But it'll come. Someday I'd like to record an album of the stuff that my father used to sing: *Songs My Daddy Taught Me*. There are some good songs, if I can get the record companies to realize that I can sing 'em." She adds, after a pause, "I have to be very selective about what I put on wax now. For these will be some of the final recordings."

Any other goals for the future? "I know there are a lot of young people that have no hope. I see it every day. And I guess that I could never become rich enough to do the things I'd like to do," she says. "I wish that I could build, somewhere down where I grew up, on some of those empty lots and fields and farms, like a little community just for kids, young people who just need a chance. I see it on the streets everyday; I see kids who've got no business in the street, just looking in space, being hip, slapping palms. There's got to be something more than that. If they had a good home to go to, they'd go home. No matter how small or how meagerly furnished it is, if there's some

love there, you want to go back to it. I want to go back to Portsmouth
so bad because my love is there. I can't make a living there, but once
I have decided that I want to stop and settle down, it doesn't take a
lot for me to live. There's no place else in the world that I would
want to go, other than back home. My roots are there, my brothers
and my sisters are there. And I have to decide what I'll do when I
get there. But I think that if I were ever to really get lucky, what I
would really like to do is take some of that vast farmland back there
and build a little community for the children, for senior citizens from
the rhythm and blues business like myself who just need a place to
pick up their dignity. Maybe a complex with playgrounds and swim-
ming pools and learning centers and little nightclub areas and recre-
ational—everything that's needed. Maybe I could do that; I don't
know. I go to sleep at night, praying that something might happen
that would allow me to do that one day. And I think that's where
I'd like to do it."

*   *   *

It's Wednesday, February 21, 1990. I call on Brown at her dressing
room in the Minskoff Theater on Broadway, where she's just finished
a matinee of *Black and Blue* and has two hours before her evening
performance. The Grammy Awards are to be presented in Los Angeles this evening. Brown's album *Blues on Broadway* has been nominated in the category of best jazz vocal, female, and a track from that
album, "If I Can't Sell It," has been nominated in the category of
best traditional blues. I'm surprised that Brown hasn't flown west for
the Grammy Awards ceremony.

    "When I got nominated, I said great—finally! I was really looking
forward to going there," she tells me. "But when I saw that the awards
for which I've been nominated would not be televised, I decided to
stay home. They give out Grammies to persons of importance in this
business—that's what it's *supposed* to be about. But they are not going to show on the telecast anything concerning the blues. They're
not showing on screen the best jazz vocal albums. Gospel music will
not be in place. All of that's like a slap in the face to the quality of
the music."

    The televised portion of the Grammy Awards ceremony will focus
on the presentation of awards to younger rock and pop artists. "Everything they got, they got from R&B. They stood on our backs to
reach and get those Grammies," she says. She doesn't care if producers feel there's more public interest in who'll be chosen the year's
best new artist [the odds-on favorite was Milli Vanilli, a manufactured

singing duo that actually had to leave the stage at one of their concerts when the tape to which they were lip-synching stopped] than
in jazz or blues. For Brown, being denied the chance for television
exposure triggers unpleasant memories of being denied exposure during the fifties.

Brown has received many honors in the past year—indeed, the
walls of her dressing room have become filled with plaques and photos (along with images of butterflies, a symbol of her career's rebirth)—but the honor that's meant the most to her was the home-
coming celebration Portsmouth, Virginia, recently staged in her
honor. "I cried for four days," she tells me. "They had marching bands
and majorettes and school assemblies. I received a citation from President Bush. Right through the heart of town, what used to be Main
Street—they've renamed Ruth Brown Avenue. And the street on
which I was born and raised, they've renamed Ruth Brown Place. So
there really is a 'Ruth's Place' now." She made a videotape for the
school children, too, in the hopes that her rise from humble begin-
nings in Portsmouth to stardom on Broadway might help boost their
aspirations and self-images.

I show Brown a few old clippings about her that I've brought her
from the Institute of Jazz Studies at Rutgers University. We look at a
copy of a magazine article—undated but from the early fifties—which
quotes Brown as saying, rather presciently as it turned out, "I'm doing OK today but what about tomorrow?" The story noted she was
earning $1,000 a performance and had a maid yet liked to press her
own skirts, explaining, "I'm not the sophisticated type." It went on
to say, "She hopes to have her own disc jockey show soon."

Brown smiles, commenting that with her current show "Blues
Stage" she's more than fulfilled that goal. "Radio affords me a wide
audience, because I have not had that TV coverage. Every home has
a radio—even if they don't have a TV or a CD player," she says. "I
hope doing the radio show will eventually allow me to go into some
of the cities where my show is heard and do some in-person things
with some of the people on the show, like the shows we did in the
fifties."

Her costar Carrie Smith drops in with some fried chicken and
greens she's cooked for Brown, then heads back to her own dressing
room. How many Broadway stars, I wonder, are eating home-cooked
meals in their dressing rooms tonight? Fourteen-year-old Tarik Winston, who's recently replaced Savion Glover as the show's tap dance
prodigy, drops in to say hello to his "Aunt Ruth"; she gets along fa-
mously with kids. She predicts big things for Tarik. Her voice drops

low as she intones—and Winston is gazing at her, wide-eyed, as if listening to an oracle—that she can see down a long tunnel and see a bright future, stardom, ahead for him. He's beaming now, and he takes a seat on the couch.

Brown is finishing off the chicken and greens when the telephone call comes. "I won! Oooh! The album!" she responds to Ralph Jungheim, her record producer, who informs her from Los Angeles that she has just won a Grammy Award—her first ever, at age sixty-two— for her album *Blues on Broadway*. She bursts into tears and asks me to hold the telephone while she runs off—"Carrie! Carrie!"—to tell Smith.

Howell Begle quickly calls, too. "You won, girl!" he tells her. She vows, "Next year, an Emmy!" Winston brings her a can of soda—she'll be going onstage soon and can't have anything alcoholic—and she celebrates with that. She wires back her acceptance of the award: "Sorry I can't be there to hold the Grammy in my hand, but I'm holding the nominating committee in my heart." "Oh, that's bad!" says Winston, hugging her as other cast members gather to give congratulations. She hadn't expected to win, she says. Although she feels she's earned this award, she believes there's no counting on anything in life. "God don't love ugly—and he ain't too pleased with beautiful every once in a while," she observes. She calls her brother, her astrologer, who'd predicted she'd win the Grammy, and her makeup man; she has a show to do—and she has cried off her lashes in happiness.

"I do believe you're lucky for me," she tells me, as if my being here somehow had something to do with it. Of her career, Brown reflects before I leave to let her get ready for tonight's performance, "It's like I say—you have to go away in order to come back. . . . I think I've still got a few good years."

2

"Like a motherless child. . . ."

"Why was I born?" implores Little Jimmy Scott, delivering the line of the anguished Jerome Kern–Oscar Hammerstein ballad so deliberately that each word registers its impact individually. "Why am I living?" The diminutive singer stretches his arms toward the audience with a curious delicacy and tentativeness—as if hoping against hope to draw you to him, to get you to share in what he's feeling and maybe supply answers to questions he's been asking himself for a long time.

When he begins singing "It's the Talk of the Town," words I'd never been aware of in other singers' renditions stand out clearly: "I can't show my face / Can't go anyplace / People stop and stare / It's so hard to bear." His face is so smooth that he looks much younger than his sixty-five years. It reminds me of my aunt's face; it's not just the set of the features, it's the particular expression of gentle kindness incompletely covering sorrow. As he gets deeper into the song, he throws his head back, eyes closed, and I notice markings running around his throat, almost as if he'd been choked.

He sings "Day by Day" as slowly as I can ever recall a song being sung, so slowly—as if in suspended animation—that it takes a while to recognize what song he is singing. "There isn't any end to my devotion," he intones, suggesting only the barest suggestion of any melody. The song that a couple of years ago rolled along brightly each Sunday under the opening credits of a television sitcom of the same name now sounds strangely taut with, perhaps, swallowed pain.

Finally, he gives "All of Me" a bit of a lilt—the only even moderately up-tempo number in the whole set. I know of no other singer who works, as a whole, at such slow tempos as Scott. When he beseeches, "Why not take all of me?" he sounds as if, under the surface cheeriness, he doubts that anyone would do that. As he stands

in the light now, his arms stretched out unevenly, his head crooked
to one side, he reminds me of a marionette whose strings are not
being held tightly enough.

Scott's voice is high, not as high and penetrating as it was in his
prime when people hearing his records on the radio often thought
they were listening to a girl, but still unusually high for a man. He
set the pace for such singers as Frankie Lymon and Frankie Valli, although he was far more inventive and emotional. His voice is not as
flexible as it was in his youth, nor is his intonation always as secure,
but his voice remains rich with pathos. His soulful, keening way of
singing is admired and appreciated by such masters as Ray Charles
and Tony Bennett.

Scott will pause here, place an unexpected emphasis there, and
flatten a melody line somewhere else until a song sounds much different from customary interpretations; his phrasing is as intuitive and
highly idiosyncratic as that of a fine jazz instrumentalist. Some of
the risks that he takes in his phrasing work, some do not. Hearing
him sing evokes the same concern that you feel for a tightrope walker:
Will he make it to the end? His singing—never loud, never uninhibited—is intense. At his best, he can communicate his feelings so acute-
ly as to leave you devastated.

Frankie Valli, who considers Scott his mentor, once told music journalist Jimmy McDonough that the truth in Scott's singing is too pain-
ful for most listeners to take. The comment perhaps explains why
Scott has never had the mass appeal of many singers—including Valli—who don't explore nearly the emotional depths Scott does. Scott
speaks particularly strongly to those who have felt hurt or oppressed,
or who in any way see themselves as set apart from the presumably
comfortable majority. In some fundamental way, he is an outsider.
Although he almost never sang the blues, Dinah Washington—billed
as the "Queen of the Blues"—used to get Scott to sub for her when
she couldn't make gigs. With his high, pure, emotionally charged
voice, he could sing almost any song in his repertoire and create the
mood of the blues. The unusual potency of Little Jimmy Scott's singing, one feels certain, comes from his life. It has been an unusual
life from the very beginning.

* * *

On July 17, 1925, a construction worker in Cleveland, Arthur Scott,
received word at work that his wife, Justine, had just given birth but
that their baby, unfortunately, had been born dead, strangled by his
umbilical cord. A fellow worker named Victor drove Scott home,

where he discovered that his baby had somehow survived. "There's a line that goes right around my neck from where the umbilical cord was. I was hanging," Little Jimmy Scott notes today. "They thought I was dead, so they rushed my father home to help my mother. Well by then, the lady upstairs had unraveled the cord and was waiting on the doctor. When the doctor got there, he said, 'He hung hisself alive!' He looked at me and told my parents, 'He'll either be a great speaker or he'll be a great singer.'" The baby was named James Victor Scott, his middle name chosen in honor of the man who brought his father home the day he was born.

Did being strangled by his umbilical cord during childbirth cause any damage to Scott?

"Not that I know except that in the esophagus, there's a hole like you see in a needle, which gave me a reaction like I had asthma—I'd be wheezing. A doctor said that in the stretching and so on, that could have caused that hole inside the throat," Scott says. "They put me on a no-milk diet, because milk caused the buildup of mucous, which helped to cause this wheezing and all, since the mucous would trap in that hole. The wheezing never interfered with my singing, though. It's a funny thing. I know times that I could sing all night long—but when it came to relaxing after I worked, I guess the muscles in the throat were tired, because then I would feel this wheezing. I took a medication called Tedrol for six or seven years for the wheezing—which recently I've outgrown—but stopped taking it after they found out it strained the heart."

Music was part of Scott's life for as far back as he can remember. "Singing was the thing in my family. It was a company-keeper for everybody. Late in the evenings, my mother would come in and play different songs on the piano that she knew we could sing. And the family would sing along together. And at church affairs, like when the youth performed at church or something like that, she would have us do the singing. Two sisters and another brother and myself had a quartet, and we'd sing in the church.

"I was fond of all types of music. My father had an old Philco radio that used to have this little green light for the dialing, that attracted me so. It gave me what I wanted to listen to. A big thing then was the concerts on harp. I used to love to hear those women who played those harps. I thought that was fantastic. Kids would say, 'Oh, he's a sissy, he don't want to go outside, he don't want to play.' But I'd be listening to music on that radio. One of my biggest hurts in my youth was when my father got uptight for money, when I was about eight or nine, and he had to pawn that radio. Back then, pawnshops more or less supported the folks in the neighborhood who had anything to pawn. And in this particular pawnshop that I passed on the way to school, I saw this radio. It just had to be my radio, because there was no other radio like mine. And I liked to die because that radio was my communication with music. We never got it back."

Scott, smaller and slighter of build than his classmates, sometimes got into fights over being called a sissy. As he got a bit older and some of his friends began growing into puberty and focusing their attention on girls, his sense of isolation increased. "I got strongly interested in singing when I guess I was about twelve or thirteen years old. I went to a boys' school, one of those training schools where they train for hand crafts and that kind of stuff. And they were having plays at school and Miss McGrath took all the boys and had us each playing parts. There was a film back then called *Ferdinand the Bull*. Well, she had me sing the part of Ferdinand the Bull. And we did shows to raise funds for the student council."

Scott says his mother played an influential role on his interest in music, adding, "The saddest part was she never got to know that I took singing as my life-style. Because this was something I wanted to do for her. It deepened my affection, even after her death, for her. The sadness was that I never had a chance to do her good. Because one of my determinations would have been to make something that would allow me to give her the joy she deserved. She was such a giving person. Back then in the late thirties, Roosevelt had this food giveaway thing; you'd go to these stations and they'd give you potatoes, peanut butter, corned beef, or whatever. She would get hers. I used to see her bring that food home. She had ten children of her own. (I was the third-oldest.) And yet she'd be running up and down the neighborhood with bags for this one and bags for that one, saying, 'Hey, they loaded up on me. I can't use it all.' Little things like that really interested me: the sharing and the caring about, 'Hey, maybe Miss Leach ain't got nothing down there for them kids. I'll take this part down there for her.' That was an example for me. She was like a teacher amongst her family. She was always teaching the girls something constructive for them and teaching the boys, 'You've got to learn how to make it.' She started me selling *Liberty* magazine, which encouraged me to work. Things like that. She had nothing, but she put it on your mind early: You had to be supportive of yourself, some kind of way.

"My Dad wasn't really interested in his family. He loved to shoot pool, he loved to gamble. That was more important to him than coming home and being with the kids. He didn't take that interest in his children—although, no matter what he did, that was your father and you had to respect him. If you disrespected that man, that little midget lady [Scott's mother] would rap you through the wall. Don't give a damn what you thought about what he didn't do for his family; that was her husband, the father of these children—and every one of those children knew, 'That's my Daddy.'

"One day when I was thirteen, my mother was on her way to school to talk to the teachers about my older sister, Shirley. And as they were crossing the street, my mother was hit by a car. It tore the right arm completely off the body and drug her for about seventy-five feet or more. She got hit like on a Friday, and that Monday following she died around 8:05. I didn't get a chance to express to her how much I would have wanted to do for her." (To this day, there is no number in Scott's repertoire that he sings more movingly than "Sometimes I Feel Like a Motherless Child," which, he says, always makes him think of her.)

"When my mother passed, we went to foster homes. My father didn't have that strength to hold his kids together. And that was bad because it caused a big void in all of our lives. It caused a separation in the family that was horrifying to all of them, because we had grown to expect more out of each other, as far as togetherness goes. And my mother was the foundation of it all, as far as the unity part in the family. Four of us went into the first foster home that I went to: a brother, Kenneth, and two sisters. Then they put two younger girls into another foster home. They put two of the others in individual homes. The biggest pain was the division that had happened to the family. You're used to communicating with your people and here's something standing in your way, or you're not allowed to see your brother or sister [he sounds momentarily like he's about to cry]—that was kind of hard to take. We lost that family unity. You're falling in a pit, you struggle to hold on yourself."

Their father, who made unfulfilled promises to get the family back together someday, never entirely faded out of their lives, however. "We always maintained to keep him somewhere in focus over the years. In fact, we took care of him to the end. Because he had his stroke in 1979 and we took care of him until he died in 1982. We shared the taking care of him all that time. Like I say, mother put in your head: 'I don't care what *you* think—that's still your father.' And you treated him like he was your father." Again, Scott sounds as if he's on the verge of tears. He adds, "And I'm glad my mother did it that way. Because when he needed you, it was so much easier to do whatever you had to do for him."

After his family fell apart, Scott devoted more of his energies to singing—at school, church, and in the community. As a teenager, he recalls, "The group that I hung out with, they were all interested in show business. We all took after-school jobs at the Metropolitan Theater, on Euclid near Fifty-fifth Street, in Cleveland. Some worked as ushers. I took care of all of the dressing rooms. Fresh towels, fresh soap—kept their dressing rooms clean and all like that. And it gave me close contact with the acts, because [bandleaders] Buddy Johnson, Cab Calloway, all of them came to this theater. It was a great place. And that was when I began branching into the business. At that theater, when I was around eighteen or nineteen, I met two tap dancers, who asked me if I could become their valet. In the back of my mind, I'm saying: 'I'll be anything if I can get in show business.' I told them, 'Yeah, I can do it,' and they took me on the road with them. After a couple of weeks, they realized, 'Hey, this cat ain't no valet.' I was just trying to get the opportunity to sing."

He got his break at a club in Meadville, Pennsylvania. By that point, he recalls, the tap dancers had gotten tired of hearing him plead, "Let me sing, let me sing," and they had heard from people in Cleveland that he actually could sing. They persuaded an all-star jazz group on the bill, which included, as Scott recalls, Lester Young, Howard McGhee, Sir Charles Thompson, Slam Stewart, and Jo Jones, to let him do a number or two with them. "I sang 'It's the Talk of the Town' and 'I'll Close My Eyes'—that's how far back those songs go—and the house came down! That was the beginning of it all. When I got that encouraging response from that audience, my mind was made up as to which way I was going to go. But right after I got such acclaim at the club, Lester and them took my feathers down. After they finished their set, they came off and said to me: 'What are you standing here for? You belong in the dressing room. You ain't nothing but a valet.' I was so hurt, man. But I learned later the purpose of them taking my feathers down was because youngsters get swell-headed. They were doing me a favor—helping me think about when you go on the stage, you do your job; you don't have an arrogant attitude. That stuck with me.

"When I came back to Cleveland, I worked with Jockey Gray, a local impresario who'd take little shows around in the Ohio area, and a comedian, Tim McCoy, out of Akron. Between the two, they kept me busy doing these gigs, in and around Cleveland." At nineteen, Scott was four feet, eleven inches tall; he looked like he was perhaps thirteen. He found that the striking purity of his clear voice, coupled with his unorthodox, laid-back way of phrasing and a nonthreatening demeanor, triggered fervent reactions from audiences. Offstage he attracted admirers of both sexes; their feelings, however, evoked no comparable responses within himself.

"And in the meantime," he notes, "I had met a young lady named Ophelia who became my first wife. I was about nineteen and Ophelia was sixteen. We went to a dance and all of us paired off. After the dance, I noticed this young lady didn't want to go home. She kept suggesting places to go. And so we went by the home of another girl. And kept sitting up all night, and I kept thinking, 'It's late. Ain't this young lady ever going to go home?' I finally realized, she was trying to stay away from home because she feared her father. The next day, she asked me to go home with her. I took her to the house, walked in the door, and her father says to me, 'You can leave now!' Later, I found out that he had brutally beat her. And I found out further that over the years he had been molesting her, sexually. And her stepmother despised her because of the attention that the father gave her. So I decided—we decided—we'd get married. He couldn't molest her then, I thought. But the damage had been done to this kid. I didn't know it at the time, but she had been reaching out to other men to rescue her from her father. Like older men that she had been sneaking out and going around with. She was unhappy for herself. Six months after that marriage, we were separated."

Hurt by the unsuccessful marriage, Scott dedicated himself wholly to his work. "I met up with Estelle Young—she was called Caldonia—who used to put shows together; this was around 1945. She got shake dancers, tap dancers, singers, comedians, a whole bunch of kids—a hell of a show, and I went on the road with it." Young treated Scott like a son. In fact, many people in the business actually thought that he was her son. "Well, she knew my mother had passed. And she took it upon herself—and I honor today the things she did—to try to be protective of me, so things would go right for me. She was sweet. She's been behind so many youngsters. Ruth Brown, Maybelle Smith, and so many artists that have done good in the business have had the support of this woman. Ruth and I became very good friends during this period. Someday I hope to be able to really do something real nice for Estelle Young. Ruth and I would both like to have a night for her. Estelle's living in Cleveland—that was her base, although originally she's from Newport News, Virginia.

"Anyway, Baltimore was one of the stops on our tour. That was where Redd Foxx and myself became real buddies—and still are today.[1] Redd used to introduce me to audiences as 'a guy that's older than baseball—breath in britches: Little Jimmy Scott.' Redd has got a big heart. He went to the Royal Theater in Baltimore where Joe Louis [the prizefighter] and Ralph Cooper [actor and emcee] were appearing and insisted to them, 'You've got to do something for this guy.' He was pushing me. So they had me come to New York, where I opened at the Baby Grand. I was supposed to be there for a week. I wound up being there for about a month to six weeks. Nipsey Russell was there, too. After New York, I went back home to Cleveland and then out on the road again with Estelle, down south. Then when I came back, I branched from her and started gigging out on my own, without the show or anything."

Scott always sounds unique, you'll never mistake him for anyone else, but it's interesting to take note of the vocalists who have influenced him. He admired a diverse group of song stylists, including many who were far less jazz oriented than he was. The singer he names as his original idol, Bing Crosby, the biggest-selling pop vocalist of Scott's youth, was greatly admired by black as well as white singers of the era. "When I was young, Bing Crosby was a guide. The tunes Bing was singing were so great. In fact that's where my interest in singing 'When Did You Leave Heaven' [a staple of Scott's repertoire even now] came from—that was a tune that he sang back then, that I really dug. And I dug the way he sang it, too. I watched him over the years. Then you had Herb Jeffries, a black singer who looked white. They were kind of idols that gave me encouragement about singing."

Scott also appreciated Billy Eckstine, Pha Terrell, Joe Medlin, Jimmy Rushing, and Tiny Bradshaw, whose song "These Things Are Love" he still sings. "Those were the guys that I fed on. Even though all of their styles weren't what you would call of my choice. But there were things that they were doing that helped me to understand more and more about the expression of singing. And then, of course, Ella [Fitzgerald] struck a note with everybody. And Billie [Holiday]. There was always a constant interest for those two in my mind. They both were strong expressionists. They were like educational guidelines for me. All of those people were. Doing concerts was considered the greatest level of presentation for a singing artist then. It was a point of mine to become that type of a singer. And that stemmed from the study of Paul Robeson, Ethel Waters. But I knew, too, I couldn't be just like them. You had to create more self-expression. Then there was Jimmy [Mitchelle], who played alto in the Erskine Hawkins band; he was a hell of a singer, too. I admired him a lot. He was very polished. Then along came guys like Cleanhead [Eddie Vinson]. Louis Jordan was the guy that started the ball to rolling to rock 'n' roll;

rock 'n' roll is a flare from what that man was expressing. In my mind each one of those singers was set in a little room—these people sit here, these sit here, these sit here—and they all were beautiful. You could love whatever they did."

Scott says he's been singing in the same laid-back style for as long as he can remember. He has no idea how he developed it. "That's just the way it comes out," he says. "Then, too, I'm very selective about telling a story. I could never sing the music just to make noise or to give a rhythm trick. If it had rhythm to it, that fit the expression I wanted to give the tune. Like 'All of Me'—I let it swing and I try to make it as enjoyable as possible. That groovy swing like that on 'All of Me'—that's my style for fast tunes. I like to swing with them."

Because Scott sang in such a slow, inwardly focused manner, some listeners speculated that he was on narcotics. Indeed, rumors that he was a junkie have followed him throughout his career. Scott scoffs at the notion, though. In his youth, he volunteers, he, like many others in the business, smoked his share of marijuana. (He won't touch it today because, he says, you can't be sure what you're buying or what it might have been sprayed with.) And he drank. He only tried hard drugs once, in the late forties. A friend persuaded him to snort some heroin, and its effect alarmed him. He felt as if everything was slowing down so completely that he feared he was dying. Panicked, he sought out a doctor he knew, who not only identified the problem immediately but also—to Scott's surprise—correctly named which of Scott's friends had supplied him with the heroin. Scott decided that day, he says, to stay away from all "powders."

Scott was just twenty-three when Lionel Hampton hired him to sing with his band in late 1948—a move up to the big time. Hampton, however, told audiences that Scott was seventeen, which seemed more in keeping with Scott's exceptionally boyish appearance and also made him seem more of a prodigy. Hampton's other vocalists at the time included Betty Carter and blues singer Sonny Parker. Scott loved singing with the Hampton band. "Boy, Hamp's my mentor. There's no one in the world like that man. When it comes to that rhythm timing that he can go with, and that laid-back thing—I do it with my voice, but if you listen to him play the vibes, you hear it. The collaboration—it was like a marriage with me and him. Because something about what he does with a phrase just fit me to a T. We really never got into a lot of extensive things with the band, but there were tunes there that were really the beginning of my being heard all over the country.

"I did none of the songs that Hamp's band already had. The tunes
I did with the band were mostly ones I had been doing over the years
in clubs and things, like 'I Wish I Knew' and those tunes. They created arrangements for them. But that tune, 'Everybody's Somebody's
Fool' [which Scott recorded with the Hampton band for Decca on
January 25, 1950]—the other singers in the band were fluffing off the
young lady, Regina Adams, who'd written the song, saying, 'Well, go
up to Jimmy Scott and take it to him.' So, it's a funny thing. I took
the tune. The meter was awkward. The guys in the band couldn't
figure out the meter of that tune and so they accepted the concep-
tion that I gave on it. I had to sing it for them and they put it together like I phrased it. That record was a hit. That and 'I've Been a
Fool' [recorded January 5, 1950]. Those two really stemmed things
off with the Hampton band. And then the other tunes, like 'I Wished
I Knew' and like that, they came up." "Everybody's Somebody's Fool"
made *Billboard*'s R&B charts for seven weeks, peaking in the number
six position.

"But my name was not on the label. The records I made with Hamp
just said, 'Lionel Hampton and vocal.'[2] On the rereleases today they
have my name, but back then the records didn't. That way, if a vocalist left a band, a bandleader could just hire someone else to sing the
same tunes. Fortunately, I had acquired a name in the business so that
a lot of people knew who was singing. When 'Everybody's Somebody's
Fool' was first released, a black disc jockey at NJR in Newark, Bill Cook,
introduced it in the area with a big contest, asking people to call in
and tell him if it was a man or a woman singing, and who they thought
it was. People have told me how they snuck out of school when I appeared in this area—like at the Adams Theater—to see who this Jimmy Scott was because of the way Bill Cook had made people curious.
That was his way of building the record up."

Sometimes, when Scott sang, women threw money at him. His tender, virginal appearance, surprisingly high voice, and songs of undy-
ing, unrequited love turned many listeners on. As he stood in front
of the band to sing, hunched over a bit, his head crooked to one side,
he projected great vulnerability. He appeared far too young to have
had much experience with love, yet there was no denying the honesty of his message. When he sang of being hurt, of feeling like a
fool, of struggling to maintain his pride, you believed him. The responses he drew from audiences were often impassioned. "Oh, man,
it was a great thing! It was greatly encouraging," he recalls. "The reaction was with both the women and the men. There were guys who
would bring their wives or girls in the clubs, and say, 'Hey man, sing

such and such a tune—I want you to hear this cat sing this tune.' This was the kind of atmosphere that was going on. So I'd sing the selections they requested. And some of the old hustlers and old guys that would hang around in those clubs, the minute I was in town, they'd bring their ladies in. So I had a great audience on the men's side, too, which was in a sense, they say, ironic."

Some people mistakenly assumed that because of the softness of his features, the high pitch of his voice, and the often heart-wrenching emotionality of his style Scott must have been homosexual. He was baffled and uncomfortable when men showed sexual interest in him. For a while, he even took to carrying a handgun so he'd feel less threatened if any man came on to him too strongly. "Having the young-looking face was rough—it was rough in lot of ways." he adds. "A lot of times I'd go places and they didn't want to believe that I was as old as I was. I'd be asked to be taken out of places because 'he ain't nothing but a teenager.' And people who knew me would say things like: 'That's an old man! That's old as dirt.'"

Although Hampton's band was filled with talent—among the fine musicians in the band during Scott's three-year stay were trombonists Al Grey and Benny Powell, saxists Bobby Plater and Jerome Richardson, guitarists Wes Montgomery and Billy Mackel, pianist Milt Buckner, and trumpeter and arranger Quincy Jones—no one made much money except for the boss. But Scott bears no ill-will toward Hampton, noting that it was Hampton's wife, Gladys, who managed Hampton and determined how much band members would be paid. He recalls that "she wouldn't give me enough money to buy a decent suit." After a couple of low-paid years with Hampton, he was ready to listen when Teddy Reig, a boisterous, self-described jazz hustler who'd recorded countless greats (from Charlie Parker and Miles Davis on down), convinced him there were big bucks to be made as a solo recording artist.

"After all, you're grown, you figure that it's time; you want to go on your own. That was when I went with Teddy Reig—a mistake, but I did it, trusting. I was no perfect guy myself, but the point is, if you said something, I took your word, I believed in you. You would have to do something bad for me to be disloyal," Scott says. And Reig, a white man who had married a black woman and chosen to live in a black neighborhood and whose love for black music and culture was obviously genuine, gained Scott's confidence easily enough. He had a rough-hewn kind of charm, and there *was* money to be made in the R&B record business, as Reig suggested, but for the Teddy Reigs of the world more often than for the artists they recorded.

Eyes closed, in a world of his own, Little Jimmy Scott's emotional intensity is well caught in this 1994 performance shot by Andreas Johnsen. (Author's collection)

A teen-aged troubadour: Little Jimmy Scott in white tie and tails, near the start of his career. (Author's collection; courtesy of Jimmy Scott)

When Illinois Jacquet, one of the all-time greats of the tenor sax, spotted Scott in the audience at the eighth anniversary celebration of New York's Blue Note jazz club in 1989, he invited Scott up to sing with his band. Singing "I Cried for You," Scott stole the show. (Author's collection; (c) Enid Farber Photography 1989)

Liza Minnelli comes to see Scott during his 1989 run at the Ballroom in New York City. (Author's collection; courtesy of Jimmy Scott.)

Nancy Wilson hugs Scott. As a girl, she'd lock herself in her room and listen to Scott's records over and over. His influence upon her phrasing still remains readily apparent in her singing. (Author's collection; courtesy of Jimmy Scott)

Madonna went to see Scott at Tavern on the Green, February 24, 1994, and told photographer Andreas Johnsen that Scott was the only singer who'd ever really made her cry. She returned to see him again the following night. (Photo by Andreas Johnsen; author's collection.)

Relaxing at home, Little Jimmy Scott holds one of his old albums. (Photo by Chip Deffaa)

In 1951 and 1952 Scott recorded a dozen sides for Reig's fledgling Roost label, based in Linden, New Jersey, including "The Masquerade Is Over," "My Mother's Eyes," "Cryin' My Heart Out for You," and "Why Do You Cry?" Reig, who seemed to know every musician of note, got such first-rate talents as Louis Bellson (drums) and Terry Gibbs (vibes) to play in the combos backing Scott. Scott recalls, "When Teddy started the Roost label, with myself and Stan Getz, I was saying, 'This is a good shot; he's started the label.' But we were just an instrument for him, you know, transferring fast bucks to another deal. As a guy, Teddy was likable. No musicians will tell you they hated Teddy, because they didn't; he was well-liked in the business. But the records didn't get much distribution. And I didn't get a dime."

Artists such as Scott didn't always know the full extent of the distribution their records received. Record producers could "give" distributors a certain number of records "off the books" (for which they'd eventually get cash that the tax men wouldn't know about), along with some other records "on the books" that would later be returned—and listed in company ledgers—as unsold. The records supplied off the books would be distributed to ghetto mom-and-pop stores, to be sold for a dollar apiece. In his autobiography *Reminiscing in Tempo*, Reig noted that R&B producers could keep their costs so low that almost all proceeds were profits. In the late forties, he recalled, Herman Lubinsky (whose Newark, New Jersey-based Savoy Records was an important independent label in the jazz and R&B fields), with whom he worked and from whom he learned, was typically able to record four sides for a total of just $180, including fees for studio rental, an engineer, and four musicians. He'd then have records pressed at a cost to him of perhaps 30 or 35 cents, meaning that if he only sold five hundred records at a dollar each from his own store in downtown Newark he was making money; if he sold two thousand copies nationwide, he was making good money.[3]

Scott reflects, "You were just an instrument for them cats to hustle with. They used to have a saying, 'Catch a fool, bump his head.' Teddy worked out a deal with Herman Lubinsky, and I wound up recording for him. And Lubinsky was something else. He was the shrewdest and the crookedest. His grandchildren, and his grandchildren's grandchildren, will live off of royalties from the material that man controlled. It seemed like he had recordings of practically everybody—Bird, Lunceford, so many people."

Lubinsky had started out with a store in Newark, where he sold radios, electronics parts, and records (a sideline, at first). In 1942 he began recording artists he knew his black customers would buy. He understood what would sell in the ghetto and—like Reig—wound up making a lot of money with that knowledge. But did he appreciate the quality of the music and musicians he recorded? "Nothing! Nobody!" Scott answers forcefully. "It was all buck-buck-buck with Lubinsky. Believe me!" Notoriously cheap and exploitative, Lubinsky generally seemed to look down on the musicians he recorded. "And when he looked at me—well, I looked like a young kid for most of my life," Scott notes. "It used to make me mad, the way he'd play that on me. He'd go, 'Oh come on now.' I'd be like, 'Treat me like I'm a man!' But this was a psychological tool that he used.

"Well, now I was under contract to Lubinsky. I didn't get royalties. Hey man, you didn't get what you were supposed to get; you got what Lubinsky wanted to give you. You'd get $50 a session. But I felt, 'I'm in a jam, because I want to sing. I want to be *heard*.'" Scott's voice sounds near tears now. There is a moving, deeply-felt urgency in his words, "I want to be heard"—the same quality that can make his singing so effective. He continues, "I was square to what the business was all about in a lot of aspects. Performing—I knew what that was all about. But the business part of it, and negotiating? I admit I did not. And Lubinsky was a monster. He was after your soul. He owned you. When I was recording with him, I couldn't record for anyone else. Say you've got a company and you want to record me, Lubinsky's got this contract back here, laying, waiting for you to do it—he's going to sue you. He's going to rip you off for money! There were companies that were interested in recording me, but they feared this man." Inevitably, friction grew between Scott and Lubinsky.

For a while, Scott (like most of Savoy's R&B artists) was being booked by an agent named Jimmy Evans, who got him gigs, he recalls, "in these little joints. They had a clique, Lubinsky and the Jimmy Evanses—they went together. If you didn't do what Lubinsky wanted done, Jimmy Evans would treat you so you didn't get gigs from his circle." Scott tried working with other agents whom he thought might be more independent. "I met other fellows who'd say: 'Come on, man, I'll manage you, I'll do this, I'll do that.' But it was always fast talk. They were after the fast buck. And that was disheartening." He eventually concluded that he could do about as well without an agent.

"I am very much appreciative of the friendships that I've made cross country—friendships that have kept me working all the years," he avows. "I thank God that in my travels I met people who respected my ability. They couldn't pay what I might have gotten had an agent been booking me around, but they paid me what they could afford and this kept me working. In Philly, I interchanged and worked at two or three clubs. Then there was like Detroit. The Chicago area. I did a few things in Louisville, Kentucky. Charles Brown and I worked in speakeasies—he'd play piano and I'd sing, and he'd sing wherever you could get a gig. There were spots here in Newark: the Key Club, the Cadillac, and so on. Not only myself worked these clubs—[organ player] Jimmy McGriff, this is where they all come from. The saloon circuit. I was working the Baby Grand from time to time, too, you dig? Most of the times, I worked in the clubs with local bands. I had a traveling group for a while, but these clubs couldn't afford traveling groups so much." Scott insists that making a lot of money was never a prime goal; being able to express himself creatively was what mattered to him. He was happy singing (for free) at an after-hours jam session at a club like Minton's in New York. "I was out there to accomplish something. Even though, as far as the material or the accomplishment goes—even though I never got it, I still desperately had that desire to do it. And I still have it."

Despite obstacles, Scott did get to make some fine recordings (as well as some inconsequential ones) during the fifties, thanks in part to the support he received from Lubinsky's longtime righthand man Fred Mendelsohn, who, unlike Lubinsky, truly loved the music and won the respect of the artists with whom he dealt. Mendelsohn had admired the way Scott had sung with Lionel Hampton's band and gave Scott freedom to record some songs he really connected with.

Scott has always been exceptionally particular about which songs he sings, finding certain ballads from the twenties, thirties, and early forties particularly appropriate. At sessions Mendelsohn produced in 1955, for example, he put his distinctive stamp on such enduring ballads as "Someone to Watch Over Me" (written in 1926), "Time on My Hands" (1930), "Guilty" (1931), "Street of Dreams" (1932), "When Did You Leave Heaven" (1936), and "Imagination" (1940)—numbers on which he was effective and convincing. When he sang earnestly (in "Imagination") of how imagination "makes a cloudy day sunny," he seemed to know what it was like to clutch dreams rather than unpleasant realities. When he declared in "Someone to Watch over Me" that he was "a little lamb who's lost in the wood," he was one lost soul communicating to all others, although the record is almost spoiled by the campy inclusion of an angelic voice assuring Scott, "I'll watch over you." He gives "Time on My Hands" the slow-as-death treatment that set him apart from all other vocalists. His involvement in some of the songs was so deep that it was not unusual for him to begin crying as he sang, earning the nickname in some quarters of "Cryin' Jimmy."

In addition to the carefully chosen older ballads he loved, Scott also had to record a mixed bag of contemporary songs for Savoy that were presumed to have greater money-making possibilities. Some were forced upon him simply because Lubinsky owned the publishing rights. The problem was simple: Because Lubinsky was never willing to pay much for anything, he was apt to wind up with the songs writers hadn't been able to sell elsewhere. Scott also believes that he was forced to record some songs because the firms that published them had paid Lubinsky to produce recordings of them. "They take great advantage of the artists," he says. "They'd shove all the material up under your nose, saying, 'This is what you got to do.'"

As it turned out, some of the newer numbers actually worked well for him. "The Show Goes On," for example, had a laughing-through-the-tears theme that he certainly understood, and the appealing "Everybody Needs Somebody" (by Fred Mendelsohn, Rose Marie McCoy, and Howard Biggs) proved to be a solidly selling record in the R&B market. Unlike many of Scott's records, it had a bit of a beat, a light but catchy swinging feel that no doubt helped it to win a larger audience. And Scott was utterly believable as he sang about how he needed somebody, how going "through life alone is living with half a heart."

Some excellent jazz musicians backed Scott's Savoy recordings. There were usually five or six, led by pianist-arranger Howard Biggs and including a featured tenor saxist (perhaps Budd Johnson) and rhythm players of the caliber of Kenny Clarke (drums), Sal Salvador or George Barnes (guitar), and Jack Lesberg or Al Hall (bass). The brilliant but volatile Charles Mingus played bass on Scott's first Savoy session but walked off because he did not appreciate Scott's unorthodox approach. One jazz giant who very much did appreciate it, however, was Charlie "Bird" Parker. The out-of-print album *One Night in Birdland* includes a bit of Scott singing live with Parker, who rarely let singers sit in. "That night I had come into Birdland and he kept waving 'come on,'" Scott recalls. "He was already blowing. He had done a chorus. He repeated the whole thing and had me sing it with him. They had a broadcast studio and recording setup back there." Scott, however, was not credited on the album. In order, he says, to avoid trouble from Lubinsky, to whom he was still under contract, his vocal was attributed to Chubby Newsom, a female blues singer.

Savoy's attempts to make Scott more commercial never really worked. When Mendelsohn left the company for a bit in the late fifties, Lubinsky tried giving Scott extra "class" by adding strings to some of his recordings, which, had it been done tastefully, Scott would have liked, but class was hardly Lubinsky's area of expertise. He also tried forcing Scott into a more contemporary vein, which only increased Scott's frustration. Scott's wife Earlene notes, "They even had him do a couple rock 'n' roll songs. But that turned Jimmy off. It definitely was not Jimmy. On one record, he just stopped singing. I wish I still had that recording, but it broke." The quality of his records declined as the fifties wore on.

The songs Scott likes singing the most are songs that make him think "that's the way life is. I mean, these songs had stories. It's like a lot of people will ask—'Why was I born? Why am I living?' There's a question. 'Why do I want the thing I daren't hope for?' The song expresses the thoughts of the people." And not just of people in general, he makes clear, but *his* thoughts. He knew well what it was to "want the thing I daren't hope for."

"Certain songs just have that give-back. You give the song something, it gives back," he says. "But we don't have the record companies today that are into caring about the sincerity of music. Everything is fast-buck now. Therefore, that kind of expression gets pushed back. I think it has an extreme importance in the world. But the media pushed those songs aside, as if it's not important how good it might be for you, for someone to tell you a beautiful story in a song. And how important that story might be for you or for the next person that may hurt of pain or be lost." As he struggles to find the right words, his voice conveys increasingly great sadness; he's verging on tears once again. The emotional tenderness in this man is striking. He's never developed the protective hardness of most adults.

Scott knew, from the effect he produced on audiences in clubs, the talent he had. One of his long-time admirers was Doc Pomus, a singer and songwriter who was coauthor of such hits as Dion and the Belmonts' "A Teenager in Love" and the Drifters' "Save the Last Dance for Me." Pomus recalled in 1987 that Scott, whom he often saw perform in Newark during the fifties, when Scott may well have been at his peak, could

> touch you in your deepest parts and even find spots that you
> never knew you had. He was frail and Indian looking. He had
> a narrow face that he kept framed with oversized thick glasses.
> His clothes were always so long and loose that he looked like
> some kind of myopic scarecrow. And he walked with a slow,
> strange stagger-shuffle. But I swear that weird-looking dude

could holler. He sang the slow notes slower than anyone else and he had a way of bending notes that was uncanny. It was like he was trying to find out how much he could control and try a note without messing up his perfect pitch. He sang behind the beat further than anyone else ever could and every time I was certain that I was certain he finally got too far back, he returned somehow. His meter was always impeccable. He had a wide vibrato and the combination of his timing, pitch, and soft sweet sound gave every song a dream-like, love fantasy quality. No one ever sang or sounded like him.[4]

Another friend and admirer of Scott's, Nathan Heard of Newark, where Scott made his home for much of the 1950s, recalled in 1987 seeing Scott, via his performances, reduce women to tears and melt the hearts of even hardened pimps who'd turn out for his club appearances. He stressed that Scott had quite a following among pimps, hustlers, numbers writers, and the like, who'd stand in line outside places where he'd be working just to get a glimpse of him. (Scott's singing particularly touched the outsiders, the disenfranchised.) Heard remembered, too, the way Scott could elicit screams from women in the audience—stressing that (in contrast to rumors concerning Frank Sinatra) no one *paid* those women to scream. In fact, he was certain that Scott's fans included many who gave up their hard-earned rent money in order to see him. When Scott first came on the scene, Heard recalled, he "knocked everybody out."

Women started imitating him, men started imitating him. . . . Of course, no one could sound like him. I think the closest we have to him now is Nancy Wilson or Etta Jones, they're pretty close to him. But that's their style. That off-key, behind-the-beat singing is just something that's uniquely his. And I know there were many good musicians who were counting 4/4 who couldn't keep up with him if they listened, because they were listening to him instead of playing their music and if you listen to Jimmy you're gonna be hypnotized. . . . Jimmy's voice at that time was, I don't know, almost like a clear unobstructed sound, almost like a whistle but yet a note. . . . When he would do songs like "Everybody's Somebody's Fool," or "When Did You Leave Heaven," or "All or Nothing at All" . . . I've never heard anyone do those songs who could evoke the emotions in people like Jimmy could. Because Jimmy went into the clubs where the music was loud and the blues singers were there and Redd Foxx was telling all his raunchy jokes and Jimmy would take this crowd, as loud and as drunk and bawdy as they were, he would touch something in this crowd with one of his ballads that would just turn everybody's head. You had to listen to him, you had to appreciate him, and certainly you had to want more.[5]

Heard remembered, too, that club owners sometimes tried to cheat Scott of his money; sometimes Heard backed Scott up in confrontations with them after shows. He also watched as the club scene changed in Newark, as it did elsewhere, as the 1950s wore on and more and more places stopped offering live music. It became harder, and increasingly more frustrating, for Scott to make a living singing. By the early sixties ghetto bars that had once regularly presented singers and bands were just neighborhood taverns with only a jukebox or a television for "entertainment."

In the meanwhile, Scott's home life through much of the fifties was far from happy. "My second marriage was to Channie, a young lady who was a barber. We got married in '54 or '55, and it lasted until '60," Scott recalls. They fought hard and often. For example, when they attended the funeral of Billie Holiday in 1959—Channie was a first cousin of Holiday's last husband, Louis McKay—Scott wore dark glasses to hide a black eye that his wife had given him. But that was the least of it. On another occasion she tried to run him down with their Cadillac. One night—drunk and frustrated by personal and professional difficulties—he put both their lives in jeopardy by slamming his foot on the gas pedal over hers. There were nights in clubs, too, when he'd get drunk after finishing his gig and pick fights with strangers much bigger than he was.

Nathan Heard was concerned by how much Scott sometimes drank and also by what he perceived as Scott's self-destructive streak. One night, Heard recalled, Scott became so angry about not being appreciated that he got out of his car on Long Island's Sunrise Highway and stood, traffic narrowly missing him, until Heard hurriedly pulled him back into the car (saving Scott's life, he believed). Heard wondered at the cause of Scott's personal anguish. Scott's marriage was coming to an end at that time, Heard knew. And Scott—uncomfortable that he could no longer be the breadwinner he once had been—had taken to staying away from home more often.[6]

There were other problems as well. Although he was never once charged formally, Scott was hassled by police repeatedly over suspicion of drug involvement. A lot of his friends in the music world—Charlie Parker, Sonny Stitt, Big Maybelle Smith—were or had been known heroin users. Police claimed that Scott had been implicated by users whom they'd arrested. He was forced to endure humiliating strip searches for drugs while police taunted him, called him "faggot," and asked whether he was male or female and other insults. He took whatever anguish he felt and put it into his singing.

Even at his peak, Scott's records enjoyed modest sales success, and as public interest in him declined it became harder for him to get record dates at all. (The only recording of Scott's that ever made the charts was "Everybody's Somebody's Fool," which he made with Hampton.) His renown was largely among urban blacks; Scott's name would have been largely unknown to white record buyers of the 1950s. Yet other singers, both black and white, paid attention to his work and offered diluted versions of it to larger audiences. You can hear aspects of Scott's style in the work of artists as varied as Nancy Wilson (who's often acknowledged her debt to him—her phrasing is obviously derived from his), Johnnie Ray, Big Maybelle Smith, Etta Jones, Larry Darnell, and young Frankie Lymon. Even the title of Lyman's high-pitched, juvenile-voiced biggest hit "Why Do Fools Fall in Love" seems to echo such Scott recordings as "I've Been a Fool" and "Everybody's Somebody's Fool." Scott helped pave the way for Stevie Wonder, Ronnie Dyson, and Michael Jackson. As Fred Mendelsohn told the music journalist Arnold Shaw, Scott "developed a very solid following. He had a style and a sound and a way of phrasing that has been copied by many, many singers. He was really an innovator who did not reap the fruits of his genius."[7]

Scott comments, "Nancy Wilson's parents have always told me— and even Nancy herself—[that] they used to take my records home to Nancy and she used to get in her room, shut the door, and she'd be just listening to them. She developed a style of singing from that. Maybelle [Smith] was a hell of a singer. A lot of people say, 'Oh, she phrased sort of like you.' OK. But they must remember—in the lean years, Maybelle and I were out there working on the same bills. Larry Darnell was another one that was working out there with us. So, I don't know. I hope whatever they got, if it was from me, I hope it did good for them. And many singers have come to me and said, 'Oh, Jimmy, I just like the way you sing such-and-such a thing and I sing it.' In show business, there was such a sharing."

Singing high, of course, came naturally to Scott. Others tried to get some of the effect he had by singing in falsetto; perhaps the most commercially successful of the falsetto singers was Frankie Valli, lead vocalist of the Four Seasons ("Walk Like a Man," "Big Girls Don't Cry"). "Frankie Valli hung out with me, all around here in Newark and everything. Frankie, little Joey Pesci [an aspiring singer who went on to become a popular actor, appearing in such films as *Goodfellas* and *Home Alone*], and myself—the three of us would all be together," Scott recalls. He encouraged Valli to try sing slower, assuring him the audience would wait for him. He also tried, unsuccessfully, to discourage Valli from singing song after song in falsetto. "You should style a song in your own voice. Frankie had a natural knack for the delivery, but he would have preserved his voice much better if he hadn't sung so much in falsetto. See, I'm listening to the vocal tones—singing high hasn't done him all that great. You know, Frankie was a guy that—it was a gimmick. He thought that gimmicks were the way," Scott says. "Many good records, of course, were made on that falsetto key. But how many voices and throat muscles were destroyed on singers that were singing falsetto! You can use your voice to make falsettic expressions that are necessary, but to sing every song you sing in falsetto—that's the worst thing in the world a person can do to their vocal cords. A lot of singers that I know, that were singing then in falsetto, they're not singing today—it's over. They can't reach those notes."

When did Scott realize his own voice was always going to stay high? There's far more in the answer to that question than may be apparent at first blush.

"Uh . . . actually, I didn't realize it until I was in my thirties. Then I realized, 'My God, my voice isn't going to change,'" Scott responds with hesitation, unsure how much he wants to explain. He zigs and zags, halting a few times, before finally making everything clear. "You know how young guys are, you're looking for . . . and I used to catch myself. . . I'd be trying the bass part and couldn't bass a lick. And sometimes I would start a song off in a baritone key just to see what depths. . . . Then I began to wonder, 'Well, why?' That's when I found out about the other conditions. But I didn't know the full extent of it back then; I was in my early thirties before I realized, 'Hey, this ain't never going to change. This is going to be like this forever.' And then you got to deal with it."

He was aware when he was quite young that he wasn't growing the way his classmates were. He didn't reach his final height, five feet seven inches, until he was in his thirties. It was more than just a matter of being a slow developer. "I remember my mother taking my brother Kenny and me to a clinic, before she passed, when we were just young kids," he comments. "They had a hormone treatment they were experimenting with, and she took us, and then after a while she stopped taking us altogether, because I guess she realized that at that time they hadn't gotten far enough with it for it to help. Then I remember after we were in the foster homes, it was brought to their attention, and they wanted us to go [renew the treatment]. But I just felt that if my mother had stopped, she must have felt that it was something that they couldn't correct at that time."

Little Jimmy Scott and two of his brothers, one of whom has died, he explains, were born with Kallman's syndrome, a rare hereditary condition in which the individual never goes through puberty. The body simply fails to produce the hormonal secretions necessary for the maturation of the sexual organs, the growth of a beard and pubic hair, and the deepening of the voice. Although scientific knowledge about the syndrome was more limited when Scott was a child than it now is, his mother understood what the condition entailed; after all, it had been passed down in the family for generations. Scott comments, "See, I've noticed and found out, in the history of the family—in my grandmother's generation, there was one boy that I know of that had this condition. He was in his seventies or eighties before he passed—my [great] Uncle Will. Then in my mother's immediate family—among her sisters and brothers—there were two boys that had it. Then among my mother's children, there were three boys that had this hormone syndrome. And my sisters each had a boy that was afflicted that way. One sister had two boys; one of them now is dead."

In his youth, his sisters, he says, tended to treat him as if he were emotionally, not just physically, immature. "I noticed even when I was growing up they'd say, 'You can't do this, you can't do that'— that was the attitude toward me: I couldn't do this, I couldn't do the other. I never thought of that particular thing being the reason until I got older and they blurted out one time: 'You ain't got no business doing this and you ain't got no business doing that.' See, that let me know that somewhere in their minds they felt that I couldn't cope with life because of it. But I was coping all the time, and they couldn't understand that."

He gave the condition more thought as he grew older. "I wanted to know, 'Why, why, why?' That was my thing, 'Why, why?' And the more I concentrated on it, the more if I'd hear something, I paid attention to it, I'd check it out, you know. And I'd come up with these different things." He felt the solution for him, ultimately, was simply to accept his condition as a given. He didn't look for help, as one of his brothers did, from doctors. "I've shared a lot of time with my brother Kenny, who was born that way—he was the one that sang with me as a boy in church and things. Ken was a person that let his heartbreaks hurt him, cut him deep. He was the type that needed support, because when he was hurt, he would do harm to himself." His brother, he maintains, viewed the condition more negatively than he did. "Kenny started taking those treatments as an adult— he's taken the shots. And he started growing hair from that. Now OK. So, what does it do? It makes a face look hairy. But it doesn't change any of the other parts. So far, I haven't heard of changing anything else. But I don't know. And it does deepen the voice some. But I think it was too late, when he started treatments. And I think they could have had an ill effect on him. . . . You know, he just had an infection that was supposed to be cancerous, down the throat, and they were giving him radiation, and at the same time, he was taking these hormone shots. I think that it was a bad move for him to continue the shots. Now his voice is gravelly and he can barely get his voice out, you know," Scott says.

The shots hold no temptation for Scott, and he certainly wouldn't want to risk changing his distinctive voice. He insists, "Something has always kept me from even worrying about the condition. I've never looked at it as a problem for me. I really didn't. And that was one of the things that I had to fight to get Kenny to understand. Because he let it interfere with his life. And he fought himself because of it, so much so that there were times I thought he hated himself, and that's no reason to hate yourself. Something that you can learn to deal with, you deal with. And that's that."

How common is the condition?

"I've rarely heard of too many others. They tell me there's more other people and whatnot," Scott says, adding after a pause, "I have an idea of some people, just by looking at them or watching their ways or their attitudes. And some guys get very indignant about certain little things, you know—because I know, in a sense, I had some of it, too, that arrogance about being picked on, like you're a little girl or something like that."

Although Scott maintains he's never viewed his condition as a problem, discussing it clearly has taken a lot out of him. It has brought powerful emotions to the surface, making it necessary for us to draw this particular interview to a close; we can continue another time. The syndrome has played a crucial role in his life. It has given him that fascinating, high, clear voice. It has also given him a sense of isolation. Even if he tried to forget his differences from most people, there were always reminders, whether from classmates in his youth, taunting him as a sissy, or from cruel police in his adult years, forcing him to strip because they claimed they'd heard he was involved in drugs. It left him far more vulnerable, far more sensitive than the average person. And he used that in his work. Did he find a greater resonance in "Why Was I Born?" than other singers? You bet. That was more than just a song for him. It was damned near the central question of his life.

*   *   *

Around 1960, Lubinsky, aware of shifting audience tastes, switched the focus of Savoy from R&B and jazz to gospel, which he felt would be more profitable for him. So he stopped recording Scott, among others. Increasingly, Scott felt like his career was heading toward a dead end. Too often he seemed to find himself working in little clubs with musicians who didn't know many of the older songs he loved or sharing bills with young rock 'n' roll performers who didn't know who he was. He was pleased when Fred Mendelsohn returned to Savoy Records, but Mendelsohn couldn't get Lubinsky to record him. "Freddy's a very likable guy," Scott says. "Deep down—even though he had to work under Lubinsky—Freddy was very fond of musicians and entertainers. He'd say to me, although he was limited in what he could do, 'Just hold on, everything will be all right.' But everything was all right for Lubinsky. Everything wasn't all right for myself and the other entertainers and musicians involved with him."

If Scott was no longer recording, he was still knocking live audiences dead. Philadelphia disc jockey Joel Dorn saw for the first time the effect Scott could have on an audience in the summer of 1960— a midnight show at the Apollo Theatre. He would later recall that Scott was "ensconced between the Coasters and Ray Charles. In those days the Coasters were a show-stopping, crowd-convulsing cartoon-come-to-life onstage. And Ray Charles . . . well, Ray Charles was *Ray Charles*. Sandwiched in between thunder and lightning, Jimmy slew that audience with a sword made of whispers. He sang four songs that night ('Everybody's Somebody's Fool,' 'When Did You Leave Heaven,' 'The Masquerade Is Over,' and 'Motherless Child'). They, and my vision of Jimmy, echoed in my brain for weeks. I had never heard or seen anything like him." The records Scott had made for Roost and Savoy, Dorn felt, "were great, and some were even classic, but they were not the Jimmy Scott I had heard that night at the Apollo. That Jimmy Scott had never been captured on record."[8]

In 1962 Scott received an offer that seemed almost too good to be true. Ray Charles, who had known and admired him since the early years of his career, had formed a new record company, Tangerine, and wanted Scott to record for him. Scott, who hadn't recorded since 1960, leaped at the chance; he and Charles respected one another. He recalls, "Ray and I sat down and came to mutual agreements for all the tunes on that album; there was just one out of the whole batch that he asked me to do. And I felt comfortable. Ray found the actual instrumentation, the style of instrumentation that I needed for presentation. He's the first one to do that, out of all of them. And there were two arrangers on that album, Gerald Wilson and Marty Paich" (both recognized masters at their craft). Charles played piano for Scott at the recording sessions, and strings were used effectively to give Scott the first-rate showcasing for which he had always hoped.

Scott had every reason to believe that the album, *Falling in Love Is Wonderful,* would mark the rebirth of his career. The first feedback was terrific. Joel Dorn would later comment that in the seven years he was on the air, no album drew a swifter or more favorable response from the public. This was the first album, he felt, to really capture what Scott was capable of live.[9] No sooner did the album come out, however, than Lubinsky obtained an injunction, claiming Scott was still under exclusive contract to him. Tangerine quickly stopped distribution. The few copies that did get into circulation are collectors' items; people have told Scott of paying from $125 to $175 for a copy. Lubinsky's action effectively scared off any other companies from considering recording Scott for the next few years.

Scott is still bewildered about why Lubinsky—who no longer had any interest in recording Scott—would want to block him from recording for anyone else. Keeping Scott down didn't benefit Lubinsky. Scott recalls in anguish, "When Lubinsky put this threat on Ray Charles's company, he was hanging over our heads a contract from 1959. But he'd never honored that contract. He never did anything for me! A contract can't be one-sided, man, all for him. In the course of time, I happened to lose my copies of my contracts, and God knows I wish I'd kept them. Because the contract itself would explain; I mean, there's *got* to be a way that album could have come out. That album I made for Ray Charles—it's still up there. The greatest album that I've ever made! That and the one I made for Atlantic with Joel Dorn—those were the greatest albums that I have ever made. And Lubinsky finagled and wangled in there, to block all of that! Deliberately. Nobody wanted to go too far with Lubinsky. He was crooked. Finally, I just got tired of his mess. And I just went away from the area." He found jobs outside of music.

In 1965, Scott recalls, "I was working at a nursing home in Cleveland as an aide to the male patients, and this young lady, Ruth, was the nurse on the shift. We got married. My attitude was, 'Just give me the simple life.' I'm not looking for unnecessary excitement out of life. But then, this young lady decided she was slick and that bought an end to that marriage. Our ideas weren't the same—and in any marriage, unless you're in one accord, it doesn't work."

Joel Dorn had enough faith in Scott to produce recording sessions with him at Atlantic in 1969 and 1972. Atlantic Records vice president Neshui Ertegun let Dorn sign Scott to a two-album deal, having been assured by Atlantic's attorneys that Scott would be free to record for them. In March 1969, accompanied by the likes of David "Fathead" Newman, Junior Mance, and Ron Carter, Scott recorded some remarkable sides for Atlantic. He was in superb voice. Arranger William Fischer gave him exquisite showcases on "Day by Day" and "Unchained Melody." Scott impressed too with his version of "Sometimes I Feel Like a Motherless Child." But Lubinsky's lawyers raised enough trouble to get that album, titled *The Source,* suppressed. Ertegun kept his word and let Scott record material for the second album (using such jazz musicians as Ray Bryant, Richard Davis, and Billy Cobham in 1972) even though he doubted it could ever be released.[10]

When Lubinsky died in 1974, Mendelsohn took over Savoy and offered to record Scott. The title of the album they made, *Can't We Begin Again?* expressed a hope that was not to be realized. At the recording sessions on May 20 and 21, 1975, in Chicago, the musicians Mendelsohn had hired faked their way without distinction through the numbers (which included "Close Your Eyes," "When I Fall in Love," and "You've Changed"). Strings were overdubbed later. The record sold too few copies to justify Mendelsohn's doing another.

Scott slipped away from show business. He took various day jobs (he worked in the shipping room of a Cleveland hotel for a while) and sought solace in religion; he even considered becoming a minister. "I've studied various religions. I'm a truth-seeker," he says. "The spiritual side of things are to me the stronger essence of a being. It seems, in some people's eyesight, to be the weaker aspect of man. But it's not. The spiritual aspect of a being is a very important part. And I've studied that." He also helped care for his ailing father, who wanted—and got from Scott—forgiveness for never having been able to provide much support.

*   *   *

By the time Scott married Earlene Rogers on Valentines Day in 1985, they had been friends for some thirty-five years.[11] "It's a funny thing. Earlene and I had known each other all through these other marriages," he notes. "She struck me as a person that needed support. Because when I met her, I got in an argument with a fellow at her house—and put him out of the house. I found out the next day, the fellow I had put out was her husband! My knees were shaking. I said, 'What? you mean to tell me I was putting this man out of his own house?' But Earlene and I always kept in contact with each other. She's a good kid."

She had been a fan of his even before she first met him. As a waitress at Newark's Coleman House Hotel in the early fifties, she used to play his record of "Everybody's Somebody's Fool" on the jukebox constantly. They became acquainted when he stayed at the hotel while touring with the Hampton band. Earlene coaxed Scott back into singing. Early in 1985 she called WBGO-FM, the Newark-based jazz public radio station to which she was a regular contributor, and suggested that they put Little Jimmy Scott on the air. She was told that "everybody knows Little Jimmy Scott is dead" but managed to convince the station otherwise. Scott was soon making a guest appearance on disc jockey Bob Porter's program. Scott was gratified by all of the supportive calls that came in for him while he was on the air—and for quite a while after.

The appearance led to a sold-out Newark club booking and a flurry of attention. He received occasional quality bookings. Before the year was through, for example, he was playing the Blue Note, one of New York's preeminent jazz clubs, and being praised by critics as one of the most original of all jazz song stylists. When Ruth Brown made her comeback in the late eighties, she got Scott to open for her on assorted gigs from her Monday night shows at the Lonestar Roadhouse to a gala 1989 New Year's Eve celebration at New York's renowned Windows on the World broadcast live over National Public Radio stations. She also helped get him an extended gig at the Ballroom, a top Manhattan cabaret, where he was backed by her regular band, with Bobby Forrester switching from organ to piano. "I love teaming with Ruth," Scott says. "And she's been working so hard to keep all of us doing something. She has to stick close to *Black and Blue* because the producers want more of her attention. She's on that stage and she has a performance to do, but half of herself's out here trying to reach out for others. And that is the honest-to-goodness truth about the woman. I've benefited by the effects of what's she's done, in so many ways. I know she's trying her damndest for the others.

"I mean, she tried hard to keep me, Bobby Forrester, and the band doing something, man, while she's in *Black and Blue*. I just want to get things tight enough that I've got enough work to keep Bobby Forrester and the cats in that band together. I really do. I want to work with those cats. I'd like to play Europe and Japan—I've never been to those places—with them. Because I think they would tear the place up. They're so soulful and they're so beautiful, man. I've got a sense of feel for the way Bobby's playing. Bobby's got a sense of feel for the way I'm singing. The horns, they have a feel. And when you get that sense of emotion going on amongst musicians, it's got to go. But you've got to get enough dates to have an itinerary. When you ain't got the work to offer these people, what you going to do? And that's all it is: *I want to work."* Scott pronounces each of the last four words separately, with equal emphasis, underscoring how desperately he would like to be working regularly.

Occasionally, Scott will get to sing a number or two, impromptu, at an all-star event in New York; for example, he sang at a gala honoring Cab Calloway at the New School. When Illinois Jacquet spotted Scott in the audience at the Blue Note's eighth anniversary celebration in November 1989, he asked Scott to come up and perform a number with his big band (including special guest guitarist Kenny Burrell), which was playing a slow blues. Scott walked up the mike to accept the unexpected invitation, saying, as the band continued behind him, that he didn't really sing the blues but that he could sing a ballad that would sound like the blues. He then eased into one of his favorites, "I Cried for You," fitting the phrases to the melody the band was already playing—words and feeling have always been more important to him than melody.

I watched his performance in suspense, uncertain whether he could make the lyrics work without the right melodic support. But as he carefully tried to accommodate himself to the band—and as the band gradually tried to accommodate itself to him—I realized that I was witnessing something remarkable. You could sense the audience—most members of which probably had never heard of Little Jimmy Scott—getting caught up in what he was doing. Burrell, with the other musicians following, subtly turned the melody around so that the band actually wound up playing "I Cried for You." Singer and band finished, triumphantly, together, and the audience thundered. Asked to do another, Scott gave "All of Me" his "lightly and politely" swing treatment, then returned to his seat, his face giving no indication that he was aware he'd just stolen the show. Tony Bennett, a longtime admirer, came over and gave him a warm bearhug. *Down Beat* magazine reported in March 1990 that "the star-studded, eighth anniversary of NYC's Blue Note brought together Tony Bennett, who sang 'Don't Get Around Much Anymore,' Jon Faddis with a rap in honor of emcee Illinois Jacquet, Milt Jackson, and Gerry Mulligan. But for pure emotion, the night belonged to singer Jimmy Scott, whose vocal styling bridged the changes of jazz into r&b and rock &

roll; his falsetto a model for Frankie Lymon, Michael Jackson, and even Diana Ross."

On other occasions, however, Scott has failed to connect with his audience. He has had moments when he has strained to stay in tune, when that idiosyncratic phrasing of his, grown more idiosyncratic over the years—his earliest recordings were much more traditional—seems to strike listeners as bizarre rather than fascinating.

Scott lives simply. The occasional bookings he gets—even when they include some prestigious venues—have not been enough to improve his modest financial conditions. "I've seen it happen to others," he reflects, "and it'll probably happen to me, too—I'll have my foot in the grave before I make a decent living."

Being included in 1989 among the first group of artists honored by the recently established Rhythm and Blues Foundation meant a great deal to Scott. "That really went to my heart. Because man, I've never had nobody ever do that for me," he says. The plaque he received from the foundation was the first such honor he'd ever received in his career, and the cash grant that came with it—$15,000—was deeply appreciated. "The money actually just came through. So I'm going and paying all of the damn bills. I want to start 1990 without owing a dime creditwise. I'm paying all of that crap up. Thank God." If he can ever get ahead of the game financially, his goal is to establish a not-for-profit foundation to help deserving youths develop their talents. He is certain that he and other seasoned performers have valuable knowledge to pass on to aspiring young performers. He'd like to give something back to the community. If he can help give some city kids a start in show business—and help keep them off of the streets in the process—he'll be happy.

Scott still voices some confidence that the renewed attention he's received in recent years will lead to an opportunity to record again. "Hey, I always felt—and still feel—I'm going to strike it right. The right thing is going to happen to me," he insists. The Rhythm and Blues Foundation, he hopes, may reissue some of his long-unavailable recordings—perhaps even the album he did for Ray Charles. (The only Scott albums in print at the time of our interviews were three reissues on the Savoy label.) In an exceptional act of generosity, Jimmy McDonough used the money he earned from his superb 1988 *Village Voice* profile of Scott to pay for the making of a new Scott demo in the hope it might help Scott get a much-deserved recording contract.

"I have good material for an album. There's really some new good writers out there. I've run across a few. And I've got more than a dozen of my own numbers that I've written. I've got to get the right opportunity, that's all," Scott says. "I want to be free to create. I don't want to have sit up and worry, what is that sucker going to do? With Lubinsky, you had to worry about everything. I came into the business with the desire to do something. I didn't accomplish those things. I'm a human being, not just a tool for people to use. Not like a hammer—if you break it, you buy a new one. This is a human being." The pain in his voice is acute.

"All of the things I'm still after and am still desiring in life, by now I should have had them," Scott says. "I should be venturing now into projects that would benefit others in some way. But how can you do it? Although your heart is there and you want to give—and I see so many things—I have to stop and say [and here Scott's voice, tinged with sorrow, drops low] you ain't got nothing yourself."

3

════════ CHARLES BROWN ════════

"I'm driftin' and driftin'. . . ."

Singer-pianist Charles Brown can still remember the tauntings he'd
get from the other boys in his hometown of Texas City, Texas. They'd
be heading off to roughhouse or play ball someplace, and they'd see
him sitting on the porch of his music teacher—her only male pu-
pil—awaiting his piano lessons. "They'd call me 'sissy, sissy,'" he recalls in gentle tones. "I'd tell my grandmother, 'Mama, I don't want
to play piano.' And she'd say, 'When those little boys call you sissy,
you tell them, 'You better shut your mouth!' They're going to be paying to see you one day.'"

His grandmother, the formidable Swanee Simpson, the first woman choir director in Texas, turned out to be right. Between 1946 and
1948, Brown sang and played piano on eleven R&B chart hits recorded by Johnny Moore's Three Blazers. Although guitarist Moore was
the nominal leader of that trio, it was Brown's smooth, sensitive,
somewhat forlorn vocals that captured the public's attention. Brown
then successfully went out as a single, recording in the next four years
a dozen R&B chart hits under his own name. His most-requested
numbers ("Drifting Blues," "Merry Christmas Baby," "Homesick
Blues," "Black Night," and "Trouble Blues") always included a good-
ly share of the blues. He describes himself, however, as a "blue ballad singer"—a singer who's particularly partial to ballads but gives
them a bluesy sound—rather than a strict blues singer. Indeed, his
singing style is indebted to the tradition of the polished nightclub
singer or band singer no less than to the tradition of the older bluesman. There's an urbanity to his work. The blues feeling—an awareness of life's tragic side—is always, unmistakably, there, but Brown's
music tends to conjure up a club that's classy (or, at the very least,
striving to be) rather than any tough, old-style blues juke joint.

Brown was right for his times. He had enough of the blues sensibility to connect with past traditions and express the ongoing disappointments of his people—and also enough poise, tender vulnerability, and even the recurring suggestion of optimism, to express the nascent upwardly mobile aspirations of his generation. There was no more militancy in his singing than there was in the rhetoric of the most respected African American civil rights leaders of the forties and early fifties. Brown was mellow and sincere, letting an audience know—but sounding resigned rather than agitated—that things, in one way or another, were harder than he'd like. His piano work combined true blues playing with a subtlety and finesse—and, at times, even delicacy—that revealed his classical training.

Brown's laid-back vocals influenced a number of artists in the late forties and early fifties. This sweet-spirited, nonprepossessing figure became a major force on the scene. Through the years that followed, he always retained a certain loyal following, although more assertive singers—perhaps reflecting an increasing self-assertion throughout black culture generally—became more popular. Brown took good care of himself throughout the lean years of his career; the fact that he neither smoked nor drank no doubt played an important part in the preservation of his voice. Even when his funds were low, he was always meticulous about his appearance and grooming; a sharp suit, a fresh toupee—these he considered good investments for his future. Still looking and sounding youthful, Brown was "rediscovered" in the 1980s when he was in his sixties. He sounds even better now than in his youth. It's not just that he's drawing upon five decades of experience as a performer; his singing has more guts. It seems more real.

Brown now sings his old songs, as well as new ones he's written, to audiences that for the most part are too young to remember him from his original success. They respond to both the feeling and the high level of craftsmanship he brings to his work. His blend of musical traditions makes him unlike any other singers they're likely to have heard. Appearing as a special guest star on a concert bill featuring raucous young rock and soul singers, he can hold the attention of listeners (who know nothing of his history) with a subdued rendition of an age-old number like "Nobody Knows the Trouble I've Seen," or a sparkling pop tune from the thirties like "All My Life," or his own (and you sense he's lived it) "Travelin' Blues." At the time of our initial interview in 1990, for example, Brown was just getting back from European dates, was about to open at the prestigious Blue Note in New York City, and, following that, would tour for a couple of months with multiple-Grammy-winner Bonnie Raitt. Charles Brown hasn't done at all badly, he'll tell you, for someone who never really set out to make a career in music.

* * *

Born September 13 in either 1920 or 1922 (depending upon which sources you accept) in Texas City, Texas, on the Gulf Coast, Brown's mother, Mattie, died when he was six months old.[1] His father, Mose, Brown says, was a cotton-picker more interested in chasing prostitutes than in raising a son. Consequently, Brown was raised by his maternal grandmother and grandfather (whom he called "Mama" and "Papa"), Swanee and Conquest Simpson. His grandmother, whom he feels was generally ahead of her time, was staunchly insistent that he make something of himself; she didn't want him winding up working on the docks or in the cotton fields as so many people did. She'd tell him often that he was lucky he *hadn't* been raised by his real father, whom she viewed as a weak man, or he'd have been nothing more than a cotton-picker, too. She also didn't want young Charles to even think of emulating his father's skirt-chasing ways and did her best to instill fear in that regard. His father, she told him, had picked up a venereal disease from a prostitute in the red-light district and had infected his mother, who had then grown weaker and weaker. Brown's mother prophetically told his father before she died (Brown's grandmother related), "Mose, you won't have nothing but bad luck for doing this to me." Indeed, Swanee Simpson believed (and young Charles could hardly think otherwise) that bad luck had dogged Charles's father. Mose Brown was struck by a train—and killed instantly—one foggy morning in 1928, the day he was returning to Texas City for the express purpose of reclaiming his son. Swanee Simpson felt that she was *meant* to raise the boy—and she had high hopes for him.

"My grandmother really wanted me to be a schoolteacher. And she wanted me to play piano. She was playing for the church, the Barbous Chapel Baptist Church. She said, 'Well, you've got to go to— I've got to send you to college when I can get able. And you've got to learn to play for the church. And you're going to be a teacher because you'll be recognized in the community.' So that was my—*her* goal. And it was customary that I should play for the church. When I took piano lessons, I'd be sitting on the porch, waiting for my turn with these little girls—I was the only boy taking lessons—and my little friends would come by, saying, 'Sissy, sissy.'" Brown began taking lessons when he was just six. His grandmother would not let him quit, although he was uncomfortable being considered the neighbor-hood sissy. "I took ten grades of piano—I can read fly specks off a sheet of music—but I didn't really know music was my talent. I didn't have no idea I was ever going to be an entertainer like I am today.

"I'd sing in the church with the choir. And they used to have me sing at the funerals. I'd sing sad. Until one day, at a Mother's Day funeral, Mrs. Johnson—Ella Johnson's mother—died. And I sang, 'This mother is gone.' Grieving, and hearing this song—it was an emotional thing—she [Ella] called out, 'Don't you sing that no more! *Oh!*' And she threw her pocketbook at me! It scared me so bad, standing be-side the casket, that I sat down. My grandmother said, 'If that wom-an had hit you with that, I don't care if her mother was in there dead, I'd have gone over and hit her over the head!' I said, 'Well, I don't want to sing for no more funerals.'"

An uncle taught him guitar, kazoo, and blues singing. He heard blues records by Leroy Carr, Blind Lemon Jefferson, and Bessie Smith. He'd sneak out to joints where he could hear the blues, too, and he'd practice playing the blues at home when his grandmother, who wouldn't have approved, was out. A niece, Joyce, would let him know when his grandmother was drawing near so he wouldn't be caught playing the forbidden music. He was also creating his own blues songs. As he entered adolescence, feeling set apart in some way from most of his peers, the blues provided self-expression. Brown says that he created "Drifting Blues," his signature song since he first record-ed it in 1945 (it became a blues anthem of his generation), in the thirties in Texas. He may have been as young as twelve or thirteen when he created that unforgettable expression of loneliness and alien-ation that he originally called "Walkin' and Driftin'."

It wasn't as if Brown chose the blues tradition whole-heartedly over the traditions of so-called respectable music, however; he found val-ue in both. He continued studying classical piano and developed a love for classical music, which again was unusual for a black youth in humble Texas City. He eventually gave a recital of all-classical music, he says, adding that he supposes he didn't have the perfec-tionism necessary for serious devotion to classical piano.

Brown's chemistry teacher at Central High School in Galveston, Texas, a Mr. James, augmented his teaching income by moonlight-ing as a musician. He led groups that played one-night stands at the white clubs on the beach front. Eventually, he asked Brown to work for him. Although Brown wasn't familiar with the pop music that James played—he knew religious music from playing in church and the classics from his piano lessons—he was a proficient enough reader to pick it up quickly. And he loved what he heard. Although he responded to the beauty of such romantic ballads as "Star Dust," however, he still didn't plan to make music his career.

After graduating with honors from high school, Brown went to Prairie View College in Hempstead, Texas. "When I went to college, I thought I knew enough piano, so I just took one semester of advanced piano, which is classical. The teacher told me, 'You should have majored in music.' I said, 'No, I've majored in chemistry and mathematics and minored in education.' I was going to teach school," Brown recalls. Teaching was considered a laudable goal for a serious, college-educated black man in Texas at the time. Although many other career options were denied to blacks because of discrimination, jobs were always available for black teachers in the segregated public school system. While in college, Brown played piano in the college band and also sang one number, "Big Fat Mama" (which Clarence Williams and Lucky Millinder had recorded), a risqué crowd-pleaser. He didn't feel that kind of song was for him, however; he preferred sweet ballads, sincerely sung.

"When I finished college in 1942, I got a job as a chemistry teacher in Baytown, Texas," Brown recalls. His principal at George Washington Carver High School felt his gentle disposition made him a natural for teaching, but Brown wasn't satisfied with the $22 a week the job paid. Nothing was left after paying for necessities. And teaching, he realized, had been more a goal his grandparents had established for him than one he had set for himself. "I put in for another job with the Civil Service since they had opened everything—Civil Service had no segregation barriers. I took an examination to be a junior chemist. Well, I got it," he recalls. In fact, he scored a ninety-six on the test, which made him, in the federal government's eyes, a most promising prospect for a junior chemist. He was offered a choice of working at arsenals in Maryland or Arkansas and chose the Pine Bluff, Arkansas, arsenal because it was closer to home. He recalls, minimizing what must have been an uncomfortable situation, "I went there and, of course, I had a little misunderstanding because they couldn't understand about a colored person being over the whites. But the major liked me and I liked him, and he told me, any trouble that I'd get into with those people to let him know. Well, I did. One little old second lieutenant kind of was prejudiced. I found that I should leave there."

After six or seven months at Pine Bluff, he decided to relocate to California, where he would be free of the heavy prejudice found in the South. "The Civil Service had a weapons research laboratory in

Berkeley. There was a job opening. But while I was on my way out here the job was closed and I was classified 1–A. I went back to Houston, Texas, to the induction center and volunteered. But they claimed that I had asthma, saying, 'Uncle Sam can't use you. He wants assets, not liabilities.' So I got a 4–F. I said, 'Well, I don't have to worry about no army no more.' I got a job first as an electrician-trainee in a shipyard, and I tried that, and I went back to Los Angeles, got a job out there in one of those shipyards. Then I got a job as an elevator operator in the Broadway Department Store in Los Angeles." Brown was also earning a little money playing piano in church on Sunday and began mulling over the idea of playing professionally. "I said to myself, 'Since there are not many people around playing the piano, maybe I should try that.'" Before 1943 was over, he was playing piano as an extra added attraction at place called the International House near Chinatown. He was also busy checking out the club scene along Central Avenue; top-quality night life was abundant in the black section of Los Angeles then.

* * *

"At that time the Lincoln Theatre in Los Angeles was very popular, like the Apollo Theatre in New York, and they had big shows, with Pigmeat Markham and all. They also had a night for amateurs, so I said I was going to see if I could win the prize of $25—it would help me—not knowing I would really win," Brown recalls. "I went down there and they had Bardu Ali, who used to be with Chick Webb, and a lot of great musicians in that band. Johnny Otis was on drums. I went on the stage and they asked me, 'Where was I from?' A lot of people had gone to California from Texas, so when I said Texas, they screamed and hollered.

"They said, 'What are you going to play?' I said, '"The Boogie-Woogie on the St. Louis Blues" by Earl Hines.' And I got on that piano and when I started that thing, oh, the house fell down! Well, I figured if I go back again, maybe I might win the prize, but when I went back to play, I played a classical number, 'The Warsaw Concerto'—because during the war that was very popular. Like Hazel Scott had done a lot of boogie on classical. And anything like that was very popular during that time. So I did that and they cheered me back, and I did a little 'Claire de Lune.' Then the guy said, 'Well, you got it made, I don't think nobody can follow you.' Everybody else who went out there, they booed. I won first prize. I didn't sing that night," he recalls.

He worked for a bit in the house orchestra at the Lincoln Theatre.

Ivie Anderson, formerly Duke Ellington's vocalist ("I Got It Bad," "It Don't Mean a Thing"), and her husband ran a place called Ivie's Chicken Shack, where Brown became the dinner pianist. He was now earning what to him a respectable sum by 1943–44 standards: $42 a week. He picked up other jobs around town, too, ultimately raising his weekly take to $68, which allowed him to live rather well in one of the better black neighborhoods of Los Angeles.

Who were Brown's influences on piano? "Fats Waller and Art Tatum. I liked [swing-to-classics pianist] Alec Templeton pretty good. I liked Mary Lou Williams because she had a lot of those interludes that she played beautifully, with Andy Kirk's band. I always liked those interludes and turn-arounds in the chord structures she had. And Dorothy Donegan, I loved the way she played, too; she was great. And Earl Hines—now, I almost forgot. Now that was really my man! I mean, because see when we first heard Billy Eckstine in Earl Hines's band with that 'Stormy Monday' and all those different things like 'I'm Falling for You' and that piano introduction that Earl Hines had—he had a terrific way of playing the piano. He was an inspiration to me, too."

How about singers? Which singers impressed Brown when he was young?

"Well, I always liked Pha Terrell as a man singer, who was with Andy Kirk's orchestra. Because he was, we called him the Bing Crosby of the colored folks' era," Brown recalls. Terrell, best remembered for "Until the Real Thing Comes Along," sang ballads in a high voice in manner that was somewhat androgynous or suggestive of some sexual ambiguity. (A hint of that quality could sometimes be discerned in Brown's singing, too, although not to such an obvious degree.) "And then I liked Ella Fitzgerald. Quite naturally, I loved Dinah Washington. But Helen O'Connell, who was with Jimmy Dorsey, was my main influence. *Yeah.* I was crazy about her. Oh, her style, it was so unique. People used to say—you should hear the black guys say—'You like *Helen O'Connell?!*' I'd say, 'I'm *crazy* about her.' She had a way of doing it. And I just loved the way she said her words."

O'Connell was at the peak of her popularity during Brown's college years. In 1942, when Brown was a senior, O'Connell—thanks to such records as "Green Eyes," "Tangerine," "Embraceable You," "Take Me," and "When the Sun Comes Out"—was voted the favorite female band singer in the nation in the *Billboard* college survey. (Brown still sings "When the Sun Comes Out," which O'Connell kept in her repertoire all her life.) O'Connell had a distinctive, somewhat exaggerated way of phrasing, with certain words particularly emphasized ("those cool and *limpid* green eyes"). Her impact upon Brown's phrasing is unmistakable. His preferences, generally, were for successful pop singers, including white pop singers, rather than for older-style, rougher-voiced blues shouters. The older-style blues shouters couldn't handle ballads well, Brown felt, and he loved ballads. He also loved singing O'Connell's ballads—emulating her style as closely as he could—although he didn't take himself seriously as a singer. He felt that playing piano was his forte.

Winning the Lincoln Theatre amateur contest, as it turned out, lead to bigger things than Brown had any reason to anticipate at the time. Unbeknown to him, the night he won the contest, "Johnny Moore, who had the Three Blazers, had been in the audience. He lost his piano player, and he came looking for me. Well, I had moved into Sugar Hill then; I got me a room. Sugar Hill was where all the black movie stars lived, like Louise Beavers and Hattie McDaniel and Ethel Waters and Ben Carter. I wanted to move out where the big shots were. I was thinking that I could make contacts out here, which I did. Johnny Moore heard that I had moved to Sugar Hill, and he was looking for me. He went next door to where I was living, and asked this white lady. She said, 'I don't know if the guy next door is named Charles Brown, but I can hear a piano.'

"Sure enough, they came—Johnny Moore and Eddie Williams [the bassist in the Three Blazers]. Johnny said, 'We'd like you to play with us, to see if we can pass the audition in Beverly Hills at the Talk of the Town. We will be making $600 a week.' Well that really turned me—$600—because I wasn't making but $68. He says 'Well, let me hear you play.' So I went in and I played, I had Art Tatum's book and I had learned 'If I Had You' and other stuff out of that. He said, 'Man, that's beautiful. Do you sing?' I said, 'Oh I don't sing. I sing Helen O'Connell's songs like "Embraceable You" and "Take Me."' 'Let me hear you do that.' I did that. 'Man! That's what we want. If you just do that with us, man that's what we could use because there ain't any piano players, they're all in the service. Let us know. Call me if you're interested.'

"So when they left, I told Reverend Davis—he was where I was staying, and he was a friend of mine, too: 'I don't know if I want to play with no trio. I play a full piano.' And Johnny Moore told me when I was playing, 'To play with the trio, you have to put your left hand behind you. You have to use your right hand. When I'm playing the lead, you use chords, and then the bass plays the bottom, you don't worry about the bass.' I kind of didn't like that. I said, 'Oh, shoot, I like to play a full piano.' Reverend Davis says, 'Charles, why don't you call Johnny and say, "Let's try it." You could be making $200 a week, if you pass the audition.' So I called Johnny Moore, and he says, 'We'll start rehearsing right now.' We started rehearsing for this job out in Beverly Hills."

It was September 1944 when they auditioned, one of maybe twenty trios to do so. "We were about the eighth," Brown recalls. "And we had been practicing, so we were together good. When we got up there, Pat Robertson, our manager, said, 'Charles, show those teeth to the audience. Put your soul into it.' When Mr. Van Der Griff, who was in charge, heard us play, he said, 'Johnny, I don't want to hear no more trios. I want yours. Ladies and gentleman, you all have to go home. Johnny, can you open next week?' And that's how we started with the trio."

The trio wasn't going into a swank nightclub for whites and stressing blues, which the audience would have considered "crude" music. They planned on playing classics and quality pop instrumentals, choosing "Warsaw Concerto" as their theme song. They spent a lot of time rehearsing—especially important because they didn't have a drummer to set the beat—to get their playing as cohesive as possible (even on challenging pieces such as "Holiday for Strings") and to get just the right tempos for the numbers. Although their repertoire included many instrumentals, Brown emerged, in the natural course of events, as the group's focal point; his vocals reached people. He sang softly, earnestly; his crooning at times took on an exaggerated, almost mooing, quality that made it immediately recognizable. Striving to sound sincere—and occasionally crossing the line to unctuousness—he could communicate self-confidence with an undercurrent of sorrow.

"We got to be so popular out in Beverly Hills," Brown recalls," all the movie stars would come into this club, like Jon Hall, Xavier Cugat, Martha Raye—everybody who was anybody. Mr. Sontag, who owned the Sontag drug stores, he was crazy about me and the 'Summertime' that I used to do. We were doing a lot of love song ballads during the war like 'I'll Walk Alone,' 'We Three,' 'If I Didn't Care,' and 'Don't Fence Me In'—different little things like that. We didn't hardly sing no blues then. We always kept 'Drifting Blues' as what they called our 'race number,' but we didn't play many blues because Hollywood was kind of sophisticated. In Beverly Hills, they only picked the trios that were sophisticated; that was Nat Cole and us.

"The audience was strictly white. We were strictly Beverly Hills and no black—at the time when we were playing, Hollywood was a no-no to the black people. In those clubs, the only way you could come in there if you were black, you had to be an entertainer." Some of the clubs—a wartime change—would also welcome blacks *if* they were servicemen. But in general, "Black folks wouldn't worry about Hollywood too much because they had their own street—Central Avenue—like Harlem in New York." The club also drew plenty of celebrities, he recalls. Tommy Dorsey came in many nights to catch the trio. Bing Crosby—drinking heavily at the time—was another frequent guest. Martha Raye and Ben Blue hired Brown (not the trio) to play at their private parties; Brown would team with a singer named Johnny Shadrack, picking up $300 for a single night's work. He became known to the movie crowd.

"We began to get pretty popular. The fellow at Riverside, Mr. Buck, wanted us in his club; the Swing Club wanted us—Billy Berg—and oh, we just had jobs galore," Brown recalls. Frankie Laine often caught the trio's performances at the Swing Club in 1945 and tried to sing somewhat like Charles Brown. (Their natural voices were different, but Brown can hear the influence of his way of phrasing in, for example, Laine's million-seller of 1947, "That's My Desire.") On Laine's first record, Brown notes, he was backed by Johnny Moore's Three Blazers. "We made our first record with Frankie Laine and got him started—'Melancholy Madeline' [in 1945]. Then we were on our way and he was on his way.

"Our popularity was growing. And when we played the Copa Club [in 1945], we started doing 'Drifting Blues' in there, then it got to be so popular that all these musicians who were out on the West Coast, like Pha Terrell, Wynonie Harris—all of them—they would come in there and pay $20 bills for us to play that tune," Brown recalls. Brown's lyrics ("I'm driftin' and driftin', like a ship out on the sea") seemed to express the feelings of many listeners. The song had an impact that the pop standards the group sang didn't have.

"And that was also when we'd go into this fortune-teller, trying to forecast who was going to win at the races," Brown adds. All three members of the Blazers, he explains, were frequent racetrack attendees. One day Moore suggested they pay a fortune-teller named Mother Davis to advise them which horses to bet on. Brown, who didn't put much stock in fortune-tellers, said he'd wait in the car while they consulted her. Shortly after Moore got his reading, he emerged from Mother Davis's, telling Brown that she insisted on seeing him, too. She said that she had a special feeling about him. When Brown saw her, she declared that the three men should bet on a horse named Lovely Millie. Then she said a prayer and told Brown, with a conviction so intense it startled him, that within twenty-four hours he was going to sign a contract that would take him across the country.

When the horse came in, netting the men some $90, they were convinced of Mother Davis's powers. Late that night at the Copa Club, record producers Sammy Goldberg and Eddie Mesner—who had been hearing about the Three Blazers and the way they did "Drifting Blues"—offered them $800 to record the piece. The contract specified a flat payment—no royalties. The producers offered verbal assurances that if the record did well, they'd be paid more. The three signed the contract without hesitation (after all, how could Mother Davis be wrong?), making what Brown feels in retrospect was a mistake of classic proportions. "Drifting Blues" would be the biggest-selling record Johnny Moore's Three Blazers would ever make, but they never earned more than the original $800 from it.

"When we made 'Drifting Blues,' that was the start of everything," Brown notes. "That was recorded for Philo Records; later they changed the name to Aladdin. It sold so many copies—350,000 or more records, which was considered a million-seller then. In the *Billboard* charts back then, there was nothing but Louis Jordan; and in *Cashbox,* too—one, two, three, Louis Jordan, four, five six, Louis Jordan, everything. But we moved him out of first place and we won the *Cashbox* Award of 1946: Best R&B—'Drifting Blues.'" "Drifting Blues" stayed on the *Billboard* Race Records charts, the forerunner of the R&B charts (*Billboard* would not switch to the newer terminology until 1949), for twenty-three weeks beginning in February 1946; it peaked in the number two position. When Moore sang with a touch of weariness how he was drifting, he seemed to be giving voice to the feelings of many blacks after World War II. Mingled feelings of disappointment, hope, uncertainty about the future, and a yearning for a clearer sense of self—such things could be sensed in Brown's song. Top stars, from Billy Eckstine and Count Basie on down, soon added it to their repertoires, but Brown's interpretation remained definitive, and he came up with other numbers in the same vein.

"Drifting Blues" opened a lot of doors for Johnny Moore's Three Blazers. "Because we were selling so many records, the jukebox operators wanted us to come to New York," Brown recalls. "So we came to New York, handled by the William Morris Agency, a big agency—they had the Will Mastin Trio with Sammy Davis, I think they had Count Basie and Pearl Bailey. But when we got to New York, Frank Schiffman [who ran the Apollo Theatre] said we weren't strong enough to open at the Apollo. The William Morris Agency said, 'You are strong enough. We'll book you, instead, into the Renaissance Casino with Luis Russell's band.' Nat Cole gave us our introduction there. Johnny Moore's brother, Oscar, played guitar in Nat's trio, so

Nat and all came down there on opening night and you couldn't get in. Seventh Avenue was crowded. So many people." Meanwhile up at the Apollo, the great Buddy Johnson band, with vocalists Ella Johnson and Arthur Prysock, wasn't drawing. The Blazers were certain, Brown recalls, that Schiffman would turn up at the Renaissance to check out the act that was stealing his audience. "And sure enough," Brown adds, "who would come in that place but Frank Schiffman? He tells Johnny Moore, 'I ain't got nobody up at the Apollo Theatre. Johnny, would you be interested in working for me?' Johnny says, 'Yeah, I'd be interested.' He says, 'I'll get in touch with your agency,' and the next day we opened at the Apollo Theatre. That was 1946. And from then on we had it made!"

Schiffman offered them $1,200 a week for their first week, with increases to follow if they drew. They would bound onstage to strains of "Air Mail Special," played by the big band at the Apollo, and then get going as a trio. Brown can still remember the cries from rapturous fans in the audience: "Do you love me?" "Do you love me?" Fans came up to the stage, hollering. Others got into the wings, to approach them as they came off.

"Sammy Davis, the Will Mastin Trio, they saw how popular we was, so they asked if they could work with us on our theater circuit. Johnny Moore told them yes, so we had the Will Mastin Trio featuring Sammy Davis; they were worth $500 a week because they were with the William Morris Agency, too. Johnny Moore gave them really their first break. And Sammy never even mentioned that until I went to see him in 1977. He said, 'I want to thank Johnny Moore because he gave us our first break.' But when you read the history, he used to talk about Eddie Cantor. And when they had that big thing on TV about Sammy—he had so many years as an entertainer—they never had the people that should know him. Me and Eddie Williams, we're the only ones left here that really know about Sammy Davis. They had all these phony people on that thing. I just looked at it and laughed. Because I know. Sammy Davis followed me everywhere I went. He and I were just like that on the road. But I don't discuss that because I remain low-key and I'm not worried about it. The Lord's blessed me to still be in good health." Moore's trio was strong enough of a draw for Moore to hire Buddy Rich to work with them on some theater dates, too.

The trio toured the United States from 1946 to 1948. Johnny Moore's name was in the spotlight then, not Charles Brown's. Brown notes: "On the records—the 78s—they had 'Johnny Moore's Three Blazers'—with 'vocal, Charles Brown' up in the corner of the label.

Johnny wanted his name listed like that. So everybody that heard us thought *I* was Johnny Moore. Our trio was a singing trio, and when it said the Nat King Cole Trio—well, Nat King Cole was the singer. When they had Johnny Moore's name on the records, a lot of people didn't see the 'vocal, Charles Brown' up in the corner—especially if they were playing the record on the jukeboxes. They'd just see 'Johnny Moore's Three Blazers' and assume Moore must be the one singing. Then when Johnny took sick and we went on the road, I had to be Johnny Moore because all these deposits had been paid for the group. The agency booking us told me, 'People don't know the name Charles Brown unless they look in the corner. So just say you're Johnny Moore.' That way, they couldn't ask for their money back. And since they never had seen us before, I could say I *was* Johnny Moore." When Moore became too ill to tour, his brother Oscar, who had been the guitarist in the Nat King Cole Trio, was brought in to play guitar for the Three Blazers. So long as Brown was still there to sing—after all, his voice had become the group's primary identifying sound—it didn't matter much who played guitar.

Brown was also writing a lot of the songs he sang, although again without much recognition; the public simply thought of the songs as being songs of Johnny Moore's Three Blazers. He was coming up with blues numbers for which the group was becoming increasingly known, and he was sometimes denied proper composer credits. One very close friend, Mark Hurley, tried to warn him to watch out lest people take advantage of him on copyrights, he recalls, but he was taken advantage of nonetheless. "I wrote 'Drifting Blues.' I had left my copyright paper with Johnny Moore's sister; it had only one name on it then: Charles Brown. But Johnny said, 'Well, anything Charles Brown writes, there's got to be three names on it.' So they put Johnny Moore, Eddie Williams, and me—the whole trio—on it, as if we'd all written it. And Johnny's sister had the original copyright paper. I didn't know that I could have written to Washington, D.C. and blocked that change. I didn't know all the laws about copyright then. So that was copyrighted with Johnny Moore and Eddie Williams's names. Anything that I did, they figured would go to the trio since we were a unit—although they didn't write nothing. Johnny Moore couldn't hardly write his name; he left everything up to me. I did all the little introductions and the little cute harmony things we did together.

"I also wrote 'Merry Christmas Baby' but didn't get the credit. A songwriter named Lou Baxter had originally brought the idea. He said, 'Charles, I need some money for an operation. Will you do one of my numbers?' So I took his satchel home and looked through it, and I saw 'Merry Christmas Blues.' The words weren't nothing like—but it gave me an idea. It said 'Merry Christmas Blues.' I said, 'What might be good might be "Merry Christmas Baby."' And so I fixed the words. And I fixed out a little arrangement and played it on the piano and told Mr. Rene, who owned Exclusive Records, about it. He figured maybe it would be a good idea to have a Merry Christmas song because there was nothing out in the market with a trio doing that. When they put the record out, we were on the road, in Chicago. I saw they'd put the names of Johnny Moore and Lou Baxter on the doggone thing; they didn't put my name on at all. I think Johnny had figured this was probably going to be a hit—which it was. I told him, 'I wrote "Merry Christmas Baby."' He said, 'Well Charles, we can't change that now. But we're putting one of your songs on the back of the record and so you'll still get royalties for every record that's sold.' They put a number I'd written called 'Lost in the Night' on the back of the record all right. But later—the record was reissued—they took my number off the back of it and put Lloyd Glenn's 'Sleigh Ride' on the back, which meant I wouldn't get nothing."

As far as Brown could tell, the trio was then about as popular as any group on the scene in the late forties. He says, "The *Pittsburgh Courier* used to run a poll for the best groups. We would always be up there on the top, but Carlos Gastell [who managed Nat King Cole and Mel Tormé, among others] said, 'Ain't nobody going to beat King Cole,' and he'd send in a thousand dollars to the *Pittsburgh Courier* for votes. Well, then they'd keep us second. But with what they called the race records—Nat Cole was into pop more than he was race—we were number one in the race records; he was number one in the pop for a black artist. Nat and all of us were good friends. Nat was living in a little old apartment and he didn't have a piano. I was fortunate to have a piano then; Nat would use my piano to rehearse on."

Johnny Moore's Three Blazers made the *Billboard* Race Records charts in 1946 with "Drifting Blues," "Sunny Road," and "So Long"; in 1947, with "New Orleans Blues," "Changeable Woman Blues," and "Merry Christmas Baby" (which also made the charts when it was reissued at Christmas the following year and again the year after that); in 1948, with "Groovy Movie Blues," "Jilted Blues," "More Than You Know," and "Lonesome Blues"; and, in 1949, with "Where Can I Find My Baby?" Most of the records were on the Exclusive label, two were on Modern, and one was on Philo.

The group was recording a lot of blues—a reflection not just of Brown's comfort with the genre but of the fact that the group was trying to make another record that would equal the popularity of "Drifting Blues," which stayed on the charts for twenty-three weeks. None ever duplicated its enormous success, though. "New Orleans Blues" was on the charts for thirteen weeks, and the trio's other hits lasted for one, two, three, or four weeks. In *Top R&B Singles, 1942–1988* Joel Whitburn calculates (factoring in the number of hit records and number of weeks on the charts from 1942 to 1949) that Johnny Moore's Three Blazers was the seventh most popular act in the field during the 1940s, surpassed only by Billy Eckstine, Duke Ellington, Lionel Hampton, the Ink Spots, the Nat King Cole Trio, and the overwhelming favorite of that period, Louis Jordan. Brown was also slowly making a reputation for himself. Audiences were becoming aware that he, not Moore, was the Three Blazers' star.

Jack Schiffman, of the family that ran the Apollo Theatre for four decades, recalled in his book about the Apollo, *Harlem Heyday,* that Brown and the Three Blazers "were one of our major attractions in those days, and our switchboard lights kept flickering on and off with calls for the tall, handsome singer all during his engagements."[2] He recalled Brown as having been, along with Nat King Cole, an obvious influence upon young Ray Charles. Ray Charles acknowledged in his autobiography, *Brother Ray,* written with David Ritz, that "Charles Brown was a powerful influence on me in the early part of my career, especially when I was struggling down in Florida. I made many a dollar doing my imitation of his 'Drifting Blues.' That was a hell of a number."[3]

Jerry Wexler points out that Brown's influence on Ray Charles can be heard on such early recordings as "Tell Me You'll Wait for Me" (written by Brown), "Hard Times" (a Brown hit), and "Funny but I Still Love You." Those only familiar with Charles's gospel-tinged later recordings, with his exuberant big band and backup singers, will be surprised by the simplicity of his earliest recordings, done in a piano-bass-guitar trio format just like Johnny Moore's Three Blazers and the Nat King Cole Trio, which had more or less established the pattern. Also surprising is how blatantly Charles emulated Brown's vocal style at times. Wexler also sees Brown's influence in such performers as Floyd Dixon, Amos Milburn, and Little Willie Littlefield, as well as in doowop singers Sonny Til of the Orioles and Eddie Rich of the Swallows. Dick Shurman of *Living Blues* magazine wrote in September 1975 that Brown's "vocal style definitely opened the door for a whole school of musicians including Floyd [Dixon]."[4] Blues authority Sheldon Harris, in his *Blues Who's Who,* cites Brown as having influenced Johnny Ace, Dave Alexander, Ray Charles, Floyd Dixon, Fats

Domino, Johnny Fuller, Candy Green, Bee Houston, B. B. King, Little Willie Littlefield, Amos Milburn, Johnny Otis, and Mel Walker.[5]

In 1947 a talent scout for Columbia Records was so impressed by Brown's potential that he followed him from New York to Los Angeles in a vain attempt to get Brown to sign—by himself—with Columbia. Brown, however, said that he felt too loyal to the trio to consider a career on his own. Perhaps at the time he lacked the confidence to leave a highly popular trio in order to try and make it on his own. He has since often felt that he made a mistake in turning down that offer, which was never repeated.

Could Columbia—one of the giants of the recording industry—have made Brown much better known, perhaps even a rival to Nat King Cole, then busy recording pop hits for Capitol? One can only speculate. Brown's style was a bit more earthy and steeped in the blues than Nat King Cole's style, but it was still much more refined and closer to the white pop tradition than that of older down-home blues singers; the potential for a crossover success in the pop marketplace appears real. Brown had proven in club performances that his mellow style could reach white as well as black audiences, but he was still known primarily to black record buyers. Although his records were big hits on the R&B charts, they were not making the pop charts. Of course, few black artists' records did in those days because they were played on a smaller number of radio stations. A major label such as Columbia could have given Brown greater distribution and promotional support and also ensured exposure to the broadest possible audience. Columbia could also have given his records generally slicker production values by spending more money on recording studios and engineers, producers, and sidemen—all of which would have helped get his recordings more airplay. But that was never to be.

*   *   *

The realization that Moore was taking advantage of him finally prompted Brown to leave the Blazers. He recalls, "I went on my own in 1949 after we had a little run-in about the money. It was supposed to be divided equally three ways, and Johnny didn't want to give the rest of my money to me—$11,000. He had used it up buying homes. That's what caused us to break up. My grandfather, who was with me, said, 'Well Charles, you should be on your own. You're strong enough. Why have arguments about money?' That gave me a little encouragement. So I went out on my own, with Ed Fishman of Federal Artists booking me. And then Howard Lewis out of Dallas, Texas, started putting me on one-nighters. People said, 'Well, you don't

need Johnny Moore. *He* needs you, because you're the main thing.'"
However, because Moore owned exclusive rights to the name "The
Blazers," Brown could not be advertised as "formerly of 'Johnny
Moore's Three Blazers.'" He could, and did, advertise himself as the
man who had sung "Drifting Blues." His bookers worked hard at
building his name. His group was originally billed as "Charles Brown
and His Smarties." "We were always dressed smart," he comments.
"I see these people today talking about the blues and dressing in jeans
with patches and the old straw hat on. That ain't the way it was. I
changed four times a night and my men changed; we were the sharp-
est things they ever had. And we were known as being sharp always—
all dressed well. I can't understand why they have the idea that black
people really got the blues. We didn't have the blues as far as our
clothes were concerned."

Aladdin Records, run by Leo and Eddie Mesner, promptly signed
Brown and for the next few years he did even better on his own than
he had as a member of Johnny Moore's Three Blazers. On records,
he continued at first to use the subtle trio format that had worked
so successfully for the Three Blazers. His initial releases carried the
billing "the Charles Brown Trio"; later they simply read "Charles
Brown." Brown scored his first hit right away. He enjoyed five weeks
on the charts in February and March 1949—peaking at the number
four spot—for "Get Yourself Another Fool." Insiders noted that the
title could be read as Brown's message to Johnny Moore: Brown
wasn't going to be exploited any longer. And Moore *did* get another
vocalist to fill Brown's shoes. He had one hit record in 1949 with Billy
Valentine. For a while, the Blazers were teamed successfully with
Floyd Dixon, the best of the Brown successors. The Blazers made their
final appearances on the charts with a hit in 1953 and in 1955—by
then, Frankie Ervin had taken the old Charles Brown role—before
fading away entirely.

Brown, meanwhile, was back on the *Billboard* R&B charts another
half-dozen times before 1949 was over, with "Long Time," "It's Nothing," "Trouble Blues" (on the charts for twenty-seven weeks, number one for fifteen weeks), "In the Evening When the Sun Goes
Down," "Homesick Blues," and "I'll Miss You" (which he had recorded before leaving Johnny Moore's Three Blazers but was only released
after he went out on his own, with his name listed first, "Charles
Brown with Johnny Moore's Three Blazers"). Brown had one hit in
1950, "My Baby's Gone." In 1951 he came through with another big
one, "Black Night" (twenty-four weeks on the charts, number one for
fourteen weeks) in addition to "I'll Always Be in Love with You" and

"Seven Long Days" (nine weeks on the charts, peaking at number two). In 1952 he recorded "Hard Times" (three weeks on the charts, peaking at number seven).

To put into perspective just how big Brown's biggest hits were based on number of weeks in the number one position on *Billboard* R&B charts, his "Trouble Blues" (with fifteen weeks at number one) was the fifth-biggest R&B hit of the 1940s, surpassed only by Lionel Hampton's "Hey! Ba-Ba-Re-Bop" (1946, sixteen weeks at number one), Louis Jordan's "Ain't Nobody Here but Us Chickens" (1947, seventeen weeks) and "Choo Choo Ch'Boogie" (1946, eighteen weeks); and Joe Liggins and his Honeydrippers' "The Honeydripper" (1945, eighteen weeks). Brown's "Black Night" (fourteen weeks at number one) was the second-biggest R&B hit of the 1950s, surpassed only by the Dominoes' "Sixty-Minute Man" (1951), which also enjoyed a fourteen-week run in the number one spot but stayed on the charts in total longer than Brown's hit did.

In 1949 and 1950 probably no male vocalist working the R&B circuit was more popular than Brown. (There were, however, three black male vocalists who enjoyed even greater popularity. Billy Eckstine and Nat King Cole, who were mining a pop-jazz vein, along with jump blues master Louis Jordan, had crossed over to success with white audiences in a way Brown hadn't.) Thanks to Brown, Aladdin was the leading West Coast R&B independent. Atlantic's Jerry Wexler has recalled that in the early fifties Aladdin was more successful than Atlantic, adding, "Aladdin was Charles Brown. Charles Brown and his fantastic California blues ballads."

With his own band backing him, Brown toured through the early 1950s in R&B package shows. When he first went out, he was the unquestioned headliner. He was grossing as much as $300,000 a year, and performers who would shortly become major R&B stars in their own right were opening for him. Agent Billy Shaw put Brown on the road with the very young Ruth Brown, who was initially getting just $50 a night, an amount that climbed to $450 a night when she proved to be a smash. Charles Brown took the Clovers, the Dominoes, Ray Charles, and Floyd Dixon on the road with him, playing one-nighters wherever audiences could be found. Dixon and Charles were both singing in styles somewhat similar to Brown's then, and sometimes people who knew Brown only from his records and didn't know what he looked like would wonder—until they heard him—whether Dixon or Charles might be Brown.

Brown doesn't feel that his early records represented the sound of his live performances, because he worked live with gutsy five-to-eight-

piece R&B bands rather than with the more subdued trios originally
featured on his records—bands he says sounded much like the bands
Ray Charles began using on *his* hit records a few years later. But when
Brown tried to persuade Eddie Mesner to let him record with the
whole band, Mesner asked why he should change a formula that was
working. And if the Mesners could hold down costs by backing an
artist with just a rhythm section and maybe a sax thrown in for good
measure, they were glad to do so. That kind of penny-pinching may
have increased their profits on a short-term basis, but it was poor
thinking in terms of artists' long-term career development. It frustrated Brown that on records he had to use simpler backing than he
liked to use when he worked live. But because his records were selling satisfactorily, the Mesners couldn't understand his complaints.
They were all making money. Why rock the boat? They gave him a
new car, which he appreciated, but he still wondered whether he was
being paid all he deserved. He had his doubts about the Mesners,
doubts that were renewed when they (and others through the years)
seemed to be treating him unfairly over composer credits.

Many of the mournful numbers Brown sang—the core of his repertoire—were ones he wrote himself. He notes, "I wrote 'Trouble
Blues' and 'My Baby's Gone.' I wrote 'Black Night'—but I didn't get
the credit for it; they put Jesse Mae Robinson's name on that one.
Oh, and I wrote some other numbers for the Hollywood label but
I'm telling you true, they did me," he says, meaning they cheated
him out of composer credits. One thing that gives Brown's account
credibility is that he is also careful to stress that he did not write one
of his biggest hits, "Homesick Blues" (1949)—for which he *did* receive
composer credit. "Floyd Dixon wrote it, but he wanted me to have
it, and he put my name on it." Brown had known Dixon (and Dixon's mother, too, he adds) before Dixon made it as a performer. He
tried to help Dixon as best he could, both when Dixon was getting
started and years later in reviving a career after a discouraged Dixon
had dropped out. "Floyd's always respected me," Brown says. Others
wrote songs for Brown, too, including Frankie Laine, Maurice King,
Bill Hanson, and even Mel Tormé (whose "Christmas Song" had been
a huge hit for Nat King Cole in 1946–47), although the number Tormé
wrote for Brown, "Humpty Dumpty," didn't go anywhere. Brown was
most convincing on songs he *felt* the most, and the songs he wrote
he felt because they came from his own experiences.

Brown was circumspect about his private life. Some of his friends
in the business were surprised when, in 1949, he married fellow Ex-

clusive recording artist Mabel Scott; they hadn't thought of Sweet
Charles as being the marrying kind. Of Mabel Scott, Brown says kind-
ly, "She was a great singer; in fact she was the greatest entertainer
I'd ever seen." Her most successful record, "Elevator Boogie," recorded
for Exclusive in 1948 (peaking at number six on the R&B charts), had
featured Brown on piano. The marriage may have been a good career move for Scott. "After I married her, she went on as Mrs. Charles
Brown. And her money went up sky high!" he recalls. But their marriage, he soon came to feel, was a mistake, and it was history by 1951.
"People broke us up by—you know how people do, telling this and
that lie," he says ambiguously, adding that in the years since their
divorce they've become friends again and have even performed together at times.

Brown spent a good deal of time touring during the late forties and
early fifties, playing places from the Birmingham Theater in Birmingham, Alabama, to the Dreamland Ballroom in Omaha, Nebraska. He
hired Dizzy Gillespie to work with him, in a "blues to bop" package,
in 1949. By contract, he recalls, they were both supposed to receive
equal billing. When Brown got to the theater in Baltimore where they
were supposed to appear, however, he saw Gillespie's name on the
marquee in large letters and his in small ones. He felt he had been
taken advantage of too many times in his career, and he walked out.
A lawyer cautioned him, however, that he risked damaging his reputation and career by not performing, and perhaps he might acquire a
reputation for being undependable. The lawyer advised that Brown "get
sick" so he couldn't be accused of shirking his commitments. Brown
found a doctor who would write a letter claiming he had been too ill
to open the engagement but was now able to perform again. By then,
though, the promoters had hired Billie Holiday to take his place, and
some doubts about his reliability had been raised.

Brown went to see Holiday, who told him that on opening night
some of the audience, who'd apparently purchased advance tickets
to see Brown, kept asking her to sing "Drifting Blues" and other of
his numbers. Brown and Holiday had met at a Los Angeles club where
he used to play piano in the afternoons before he'd made a name
for himself. She and a female companion would come in every day,
bringing a small dog with them. She told him then that someday he'd
be a star. Brown adds that of all the songs he used to sing, the one
Holiday was crazy about was "My Baby's Gone." He remembers, too,
her asking plaintively, "Where do you get all those sad songs?" And
he told her, directly, honestly: "The same place you got yours."

Charles Brown, early in his career. (Author's photo; courtesy of the Institute of Jazz Studies)

With this ad on April 16, 1949, the now-defunct Aladdin Records company introduced Brown's recording of "Trouble Blues" to readers of the trade publication *Billboard*. The following week the record began a twenty-seven-week run on the *Billboard* R&B charts, including fifteen weeks in the number one spot—the biggest chart success of his career. (Author's collection)

Charles Brown costarred with fellow R&B pioneers Ruth Brown and Floyd Dixon in a package show entitled "Los Angeles R&B Caravan 1980," which toured Scandinavia from June 13 through July 7, 1980. (Author's collection; courtesy of Kathleen Barlow)

LOS ANGELES
R&B CARAVAN 1980
13 JUNE – 7 JULY IN SCANDINAVIA
FEATURING

CHARLES BROWN
vocal/piano

RUTH BROWN
vocal

FLOYD DIXON
vocal/piano

PRESTON LOVE
saxophone/flute

SPECIAL GUEST
PEPS PERSSON
vocal/guitar/harmonica

CHUCK NORRIS
guitar/vocal

SLIM NOTINI/piano
ULF ANDERSSON/saxophone

ALI LUNDBOHM/drums

Production/ROUTE 66 RECORDS

Brown and Little Jimmy Scott. (Photo by R. J. Capak; author's collection)

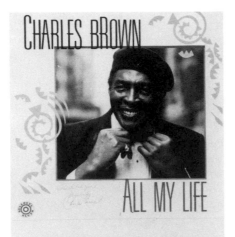

A poster publicizing Brown's 1990 tour with Bonnie Raitt and debut release for Bullseye Blues/Rounder. In 1995 both Charles Brown and Ruth Brown joined Bonnie Raitt in a national tour. (Author's collection; courtesy of Myers Media)

Brown in performance at the New York club S.O.B. (with Earl May on bass), 1991. (Photo by Chip Deffaa)

Charles Brown, 1994. (Photo by Michael Terranova; author's collection; courtesy of Bullseye Blues/Rounder Records)

*   *   *

Brown had hits on the charts—either as a member of the Three Blazers or on his own—every year from 1946 through 1952. Then the hits
abruptly stopped coming. With the exception of "Please Come Home
for Christmas," which put Brown on the charts for two weeks around
Christmas of 1960, he never had another hit. What happened?

For one thing, in 1952 Brown and Aladdin Records had a major
falling-out. He sued the company for royalties, and it, in turn, accused him of not living up to his obligations. Although he ultimately won the suit, it proved to be a Pyrrhic victory. He was awarded
$8,000, less than he felt he deserved but still satisfying in that it con-
firmed his feeling that the Mesners had exploited him. But now Aladdin Records "punished" him, as he perceived it, by neglecting him.
The atmosphere cooled, and Aladdin no longer promoted him. It
concentrated on building such other artists as Floyd Dixon and Amos
Milburn. Because Brown was under exclusive contract, the company
knew he couldn't go anywhere else, and most companies would be
wary of an artist "uppity" enough to dare sue for royalties. From Aladdin's point of view, no doubt, Brown was a troublemaker whom it
could not afford to reward for his transgressions lest it encourage other artists to sue for royalties. The flow of Brown's records slowed. He
was still on the road doing one-nighters, but the fact that he was giv-
en the cold shoulder as a recording artist made his career lose momentum. When Brown's contract finally ran out and he was free to
record for other labels, he was no longer a hot property. Once a performer has gone a couple of years without a hit, the public tends to
forget and develop new favorites.

Maintaining a cheerful front, Brown continued trying to do his
work as if nothing had happened. When a black magazine called *Jive*
asked Brown in February 1955 to tell his story in the hope that it
would help inspire black teenagers, he was characteristically upbeat.
He recalled, "I organized the 'Charles Brown Trio'; after disappointments we made a hit, and since that time things have been running
along smoothly, that's why I can say here in America your locality
and family background don't determine how high up you can go. It
is the privilege of every individual American to make his or her future a successful one, whether rich or poor. All any of us has to do is
to take advantage of the opportunities offered in this wonderful land
of plenty."[6] He kept to himself the resentments he felt about the way
he'd been taken advantage of.

The falling-out between Aladdin Records and Brown, of course, was only part of the reason Brown's career faded. As the fifties wore on, tastes were changing. Rock 'n' roll was coming up. The growing preference was for more emotionally uninhibited, harder-hitting singers. Brown was never one to "let it all hang out." He was personally more reserved. His style was not just a matter of temperament; it reflected, too, his upbringing and the times in which he had been raised. One didn't show too much anger; one tried to maintain a pleasant facade. Brown's comparatively decorous, laid-back blues crooning, rooted in the pre-rock era, was too polite for some younger listeners. They preferred hearing feelings expressed more passionately, more outspokenly. Often, too, they wanted to hear more of a big beat in their music than they were apt to find in Brown's records.

Brown's fame gradually declined. He remained a solid draw on the R&B circuit, but without any current hit records he could no longer command fees as before; nor could he justify touring with his own five-to-eight-piece band. When, for example, in the summer of 1954 Brown toured in a package with Johnny Ace and Willie Mae Thornton, playing southern tobacco warehouses and the like, he was backed by Ace's band rather than a band of his own. Brown's grandfather traveled with him on that tour; he used to hold Ace's gun for him when Ace would perform, Brown recalls. (By year's end, Ace would be dead from that gun. By most accounts he died playing Russian roulette, but Brown says Thornton assured him that Ace was fooling around with the gun, thinking it was unloaded. Whatever the reality, it gives Brown pause now to reflect on how many of his contemporaries in R&B died prematurely.) After the tour ended, Brown did one-nighters as a single attraction in California, accompanying himself on piano or organ as he sang, sometimes picking up one or two local musicians to work with him. He hoped brighter days lay ahead.

By 1957 Brown was free to record for whomever he pleased. He went to Atlantic Records. At one time Atlantic would rather have had Brown on their label than Ray Charles—during the late forties and early fifties Brown's name was bigger than Charles's—but by 1957 Charles (with hits like "Hallelujah I Love Her So" and "I've Got a Woman") had become the considerably more popular artist. Brown also had an idea that Ray Charles's manager didn't want Atlantic to have Brown recording for them. Why should the company have two artists in a conceivably competing vein? Jerry Wexler produced a couple of recordings by Brown for the company, including "When Did You Leave Heaven?" and "Sentimental Journey," which were issued on an Atlantic subsidiary label, East West. Sales were poor.

Curiously, the last title Brown had recorded for the Mesners, "Con-

fidential," became a minor hit in 1957 after he had stopped recording for them. On the strength of its success, Brown was given the
opportunity to become part of a big package show with Fats Domino, LaVern Baker, Chuck Berry, the Five Keys, Bill Doggett, and Otis
Williams and the Charms. Then he got his own band again and
toured through the rest of 1957 and into 1958 doing one-nighters.
It looked like his career was gaining momentum once again.

While he was in Florida, however, almost everything he owned was
stolen, leaving him with little beyond the clothes he was wearing.
He called his grandfather in Texas, who told him to come on home.
The grandfather said he was tired of seeing his grandson mistreated
and living a hard life on the road. He wanted to do something for
Brown and soon bought a clubhouse on the bay where he could perform. Brown's grandfather became ill, however, and Brown took him
to Los Angeles to be treated by a specialist.

By this point, Brown's career was in shambles. He had failed to
make contracted appearances, which led to problems with the union.
"I'd gotten on what they call the 'unfair list' because I'd left [agent]
Billy Shaw to go home to see my grandfather. They'd sued me and I
had to be a scab musician. And everywhere I played, if the promoter
wanted me, he would pay the union to let me work. And I went
through this. I never was on a major scale no more."

Brown explains how failing to fulfill a contracted appearance can
place a performer on the unfair list. "When you don't show up—like
if you go home for some sickness or anything—and they've got deposits, well, the bookers don't want to give back that money. So they
say, 'Well, we don't know, he's supposed to be there and he didn't
show.' And they write to the union, and you can be placed on the
unfair list. Then you have to pay so much into the union on the
claims. So that's what knocked me out. Finally I got tired of paying.
Things had been so hard." Even when he had legitimate excuses for
not making gigs, he felt the union ignored him. "I asked the guy,
'How come the union didn't recognize my rebuttals, didn't listen to
me?' But New York was the type of place where if one person put
something against you and you weren't in the New York area, then
the New York people would believe it. They would win. I was on the
blacklist from the latter part of '58 all through until about '62. Finally I was told, 'Charles Brown, you can get back into the union
now. Everybody that held a claim against you is dead.'"

During the time he was blacklisted by the union, he notes, he continued to work but under far from ideal circumstances. "I had to go
to Newport, Kentucky, and work with the gangsters. That kept me

going. The big boss had me over the music department. And so I hired Jimmy Witherspoon to play with me because Jimmy was having a bad time himself. Then I had Little Miss Cornshucks. Then I brought in Amos Milburn. [Brown and Milburn recorded an album together around this time for the Ace label.] I was bringing in all the people who were having a little bad time. And so when Jimmy Witherspoon got a little break to go to the Monterey Jazz Festival, he left me and I borrowed $600—I got it from the old boss, and Jimmy never did come back to Newport. He was on his way; he got out to California to stay. He didn't come back no more."

The gangsters, Brown recalls, had turned Newport into a small-scale Las Vegas. Where Brown worked, they had slot machines, numbers, and other forms of gambling in addition to legitimate entertainment. The boss took quite a liking to Brown and would think nothing of giving him $100 tips. But he was also rather possessive and soon made it clear that Brown wasn't to think about leaving. Brown told Jerry Wexler that when he mentioned that he might like to go back to California, the boss explained the situation with these unforgettable words: "Charles, you're pretty and I love you, but you wouldn't look too good with a bullet in your brain."[7]

Brown stayed put. When Dinah Washington came through Newport, headlining at the club in October 1960, she expressed surprise at finding him seemingly trapped there with little public visibility. She could remember when he was the big star on touring shows they did together and she was considered a lesser draw. Washington asked him to open for her the following month at Robert's Show Lounge in Chicago, but Brown said he was afraid to accept her offer.

During one season of the year, however, Brown's voice was sure to be heard on the air: Christmas. Every year, disc jockeys still played his "Merry Christmas Baby" as well as cover versions by others—even Elvis Presley recorded it. The song had become, along with "Drifting Blues," one of Brown's defining numbers; he was asked to do it at almost every appearance, regardless of the season. Over the years, he notes, he's recorded "Merry Christmas Baby" a number of times. Once he was even tricked into recording it. A sharp operator asked Brown to sing "Merry Christmas Baby" to someone else's piano accompaniment, supposedly as a kind of demo for a proposed album. Brown never heard another word about the album, but the recording, with a full band dubbed in afterward, was released as a single to catch the holiday trade.

Syd Nathan, head of King Records, asked Brown if he could write a follow-up that would equal the success of "Merry Christmas Baby."

Brown felt doubtful but agreed to give it a try, and Nathan locked him in a room until he delivered. Most Christmas songs are relentlessly cheery, but Brown wrote with the awareness that holidays can be sad times for people. He wrote, he recalls, of how you felt at Christmas "when you don't have nobody." Once again, he struck a chord. The record was a success. King put out *Christmas Songs* as well as another album of assorted songs sung by Brown, *The Great Charles Brown That Will Grip Your Heart.* "Please Come Home for Christmas" made the R&B charts for two weeks, peaking at number twenty-one at Christmas in 1960 and giving Brown his first chart hit in eight years. (Years later the Eagles also covered it.) Brown once again had a record that would resurface in subsequent years. The composer's royalties alone should have been a nice source of income, but Brown received nothing. "They tried to take 'Please Come Home for Christmas' away from me," he notes. "I just got that song back after twenty-eight years, two years ago. I'm telling you, everybody—Syd Nathan and all—did dirt to me.

"Meanwhile, I stayed in Newport from '59 through a little after '61. Because when the Kennedy administration came in, with Robert Kennedy, they busted all those gangsters. So when they did that, it gave me a chance to leave," Brown recalls. He adds that the boss who had once told him, "Charles, you're pretty and I love you, but you wouldn't look too good with a bullet in your brain," committed suicide.

"I left Newport to come to California, and Mr. Sullivan took me in '62," Brown continues, referring to Charles Sullivan, a prominent, West Coast black booking agent who was later murdered in an as yet unsolved gangland-style slaying. "And I stayed out West from '62, working in and around Denver, working over in L.A., until '66." Brown recorded a couple of albums for Mainstream (*Boss* and *Ballads My Way*) in 1963 and 1964. He did gigs with Johnny Moore, Mabel Scott, and—quite often—with Amos Milburn, whose style he had considerably influenced. For a while he worked around Columbus, Ohio. One club owner liked him so much he put Scott up in a house behind the club. Brown also taught piano.

If he was no longer making the charts himself, he took a kind of paternal pride in seeing younger performers occasionally score with songs he had created. After seeing Brown perform, for example, Sam Cooke in 1962 said he wanted to do one of Brown's numbers, "I Wanna Go Home." Cooke recorded a loose adaptation of it called "Bring It on Home to Me," which reached number two on the R&B charts and number thirteen on the pop charts. Bobby "Blue" Bland's recording of "Drifting Blues" reached number twenty-three on the

R&B charts in 1968. By that point, however, Brown had nearly dropped out of the music business. He was living in Cincinnati and working in the used furniture business.

He still had periodic recording dates, however, doing albums, for example, for BluesWay in 1969; Jewel, around 1971; Reprise (with T-Bone Walker) in 1973; Blues Spectrum (on which Johnny Otis played guitar and Otis's son overdubbed bass and guitar) around 1975; and Jefferson in 1976 (a live recording of a San Francisco Blues Festival appearance). Most of the albums didn't do much for him. He was disappointed with the sound quality of the Blues Spectrum and Jewel releases in particular. The poorly mixed Jewel album had been hurried out after the producer died unexpectedly. Too often, Brown felt, his recording projects were executed without sufficient planning or attention to detail and thus did not capture him at his best. If asked to cover a current pop hit like "Go Away Little Girl," he would do it and personalize it a bit, saying over the organ things such as "Charles Brown belongs to somebody else" (he often refers to himself in the third person), "yeah, I got to be true, so true." But what a waste of Brown's highly individual performing style, not to mention his abilities as a blues songwriter, to have him recording cover versions of other performers' latest hits. In terms of career development, that's traveling a dead-end road.

One of the few albums Brown felt really captured him was *Million Sellers* on Imperial. That title, of course, was hyperbole; none of Brown's recordings, even at his peak, had actually been million-sellers, and his sales had fallen off precipitously. Although he enjoyed singing his old hits again, his career appeared to have run its course. Meanwhile, he saw old friends such as Nat King Cole and Ray Charles working with top producers, recording engineers, and first-rate orchestral backing; they were introducing new songs and turning out certified million-seller records during the sixties. Given the same quality of packaging and promotion Cole and Charles received, Brown would likely not have been equally big over the long haul, for they had truly exceptional gifts. Among other things, Cole was blessed with a silky voice of strangely attractive timbre, and Charles had great soul and conviction coupled with a strong rhythmic verve. But having, for example, first-rate orchestral backing on their records helped get them airplay on mainstream stations that would never have played the rougher-sounding, lower-budget albums Brown got to make during the sixties and seventies. How an artist is packaged can make a big difference. Brown would have liked more of a chance to demonstrate his capabilities.

In the sixties and seventies there were large-scale blues revivals as white college youths discovered the music, but Brown was still over-looked. Younger blues critics who had grown up listening to rock found it easier to relate to hard-edged, electric Chicago blues than to Brown's gentler, more laid-back sounds. The electric blues were closer to the rock music they preferred, and they were apt to consider impassioned vocals—howled rather than crooned, furies vented rather than reined in—to be more honest. Furthermore, young blues aficionados who explored the roots of the music were more likely to investigate artists from the era before Brown: Bessie Smith, Ma Rainey, Robert Johnson, Leadbelly, and others. To them, someone like Brown—unlike the "purer" blues performers of an earlier era—seemed tainted by plastic white pop torch-singing traditions.

Little call remained for Brown's services other than bookings performing for aging fans who remembered the years of his original success fondly. Sometimes, too, he was hired to work lounges and entertain people who had no idea that he had ever "been somebody." For them, he would have to sing standards and current pops but not much blues. But he told himself things could be worse; he had his health and there was nothing more important than that. When Amos Milburn and he reunited for a gig in Cincinnati, he was saddened by Milburn's excessive drinking. The songs Milburn sang, "One Scotch, One Bourbon, One Beer," "Bad, Bad Whiskey," "Thinking and Drinking," and "Let's Have a Party," all reflected his life. "He'd party all night long," Brown comments. And Milburn made it clear that he'd rather have Brown join him for a drink than caution him about his health. One night, Brown recalls, he had a dream he's never forgotten. People he'd known were going into a dome: Dinah Washington, Syd Nathan, Nat King Cole. They had all died in recent years. "And Amos is saying to me, 'Let's go in there.'" The meaning was clear to Brown: Milburn was killing himself and he would lead Brown down the same path. "I tried to get Amos to stop drinking. He had the shakes, but he wouldn't stop," Brown recalls. Milburn suffered a seizure in 1970, which forced him into semiretirement for his ten remaining years.

Brown kept plugging, traveling to wherever he could find work. "From Cincinnati, I went to Denver in '70 and I worked there until '72 when I went to Nashville, Tennessee, and a company gave me a job fixing lead sheets [sheet music used by performers] because they owed me money," Brown recalls. "From there, in '72, I went to Atlanta, Georgia, and I got a job with Reverend Stafford playing in his club called Top of Peach Street. And I did so well there, I stayed there until '73. The Brothers Two Restaurant hired me to work next to the Fairmount Hotel. And I did such great business for them, from '74 to '75. And then I went to the Ramada circuit. I played the Ramada Inn out in Mansville, Ohio, in '75. Then from '75, I went back to San Diego, and I kind of laid low just doing little gigs like Thanksgiving gigs around L.A. or something, one-nighters. And then in '76 I came up to Berkeley, and I started living with some friends of mine, Pat and Bob Jordan, and then I did a few little gigs up here and then in '77, I went on the road again, and this guy beat us out of our money. Then I went and stayed back in L.A., working a few little gigs around there in '77. In '78 I was back up here in Richmond, California, doing a few little gigs." He took menial jobs outside of music, as needed, to get by. But, as the saying goes, everything that goes around comes around. By the time Brown's turn began coming around again, he had nearly given up hope of ever receiving significant appreciation as a performer.

* * *

"In 1979, Terry Dunne asked me to play at his club, Tramps, off of Third Avenue in New York—and that was the start of everything," Brown notes simply. Dunne, an Irishman with a deep interest in the blues and R&B, had started the club in 1975 and had gone to considerable lengths to get older performers whose work he respected, even if they'd dropped completely out of sight. Dunne had found, for example, Big Jay McNeely working in a post office in California and Nappy Brown running a church and hog farm in North Carolina. He was also helping cultivate such rising young performers as Buster Poindexter [David Johansen], who made Tramps his base. Brown notes, "When Terry first said, 'New York is ready for you,' I didn't want to come; I said, 'Oh, New York is not ready for me yet.' He said, 'Yes, your music is coming back, Charles; they're ready for you.' And when I went, he kept me at Tramps almost three months! I did so well. Alberta Hunter, who was singing at the Cookery, and I were the only people staying around New York that long."

Audiences in the club were often small, but it didn't matter. Brown—who hadn't played a major New York booking in more years than he could remember—was being seen, appreciated, and written about by a new generation of New York critics, and things were beginning to break for him. Dunne brought Brown back for return engagements. Stephen Holden of *The New York Times* noted on April 30, 1982, that Brown "has the stamina and enthusiasm of a man twenty years younger and a voice that is in remarkably fine shape.

In his set on Wednesday, Mr. Brown sounded like the missing link stylistically between the husky gentility of the late Nat King Cole and the gospel-based blues of Ray Charles. In his version of 'So Long' . . . he modulated his voice from a gentle whisper to a powerful, raw vibrato in a series of beautifully articulated sliding phrases." Jon Pareles also of *The New York Times* observed April 24, 1984, "Mr. Brown is still in top form. . . . He even found some genuine emotion in Billy Joel's 'Just the Way You Are.' Although Mr. Brown has been working for four decades, the power and pleasure of his music have nothing to do with nostalgia."

The bookings at Tramps greatly renewed interest in Brown. "That was the start of it, and since then, everything else has come up," Brown notes. "I've been on the festivals. Everybody wants me in the Swedish things. After I did my first one there, I got Ruth Brown to go with me the next time. We went and had the Los Angeles Blues Caravan. And we played at the Northsea Festival with Bruce Springsteen," who subsequently went on to record Brown's "Merry Christmas Baby."

In 1986 Brown cut an album called *One More for the Road* for a small label, Blue Side. Released in 1987, the album—although it offered less variety in terms of tempos and material than it ideally should have—proved a solid come-back vehicle. Well recorded, Brown had backing from jazz pros Harold Ousley (tenor sax), Billy Butler (guitar), Earl May (acoustic bass), and Kenny Washington (drums). His voice, smooth and unblemished, sounded like that of a man much younger than sixty-six.

The album received considerable, and overwhelmingly favorable, coverage during 1987. In a review syndicated in the *Los Angeles Times* newspaper network Anthony DeCurtis wrote, "*One More for the Road* is perfect for late, lonely nights when feeling bad somehow feels good." The *Gavin Report* noted on February 13 that "Charles Brown wears a blues ballad like Humphrey Bogart lit cigarettes—perfectly. . . . Here's a voice that's seen and felt it all. He's a contemporary of Nat King Cole and Ray Charles with equal the soul." Don Palmer noted in *Music and Sound Output* in February that "his crooning baritone can sound like food for lounge lizards, but Brown has much more to offer. *One More for the Road* shows Brown in fine fettle as he transforms even the most maudlin of standards into pensive remembrances. Brown's blues, so adult and post-WWII middle-class in their resignation, are a predecessor to the younger [Robert] Cray's almost sentimental lyrics." The *Philadelphia Inquirer*'s Ken Tucker observed on February 15 that "sometimes his choice of material is dull, but his vocals are always sly and sure, and both 'I Cried Last Night' and 'Get Yourself Another Fool' suggest a world-weariness more mature than most pop performers ever achieve." Reviewer Jill Pearlman (in a clip of unknown origin) reflected on the fact that "instead of heralding him, the blues revival [had] passed over his urban sound—though deep blue in feel—for the 'authentic' raw blistering Chicago sort," adding that, ironically enough, white audiences had once looked down upon his "dirtying up standards." Brown's new album, she wrote, "paves the way for a new generation to discover his timeless work." On June 10 Robert Christgau of the *Village Voice* gave the album a "B plus" rating, noting "this long-overdue piece of record making hits you with its craft and taste," but Christgau expressed reservations over the way Brown's voice slipped too reflexively "into the lugubrious"; he suspected that Brown might be best appreciated "like so many chart-toppers before him, in three-minute doses." *Billboard's* Peter Keepnews noted that although Brown was an R&B pioneer, his album was being played "on some 150 jazz radio stations, including such major outlets as KKGO Los Angeles, WBGO Newark, and KJAZ San Francisco, and it's not hard to understand why: Brown . . . establishes a mellow, lightly swinging groove . . . that is completely at home in a jazz format."[8]

Brown had not gotten such critical attention in years. Unfortunately, the record didn't get the distribution it deserved—minor-label releases, no matter how well received by critics, simply don't make their way into a great number of stores and, to make matters worse, the record company failed not long after the album's release. But Alligator Records—a leading independent in the blues and R&B fields—came to the rescue. In 1989 they reissued the album, adding a couple of unreleased tracks from the recording session and deleting a couple they felt were weak. Alligator president Bruce Iglauer, aware that Brown's singing would be an acquired taste for most young blues listeners, cautioned in the liner notes: "For the fans of Alligator's rough and ready 'genuine houserockin' music, this album may come as a bit of a shock. Charles Brown is most definitely a blues musician, but he inhabits the melodic, jazzy, after-hours region of the blues world. His style of blues has been neglected in our recent years. It's our hope that his deep feeling and brilliant musicianship will transform him from a shock to an exciting revelation for younger blues fans."

Iglauer needn't have worried; the rediscovery of Charles Brown was picking up speed. In 1988 he was featured, along with Ruth Brown, in a documentary aired on public television, "That Rhythm, Those

Blues." Ruth Brown had him appear with her at the Lonestar Road-house. He also played New York's prestigious Blue Note, which bills itself as "the world's greatest jazz club." And he was pleased to discover that he had admirers among current stars. Brown recalls, "I went to the Blue Note and everybody said to me, 'Meet Dr. John.' And *he* said, 'Charles Brown, you remember me! I played with you and Johnny Vincent down in New Orleans.' And I just couldn't believe it; it was just amazing. He was a young boy when he played guitar with me, when I did a thing down there in New Orleans years ago [around 1959]. But he wasn't called Dr. John back then; he was called Max Reben-nack. After meeting at the Blue Note, we got to be close again. He's even dedicated a song to me." Dr. John, Malcolm John Rebennack, is still called "Mac" by old friends—"Max" in Brown's locution. Recognition kept coming: Elvis Costello said Charles Brown was one of his favorite blues singers; Buster Poindexter presented Brown on the Show-time cable television network's "Coast to Coast" music series in 1990; and Bonnie Raitt (who in 1990 was enjoying her own substantial come-back after a period of low visibility—she won four Grammy Awards that year) invited him to open for her on her national tour. Raitt had loved his appearance at the Vine Street Grill in Los Angeles. Brown notes, "I'm on all her dates from July 24 to September 30 [1990]. We play all the West Coast, East Coast, we go to Universal City—all big places, twenty-five thousand people. She thinks the world of me. They've sold out most of the places, they tell me. So, they're very hap-py." Raitt told the *Boston Sunday Globe*'s Steve Morse:

> We're just flabbergasted to be touring with Charles. He's a legend . . . one of the founding fathers of this type of music. And Charles hasn't dissipated himself at all. He's sharp as a tack. He's got a great heart and a great attitude—and he's so elegant. . . . He's all there. Like all the best people who have aged beautiful-ly, whether it's Jessica Tandy or Helen Hayes or Alberta Hunter or Sippie Wallace. . . . It's just a great lesson for those of us who are getting older and wrestling with middle age, to know that role models like Charles, Muddy Waters, Fred McDowell, and Sippie just get better and better as they get older. If you're lucky enough to have your health, you're going to play with all those years of experience. And that was my first impression of Charles. If this is what his age is all about, then I can't wait.[9]

Raitt was equally enthusiastic to *Rolling Stone*'s Sheila Rogers on September 20, 1990. She said that bringing Brown on the tour "is sort of a gift to myself." She added, "In my opinion, he's the greatest living piano player." Brown acknowledges that Raitt loves his piano playing but seems embarrassed by such extreme praise. "Well, I don't know," he says in a self-deprecating way. "I'm from the older school. I play accordingly. Because Art Tatum was my inspiration; those people were my—I don't play like them but I get my inspiration from them."

He knows he's not "the greatest living piano player," but he *is* quite a skilled one—and a self-aware one. When Alan di Perna of *Musician* magazine got Brown to talk about his playing in April 1991, Brown suggested that a secret to his success was the way he'd cross between major and minor chords, citing as an early example the Three Blazers' original recording of "Drifting Blues": "In most blues, say if you're in E, you'll just hear straight major chords from an E scale. But we went between a major and a minor and that was the key to our success."

Di Perna found repeated examples of the principle throughout Brown's CD *All My Life* (Bullseye Blues/Rounder Records, 1990), noting, for instance, that "Early in the Morning," a twelve-bar blues composed by Brown, departs from the standard blues I-IV-V chord structure: "In the ninth bar, which usually moves to the V chord—B major in this case—Brown alternates between an Fmin7 and a B7. Minor to major, just like the man says. And in the third bar, where most bluesmen would be content to rest on the tonic E, Brown divides the measure between E and—depending on his mood in each chorus—either B7 or B7 augmented." Analyzing the second solo piano break that Brown takes on an original piece entitled "Joyce's Boogie," di Perna noted, "While his right hand plays a very orthodox tonic-to-dominant-seventh pattern in octaves, his left is adding some harmonies George Gershwin would have been proud of. Here's an example in C: When the right-hand note is C, the left hand's playing E, B flat and D beneath it. And when the right hand goes to B flat, the left plays F, B natural, and E flat."[10]

You don't have to be a musicologist, however, to appreciate Brown's playing, which is sparkling and often surprising. I've seen him, in concert, play an ornate introduction to "When the Sun Comes Out" with such urgency and fluency as to elicit enthusiastic shouts of "whoo!" from the audience before even he's started singing the song. I wonder whether some of Brown's past record producers really appreciated his contributions as a piano player; precious little of his playing was heard on some records, and one label—Jewel—just had Brown sing, getting someone else to play piano throughout the album. Brown's piano—and, on some tracks, organ—is very much in evidence on *All My Life*.

All My Life may well be Brown's best album to date. He's not necessarily in the best voice; his voice is not quite as clear as on *One
More for the Road*. Detectable traces of huskiness and strain may reflect the aging process, or he may simply have been a bit tired. But
he's singing with great self-assurance, naturalness, and ease. And, significantly, there's more variety in terms of tempos, types of tunes,
and instrumental color than on the justly acclaimed *One More for the
Road*. Producer Ron Levy deserves recognition for the care he's obviously taken with the *All My Life* recording project; one can only wish
Brown had been so well showcased throughout his career. Featured
on alto and tenor sax is Clifford Solomon, who'd worked with Brown
in the early fifties then spent some fifteen years working with Ray
Charles. He's now back working with Brown regularly. On some cuts,
Heywood Henry's baritone sax helps create a classic R&B sound. And
why not? It was Henry's baritone heard on some classic fifties' R&B
records. Dr. John is heard playing piano and organ on a couple of
tracks and singing on one a new Brown composition entitled "A Virus Called the Blues," which the two performers really sing to each
other: "Max, I've got a virus called the blues." "Charles Brown, I've
got a virus called the blues." Ruth Brown joins with Charles Brown
for "Tell Me Who," a ditty with a happy-go-lucky mid-fifties R&B feel
to it. Ruth Brown is by no means in peak voice on the track but it
hardly matters; the duet of these two survivors radiates such joy and
sentiment—it sums up an era—that it is one of the high points of
the album. (Let's hope they get to record together some more.)
Charles Brown gets to remake "Trouble Blues" and "Seven Long
Days"; pay tribute to Amos Milburn with "Bad, Bad Whiskey"; and
offer a lilting, economical "All My Life" and a subdued, brooding
original that shows well his strengths as both a singer and player of
the blues, "Early in the Morning." It's steeped in the blues yet—characteristically—is not bitter. Doesn't Brown ever feel any resentment
toward the people who've cheated or taken advantage of him during his long career? He responds quietly, with equanimity, that he's
outlived most of those people.

It's April 29, 1991. Charles Brown is to appear tonight at the popular downtown New York club, S.O.B.'s. I arrive long before show time.
Walking into the club—deserted except for waitresses and the like—
I am surprised to hear music by Debussy being played with a con-
templative air. It's Brown, warming up at the piano with some of his
classical repertoire. I take a seat quietly in one corner, enjoying the
unexpected private concert. When he finishes, I go to say hello. He
makes me feel he's genuinely pleased to see me once again, radiat-

ing a gentle warmth. I ask him whether it's okay to talk for a bit; I know that some singers—Jimmy Witherspoon, for one—don't like talking much before performing because they're anxious to conserve their voices. Brown says he doesn't think like that. "If you have it here," he tells me, putting one hand to his heart, "you don't worry about how it comes out."

I remark on how youthful he appears and sounds. He notes that his voice is heavier now than it was in his youth, but he's still got plenty of energy. He reflects, with a bit of wonder, on how his career has turned around in recent years. On Saturday night he had given a concert at Columbia University—where there were lots of college students, much too young to remember his early successes—and he had to do four or five encores.

An older woman fan comes in and says she's sorry to interrupt us, but she'd just like to give Brown something she's made for him. She hands him, wrapped in foil, a container of black-eyed peas and a little cake. He tells her how grateful he is and later, during the performance, also thanks her publicly. Black-eyed peas are a favorite. He rarely eats meat anymore because he says that he doesn't need all that cholesterol. High blood pressure is a problem for a lot of black people—it runs in his family—and Brown tries to watch his diet.

Now the audience is drifting in. A few are older fans; they're the ones who will start clapping as soon as he sings the first words of his forty-year-old hit "Black Night": "Nobody cares about me. . . ." Most, however, are young and probably know him only from his last album or two. They're the ones to whom he will address remarks like, "I first recorded this next song in 1945. You were little angels up in the sky, but Charles Brown was right here."

The lights dim. Brown is introduced as "one of the founding fathers of American music in rhythm and blues. There would be no Ray Charles without this man." Charles Brown doesn't electrify you the way Ruth Brown, when she's inspired, can. But he maintains an even pace. He can create a late night mood of loss and longing and sustain it, in song after song, until it gets inside of you. In his subdued voice, he can sing that he's lonely and then add, conversationally, "I can see some of you are lonely, too." He's singing to—and for—those of us who are lonely. And you forget there are four other musicians on the stage with him, forget there's a room full of people watching him perform; he's communicating with you personally.

Yet if his words are on the "down" side, he seems so clearly at peace with himself, so secure, that there's something fundamentally buoying about him. Singing "I Wanna Go Home," he coaxes the audience to sing lines along with him; by now, he's gotten us under his spell. He breaks the rhythm of the song and, with a preacher's cadence, calls out places to where he feels tugs to return: "I've got relatives in Watts, California; De-troit, Michigan; Harlem, New York." You half expect the audience to respond with calls of "Amen!" Almost campily, he raises a handkerchief to his face as he utters, "It brings tears to my eyes," breaking the mild tension he's created.

There are shifts of mood. He can project poignance on "Cottage for Sale" then good cheer on "All My Life." He can hint at a suicidal despair one moment (singing a line like "I won't be trouble for long") then suggest a curious innocence the next (folding his hands like a choirboy as he vows he'll "pray you'll come back to me"). His piano playing can be spritely in one song, then show an unexpected strength and even aggressiveness the next. Often he'll sing words that may be sad, but he sings them with a voice that retains hope.

He banters with us: "I wrote this next number before I got married: 'I Cried Last Night.' After I got married, I really cried!" He declaims the sufferings of unrequited love: "I got so disgusted, I thought I'd end it all. / I went out into the Bay Bridge and said—'That's too far to fall.'" The band revs up and he sings about how he cried last night. A bit later he's talk-singing again: 'Well I went out to the Hudson River, I thought I'd jump in. / I heard a little voice say, 'Wait, Charles Brown, she'll come back again!'" And he's got us smiling, even as he's ostensibly singing of how he'd been hurt.

By the time Ruth Brown has finished a set, it's as if she's picked you up with both hands, given you a thorough shaking, and set you down again. It's not like that with Charles Brown. He doesn't aim for big, emotional moments the way she does. But he's an effective performer in a low-pressure way, and he does leave you feeling relaxed and together. Checking my watch at the conclusion of Brown's set at S.O.B.'s, I'm surprised to realize that he's sung, without an intermission, for a full two hours. Midway through, he had given his band a break, doing a few intimate numbers just by himself. Many performers would have made me restless after an hour or so, but I'd gotten caught up in the calming spirit of his music.

Afterward he chats—with more graciousness than I could ever imagine mustering after working so long—with fans who want to ask questions or take photos. He assures me that he's getting *plenty* of work these days, both in the United States and abroad. He's getting more offers to record and even, perhaps, do some videos. He takes it all in stride. "If all the records come in now, I'm not excited about it, because I've been low-key so long," he says evenly. But he admits that he is pleased, at his age, to get this attention. "I think I deserve some kind of recognition," he acknowledges. "When you do leave, you know, you want to say you left a little mark for somebody to remember."

4

"Hard living alone. . . ."

"See, in the type of music we played, me and Charles [Brown], we caused less fights across the country than anybody in the music business. You listen to some of that other music, it don't cause nothing but riots. But everywhere I played, everybody leaved peaceful and happy, and there wasn't none of that hully-gully," reflects Floyd Dixon. He was, along with Charles Brown and Amos Milburn (like him, both Texans transplanted to California), a major figure in West Coast R&B.

Although he's often been compared with Brown (eight years his senior), it would be a mistake to think of Dixon as merely a Brown clone. Singing of loneliness and unrequited love with a simple yet elegant trio backing, as he frequently did in his heyday, Dixon could create a subdued late-night mood similar to that characteristically created by Brown—a significant early influence on him and a long-time good friend. The stylistic similarities between the two men reflected some temperamental similarities, as the fact that Brown at his peak exerted an influence upon most upcoming R&B singers. But Dixon had a markedly buoyant side, too. He did more exuberant jump-blues numbers than Brown did and seemed more at home doing them. Dixon's singing also often seemed warmer and more down to earth.

Both Brown and Dixon created good vibes, but, to oversimplify a bit, if Brown imparted tranquility to his listeners, his repeated, cool-ly voiced expressions of sorrow and self-pity proving cathartic, Dix-on—with a bit more upbeat emphasis and mixing songs of loss with some that were cheerily risqué—imparted more of a glow of joy.

But whatever a performer's particular style happens to be, Dixon believes, generating genuinely good vibes is part of a musician's responsibility—and he's given the matter considerable thought. "When musicians get away from it, you come up with all types of evil. See, I know; I know!" Dixon says. "You can have good music and bad music; I'm telling you. And the worst thing in the world is for a musician to be mistreated. Because if a musician really knows music, he can play in the key of D natural and—if he throws it out of tonality—mess up the whole country. You think I'm lying, you go to the library and read. Chinese people know about it. A musician can be more detrimental to society than anything on earth. He can mess up all of the government officials with his playing. With just his playing! On the other hand, music can be a natural healing power. So you want to keep musicians happy, because they're trying to keep you happy. That's right," Dixon affirms. He notes that he became aware quite early in his life of the power a musician has to make people happy.

* * *

"I first decided to become a musician by hearing the [music at] house-rent parties in my hometown," recalls Dixon, who was born in Marshall, Texas (153 miles from Dallas and 39 miles from Shreveport, Louisiana) on February 8, 1928. At the house-rent parties he met the man he admired the most as a young boy in Texas, a regional-favorite piano player who went by the name of Roadmaster. "He could really play the piano and talk to the piano. He had so many gimmicks. I never heard a straight-out blues piano or boogie piano of today that could play like Roadmaster. He was just something! I can just see him now sitting there playing. I wish someone had recorded him. And anyone *ever* heard him—and there was thousands, because he played all over Shreveport, Marshall, Longview—anyone ever heard him, they will tell you that nobody could come up to Roadmaster. If he was living today, you would know what I was talking about. And I just decided I wanted to play. So I started *trying* to play," Dixon says.

Thinking of Roadmaster prompts many pleasant memories. "I still remember the melody of 'Road's Boogie' but I'd have to practice awhile to get it back. Oh, I'll tell you, every night when I was out on the road in the fifties I used to play two or three choruses of it, and people would just shout, shout—it was a different type of boogie." Now Dixon begins scatting the piano number he remembers from his boyhood, gradually adding the vocal interjections he remembers Roadmaster making, and suddenly—here in the Los Angeles boardinghouse Dixon calls home—it's as if Roadmaster is alive again: "He'd say, 'Now talk to me, Mr. Road. Oooh, that's old Pinetop come

out; I believe he done stole from Roadmaster.'" And Dixon scats something that sounds very much like "Pinetop's Boogie-Woogie," the
seminal boogie-woogie piece Pinetop Smith recorded in 1928. "He'd
say, 'Now talk, Mr. Road! Now ride your horse across the prairie.' Aw,
he'd talk. And I mean, he could play. I mean, Mr. Roadmaster was
just top. He'd say, 'Now, I'm going to hop this freight train now and
I want all of you to see this train; it's ninety miles an hour.'" Dixon
scats some more of the rollicking boogie-woogie patterns that could
suggest one minute a galloping horse, the next a barreling train.
"'Now, hop it, Mr. Road,' he'd say. And boy, he was a comedy, but
he could really play. You know, when you can really do it and talk
that talk, it's all right. Well, he could talk that talk and really do it.
And he'd have the whole house crying and just jumping! And they'd
say, 'All right, Mr. Road, I want to hear you, I want to hear you tell
me to stop.'" Dixon scats some more, then commands: "'Stop!' Now
pat your feet a couple of times. Bop-bop.' He'd say, 'Now I want you
to boogie a little while.' Oh, and he'd get—and the house would be
just rocking! And they'd be stomping! Oh man, it was something else.
That was really the fun.

    "And oh, the kids, they'd be mobbed around the house! The adults
wouldn't let them in there. I was the only one who could be in there
because they said one day this boy might be a piano player. And I
could be in there with them because I liked it so much I'd have
crawled through the window anyway. And boy, he could play a piano! I've heard 'em all. *I've heard 'em all.* But he must have been *five
hundred* years ahead of time. You have no idea of what I'm really talking about. You would have to really see him for yourself to get the
real, know-what-I'm-taking-about. Like that song said, 'If you've never
been mistreated, you don't know what I'm talking about.'"

    Dixon was so inspired by the exuberant Roadmaster that by the
time he was perhaps twelve he decided to seek formal piano instruc-
tion. "This guy named Julius Jackson, he taught piano lessons. So, I
took one lesson from him in Marshall and he beat my hand so much
with that ruler, I wouldn't go back! I just practiced on my own." In
the meantime, Dixon had also begun singing. "Well, I started off singing church songs. [He sings] 'I'm packing up, I'm getting ready to
go,' those kind of songs. Me and a guy named Gaylord, we used to
have us a little choir, like. We'd called it having a little choir; we'd
be singing 'Precious Lord' and all of them things. Back in Texas, we'd
sit on the porch at night. One of them would be playing . . . and we'd
be singing." In Dixon's memories of Texas, music plays a major role.

    He was twelve when his mother decided they would move to Los

Angeles. "The reason I moved out here was my mother's sister was out here. And my mother's brothers had passed and then my grandmother wanted her to come out here, and my mother wanted to be out here with her. So we moved. And I didn't like that. When we first moved to Los Angeles, I would go around and see if anybody had a piano," he recalls. He wanted to keep up his piano playing, but in a more general sense he was striving to re-create the scene he had known in Texas. "After about a month here, they had to send me back to Texas because I was bickering so much; I was crying every day. And I had a dog back there in Texas named Jack, and I missed him. They sent me back and let me stay a while with my animal. I stayed a year in Texas and then come back here."

He lived alone during that year, he says, and made money as best he could. "Home" was a treehouse in the woods, which friends Bill and Lawrence Whaley helped build for him. Sometimes he'd catch a meal at their house; more often he'd fend for himself. His dog, Jack, was good at catching rabbits, which he'd cook, and he'd gather hickory nuts, huckleberries, and other wild edibles. For a while, he worked at a bowling alley, setting pins from four in the afternoon until midnight; it'd be around two in the morning by the time he'd walked back to his home. Later he found work as a laborer, setting pipe in the ground. (It was a man's job, really, but by then the draft had been instituted, and as laborers got drafted bosses became less choosy about who they hired as replacements.) When his grandmother came to visit, he was proud to be able to offer her money he'd earned, but he was hurt sorely when she simply took it all and returned to California without taking him back with her as he'd hoped she would. He eventually wrote a song about that occurrence, but it wasn't one to be performed publicly; it was simply too personal. However, the pain and alienation he felt would, in a general sense, go into any number of songs.

When Dixon finally returned to California he tried living with his family once again, but it didn't work out. He doesn't say that he felt rejected, although he must have; he believes that he was a wayward youth. For a while, he lived at his cousins' house. "But I didn't wash dishes for eight days and I got put out. So I just started going to church. A friend saw me and told his parents and I stayed with them a while, first. At Bobby Williams's house. They had a piano that I could practice on. And then when I left there, I practiced down at T-Bone's sometime [the home of bluesman T-Bone Walker].

"Then a white fellow by the name of Mark Hurley asked my mother one day, could I live with him. She said, 'Yeah, if you think you

can do anything with him, Mr. Hurley, take him on.' So he did."
Hurley, whom Dixon remembers with great affection and appreciation, became a key figure in Dixon's life. He provided emotional support, encouraged Dixon in his playing, singing, and songwriting—
Hurley also wrote songs—and guided and managed his career as it
began to develop. Hurley was close to the members of Johnny Moore's
Three Blazers and had written many songs for them; he believed Dixon had the potential to be as successful as they. Unmarried, Hurley
focused considerable attention on Dixon, whom he called "Dick." He
played banjo and piano and made sure that Dixon practiced the piano. Were it not for Hurley, Dixon believes, he would not have become a professional singer and pianist despite his strong yearnings
to do so. The "wayward youth," who had not fit in at home, found
a sense of belonging in Hurley's home.

Dixon recalls, "I had come back to California from Texas and won
the amateur hour at the Million Dollar Theater [in Los Angeles]. And
then I met Mark. I remember just like yesterday. If it had been three
hundred years ago, it would have been just like yesterday with me. I
lived with him over there across from the Universal police station a
long time. Oh, I was fourteen or fifteen. But I was around with him
when I was sixteen, seventeen, eighteen, nineteen. And he'd say,
'Dick, you got to practice. You got to practice that now because we're
going to get out here and make a good tour set.' And he gave me $3
a day to sit and practice." Dixon laughs warmly now at the memory
before continuing.

"I don't know the exact age when I started staying with him, but
I was young enough not to even get in the [musicians'] union or
nothing. I started staying with him *some* when I was fourteen—maybe
two nights a week and then come back. See, I stayed with him way
before I lived with him. See, when you stay with somebody, that's—
staying and living is different. So I'd stop by there, I'd be coming
home; curfew was 11:30, you were supposed to be in. I'd get into
Mark's sometimes at 11 and I'd know I couldn't make it all the way
home. I'd jump up there and knock, wake everybody up, and Mark
would let me in there and I'd stay in there; he had an extra army
cot like for me, and I'd stay right there. . . . And that's the way it was.

"Mark was about fifty-something then. But he was still a good old
man when he got to seventy. He was really, really—you wouldn't
know it. Because every morning he'd get up and he'd say, 'Ah, how
do you like that punch, Dick?' [Dixon pantomimes giving a playful
punch.] And he'd tell Johnny Moore and Charles [Brown] and all of
us—he really liked us—'You guys ain't worth a dime. I hit you one

time, I'll knock your clothes off.' And boy, was he strong! He was a strong guy, that's right. 'Hold that, Dick!' Bup! We couldn't hold him for nothing.

"He loved old Charles, too. He wrote a song for Charles. And he loved old Johnny Moore, too; Johnny Moore could get away with anything. And he had great big pictures, as big as that [Dixon points to a mirror over the mantelpiece, about as wide as the fireplace] made of Charles Brown, Johnny Moore, Oscar Moore." Dixon notes that he has Brown to thank for introducing him to Mark Hurley. "Mark met me at Charles's place," he recalls, "and we started talking about songwriting and singing and different things like that."

How did Dixon first come to know Brown? He backtracks a bit. "I was about fourteen, I imagine, when I won that amateur contest at the Million Dollar Theater," Dixon says. The Three Blazers, including Brown (a member of the group from 1944 to 1948), were also performing at the theater that night, and Brown enjoyed the newcomer whose style reminded him so much of his own. Dixon is not certain about exactly how old he was when he won that first amateur contest (he soon went on to win another one at the Barrelhouse Club in Los Angeles), and it is possible he may have been a bit older than fourteen. He remembers doing such numbers in amateur contests as "Dallas Blues" (which he would later successfully record), "Blueberry Hill," and "Changeable Woman Blues."

If Dixon's recollection of doing "Changeable Woman Blues" is correct, it would suggest that he may have been nearer to eighteen than fourteen, because that number—a big hit for Johnny Moore's Three Blazers—did not come along until 1947. He says, "Charles talked to me backstage and gave me his address—1275 West 35th Street is where he lived then—and told me I could come by there that weekend because they wasn't leaving town then. So I got a couple of my friends from high school and went over there, and he had it really fixed up. And he treated me just nice. Charles has always treated me nice, all my life, just like he was my brother or something. Oh, I'd get mad sometimes—dislike some of his ways. He might want to go across town or to the track and I didn't want to go or something. Just little things like that. But he would always, like if he'd be traveling uptown, maybe he'd say, 'Let's get this. I'm going over here and get this jacket. You ought to get yours.' 'I don't want that jacket.' 'Well, Floyd, so-and-so-and so.' But we always was friends. Oh, and he taught me. He went to conservatory. He played Tschaikowsky's book or Beethoven's with one hand. He's really a conservatory piano player. And he taught me all my triads. He taught me a lot of different things, how to hit my relative chords and minors, majors, subdominants."

Brown not only influenced Dixon's piano playing but also his singing. Asked which singers he had admired when he was younger, Dixon responds without hesitation: "Charles Brown, definitely. Uh-huh. And Louis Jordan. Wynonie Harris. I liked his style. I used to go around singing 'Play for Baby.' [Dixon sings a bit of it, in a high voice.] 'I like to play for the baby, the way she plays all night.' I liked his songs because a lot of them was a little risqué. 'She loves to play it in the day, and I love to play it at night.' You know, a kid would get that in his mind. So that's why I liked all of his songs. If my mom had heard me, when I was little, singing a song like that one, she'd have beat all the bark off me! She didn't like those kind of songs."

Although he enjoyed Wynonie Harris, a blues shouter who helped pave the way for rock 'n' roll, Dixon notes that he never tried to sing like him. He drew more inspiration from the smoother stylings of both the extroverted, ebullient Louis Jordan (his favorite entertainer at the time) and the cooler, more laid-back Charles Brown. He recalls studying Brown's piano and vocal on "Changeable Woman Blues" when it came out until he could do it so like the original that some who heard him thought that it was he on the record. (He adds that some friends who heard him sing told him that he reminded them of Charles Brown even before he'd heard Brown himself.) Not surprisingly, he also liked Amos Milburn (whom Brown had influenced) and Joe Liggins and the Honeydrippers. Pianists he liked included Pete Johnson (the boogie-woogie specialist), Art Tatum, Fats Waller, Bill Doggett, and Milt Buckner.

In 1948 Charles Brown left Johnny Moore's Three Blazers to make it on his own, leading a Blazers-type group. Bassist Eddie Williams decided to strike off on his own, too. Williams wasn't doing much when Mark Hurley had a good idea: put Dixon with Williams plus another musician or two. Williams could lead a group that, with Dixon on piano and vocals, would appeal to anyone who'd enjoyed the Three Blazers. It was a logical proposal and a good way to get Dixon's career going. If they'd rehearse until they could execute a decent-sized repertoire with some polish, Hurley was sure that gigs and recording opportunities would follow. Dixon, by then living with Hurley, recalls how Hurley strove hard to get them to practice every day, which wasn't always easy because Williams sometimes had other priorities. "Mark would get up and then we'd go over to Eddie's. He'd make sure. Eddie had a piano in a garage over there. Now Eddie really liked Mark but he was drinking a little Ballantine at that time, and he would drink a little and say, 'Shut up, Mark! We're going to rehearse in forty-five minutes or an hour, man, but let us drink.' 'No, you've got to practice, you've got to practice everything.' Eddie'd look at me and wink his eye. He'd say, 'So all right, man. Well, go get us some pop.' And then Mark would laugh and say, 'I'll be with you in an hour.' I'd say to Eddie, 'Mark really think the world of you, boy. That old man, we ain't going to give him no trouble because if he had heart failure or something, I never would get over it. We don't want to hurt his feelings.'"

Meanwhile, Dixon had the idea that if he took his song "Dallas Blues" to a record company he might persuade someone that a professional singer should record it. A friend drove him over to Modern Records, an independent company run by the Bihari family (Jules, Joe, Saul, Lester, and others). "See, I even did that without Mark. Mark didn't even know. He didn't think I was ready or nothing," Dixon notes. For that matter, Dixon himself—then working at a drug store—didn't think he was ready yet as a singer either. "I didn't want to sing the song myself," he explains. "I wanted some big artist to sing it. God, I wanted someone finally to sing it that I had heard of, like anybody. I guess most singers begin like that. They want to hear some other artist sing their tune to make them feel a little better." His mother, he recalls, had her doubts. But one friend decided that if Floyd had that much nerve he would drive him across town to the record company.

Modern Records was representative of any number of small R&B record companies. It had been founded just a few years earlier, in the spring of 1945. Jules Bihari had operated jukeboxes in black neighborhoods before then. During the war he had trouble getting enough new records to stock his jukeboxes fully, and he hit upon the idea of producing records himself. They'd help keep his jukeboxes filled, and the records in his jukeboxes would promote sales in the area.

His entire family became involved in the business: one brother would concentrate on recording sessions, one on manufacturing, one on sales, and so on. Recording sessions were done simply and economically, and artists were recorded with minimal interference. The Biharis didn't interrupt takes or order countless retakes as more experienced producers with bigger budgets normally would have done. They let the artists go, and what the results lacked in polish they often made up in naturalness and spontaneity. When things worked right, the Biharis' records had feeling that was sometimes missing in more professionally produced, bigger-label recordings.

The Biharis recorded artists and also sold records in smaller outlets that bigger labels overlooked. They hustled personally, going from store to store in black communities, not just record stores but all kinds of mom-and-pop operations: stationary stores, five-and-dimes, and grocery stores. If the owner of such a store assured trusting customers that a new record was really good, copies would sell. The Biharis' records received limited exposure on radio, but they found plenty on ghetto jukeboxes, which also spurred sales.

The Biharis soon developed a reputation for knowing the community, and jukebox operators from other black areas also began to trust their judgments. Some became distributors for them, placing records at record stores, candy stores, and shoeshine stands, for example, in the new areas. In addition, the Biharis cultivated the comparatively few disc jockeys who did play R&B records. In the Los Angeles area, for example, perhaps the most important disc jockey for R&B during the late forties was the wildly exuberant Hunter Hancock, who was white but sounded, by timbre and cadence, black. His sponsors, whom he solicited personally at first, included Central Avenue stores likely to carry the records he played. As he—and R&B—grew more popular during the early fifties, his show, on tape, was syndicated into a growing number of cities, increasing his ability to make a new record a hit.

Nationally, distribution of the Biharis' records was spotty during the forties. They didn't reach all areas, only some with concentrations of blacks, although distribution would get stronger in subsequent years. Occasionally, they might score with a big hit that would sell hundreds of thousands of copies. But with costs kept low, they could make good money on records that sold many fewer copies. They were able to produce and market profitable records—records that over a five- or six-month period might sell seventy-five or a hundred thousand copies almost entirely in black neighborhoods—with the major labels barely seeming to take notice. And they turned out new records steadily.

This was the situation when Floyd Dixon walked into Modern Records. He was asked to record what he was told would be a demo version of his song "Dallas Blues." It just happened—at least far as Dixon could tell—that a guitarist and bass player were present. "And Joe Bihari said to them, 'Try that with him.' So I played my song. I played 'waah, waah,' the introduction, and they just fell right in like that. Yeah, Joe and all of them will tell you, I didn't cut 'Dallas Blues' but one time! And it wasn't supposed to come out. I just thought he was going to give the number to somebody else to put out. And I played a thing called 'Helen,' too, just to try it. I was eighteen, going on eighteen, because when I cut the record, Joe was saying, 'Are you in the union?' I said, 'No.' He said, 'Oh, my goodness! Go and get in the union.' There weren't integrated unions at that time, so I had to go over on Central and join Local 767. I'd taped 'Dallas Blues' just for him to give it to another artist. That's the way I went in. But he said, 'That's good enough to put out.'" Dixon was delighted when they offered him a check on the spot, flat payment, of course—no royalties. "And the next thing I hear Hunter Hancock was playing it and all that!"

Modern Records released a 78 rpm single of "Dallas Blues," with "Helen" on the flip side by "Floyd Dixon's Trio." Both the singing style and instrumentation showed the influence of Charles Brown and Johnny Moore's Three Blazers. On March 12, 1949, "Dallas Blues" made the number ten spot on *Billboard*'s "Most-Played Juke Box Race Records" chart. Dixon was so delighted to have a hit record that he didn't worry about whether he had gotten a fair deal financially. And Eddie Williams was convinced—even though he had not been on Dixon's record of "Dallas Blues"—that its popularity proved their group, featuring Dixon, would click. "Dallas Blues" sold especially well in Texas; Dixon heard from old friends there who wondered whether the record had been made by the same Floyd Dixon they had known. In his youth he had been known by the nickname "Skeet" rather than Floyd. There shouldn't have been much question; besides singing about how he was longing to go back to Dallas, he threw in a line about "a little place called Marshall" where he was better known.

Despite the record's popularity, Dixon recalls, "We didn't start touring then. Mark said, 'Well, you got to have the material to do a half-hour set. And you need to go get with BMI [Broadcast Music Inc., which would ensure that he'd receive some royalties as a songwriter]. Joe's not going to pay no royalties on a thing like that.' 'Dallas Blues' was my first hit, but I didn't make money on it. I didn't know anything about the record business." On "Dallas Blues," composer credits were attributed to Dixon and "Jules Taub"—a pseudonym the Biharis used. He was to share credit with Jules Taub on other recordings, too. Claiming composer credit was particularly rewarding for an R&B record producer if a record subsequently got "covered" by other singers on bigger labels, because the supposed "composer" would make money from the sales of all those records. On "Doin' the Town," which Dixon later recorded and says he wrote, he found that the *only* composer credited was Jules Taub, meaning that all composer royalties went to the Biharis.

In retrospect, Dixon feels that the Biharis treated him better than many other record company people he dealt with later. At least Jules Bihari "sent us out to pick up a new Mercury wagon for the band," which was more than the others in later years would do. He later let Amos Milburn use that car to make some dates when Milburn's car broke down. Milburn returned it damaged and said he couldn't afford to repair it because he'd lost all his money at the track. Dixon, never big on confronting people, let the matter slide; he and Milburn remained friends.

Dixon continued recording for Modern and toured regionally. Hurley sought to make sure that he was compensated fairly for his work, both as a songwriter and as a recording artist. Dixon recalls, "Mark said, 'Let's go and get a good contract.' Mark liked Supreme Records." Supreme, a tiny, independent label run by a black dentist named Al Patrick, appeared to be on a hot streak thanks solely to the popularity of two artists on the label: Paula Watson and Jimmy Witherspoon. Watson's "A Little Bird Told Me" enjoyed a fourteen-week run on the *Billboard* R&B charts in 1948–49, and Witherspoon's smash hit "Ain't Nobody's Business" enjoyed an extraordinary thirty-four-week run on the charts in 1949.

Hurley, Dixon, and Williams went to meet with the people of Supreme Records and see what they had to offer. Dixon appreciated the fact that Hurley looked out for his interests. He comments, "Mark's a straight fellow. He said, 'Whatever Floyd says is all right with me.' So we decided, 'We want to do a session for them.' But Eddie drinks that Ballantine, and he says to them, 'Well, we already got a record out so. We're going to make you a quarter of a million dollars in a year.' Eddie would say to me, 'Dick, you don't know the game. There's a lot of money in this. Ask for a quarter of a million dollars.' And Mark says to me, 'We've got to ask for some money.'" Dixon left the financial negotiations to his associates. Whatever deal they worked out—and he knew there was no way the record company was going to go along with Williams's pipe dreams—he figured he could live with it. He just wanted to make records. They signed a one-year contract that day—on Supreme's terms, not Williams's—and Supreme had them in the studio, recording, that night.

They'd cut a few tunes, including "Red Head 'n' Cadillac" (by Eddie Williams and drummer Ellis Walsh) and "Prairie Dog Hole" (by Hurley), Dixon recalls, when the record company people asked, "'You got any deep blues?' I say, 'Well, one. I've got the paper in my pocket here. It's "Broken Hearted." John Hogg give me this.' I put it up on the piano. I said, 'Let's start this, I'm going to do it in E flat.' I

did it one time. We played it back. Eddie said, 'What do you think
about that?' I said, 'Well we don't need to fool with it no more.' He
said, 'Well, don't fool with it no more. Press that! That's it.' So that's
the way we did that—one cut." A September 1949 *Billboard* review
of the disc accurately predicted success: "Dixon warbles a strong blues,
ably backed by the combo, setting a warming after-hours mood that
should snare heavy attention." "Broken Hearted" was not billed as
Dixon's record, however. "It was under the billing of 'Eddie Williams
and His Brown Buddies'; I was the vocal/piano," Dixon says, adding,
"Well, at that time I was a little young and didn't know the business
at all. I'd told Eddie that that was all right."

Not long after the recording session, Dixon went to Texas on his
own. To his surprise, "Every jukebox in the town, anywhere I could
go, I'd hear that record—it was a big hit in Texas. I picked up a *Cashbox* and all the way across there, 'Broken Hearted' was number one
in every little town." But when he tried telling friends or relatives
he'd made the record, he encountered skepticism. When he told one
friend, "'I put that record out,' she told me, 'No, that's by Eddie Williams.' I said, 'That's me singing.' 'No, that ain't you neither, Skeet!
Shut up! Don't tell anybody. Nobody would believe you.' I said, 'Well
OK. I'm going to go back because they probably is getting ready to
book me now. Will you lend me $15 so I can catch the train to go
back to California?' See, I had gone away and nobody knew where I
was, and I was ashamed to call and ask for some money. This is the
honest-to-God truth. She lent me that $15. And I sent her $30 back!
And I come on back to California and Mark said, 'My goodness, we've
got a hit! The William Morris Agency, which handles Nat King Cole,
wants to put the group on tour.'

"Broken Hearted" was our biggest tune," Dixon notes. "It stayed
in *Billboard* longer than any other thing I cut." In fact, "Broken Hearted" was on the *Billboard* R&B charts for seventeen weeks, beginning
September 17, 1949, peaking, on both the retail sales and jukebox
play charts, at number two. It garnered enough attention for at least
one other artist, the popular R&B singer-trumpeter-bandleader Joe
Morris, to record a cover version of it. In the meantime, Modern was
still releasing sides Dixon had previously recorded for them. On December 17, 1949, Modern's release of "Mississippi Blues" by the Floyd
Dixon Trio reached the number fourteen spot on *Billboard's* "Most
Played Jukebox" R&B chart, giving Dixon two hits on the charts at
the same time.

Ironically, Supreme declined to release one side, recorded at the
same session as "Broken Hearted," which Dixon feels might have been

bigger yet. That number was "Saturday Night Fish Fry," an original composed by the group's drummer Ellis Walsh. Walsh, Williams, and Dixon had agreed that they would all share equally, in terms of composer royalties, on tunes that any member of the group created. "We were all supposed to have a third; we had it agreed, signed," Dixon recalls. "But Ellis had lost his house up there, on Second Avenue right off Adams, just before we hit. So I didn't want a third of his song. I told him, 'Well, Ellis, I don't want any of your tune. You take out yourself for my part. And Eddie feels the same way.'" They both gave up their claims to the number, which Supreme had decided not to release because it was thought to be competition for "Broken Hearted." Walsh took the number to Berle Adams in Hollywood, who handled Louis Jordan, and Jordan recorded it promptly. On October 8, 1949, it began a twenty-three-week run on the R&B charts. "Saturday Night Fish Fry" would be the best-selling R&B record in the country for twelve of those weeks, reaching the number twenty-one spot on the pop charts as well and becoming one of Jordan's all-time best-known numbers. Dixon says the first royalty check alone that Walsh received was for nearly $5,000, and the house Walsh had lost for inability to keep up payments had been worth a total of perhaps $6,000.

Meanwhile, Dixon notes, "The version of 'Saturday Night Fish Fry' we'd cut first was still on the shelf. I think Louis Jordan listened to it and cut his version exactly the same way, exactly. The only difference was, the one said, 'Hey, boy, get away from that fish' at the end." There's no way of knowing, of course, whether Dixon's recording would have sold as well as Jordan's. Jordan was phenomenally popular during the forties and early fifties, and people bought his records to hear him, not just the songs. His 1949 recording of "Cole Slaw," for example, far outsold the recording that its composer, Jesse Stone, made of it. But Dixon would have welcomed the chance.

Dixon's insouciant singing of "Houston Jump," an original, related how a friend had told him that in New Orleans "there are some of the finest queens that he ever has seen" yet *he* believed the "Houston queens" were best. Less of Dixon's personality came through on "I Saw Stars," a trite, conventional love song about seeing stars when falling in love, coauthored by Hurley and one A. Swenson. His limitations as a singer of deep blues are apparent as he drifts along in a Charles Brown-influenced way on "It's Getting Foggy." The original's grim theme—that his ailing woman didn't have long to live—called for an artist with greater emotional impact, such as Jimmy Witherspoon.

In the meantime, "Homesick Blues," one of several numbers that Dixon had written for Brown, had become a big hit for Brown. It ran nine weeks on *Billboard*'s R&B charts, beginning December 3, 1949, peaking at number five. Homesickness was a topic that Dixon, uprooted from Texas as a boy, understood. He believes the record sold something like seven hundred thousand copies, although he received no composer royalties. At first, he thought that a check would be sent to him eventually. He was so busy with live appearances with Williams's group that he had no time to chase the royalties owed him. When he finally tried to call Eddie Mesner (who ran Aladdin Records, which had released "Homesick Blues") to ask when he'd be paid, Mesner's secretary told him Mesner was out of town and she did not know when he'd return. Dixon, never one to put up much of a fuss, let the matter drop. By training and temperament he wasn't one to protest, and he could rationalize that with the group in such demand there wasn't much point in wasting more time on a futile effort.

"We were recording. And then William Morris took us out of here—Eddie Williams's group featuring Floyd Dixon—on forty-five straight one-nighters," Dixon recalls. It was a memorable trip for him. "Boy, Mark went on the road with us! He went all down in Georgia and Texas. And when we first hit Texas, they didn't want him staying with us. Until I'd say, 'Well, if he can't stay, I ain't staying either because he's my manager.' So, he stayed. They said, 'Well, all right.' I told Mark, 'That's just a rule down here. In the black hotels, they don't want whites—there's liable to be a lot of trouble.' So he shut up. He couldn't understand it, though, because he had never been south. And he didn't believe certain things we saw. We had to go to the back of the cafe and wait outside, where we could drink water; when he was there we couldn't usually eat. That disturbed him. He'd say, 'What is going on?' I'd say, 'Well, that's just the law, Mark, that's all.' 'What kind of law?' I'd say, 'Well, it's the state law, here. When in Rome, do as the Romans do.' He never did. He just said, 'Well.'" On at least one occasion, Hurley had to stay in a separate hotel from Dixon.

Hurley went back to California before that tour was over. By now, Dixon's career seemed to be progressing nicely. None other than Joe Glaser—Louis Armstrong's manager—wanted to bring the group, which now included a sax in addition to piano, bass, drums, and guitar, into New York. They seemed bound for the big time. "What happened was, I got a little cocky there," Dixon says. "I had my new wagon I'd got—I'm going to tell the truth about it—so we were traveling and I said to Eddie, 'Watch your bass, it's going to crack my window there.' 'It ain't going to happen,' he said. So I get down in Beaumont and, so help me, his bass—that big upright—cracked my window. When we got paid I told him, 'You owe me $25 for my window.' We had almost $700 apiece that night because that was a real sell-out, it had run the percentage way up. I was getting all by percentage then. He said, 'No.' He got to drinking that Ballantine and he said, 'My bass can't talk. And I ain't bothering nobody. And ain't giving nobody no harm.' So I said OK. I just said that this is it. There wasn't no fighting or anything. I just wanted the window paid for. That was it. I let him out. And I cut right on back out of there. Made time on the highway. He took the train back to Los Angeles." That marked the end of the group. Dixon adds, "If Mark had have been with us, it would have probably been better, but he had left in Dallas on that trip—him and all his harmony."

Dixon, as was his custom, went off by himself to lick his wounds. When things would get stressful, he wouldn't voice anger, he'd withdraw. "I come on back to Los Angeles. And I didn't really like playing no more because I started to work in a sauerkraut factory." Later he took a job at National Storage. "I had to lift hundred-pound sacks there. I remember a white guy who had just been passing by walked over to me one day and said, 'Listen. This is unlawful for each one of you all to lift them hundred-pound sacks and set them up there. How long have you doing this?' I said, 'Well, we've been doing it ever since we've been here, three or four weeks.' He said, 'That shouldn't be no one-person's job, lifting them hundred-pound sacks like that. When you get fifty-five or sixty you won't be worth a dime, your back will be so bad.' But I just worked there six weeks. It didn't affect my back. The first three days, you'd be really sore. You'd have to take Absorbine Jr. After the third day, you can lift them hundred-pound sacks like they're nothing. There's a swing to it."

Meanwhile, Supreme Records, to the surprise of the artists who'd recorded for it, had declared bankruptcy. Dixon's career could have come to an end at that point. But Hurley helped coax him back to writing songs and performing and suggested the next move in Dixon's career. "Mark's such a nice friend of mine, I can't refuse him," Dixon says. "And then, after I got back with Mark, he said, 'I've got Johnny Moore. Now y'all will get together. Y'all will be all right. I know I got to look out for y'all or y'all will wind up killing another and acting crazy as it gets. If it don't be for me, y'all act like a sack of hogs. Well Dick, I can handle you but these other nuts, I so-and-so-and-so.' And he'd talk [Dixon chuckles at the memory], and Johnny'd scratch his head. Because he'd know Mark. They liked Mark. Everybody liked him. So Mark would get back in there, and we rehearsed and got it together."

In the meantime, Dixon's mother died. Swallowing his pride, Dixon approached the Biharis to ask whether they could give him some money so he could bury her. No deal. He next approached Don Robey of Peacock Records, who said that he would advance funds if Dixon, who agreed, would record some sides. Some said Robey was a gangster, and Dixon had heard that he'd pistolwhipped performers but that didn't concern him. He was just glad to be able to treat his mother with respect. He recorded eight sides for Robey, including the moving "Sad Journey," the mood of which was likely affected by the loss of his mother.

Robey made minimal efforts at promoting the records, saying that he couldn't afford to spend much on promoting Dixon unless Dixon could make a long-term commitment to the label (Robey had a reputation for signing artists to long-term exclusive contracts for little money), which Dixon was unwilling to do. Instead, Dixon soon signed with Aladdin Records, a company small compared to the major record companies but significantly bigger than Peacock. The idea—Hurley's idea, actually—was that Dixon would record for Aladdin backed by Johnny Moore's Three Blazers. Aladdin would be getting two names with proven drawing power. Dixon recalls, "Eddie Mesner said, 'I'll take a chance for a different sound; I'll gamble with you.'"

Although Mesner may have talked as if he were taking a big gamble, he had enough confidence in Dixon's sales potential to buy rights to the eight sides that Dixon had cut for Robey. Dixon's understanding was that Mesner paid Robey something like $5,000 up front and then monthly payments of $1,000 for eight or nine months. One of the sides initially released by Peacock and now released by Aladdin, "Sad Journey," made the number eight spot on *Billboard*'s "Most Played Jukebox" R&B chart in November 1950. Mesner knew that he had a valuable property.

The combination of Dixon with the Three Blazers also proved wise. Aladdin's recording of "Telephone Blues" by Floyd Dixon backed by Johnny Moore's Three Blazers, for which Dixon shared composer credits with Eddie Mesner, enjoyed a six-week run (peaking at number four) on *Billboard*'s R&B charts, beginning January 20, 1951. The song projected the anguish of trying to reach out to a loved one who wasn't there. In the song, Dixon begs the long-distance operator to try his baby's number once again. It was a theme to which he would later return for one of his biggest hits, and music historian Arnold Shaw wrote that Dixon's "recording career was focused on a single subject."[1]

Shaw, however, was grossly overstating things. Throughout his career, Dixon recorded considerably varied material and, he adds, he would have recorded even more had record producers permitted him to do so. Consider just the numbers he recorded for Aladdin in the year or so that he was backed by the Blazers (Johnny and Oscar Moore on guitars, Johnny Miller on bass, and Ellis Walsh on drums, with Maxwell Davis sometimes added on tenor sax), most of which he wrote himself. Among the more memorable sides were the jumping "Real Lovin' Mama" (which gave Dixon a chance to play some of his boogie piano), the brooding "Bad Neighborhood" (which began with the idea that people gossiped too much when he wished they'd mind their business and leave him alone—an unusual and perhaps revealing line), the laid-back "Married Woman" (performed Charles Brown-style), and the sensitive "Do I Love You?" (on which Dixon was backed just by Oscar Moore, who played an exquisite solo, and Miller; to achieve the finesse they desired, they rehearsed the number for a month before it was recorded). Further variety was obtained with "Blues for Cuba" (which had a calypso beat), the more conventional "San Francisco Blues," "Time and Place" (an earthy, exuberant celebration of drinking and "messing around"—"we'll have lots of fun making love to each other"), "Empty Stocking Blues" (an obvious attempt to duplicate the success of Charles Brown's "Merry Christmas Baby," with composer credit shared by Hurley and Johnny Moore), and "Girl Fifteen."

Most radio stations couldn't play "Girl Fifteen," Dixon's spirited ode to jailbait ("I like them young, when they're in their prime. . . . When they get old the feeling gets cold"). Mari Jones, sharing vocal duties with him, noted that she was fifteen but "not green" and vowed that everything she had was his and that when the police came to take him away, they'd have to take her, too. They had fun performing the number in concerts, too. They were so convincing, singing to one another, that fans assumed they were involved off-stage. Speculation grew more lively as it became increasingly obvious that Jones, a minor, was pregnant. But there was never anything between them. Jones and Johnny Moore were a couple, according to Dixon, and they had two children. Nor was there any truth to the notion—although Dixon encouraged such reports in the black press—that anything was going on romantically between Dixon and Ruth Brown; that was simply publicity. Fans loved such gossip, which many found easy to believe because Dixon's songs sometimes presented him as a womanizer. Of course, anything that kept a performer's name before the public helped draw crowds.

By Dixon's standards—considering he hadn't had much money growing up—he was making great sums on the road. Conversely, he

wasn't making much from his records. He was pleased that the contract he'd signed with Aladdin entitled him to royalties as a recording artist: one-quarter of a cent per record. That meant that if a record
sold a hundred thousand copies, he would be entitled to $250 in roy-
alties. He was too naive about the business, he now realizes, to have
known whether he had been given a fair contract. In fact, Dixon recalls being surprised one day to hear Leo Mesner tell his brother Eddie that the contract's terms really weren't good enough for Dixon.
Eddie Mesner replied that he'd try to do better by Dixon in the future. At that point, though, Dixon had no complaints. Aladdin was
promoting the records well, advertising in trade publications like *Billboard,* and getting jukebox and radio play wherever possible. Of
course, the records helped spur interest in his personal appearances.

For five or six years, until demand tapered off, Dixon estimates
that he was on the road eleven months a year, hitting nearly all of
the country. In the early years he often booked himself, with his own
band and maybe an opening act; in later years, when his own name
didn't have as much drawing power, he performed more often as part
of multi-act package shows. He played everywhere, from New York
to Providence, to Atlanta, to Wilmington, to Lynchburg, to Boston—
and always, always, in Texas, where he had an especially loyal following and felt particularly at home. He loved playing Texas so much
that in order to return there he would agree to flat payment deals
rather than insisting on a percentage of the gate. Some bookers likely took advantage of him, but he had plenty of money for the time
being and plenty of fans (even some fan clubs), so he didn't worry
about being used. He'd hear his records on jukeboxes in many areas
he visited. Although they never made the national *Billboard* charts,
they were apparently regional hits.

Performing was almost a calling for Dixon. He was well aware of
the impact he could have upon people. "Well, you get out there and
you're doing it. You're trying to make people happy and there's a real
power—I saved a few lives playing. I know this to be a fact," he says
emphatically. "I know a boy was going to really go harm three people one night. And it just so happened I walks up—we were going in
to play a dance there—and one fellow said to me, 'Floyd Dixon, I'm
definitely coming to your dance tonight.' And when this other boy,
who hadn't known it was me standing there, heard that, he went
on about, 'Is that Floyd Dixon? Well, I'll be dogged! I got your record
"Mississippi Blues." Well, I've just got into town from Memphis and
I didn't know nothing about your playing here. Let me go get me a
ticket now.' And he just completely made a different change altogeth-

er. Right there he settled down. He forgot about hurting anybody. And everybody know he was off. I'm just showing you how different things happen. And I saw what some people can do by music. Just completely turn into another human being."

But the constant touring was exhausting, and the periodic difficulties in finding accommodations due to racial prejudice didn't help matters. Promoters tried to line up dates for him as close to one another as possible, but their main goal was to keep him working as many dates as possible, ensuring a steady flow of earnings for him—and them—even if it meant, sometimes, bone-wearying jumps of four or five hundred miles between gigs. Promoters had ways to get him plenty of bookings, even in regions where he wasn't well known. "Oh, I was busy all the time. There wasn't no such thing as 'being off.' Yeah, they kept a solid book," Dixon recalls. "I'd tour down in Florida twenty-five days, and then up in around Ohio, would take thirty-five or forty days. You'd go from one string of dates to the next date. It wasn't like you'd work three days and you're off six. You'd have to have twenty-five days and then off one. Yeah. Or forty-five days and no day off. And the promoter would be telling people booking us, 'If you lose on that, I'll send you a powerhouse the next time. Or two of the biggest acts to come through here.' But you'd have to take some of the lower stuff, too. Just like with a record company. When I'd put out a hit record, maybe Amos Milburn would put out one then that wasn't doing so good. The record company would say, 'You can buy fifteen hundred of Floyd Dixon's "Operator 210" but you've also got to get eight hundred of Amos Milburn's so-and-so or Charles Brown's so-and-so.' Even if it wasn't selling, you had to do it. Or maybe somebody'd be saying to the record company: 'I want five thousand of Charles Brown's "Black Night."' They'd be told: 'Well, you've got to take fifteen hundred of Floyd Dixon's "Tired, Broke, and Busted."' Yeah. They was good at it then.

"I would tour with a band—like two saxes, guitar, bass, and drums. Chuck Willis used to be with me. We grew up together nicely. And T-Bone Walker was with me three or four times. His son—T-Bone Junior—and I had finished Jefferson High School together. And B. B. King's first professional dates, we were together at the Robertson Auditorium in Little Rock, Arkansas. And oh, Larry Davis, yes indeed—before he cut 'Texas Flood.' Oh my, I heard him down in Arkansas, and I got his band to play about fifteen or twenty dates with me. I liked his bass so much, and boy, he could play a tune.

"Some that have toured with me, at one time or another, include Ray Charles, Jimmy Witherspoon, Lowell Fulson, Charles Brown,

Margie Day, Ruth Brown, John Lee Hooker, the Clovers, Etta James. I've played on packages with some of everybody," including, through the years, Big Joe Turner, Esther Phillips, Ivory Joe Hunter, and Bo Diddley. And he wasn't always teamed with rhythm and blues acts. He was thrilled to be paired, for example, on dates with Louis Armstrong's All-Stars, and to play piano with Harry James's band for a March of Dimes benefit. Dixon especially loved the way Armstrong and James played trumpet and would have had a trumpeter in his band had he been able to find a good one who played in their styles. He got to work on some bills with Lionel Hampton, and Hampton also used him as his pianist on one recording session (on October 16, 1951), cutting "Samson's Boogie" (composer credits shared by Dixon and Hampton), "Crying," "Helpless," and "Jumpin' with G. H." for MGM Records.

Ray Charles—who, in the opinion of blues authority Sheldon Harris, was influenced somewhat by Dixon—was not yet famous when he toured for awhile with Dixon around 1951 or 1952. He had been touring as pianist in Lowell Fulson's band and recording on his own as a singer and pianist for a tiny record label called Swing Time. Charles was then working mostly in a Charles Brown-Nat King Cole kind of vein, sometimes even recording with musicians from Johnny Moore's Three Blazers; producers always like copying proven styles. He would croon derivatively rather than apply the gospel feel to pop music as he later did so successfully. When he toured with Dixon, Charles hadn't yet found his own identity, although suggestions of a future style would surface occasionally. Dixon recalls one night when they were playing "at the Armory in Muncie, Indiana. I heard Ray singing [a gospel number], 'Lord, Do Something for Me.' Sounded good. So when he come back to the dressing room, I said, 'Ray, when you get to New York, you get on the church kick and you're going.' He said, 'You think so?' I said, 'I know so.' He said, 'OK.' So when he went up there, I guess he was planning on getting on that. I'd wanted to do it myself. But the record companies wouldn't cut me on country and western and religious. I said, 'This is coming in— country and western and the church kick.' I wanted to cut it with a band behind me. Whoo! But they wouldn't let me do that. Well, Ray got on it and he was gone: 'Hallelujah, I Love Her So' and all that. Now you ask Ray—didn't I tell him that?" Despite having grown up in Texas, the only record Dixon had recorded with a country and western feel to it was "Prairie Dog Hole." He had recorded a couple of traditional gospel numbers in 1949, "Precious Lord" and "Milky White Way," but sales had been slight. Mesner wasn't interested in

Dixon getting on any "church kick" or "country and western kick," much less backed by a costly band.

In those days, Dixon was making more money than Charles—not that it always seemed to matter much. At one point when they were touring together—in Lexington, Kentucky, Dixon recalls—Charles came to Dixon, asking for his pay, and they discovered that the show's emcee had pocketed everyone's money and skipped town. Dixon called booker Billy Shaw in New York, who wired funds so they could continue their tour. Such incidents were just considered the hardships of life on the road. Simply getting from gig to gig was not always easy. For example, in 1952, when Dixon was probably at his zenith of popularity, he recalls, "Eddie Mesner gave us a car that got busted before I got to El Paso, and I missed three of the biggest dates. Herbert Walker said it was the biggest crowd he had ever had in Waco, and at the Rose Room in Dallas it was a sell-out, too. He kept a little money owed me from another date, which I agreed to because he had lost money when they'd had to give people their money back because I'd never showed up. It was just something out there on the road, then."

One recurring source of frustration for Dixon on the road, whether working with set bands as he did in the early fifties or with pick-up musicians as was more common in later years, was having to deal with drunken or less than conscientious musicians. Although his songs often celebrated drinking—a familiar theme in R&B—liquor didn't play an important part in Dixon's life, and eventually he swore off drinking altogether. Today, he neither drinks nor smokes.

Dixon's recording association with the Three Blazers had ended within a year, although from time to time he still worked with individual members of the group, either on record dates or live gigs. He considered Oscar Moore, who had taught him a lot about music, to be about the finest jazz guitarist anywhere, and Johnny Moore the finest blues guitarist. He continued using similar instrumentation on his records, and fans probably didn't notice any dramatic change when he changed personnel. He used Eddie Williams as bassist on dates when opportunities permitted, too.

Being almost constantly on the move made it hard for Dixon to maintain close personal ties. (He became quite a good letter-writer, though.) Although he still considered Los Angeles his home and tried to maintain contact with old friends whenever he happened to be home, most of time he was traveling from gig to gig. He was no longer managed by Mark Hurley, and although they were no longer as close as they had once been the two shared a bond until Hurley died nearly thirty years after they'd met. Because Hurley was important to him, Dixon takes time to talk of his later years: "Mark married this lady in his older life—when he was close to eighty—and she didn't want him doing anything, period. But she didn't stop him from *every day* coming to see me. *Every* day. Seven days a week, he'd be over to see that everything was OK with me—then he'd go by Eddie Williams. 'Y'all need anything?' He'd get us anything we wanted. We never did—I wouldn't have took it because he's too nice. You don't take kindness for weakness. Eddie wouldn't take nothing either, at no time. He said, 'That's a good old man, boy.' I said, 'You better believe it is.' When he died, Eddie and his wife went to his funeral, and I didn't know about it 'til after he was buried. Well, of course it wasn't Eddie's fault that I wasn't in town. But, he was a good man. And his wife was good. She was just a lady that wanted her husband home with her. Her name was Helen. I went out to his house. They lived in the Valley. Nice home and everything. She just wanted him, uh, she didn't know me like he did. And she wanted her husband to herself, that's all. I don't know just when Mark died. It seems like yesterday to me. Because old Mark's a good cat, man. They don't make 'em like him. He was a good fellow. Charles Brown will tell you the same thing, Eddie Williams or anybody else that knew him."

Dixon remembers plenty of times in his career when he wished Hurley could have been there to voice concern over missing royalties. So long as Dixon had money in his pocket, he wasn't overly worried about contracts or royalties. In 1952 he scored heavily with a new number he'd written, "Call Operator 210," in which—just as in his earlier hit "Telephone Blues"—he was trying to get an unresponsive girlfriend to return his calls. Beginning July 26, 1952, the record stayed on *Billboard*'s R&B charts for eleven weeks, peaking at number four. Other artists' cover versions of "Operator 210" sold well, too, validating Dixon's abilities as a songwriter. Johnny Otis's orchestra, with vocalist Mel Walker (who had gone to Jefferson High School with Dixon), recorded a cover version for Mercury Records that made *Billboard*'s charts for four weeks, rising as high as number four on the "Most Played Juke Box Rhythm and Blues Records" chart. Another artist, whose name Dixon has forgotten, also recorded a cover version with a country and western feel. Dixon *should* have made some decent money on composer royalties. But, he says, "I didn't get a penny out of Johnny Otis's recording 'Operator 210' for Mercury. I really should have gotten a lawyer for that, because it's my song and I had it copyrighted and everything. That's when I got kind of poison-minded on the music business, behind that tune, because I was just coming in to realize that a person should be paid for what they do."

Dixon knew that he was worth more than Aladdin was paying him. He was a hot property as both a performer and a songwriter. That was confirmed, he recalls, when Atlantic Records made him a verbal offer of a $50,000 advance on royalties, with the assurance of continuing good royalties in years to come, if he'd sign a ten-year contract. "I was talking to Atlantic Records in New York—Ahmet Ertegun," he recalls. "But Eddie Mesner wouldn't give me a release from our contract; I still had nine more months with him. And I offered to give *him* $10,000 cash money to get out of the contract. But he wouldn't give me a release. Because he hated for Atlantic to give me that $50,000 advance, and guarantee me 150,000 records behind each release. That's what they were doing. See, they know Atlantic would put them records everywhere."

Dixon is convinced he lost out in a big way because Eddie Mesner held him back. "I couldn't call that a friend," he says of Mesner. "If I try to hold somebody to a deal when he's got a better opportunity somewhere else, then I'm not his friend. I'm only looking out for my own protective selfish self. And I'm envious of him to get a little ahead. That's what you call envy, malice. I would say Eddie was envy and malice and didn't want me to get in a position because at that time, with the stuff I had written and the stuff I had, I'd have had been able to buy Atlantic. They wanted to give Joe Morris 50 percent of Atlantic Records so they could keep all the money on 'Shake a Hand,' which he wrote. I told him, 'If someone would offer me 50 percent of the company, I wouldn't even ask nobody about that. I'd get that signed and notarized and give him all of it.' Joe Morris could have had 50 percent of Atlantic. That was a dumb move he made, because 'Shake a Hand' died right after. My goodness! That was the deal of the year, man." Dixon was in a comparable position. Public interest in him was as fervent as it would ever be. Although he had no way of knowing it at the time, "Operator 210" would prove to be his last chart hit. He would continue to score with some regional successes and would continue to be a solid draw on the road, but his popularity had reached its zenith.

Atlantic would no doubt have welcomed having any of Aladdin's stars on its label, for in the early fifties Aladdin had the hottest West Coast R&B singers, with Charles Brown, Amos Milburn, and Dixon all tightly under contract. Brown was turning out such hits as "Seven Long Days" and "Hard Times." Milburn's recent "Bad, Bad Whiskey" and "Let's Rock a While" were but two of nineteen R&B chart hits he recorded for Aladdin between 1946 and 1956. Of course, Milburn wasn't about to leave that label; he was married, Dixon recalls, to Eddie Mesner's niece. In 1952 Atlantic Records was still small but it was steadily growing, its owners wisely investing in its future. They thought bigger—more in terms of what was best for long-term development—than did the Mesners or the Biharis.

In 1952 Atlantic bought Ray Charles's contract from the financially strapped Swing Time record label for a paltry $2,500. In the next couple of years, Charles—with Atlantic's support and encouragement—moved away from polished crooning in the style of Charles Brown to a gutsier, more individualistic, gospel-inflected sound, sometimes boldly reworking church numbers into pop tunes. His 1955 smash "I've Got a Woman," for example, was adapted from a gospel number he'd liked called "I've Got a Savior." He later branched out into country and western recordings as well. Dixon, naturally, has enormous respect for Ray Charles's talent, but he's also firmly convinced Charles never would have become the great and enduring sensation he became had he not signed with Atlantic Records. There was a limit to what a label like Swing Time could do, even with a Ray Charles. Atlantic recorded him right and committed the resources needed to promote him right. Charles had his first R&B chart hit for Atlantic in 1954; he would have no less than twenty-one additional chart hits for them before leaving the label in 1960. Dixon, reflecting on Charles's phenomenal success, can't help but raise thoughts of what might have been in his own career.

Dixon continued recording, although he was growing increasingly disenchanted with Eddie Mesner. On Dixon's original "Tired, Broke, and Busted," he sang of feeling like a fool, of feeling used—by a girlfriend in the lyrics of the song—but he was definitely feeling used in real life by Mesner and people like him. On "The River," which had the most despondent theme of any Dixon recorded, he sang of not wanting to see another day, of being irresistibly drawn to the river. The record seemed to be a bargain-basement answer to Billie Holiday's classic "Gloomy Sunday," which reportedly had actually impelled some listeners to suicide. Minimal backing was provided by a guitar, bass, and flute—Maxwell Davis, setting an eerie mood. The sound, not uncharacteristically, seems a bit on the boxy side (Atlantic's recordings generally sounded fuller and more vibrant, thanks to superior recording engineering by Tom Dowd). The record concluded with the sound of water splashing—presumably Dixon jumping into the river to end it all—a schlocky production touch that lent an almost camp sensibility.

Floyd Dixon, 1991. (Author's collection; courtesy of Right Time Productions)

Floyd Dixon in the late forties—a publicity shot taken in North Hollywood early in his career. (Author's collection; courtesy of Right Time Productions)

When the now-defunct Supreme record label placed this ad in *Billboard,* September 24, 1949, Dixon was featured on piano and vocals with bassist Eddie Williams's group. The ad shows (left to right) Floyd Dixon, Eddie Williams, Tiny Webb, and Eddie Walsh. (Author's collection)

When Aladdin placed this ad in *Billboard,* December 2, 1950, Dixon was being given star billing, singing and playing piano with Johnny Moore's Three Blazers (a role that had previously been filled by his friend Charles Brown). (Author's collection)

This rare record sleeve, which Aladdin used for its 78-rpm singles in the early fifties, depicts four of Aladdin's R&B singing stars—Charles Brown, Floyd Dixon, Amos Milburn, and Calvin Boze—along with jazz tenor saxist Lester Young. (Author's collection; courtesy of Right Time Productions)

Charles Brown drops in to catch Floyd Dixon at the China Club in Hollywood, February 1991. (Author's collection; courtesy of Right Time Productions)

Dixon was disappointed that Aladdin opted not to release some recordings he made that he liked, such as "Blues in My Heart" and "The Glory of Love." He would have liked, too, to have recorded more jazz piano. His brighter side came through on "Red Cherries" (a double-entendre number) and "Wine, Wine, Wine." If the latter, celebrating how good wine makes you feel, did not sell as well as other R&B artists' songs in the vein, at least one liquor manufacturer—whose brand of wine Dixon had mentioned in his recording—gave him cartons of wine in gratitude.

Aladdin's studio recordings captured only a fraction of the spirit Dixon exhibited in actual performances. He sounds wonderfully relaxed, ebullient, and uninhibited on "Baby, Let's Go Down to the Woods" and "Too Much Jelly Roll," live 1951 concert recordings taped at Frank Bull and Gene Norman's Blues Jamboree at the Los Angeles Shrine Auditorium (both included in the album *Floyd Dixon: Opportunity Blues*). As soon as Dixon utters the words, "Baby let's go down to the woods," the audience, titillated by him, laughs appreciatively. He's suggestive, yet with a disarming kind of innocence. He promises, "You'll sure come back feeling real good," and his fans laugh some more. He's thoroughly up front about his desires but there's no leering quality, rather an open acceptance of sexual feelings. In that regard, he was earthier than Charles Brown, who had a touch of prim dignity. Dixon came across as more of a scalawag. He beckons his girl, in the song, to invite him to her house when her folks aren't at home. He proclaims candidly, "I'm getting tired of sleeping by myself." That line that would have been far too explicit for most radio stations in the early 1950s, but it's apparent on the live performance that he has thoroughly connected with his young audience. He scats a bit, too, in a charming, modern-jazz inflected way that was never captured on his studio recordings. The band sounds utterly at ease, and the guitar and sax get to play more than on a typical studio recording.

Overall, "Baby, Let's Go Down to the Woods" is a winning performance. It's not wholly polished and ends a bit weakly, but it's filled with life and makes much of the pop music of the era sound plastic by comparison. You can see why this music so appealed to all who heard it. You can also hear in this music a predecessor to early rock 'n' roll. "Baby, Let's Go Down to the Woods" was, like most of the songs Dixon performed, an original. "Too Much Jelly Roll," by contrast, was the creation of two eighteen-year-old whites who had a deep interest in black popular music and were soon to become major rock 'n' roll songwriters: Jerry Leiber and Mike Stoller. Although "Too Much

Jelly Roll" is hardly one of their most original creations—Billy Eckstine had scored one of his biggest hits singing "Jelly Roll" in 1940 (and
he had based his song on a still-older black vaudeville routine)—it's
catchy and fits Dixon's personality. He has fun singing such lines as,
"Well, I'm twenty-seven but I look like I'm ninety-fo' / The cause of
my condition is too much jelly roll" and urging his tenor saxist, "Blow,
Max!"—which Davis, of course, proceeds to do. It's a pity that more
of the high-spirited vitality heard in these live performances could not
have been captured in Dixon's studio recordings.

It's also a pity that Eddie Mesner couldn't have done more to keep
his artists satisfied. He would have served his own long-term interests by being more flexible. Around this time, Charles Brown sued
Aladdin for underpayment of royalties, and Dixon, because he wasn't
being given enough freedom to record the way he wanted to, was
losing interest in recording. How did it profit Aladdin to have de-
moralized performers under contract? Dixon says, "I just recorded
with Eddie Mesner until I got to see he wasn't treating me fairly.
Maxwell, a guy I knew that loved all musicians and strays, he saw
how Eddie was doing me and all of that. Maxwell said to me, 'Go
ask that man for $25,000. You're putting all these hits out and ev-
erything like that. He hasn't sent you a royalty check. That's not
right.' But I did ask Eddie for $5,000. Eddie pulled a bunch of $500
bills folded like that, out of his pocket, and said, 'I'll see you when I
come back from the race track.' He went out there and he just never
gave it to me."

By this point, public tastes in R&B had shifted markedly from individual singers to vocal groups. Not everyone had recognized the
significance of the shift, but *Billboard*'s rhythm and blues reporter Bob
Rolontz had noted presciently as early as September 15, 1951, that
vocal groups were generally selling stronger than individuals; he
wrote of a growing trend. By 1953 and 1954, it was obvious to anyone in the record business that vocal groups were where the action
was, a reality that lowered the market value of recording artists such
as Dixon.

"When I did get released from the contract with Aladdin, I cut a
couple of sessions for Art Rupe, but I didn't sign no exclusive thing
with him," Dixon recalls. In the late forties, Rupe had established his
company, called Specialty because it specialized in black music—blues
and gospel—with an investment of only $600. Through the fifties and
sixties he went on to sell some two hundred million discs, invested
his profits in oil and real estate, and retired from producing records a
far wealthier man than nearly all of the artists he'd recorded. Dixon

was satisfied with the way some of the sides he made for Rupe in 1953 and 1954 turned out, notably "Please Don't Go." And in his "Hard Living Alone" he gave as effective a blues performance as any he'd recorded, touching in its heartfelt simplicity. Singing how hard it is to go through life alone, obviously Dixon drew lyrics from his life: "Never had no father to call my own. . . . I had a mother but now she's dead and gone; yes, and Marshall, Texas is my home." There is a note of wariness, too, from a man who's been burned too often, in a line like: "Don't have nobody I can have faith in." This is Dixon at his most natural and convincing. Several years later when Art Rupe and his wife, Leona, divorced, she started her own record company, called Ebb, and got Dixon to record a couple of sides for her. By then Art Rupe's biggest-selling artist was Little Richard; she tried to compete by having Dixon record a number called "Ooh Little Girl" in Little Richard's style, which didn't sound convincing.

Dixon kept on touring, appearing in clubs and theaters that included the Flame Show Bar in Detroit, the Riviera Club in St. Louis, the Regal Theater in Chicago, the Howard Theater in Washington, D.C., and the Royal Theater in Baltimore. The number of radio stations carrying R&B was increasing, and more and more white teens were discovering—and coming out for—R&B shows. Some in the record business understood clearly that growth in the R&B market would depend on white consumption. They did whatever they could to expand the market, from paying off disc jockeys to give their records airtime ("payola") to getting white performers to record cover versions of songs blacks had introduced. Some whites "blackened" their style a bit, and some black performers developed more "polish"—at times diluting their impact—so they'd be more acceptable to white mainstream tastes. They wanted records that would have a broad appeal. This was the atmosphere from which rock 'n' roll would emerge.

In April 1954 Atlantic Records started a subsidiary label called Cat. The name, as Atlantic told *Billboard*, was deliberately chosen to appeal to that subset of mostly poor southern white teens who preferred black rhythm and blues to white hillbilly or pop music and who had taken to calling themselves "cats." They often lived in slum communities along with blacks, took the same kinds of low-paying jobs as were then typically available to blacks in the South, and—in marked contrast to most whites in the segregated South—sometimes shopped at stores that mostly served blacks. Brightly colored clothes, for example, from Lansky's in Memphis, were popular.

Atlantic signed Dixon to cut sides for the new label. He was glad to be connected with Atlantic finally, although he notes, "I just got a few thousand bucks, not the deal they had offered me back then." He recorded, in April and November of 1954, such numbers as "Roll Baby Roll," "Is It True," "When I Get Lucky," "Two Piano Blues," "Floyd's Blues," and "Hey Bartender." They were lively and fetching, but sales were disappointingly low. Dixon recalls, "I'm going to say one thing—Atlantic was the only clean company. They did more for any artists in the business; they paid more royalties than anybody." He still gets some royalties from Atlantic, he notes, for reissues it has on the market currently of his recordings "Hey Bartender" and "Floyd's Blues." But Atlantic didn't see enough public interest in Dixon in the mid-fifties to continue with him. The company was then doing great business with singers such as Ray Charles, Ruth Brown, and Joe Turner and with such vocal groups—for which the public seemed to have an especially strong appetite—as the Clovers (twenty chart hits for Atlantic between 1951 and 1956) and the Drifters (thirty-six chart hits for Atlantic between 1953 and 1967).

In 1957 Dixon recorded for John Dolphin, who owned a Central Avenue record store, on his Cash record label. Although Dixon came to feel that Dolphin was a fast-talker, forever promising more than he delivered, Dolphin did it so transparently that Dixon laughed off his behavior—or at least tried to. Others viewed Dolphin's wheeling and dealing less charitably; one fellow took a shot at him. Dixon recalls Dolphin saying, for example, that he would make Dixon rich, promising him $50,000 for eight sides. When Dolphin gave him a thick wad of cash in payment for recording, Dixon put the money—which he believed totaled $5,000 or more—into his pocket quickly. Upon later examination, Dixon found that although a $50 bill was on the top and a $20 was on the bottom, the rest of the bills were merely ones; the whole wad totaled just $175. Dixon sought to see the humor in the situation—he wanted to get along with the people he dealt with—but, ultimately, working for such pay was demoralizing.

He kept recording for one small label or another such as Pearl (around 1956), Checker (1956), Kent (1958), Swingin' (1960), Dodge (1961), and Chatta-Hoo-Chie (1962), striving—not always wisely—to stay contemporary. He also continued touring, doing a lot of midwestern one-nighters, into the early sixties. When J. Fleming, Amos Milburn's manager, got Dixon ten Chicago gigs, he was so grateful that he listed Fleming as the songwriter for a couple of songs Dixon had written and recorded, "Alarm Clock Blues" and "I'm Ashamed of Myself" so Fleming would receive any royalties due the songwriter.

Dixon scored one last regional hit in Texas with "Tight Skirts," a

1960 recording in which he was backed by Buster Smith's exuberantly rocking band. Smith was a gifted saxist and arranger who should
have become better known than he did. He had been a key element
in the original, Kansas City-based Count Basie Band—he was largely
responsible for devising "One O'Clock Jump"—but spent most of his
career in the relative obscurity of Texas. On the cut, Dixon is in fine
form, exulting about how tight skirts really move him and relating how
one chick had told him, "Don't waste my time if you don't have no
money." "Sure as a dog's a pup, dead presidents [money] really cracks
her up," he adds in his highly idiomatic speech. The impact of Dixon
and Smith's strong band is undercut, however, by the low-budget recording sound. Had the same side been cut in a first-rate studio with
a first-rate engineer in New York—as, for example, Ray Charles's sides
were by this point—it would have had greater marketability.

In 1961 Dixon recorded an original in Houston, Texas, called "Opportunity Blues"; in 1963 Louis Jordan paid him the compliment of
recording it, retitled as "My Friends." But that year Dixon dropped
out of sight. He had become worn down by the long years of travel
and exploitation. At thirty-five he hadn't the heart to keep pushing
any longer. He picked a good time to get out. Public interest in R&B,
which had long been on the decline, was about to take a nosedive.
In January 1964 the Beatles broke through with their first chart-topping hit, "I Want to Hold Your Hand," and opened the floodgates
for British groups, which soon thoroughly dominated popular music. In the mid-sixties almost no one would have been listening to a
middle-aged R&B singer-pianist struggling to make a comeback.

Now that he was no longer touring, Dixon could devote time to
studying and reflecting upon matters of faith, a topic always of considerable interest to him. He takes time to expound on his personal
beliefs, almost preaching to me in words that gradually fall into a
compelling cadence: "Well, I'll tell you one thing—I recognize God
before anything else. And not in some of my activities, but in all of
them. I believe that the universe can be your friend or your enemy.
And I believe that God is *mind*. A person live and move and have
his being in mind. That's why Christ said, 'Let this mind be in you
that was in Christ, Jesus.' Mind is all there is. Mind. Sound mind.
Immortal mind. But mortal mind is of error. A person is immortal,
so if a person would ever know how to keep that spirit pure on a
pure level, et. cetera, that knows all there is. There's something up
here in your mind that knows all there is. That's why the Bible said,
'He that is in you is greater than he that is the world.' It means that
spirit of mind. And it knows all, sees all, and is all. There's no knowl-

edge that it does not know. You might not comprehend it because the channels of your idiosynthesy of senses might not be open. But it's still there and knows all. It's omnipresent. *Any present.* See. 'I give life without beginning and without ending because I am life. I am the substance of all because I am that I am.' All spirit. Substance of all. Out of one blood, all nations was built. One blood. *All* nations was built." If the points he is trying to communicate are not always clearly verbalized, the intensity of his convictions comes across strongly. He has written songs, too, that are rooted in his spiritual beliefs, songs—less marketable than his blues songs—dealing with the need for wisdom and harmony.

From time to time, Dixon would reemerge on the performing scene briefly, only to vanish into obscurity shortly afterward. In 1970 he recorded a few sides for an obscure label called Boxer. In 1971 Charles Brown coaxed his old buddy to sing a duet with him, "For You," on Brown's album *Blues and Brown* (Jewel) and prodded him to get out and entertain. Before dropping out of sight again, Dixon gigged a bit, performing around 1971 at such clubs as Sweet Pea in Santa Monica and Mr. Jones' Pub in nearby Venice and on dates in the Beaumont, Texas, area with Z. Z. Hill. Reports of his whereabouts surfaced, but irregularly. In 1973, for example, he worked outside of music and lived with the popular rock 'n' roll disc jockey Wolfman Jack.

San Francisco blues disc jockey-writer Tom Mazzolini had no idea what Dixon was doing, but he occasionally played Dixon's recordings on his show on KPOO-FM. He consequently wasn't sure whether the fellow who walked into his show one Saturday night in 1974 and said that he was Floyd Dixon was the real item—even if the fellow did resemble old pictures of Dixon. (During the peak of Dixon's popularity, at least two "Floyd Dixons" were known to have booked themselves in Texas and in Florida.) Mazzolini wasn't accustomed to having "lost" legendary bluesmen simply drop by. But they talked, and Mazzolini helped Dixon get a gig a few weeks later at a club called Minnie's Can-Do. Hearing Dixon sing a bit of his "Hey Bartender" there dispelled any remaining doubts Mazzolini may have had. On March 22 and May 17, 1975, he taped two and a half hours of interviews with Dixon. He noted, "Dixon was open and freely discussed his musical career. He was less free about his personal life, and call it writer's instinct or what, I felt some regions were better left unexplored."[2]

Mazzolini learned that Dixon lived in a hotel south of Market Street, a poorer neighborhood in San Francisco, and worked for an old friend from Marshall, Texas, R. L. "Smitty" Smith. He was rehearsing daily, sometimes alone, sometimes backed by white musicians.

He'd written new songs, which he'd taken care to copyright, and seemed ready to come back. And with Mazzolini helping to champion him, Dixon's career did start up again. Mazzolini gave Dixon exposure not only through his radio show but also through a substantial profile of him in the September 1975 issue of *Living Blues,* the leading magazine in the field. "The role Floyd Dixon has played in the evolution of the West Coast blues scene has long been overlooked," Mazzolini noted in his piece, which simultaneously alerted older blues fans internationally about Dixon's availability and helped introduce him to many too young to have known his early R&B hits.[3]

Dixon became much more visible in the region, performing in 1975, for example, at the San Francisco Blues Festival, at the Cat's Cradle and Exploratorium in San Francisco, at Ruthie's in Berkeley, and on a local television show, "Perspective" (KGO-TV). He performed at the University of Chicago's Festival of the Arts in 1976 as well. Although he didn't get an American record contract or do the national touring that would have been necessary to revive his career in the United States fully, he was invited to give a concert for the Scandinavian Blues Association, in Orebro, Sweden, in 1975. The appearance led to further exposure in Scandinavia via recordings (on the album *Live in Sweden* [Great Dane, 1975] he was accompanied by Swedish musicians), concerts, and television. In 1978 he played the R&B Festival in Groningen, Netherlands. In 1980 Dixon, Charles Brown, and Ruth Brown toured Sweden, Norway, and Finland for several weeks with the "Los Angeles R&B Caravan." Scandinavian blues aficionados read about Dixon in *Jefferson* blues magazine published in Sweden. Although his records were out of print in the United States, European buyers were soon able to choose from three Floyd Dixon reissue albums, compilations of recordings he'd made between 1947 and 1961 issued on the Route 66 label. Dixon was the first artist chosen for release by that label, which has become a valuable source for classic R&B.

Dixon's European admirers found him an intriguingly complex individual. Jonas Bernholm, who wrote the liner notes for one of Dixon's Route 66 albums, observed that Dixon struck him as often overflowing with joy but periodically brooding and withdrawn. Bernholm was surprised to discover that Dixon was capable of quickly multiplying multiple-digit numbers in his head; that he had taken night school courses in business; that he sometimes had premonitions about future events; and that he could be difficult to understand, giving answers that didn't always seem to relate to questions asked.[4]

Dixon often sang about women and could often be found chatting, bantering, or flirting with women on his tours—Bernholm noted that Dixon seemed to bring out the maternal instinct in them, and yet Dixon took care to point out that "for seven years I didn't even talk to a woman. I lived in Paris, Texas, a small place with two hundred people. I had saved $15,000, bought a lot of canned food, and met nobody while staying there. [Singer] Ivory Joe Hunter used to tell me to be careful with women. His wife had stolen everything he had after the divorce. He was bitter and carried a gun. So I never married. I would spend a week, maybe eight days with [a woman], then I left."[5]

By the mid-seventies, an American actor named Bernie Hamilton had become Dixon's manager and also collaborated with him in the writing of new songs. Dixon recorded occasional 45s. He enjoyed seeing his influence touch younger artists. For example, blues singer-pianist-songwriter Dave Alexander (a.k.a. Omar Hakim Khayyam), described by John Norris of *Coda* magazine as "one of the most individual and satisfying blues performers in action today," has cited Dixon as an influence.[6] And after "Saturday Night Live" comedians John Belushi and Dan Ackroyd decided to turn two comic characters they'd created, the Blues Brothers, into recording artists (and eventually the stars of a successful film musical), they asked Dixon to coach them. Their recording of his "Hey Bartender" became a hit in 1983, winning the *Billboard* blues award the following year. Then, in 1985, another recording of "Hey Bartender," this one by Johnny Lee, won a *Billboard* award in the country category. As composer, Dixon received $35,000 in royalties, which he has invested. He was thrilled to hear his old song on radio again and between the Blues Brothers' and Lee's versions he noted that his song had a longer run of popularity than had some of Michael Jackson's. "But Michael is a gone cat, boy," he's quick to add. "I like Michael. I *love* him. Yes I do. I really like him, and I like a lot of his stuff. Quincy's doing them good arrangements behind him. Can't take nothing from him."

The popular country singer-songwriter Willie Nelson commissioned Dixon to write songs for him ("Wisdom Speaks" and "A Love Somewhere for Me"). Duke Robillard and other younger blues artists asked Dixon to do gigs with them. Los Angeles R&B disc jockey Billy Vera—a long-time admirer who used to have a bit of one of Dixon's recordings on his answering machine message—devoted a show to Dixon on KCRW-FM on October 20, 1990. On that show, Dixon reminisced, listened to his best early recordings, and also played and sang live in the studio. In 1991 Vera (or "Mr. Billy Vera," in the deferen-

tial way Dixon characteristically refers to him) produced an album
for Fantasy Records that was compiled from Dixon's 1953 Specialty
recording sessions.

Managed since December 1989 by a personable young go-getter
named Kathleen Barlow, Dixon is maintaining a busier schedule than
he had for many years. Barlow has also been active in setting up a
Floyd Dixon fan club, selling tee-shirts, buttons, and recordings by
mail, and doing her best to keep his activities publicized. She has tried
to make him more visible. As Dixon observes, "These days I'm traveling for Right Time Productions, playing quite a few engagements.
Miss Kathleen Barlow is head of Right-Time Productions, and her
husband, Mr. Port Barlow, is the guitarist with them. Very good guitarist. Oh, we've been back East and down in Atlanta, Georgia, and
over in Italy and France and Switzerland. And Texas, yes indeed.
Rhode Island. Massachusetts. Connecticut."

"He's just about getting ready to leave for the Amsterdam Blues
Festival," Barlow interjects [in February 1991], "then Atlanta after
that. He's going to Washington, D.C.—the Kennedy Center—in June.
We have a festival that we're doing on June 8 in Topanga, here in
California. I'm trying to get a tour together right now to go down to
Arizona, and another one up into upstate—northern California."

Tonight, February 14, 1991, he is to appear at Fleetwood's, the classy
new Los Angeles blues club opened by Mick Fleetwood of the popular, blues-based British rock group Fleetwood Mac. It's the first night
the club will be open to the public. Barlow has been assured that the
club will be booking Dixon regularly; it has been getting a lot of press
attention, and she's thrilled to have a prestigious, high-visibility out-
let for him. But attending the opening, I'm less than thrilled. Dixon,
I find, is to be but one of four acts—the first on, to help warm up the
crowd for the eventual appearance of the headliner, Bo Diddley, who's
more of a rock 'n' roll than a blues or R&B figure. Following Dixon
will be a young British band that plays mid-fifties-style American R&B
in almost a caricature of the original manner.

The club obviously doesn't place a premium on authenticity. It's
a gorgeous, spacious place—done up in what appears to be white
marble, it looks like some Hollywood set-designer's idea of a nightclub—and it's jam-packed with a young, affluent, talkative, all-white
crowd. I wonder how many of those in attendance, who've either
paid the $20 cover charge—steep by L.A. club standards—or gotten
on the guest list, know who Dixon is. The club makes no effort to
inform them, nor, for that matter, does Dixon. Resplendent in a white
suit, he simply performs his songs, one after another, without stage

patter. Ruth Brown has a way of talking about her songs before she sings them that can make even young fans feel nostalgic, and she also lets you know these songs *were* hits. The yuppies filling this club tonight would have no way of knowing the numbers Dixon sings are early R&B hits and, for the most part, his own compositions.

He is a congenial, warm—if not forceful—personality. I'm reminded of Fats Domino, even more so when Dixon does "My Blue Heaven," his piano playing and singing—if tinged with huskiness tonight—very much in a Domino vein. He offers some slow blues, but it's on the free-and-easy, happier ones that have a beat that he communicates best. He seems to radiate joy. Finally, he goes into "Hey Bartender," the number in his repertoire that—thanks to the Blues Brothers and Johnny Lee—is probably most familiar to the audience; it's obvious that he's saved it to be his strong finish. But as he's doing the song, the management decides that he should perform for another five minutes. I can't tell whether the next act is ready, but Dixon is simply told to do another number. It's an unprofessional way to treat a performer who has built to a climax. He voices no complaint but follows the exuberant "Hey Bartender" anticlimactically with "C Jam Blues." He gives it a spritely interpretation, playing economically, reminding me now of Count Basie. It's interesting that he's chosen to close with an instrumental; they wanted five more minutes from him and they got it—but not his singing. Is that a subtle protest?

Dixon's appealing naturalness is missing in the British R&B group and the young American doowop group that follow him, both of which are trying to re-create sounds of an earlier era. Dixon doesn't have the magnetism of a Charles Brown, much less a Ruth Brown, but he has something good and real and satisfying to offer. I'm convinced that if some wise record producer were to do for Dixon what the producer of Charles Brown's last two albums did for him, he, too, could enjoy a rediscovery. Barlow says that one album is already taped and waiting to be mixed and another one is planned, which she will try to shop around. When Dixon is at home, he can often be found at the piano his landlord bought for him, working on new songs. He says that he is getting a lot of material together for future albums.

He still is hoping—perhaps grandiosely—for a big record deal, the kind that could right all the wrongs he's very much aware he's suffered. "If I signed a long-term exclusive deal with anyone, I'd want *$700,000*—if I'd sign for three years with a two-year option. That's how much money I would want. I know how much is in it—and if it ain't in it no more, still it's how much I want. Because them record companies is a goof, man. Yes, indeed. That's what I'd ask for. And that ain't no money behind a record if they really get behind the thing, really like you. If they want to take a chance with you."

There's no evidence that any company wants to take anything like that kind of a chance with Floyd Dixon at this stage of his career, though, and it rankles him that he wasn't paid better when he was a solid draw on the R&B circuit.[7] Of course, he wasn't the only one who got gypped in those days; it was commonplace. "Bo Diddley said in his younger days he had a big record out—a million-seller—and his wife and him were scuffling and couldn't hardly eat," he comments. The industry treats artists more fairly today, he observes, but the changes have come too late to be of much benefit for most artists of his generation. "You have missed a lot of the good times in life that you could have had with your family and things like that. And I can see a lot of musicians' families broke up because of not being able to make a living," he says.

He recalls that one of his relatives in Texas, who married a judge, had offered to help him fight for back royalties. "She told me, 'We'll straighten it out. We'll get Percy Foreman, who never lost a case in Houston.' I was supposed to go down there but I didn't go. If Mark had been living then—because Mark was the whole thing, into that scene—he'd know all about it; he was always talking a lot about it, mechanical and performance artist, and all them different royalties. But when I was young, I didn't know the meaning of money. It didn't mean nothing to me. And I didn't think that people would really do what they did to me. I just didn't believe that." He had been brought up to treat whites—particularly those in authority—with respect.

Looking back, he can't understand how he—and so many other performers he knew—let himself be so thoroughly exploited while offering only mild protests. "There's something wrong somewhere," he says, struggling for an explanation—no matter how tenuous it may be—for what happened. "And it's going to come to pass that it's going to really be checked out. I know a group that's studying on this now: why these people wasn't being paid, and what caused—they study the mind now. It's something about them mesmerizing people's minds or using sorcery or something. I know a group that's secretly studying about it, and they say they'll come up with it—they're finding out that it was something about the mind that they was doing to make people not get mad enough to kill them or do something terribly wrong and not get their money, to be living like they was living. They got an organization here now is studying about that. They really believe that. It's something unordinary. And they're going to find out why they could take advantage of everybody."

How were so many of the creators of R&B taken advantage of, he wonders, and by individuals who for the most part seemed likable. "I liked all the peoples I was with. I really liked them, almost as a family," Dixon stresses, a touch of bewilderment coloring his speech. "But it don't mean nothing to them. A lot of them. You know, when you like somebody and you're in harmony together, you feel, you trust, you become honest with them. And you become obedient to their command, like. That was the only thing. When you get kind of crippled in the mind, it changes your prolific style. And until you reach the right person, you're going through strange strategic statistics. That's where you're going," he declares, his voice trailing off. "But I won't jump from impulse no more—quick-like. I think."

5

LAVERN BAKER

"Where ya been so long?"

"This is like a last chance around. Now how many old women you know get a second chance at it? And do it?" asks sixty-one-year-old LaVern Baker, eyes twinkling, in her dressing room at New York's Minskoff Theater. After an absence from the American scene of more than two decades, she returned to the United States to take over, as of June 25, 1990, Ruth Brown's role singing vintage blues songs in the Broadway hit *Black and Blue*. It's not the first time Baker has followed Brown, for in the mid-fifties she supplanted her as Atlantic's best-selling female recording artist. Brown had reigned unchallenged from 1949 to 1955, but the public periodically seeks new favorites. From 1955 into the early sixties, Baker, introducing such songs as "Tweedlee Dee," "Play It Fair," "Jim Dandy" and "I Cried a Tear," had one hit after another on the R&B charts before dropping out of sight.

Where has she been hiding for the past twenty-odd years? "In the Philippines," she says. I can't help asking: Wasn't she bothered by all of the fighting and civil unrest there? "Hell! I went through all of that in the south!" Baker responds, recalling her tours as a singer in the years before integration. "We went through cities where the riots were going on—people would push on the bus and stuff." But that's getting ahead of the story, she lets me know. She's been singing much longer than most of her fans might imagine, and if we're going to tell her story, we must start at the beginning.

* * *

Black and Blue hardly represented Baker's first exposure to vintage blues. Her aunt—her father's sister—was blues singer Merline Johnson. Known as the "Yas Yas Girl," Johnson recorded more than seventy sides in Chicago during the thirties and forties (including such numbers as "Blues Everywhere," "Patrol Wagon Blues," "New Muddy Water Blues," "Pallet on the Floor," "Jelly Bean Blues," "He May Be Your Man," and "Don't You Make Me High") accompanied by such well-known bluesmen as Big Bill Broonzy on guitar and Blind John Davis on piano. She sang both sorrowful and slyly risqué material.

In addition, a distant relative of Baker's (misidentified in some Baker publicity material and consequently in various articles about Baker as an aunt) was Memphis Minnie (Lizzie Douglas), who was also based in Chicago during Baker's formative years and associated with Big Bill Broonzy. Memphis Minnie was, according to Steve La-Vere, "the most popular female country blues singer of all time."[1] Music publisher and A&R man Lester Melrose, a dominant figure in the Chicago blues scene of the era, handled many recording sessions for both Merline Johnson and Memphis Minnie, and eventually La-Vern Baker would have opportunities to perform with both of them.

Although Baker greatly admired Ella Fitzgerald and some other popular performers of the day, she says that Merline Johnson was her "biggest influence. I just wanted to be like her. I would sit there in the studio and watch her record. I guess this is why I wanted to do it, as a kid. It was nice. I think I was about eight or nine when I told my mom, 'I want to sing like my Auntie Merline.' My daddy didn't like it so hot. Well, he didn't want me to pattern too much after her, but he didn't mind me being a singer. After I was grown, that was OK. I saw him after I started to really get in the business and I had a couple of hits. In fact, one of the big shows that they booked, we played Milwaukee and my father turned out to see me. That was the last time he saw me.

"My first recording—nobody knows anything about it—was with the same man that recorded my aunt—Lester Melrose. Oh, I knew him since I was a little girl. The record was nothing; it didn't move. But at least I did something. That's when I was just trying to get started. I recorded for RCA when I was maybe twelve, thirteen, or fourteen," Baker says. She's only met one collector who has that obscure first record (which she doesn't possess herself, she adds), and he won't copy it for her.

Baker was born in Chicago on November 11, 1929. "LaVern" is not her real name, but rather a stage name she has long used. Baker, she says, was her father's last name; "I use it," she remarks in an offhand way, adding that early in her performing career she experimented with various other names. Among billings she used at one time or another before making it big were "Little Miss Sharecropper," "Bea Baker," and "Dolores Williams." Standard sources that give her real name as Do-lores Williams are incorrect; that was her name when she was married to a post office worker named Eugene Williams. The marriage, which lasted for about two years, began when she was eighteen.

Her upbringing was split between her father and mother "because they were separated. So I'd go to Milwaukee sometimes with my father and then back with my mom." Did she see much of her aunt? "Oh yeah. Whenever she came, I went with her. Whenever. They never held me from going with her. Anytime I wanted to be with her, I could. Especially when she came over to Chicago. Because any time she came, she was going down to the RCA Victor [studio]. So I could go with her all the time." Poor and sometimes hungry as a child, she felt that her aunt—who could wear a feather boa with style—represented the epitome of success and glamour.

Baker sang first in a Baptist choir. She was ten when she began making appearances in Chicago clubs. She and a friend had won one club's amateur contest by jitterbugging. After being announced a winner that first night, she was asked if there was anything else she'd like to do. She said that she wanted to sing—which she proceeded to do with such verve that the club hired her to work weekends for $5 a night. She went on to sing in one little club after another for black audiences, often skipping school and hiding whenever the police appeared. Her earnings helped her mother to get by. Another upcoming singer on the Chicago club scene of that era, whom Baker admired greatly, was Joe Williams.

The people who ran the Club DeLisa (one of the best-known black clubs in Chicago, with a seating capacity of more than a thousand) told Baker after seeing her perform someplace else that they'd hire her once she was old enough to work legally at a club where liquor was sold. On November 11, 1946, her seventeenth birthday, she received a contract. The DeLisa's six-times-a-year revues were important showcases for up-and-coming talents. Baker recalls, "I was so shocked when I went into the Club DeLisa. Wow! I finally made it!" Her first billing in a Club DeLisa advertisement, which appeared in the *Chicago Defender* on February 8, 1947, was, curiously enough, as "Midget LaVern."

Over the next few years, she worked various clubs around Chicago under the billing of Little Miss Sharecropper (a club owner's idea). Advertisements in the *Chicago Defender* have her appearing as Little Miss Sharecropper at the Brookmont Lounge (August 7, 1948), at the Blue Dahlia (April 23, 1949), at the Miramar Ballroom (December 24, 1949), and at the Club DeLisa (May 13, 1950). As Little Miss Sharecropper she kept her hair in pigtails, wore tattered overalls, and carried a basket. "It didn't turn me on. It didn't turn me on at all," she says of the stereotypical image she was asked to project. Why was she billed as Little Miss Sharecropper? "Well, there was a girl who was quite a big hit in Chicago at the time called Little Miss Cornshucks. And she turned to be, well—let's just say not what they expected; I don't want to belittle anyone. And so they were trying to bill me to take her place." Virtually forgotten now, Miss Cornshucks had an emotional, broken-note style of singing blues and torch songs that impressed all who heard her. Some felt she had the potential to have become as successful as LaVern Baker or Ruth Brown eventually became. In fact, one reason Atlantic had Brown record "So Long," her first hit, was that the company liked the way Miss Cornshucks had done the song.

"Right from the beginning, I was singing the same sort of songs as I do now. Well, I was doing other people's songs back then because I didn't have hit records of my own. I sang a lot of Dinah Washington things. I used to love Dinah Washington. I used to do all of her blues things." Fletcher Henderson, whose band was in residence at the Club DeLisa from February 1946 until May 1947, was so impressed with Baker's abilities that he wrote a song for her, "When I'm in a Crying Mood," and helped get her a chance to record it.

She cut sides for various labels, although none created much of a stir. She recorded, for example, with Eddie Penigar's band for RCA in 1949, with Maurice King and his Wolverines for Columbia in 1951 (as Bea Baker), and for National in 1951 (as Little Miss Sharecropper). She recalls recording sometime during this period for the Chicago-based Chess record label, too. Her bold yet sly and sexy way of putting over a song was winning her a strong but strictly local following, and her records received local airplay. She was glad when she was able to make $125 for a week's work, but making a lot of money wasn't Baker's primary concern. In fact, she criticizes some of today's younger performers for getting too hung up on the money issue when they should be concerned about learning the ropes as a performer. "I've noticed that everything people do now, they've got to get paid for it," she comments with disapproval. "Well, what about the write-ups and the beautiful press that you can get? Which is worth more than the $50 or $60 that you're going to get. That's the way I look at it. The money's only good for while you've got it. Once you spend it, it's gone. But that write-up that you're going to get, at least you've got that. And you can use it to show for other jobs."

According to advertisements in the *Chicago Defender,* she headlined at such Chicago nightclubs as Ralph's Place (October 21, 1950), Joe's Rendezvous Lounge (January 27, 1951), and the Crown Propeller

Lounge (September 22, 1951). The last-named was, during the early 1950s, perhaps Chicago's most prestigious club; unlike the Club DeLisa, it regularly booked name talent. During the Crown Propeller Lounge engagement, Baker, billed as Little Miss Sharecropper, "Empress of the Blues," appeared in a midnight "battle of the blues" at the Indiana Theater with Memphis Minnie, the "Queen of the Blues." Baker had become a star, at least in Chicago.

Detroit's renowned Flame Show Bar, which drew a racially mixed audience, was Baker's next major venue, becoming her base for a couple of years. Its boss, Al Green, signed her to a personal management contract, and she began the slow process of trying to increase her visibility. In the spring of 1952 she succeeded Kitty Stevenson as vocalist with the Detroit-based Todd Rhodes Orchestra, which had had two R&B chart hits. In July and October of that year she recorded with Rhodes's band for the Cincinnati-based King Records. Baker recalls, "My manager put me out with Todd Rhodes—a big bandleader at that time—to let me feel the one-nighters, let me know the clubs, how to work this system and all that: to get my feet wet."

King Records' promotional material from this period billed Baker as "Little Miss Sharecropper, the Gal with the Singing Soul" and quoted Chicago's top R&B disc jockey, Al Benson, as saying, "I had her on my television show for sixteen weeks. I play her records because I think she's the greatest." The *Pittsburgh Courier*'s Phil Waddell added that Baker had enough polish "to be big time material. She's in this spot giving name stars the headache . . . stopping all the shows. Stop by the Flame and lend an ear to the gal with the TNT voice named 'Sharecropper.'" And Flame Show Bar bandleader Maurice King said, "In the three years my band and I have been here, no other artist than Johnnie Ray has ever left me with a feeling of wanting to hear them over and over again."[2]

Baker notes, "During that time I met Johnnie Ray, who just recently passed away [on February 24, 1990], and I helped him. And we became like bread and butter. It was nice." Ray, several years older than Baker, had not yet made any records when they met. A white singer with an emotion-packed, largely black-influenced style, Ray was thoroughly comfortable in black culture. He and Baker, whom Ray knew initially as Little Miss Sharecropper, developed a lasting friendship. She still remembers the way he'd holler up to her, standing outside her apartment, "Sharecropper! Sharecropper!"

Al Green, who introduced Ray to Baker as a young fellow who was striving to sing the blues, asked her to teach Ray what she could, and she did. She knew far more about showmanship than he did. She remembers telling Ray about Al Jolson; she soon had Ray dramatically bowing down on one knee in the famous Jolson manner, which went over well with the crowd. That Baker, who is black, would be teaching Ray about Jolson, who was white, is a reminder that the issue of black performers influencing whites and vice versa is more complex than many writers have suggested. Influences go both ways.[3]

Baker and Ray worked many times together on the same bill; a typical Flame show would include a comic and a couple of singers. After the show, they'd often go to an all-night movie theater or an after-hours joint—one of which was raided by the police when they were there. They were among those hauled off to jail for a few hours. Ray became an overnight sensation in 1951–52 with such songs as "Cry" and "The Little White Cloud That Cried." In later years he and Baker would have numerous opportunities to work on the same bills and use some of the same songwriters; both would make successful recordings of "Shake a Hand," and both would, late in life, be managed by Alan Eichler. King's promotional literature of the early fifties quoted Ray as saying of Baker: "I owe so much of my success to LaVern, because she gave me faith and a helping hand towards the success I now enjoy."[4]

Eventually, Baker recalls, "I sat down and told my manager, 'I don't like this Little Miss Sharecropper thing. I want to wear pretty gowns and stuff like that.' He said, 'OK, I agree.' So we changed it." She felt her career starting to move and didn't want to be trapped forever with the raggedy sharecropper image. "The people's eyes were starting to open to me."

In 1952 Baker appeared on several of disc jockey Alan Freed's first R&B concerts, stopping the shows. Freed was to prove a leading figure in making R&B—and the rock 'n' roll that came out of it—more popular, and Baker's connection with Freed would prove good for both of them. Freed, the best-known rock 'n' roll disc jockey in the business during the mid-fifties, appreciated Baker as an artist, and as his importance grew so did his ability to help promote her career. Freed had begun programming R&B on Cleveland's WJW in mid-1951 after a local record store owner who advertised on his show told him of a curious development: increasing numbers of white youths were buying records by black performers. Freed used a Todd Rhodes instrumental, "Blues for Moon Dog," as his theme—sometimes he'd howl over it as it played, thumping out a beat on a telephone book— and rapidly attracted a growing audience by playing record after record by black R&B artists. In an excited, gravelly voice (his vocal chords had been damaged during treatment for polyps), using black slang and black inflection (for a while he actually tried to conceal the fact that he was white), he didn't just play R&B—he championed it.

When Freed began calling the music he played "rock 'n' roll," he was simply playing the same black rhythm and blues he had been playing. The term *rock 'n' roll* was intended to signal that the music was for everybody—whites as well as blacks—because many people thought of R&B as music for blacks. As more and more white performers eventually got into rock 'n' roll, Freed continued giving heavy exposure—both on the air and in concerts he organized and hosted—to black artists he liked. Unlike many disc jockeys of the fifties, he favored records by black originators rather than the white artists he felt were copying their styles. Many black artists of the early and mid-fifties recognized the importance of Freed's support, and he should be remembered for that, not just that he, like many DJs of the era, became involved with payola. Freed became nationally syndicated within a few years. He moved his base of operations to New York in 1954, quickly opening that city for R&B, and soon moved into television and film work as well, bringing the music he favored to an ever-widening audience.

Meanwhile, in 1953, Baker recalls, "My manager brought me to New York and put me on Atlantic." By now, she was able to make as much as $300 a week, when she worked a full week, which she thought was great. When a chance came up to do even better overseas than in the United States, she took it. "We went into New York and recorded [in June 1953], and about four months later I left for Europe on a show called *The Harlem Melody*," she remembers. "Eventually, everybody else left and they left me over there. I got a job at this club in Milano, Italy, and worked there until I went home. You don't have to speak the language, just be able to sing. And I met Anna Magnani, the big movie star, and a few other real nice people—the Peters Sisters; I did a live TV show over there with them. And I met an agent from France; he booked me in France. I didn't want to come home. But, remember, I had already recorded for Atlantic when I left for Europe. And now the record 'Soul on Fire' was hitting. My manager cabled me, 'Come home, you've got a hit record.'"

"Soul on Fire" was a terrific recording, capturing Baker at her most dynamic, with appealingly laid-back backing from a blues-tinged combo consisting of a tenor sax, a baritone sax, and rhythm. Singing about how she's played the "love game" in the past with "boy friends and good-time men friends," her voice quivers with excitement. With rising intonation, like one testifying in church, she declares, giving each word separate emphasis, "You set my soul on fire! Whoa! She's burning." America's youth weren't hearing songs like that on "Your Hit Parade." Although "Soul on Fire" (for which Baker shared composer credit with Ahmet Ertegun, using a pseudonym) did not make the charts, it sold well enough to convince Atlantic that it had a talent worth nurturing.

Back in the United States after nine months abroad, Baker recorded "Tweedlee Dee" (by Winfield Scott) on October 20, 1954. Early in 1955 it became a smash hit. It had a catchy samba beat that Ahmet Ertegun had suggested trying during the course of a long recording session while those present munched on fried chicken Baker had cooked. Its lyrics are innocuous, a fact connected with its great commercial success, with such lines as "Tweedlee Dee, I'm as happy as can be . . . you make my heart go clickety-clack." These are lines any twelve-year-old girl could sing in the schoolyard, and melodically the song is no more involved than a schoolyard chant.

"Tweedlee Dee" was not half the number "Soul on Fire" was, but some disc jockeys who were afraid to play a record of a sexy black woman frankly singing "you set my soul on fire" could play a record by that same singer proclaiming the far tamer "you make my heart go clickety-clack." Even on "Tweedlee Dee," though, some of Baker's sexuality came through. In a vocal fill she sang something that sounded like "humpy-um-bum-bum" with an over-brimming sensual vitality. No matter how sexless the lyrics Baker was asked to sing ever might be, her appearance—she was, in the parlance of the day, "stacked," and wore tight-fitting gowns accentuating that fact—and her body language tended to convey a message. Even the way that she sometimes innocently yet coyly stuck a finger in her mouth at the conclusion of a song struck some fans as sensual. At one Brooklyn theater appearance, one Baker fan was so excited by her performance that he jumped onto the stage, screaming, and bit her while she sang. She kept singing—with his teeth locked on her hand.

She could, without much effort, imbue seemingly any kind of lyrics with a yearning that was decidedly grown-up; one clear example is the flip side of "Tweedlee Dee," "Tomorrow Night." It is important to remember that in the mid-fifties artists such as Baker ran up against not only ingrained racism in American society but also ingrained sexually repressive attitudes. People who wrote angry letters to radio stations that played rhythm and blues to demand (at their crudest) that broadcasters not give "nigger music" such exposure or (in more "refined" language) play such "low-class music" were often not only racially prejudiced but also uptight about, and threatened by, the atmosphere of sexual freedom they perceived in the music. Some seemed to fear that when masses of white teens started buying records by sexy-voiced black women like Baker it meant the end of civilization as they knew it.[5] (Who was more hysterical, the teens discovering such music or the adults who protested so vigorously against it?) West Virginia disc jockey Marc Jennings (of WCMI) declared that recent hit R&B "tunes like . . . 'Hearts of Stone,' 'Ko Ko Mo,' and 'Tweedlee Dee' are products of the mass hysteria prevalent in our world today."[6] No one wanted to admit to racism, but many disc jockeys who weren't comfortable playing songs by black R&B artists apparently felt quite comfortable playing recordings of those same songs so long as they were sung by whites—a reality record companies were all too happy to exploit.

As soon as Baker's recording of "Tweedlee Dee" began selling, Mercury Records, which was bigger than Atlantic, rushed to record a cover version of it using a white pop singer, Georgia Gibbs. Gibbs's version followed the original so closely that her voice almost seemed to have been overdubbed onto Baker's Atlantic recording. Atlantic recording engineer Tom Dowd has said that Mercury asked him to do the session for them but he turned the company down. He was told that the same musicians would back Gibbs as had backed Baker. When Baker's record of "Tweedlee Dee" rose to number fourteen on the pop charts, Atlantic's heads knew they had a star on their hands. For perspective, only one of Ruth Brown's records had ever made the pop charts by that time; "Mama, He Treats Your Daughter Mean" reached number twenty-three. But Gibbs's clone rose to number two on the pop charts, staying on the charts nineteen weeks beginning January 29, 1955, just two weeks after Baker's original made the charts.

An examination of how the recordings did on specific charts provides evidence that racial prejudice limited access to the airwaves. Baker's version rose to number fourteen on the pop jukebox charts and number twenty-two on the pop bestseller charts, meaning that teens were buying the record and selecting it on jukeboxes. It did not make the pop disc jockey charts at all, meaning that most disc jockeys simply weren't playing it. By contrast, Gibbs's version reached the number two spot on the pop disc jockey charts. Clearly, white jockeys who wouldn't play a black original were playing the white copy. In the early fifties, as producer Bob Shad of Mercury Records acknowledged to music historian Arnold Shaw, "If you brought a record by a black artist to pop disc jockeys, they would refuse to play it."[7] And Mercury, like some other labels, sought to take advantage of that reality.

Boosted by heavy airplay, Gibbs's version of "Tweedlee Dee" rose to number three on both the pop bestseller and pop jukebox charts. Baker reckons that she lost $15,000 in royalties on just that one record because people bought Gibbs's version rather than hers. Some in the business warned Baker to resign herself to the injustice; being covered by white artists simply went with the territory. She soon found that subsequent releases of hers would, indeed, be covered. She was not just losing out on sales of a specific record when that happened, however, she was also losing out on publicity and other intangibles that would have boosted her stock as a performer. Baker tossed off quips to the press to the effect that maybe imitation was the sincerest kind of flattery but she could do without such "flattery."

The close copying of the arrangement Baker had used on "Tweedlee Dee" makes it as blatant and egregious an example of a white artist profiting from the creativity of a black artist as can be found. It must be emphasized, however, that this example, while extreme, was far from isolated. Over the years, countless white performers (including many who were not at all racist themselves but who benefited from the system nonetheless) have reaped financial rewards by using material of black performers, although customarily modifying it, at least somewhat. The first jazz band ever to record—the white Original Dixieland Jazz Band—advertised itself as having originated jazz even though it had borrowed freely from music that black bands played in New Orleans. White entertainer Gilda Gray was presented in the twenties as the creator of the shimmy—an uninhibited dance new to white audiences but familiar to black performers and nonperformers alike. When the pioneering white radio stars Charles Correll and Freeman Gosden—radio's "Amos 'n' Andy"—borrowed from routines that the black vaudeville comedians Flournoy Miller and Aubrey Lyles had devised, Miller threatened legal action, a bold step for a black performer to take in 1930. Correll and Gosden later hired him to write for them. Tommy Dorsey's special and often-imitated arrangement of "Marie"—his first big hit—originated with an obscure black band in Philadelphia, Doc Wheeler's. Benny Goodman made far more money playing arrangements of pace-setting black bandleader and arranger Fletcher Henderson (whom he always credited) than Henderson himself had ever made. When Goodman started, it was much easier for a white bandleader than a black bandleader to get a radio sponsor.

In the rock 'n' roll era, such "Elvis Presley songs"—as many Presley fans considered them—as "That's All Right," "My Baby Left Me," and "Hound Dog" had previously been recorded by black R&B artists. ("Hound Dog," however, had been written by white songwrit-ers—a reminder that the issue of "ownership" of material isn't always black and white.) Bandleader Buddy Morrow's biggest hit, "Night Train" (1952), had earlier been an R&B hit for tenor saxist Jimmy Forrest (and that, in turn, had been derived from a Duke Ellington number). Morrow's RCA Victor producers looked for freshly break-ing, small-label R&B and rock 'n' roll hits by black as well as white artists for him to record. Morrow's band also made the pop charts, for example, with "One Mint Julip," which the Clovers, a black R&B vocal group, had introduced, and "I Don't Know," which Willie Ma-bon, a black Chicago bluesman, had introduced. (Ironically, Morrow was also asked to cover LaVern Baker's "Tweedlee Dee" when it first began to break but turned it down—a mistake in judgment, he feels, because it turned out to be such a popular number.) Georgia Gibbs's 1955 pop chart-topper "Dance with Me Henry" was a cleaned-up ver-sion of an earthier song that had been an R&B chart-topper for Hank Ballard and the Midnighters the year before: "Work with Me Annie." The charming Irish rocker Ian Whitcomb made the pop charts in 1965 with an "original" called "N-E-R-V-O-U-S," which was reminis-cent enough of an earlier song called "Nervous" by Mississippi-born bluesman Willie Dixon that Dixon eventually succeeded in having his name added to the sheet-music credits as coauthor. And on and on, and on and on. Borrowing, of course, went both ways. Many black performers borrowed from white performers, for example, tak-ing a country and western number introduced by a white artist and making an R&B version of it. But the playing field was not level. It was far easier for a white artist, who had greater chances of getting major record label backing and radio and television exposure, to reap benefits by exploiting the creativity of a black artist than it was for the reverse to happen.

Now, Baker tries to look at the whole issue of being covered philo-sophically: "Well, you get a little upset when someone covers you, but it makes you try harder for the next one. It's a gas to fight back. It's a challenge to me. Because you've got this inner thing: 'Well, I'll do better.' And then you feel the greatness, OK? I started to think, 'Heck, I must be really something. She [Georgia Gibbs] can't get noth-ing; she has to use me.' And I said, 'Oh, she only made my name bigger' because so many people bought the two records, hers and mine. This was back then when the payola and stuff was going on, and you couldn't fight this."

Gibbs, meanwhile, continued copying Baker. On December 8, 1956, she scored a hit with a heavily promoted version of another number

Baker had introduced, "Tra La La." Gibbs's version spent seven weeks on the pop charts, rising as high as number twenty-four on the pop disc jockey chart, thirty-nine on the pop Top 100. Baker's version rose no higher than ninety-four on the pop Top 100 and did not make the pop disc jockey chart at all. "After 'Tweedlee Dee,' Georgia Gibbs covered 'Tra-La-La,' too," Baker recalls, adding, "but the back side of that record was the real hit! She covered the wrong side." Baker's version of "Tra-La-La" made the pop charts for just one week; however, the other side of the record, "Jim Dandy," made the pop charts for nineteen weeks (beginning in December 1956), reaching as high as number seventeen and reaching number one on the R&B charts. Did Baker become upset about Gibbs's copying her? You bet! But she handled it with sly humor. When she boarded one airplane in 1957, she named Gibbs as the beneficiary on her flight insurance, explaining that if she were to die in a plane crash, leaving Gibbs with no one to copy, she would still have a source of income thanks to Baker. Baker let Gibbs know what she'd done; Gibbs was not amused.

Baker told *Our World* in June 1955 that "I bitterly resent their arrogance in thefting my music note for note." That magazine, produced for black readers, complained that white artists were stealing Baker's thunder. A lot of other people were also coming to see the injustice. The New York *Post,* on October 14, 1956, called Baker's "Tweedlee Dee" "the first major Rock and Roll hit" and reported that Gibbs's covering of "Tweedlee Dee" had become "a cause célèbre in the industry because the version of Miss Gibbs was virtually the same as Miss Baker's" and quoted Baker as saying, "She used my arrangement note for note. We worked all night to get the arrangement; it didn't seem fair to have someone get all the gravy for nothing." The *Post* said that artists had also covered Baker's recordings of "Play It Fair" and "Sleepyhead."

What Baker considered really unacceptable, she stresses, was that Gibbs's records copied her arrangements, adding, "Congress passed a bill after that, that you could do the same song but it must be sixteen to twenty-four bars different. Oh, that's standard now. Ever since then. You can do the same song, but it must be a little bit different. Not straight note-for-note. That's what got me, because I paid for my own arrangements. When you do a session nowadays, that's yours." Baker feels good about the modification in the law, noting that she had written to her congressman, Democrat Charles Diggs Jr. of Michigan, to implore that something be done about the problem of artists covering other performers' creations. When the bill became law, she kept a copy of it in her home for quite a while.[8]

How did Georgia Gibbs feel about the covering issue? She told John Milward of the Los Angeles *Times* on April 14, 1991, that "it was a tragic thing that happened to black artists in the fifties, but I don't think I should be personally held responsible for it." She maintained that she had no say in what songs she recorded then, much less in how they were arranged. She had simply come into the studio and done what was asked of her. The popularity of white cover versions generally declined as the fifties wore on; increasing numbers of white record buyers came to prefer the stronger original black versions to the white counterparts, and increasing numbers of disc jockeys were playing them. The color line gradually faded.

Baker seems reluctant to fuss too much over the covering problem. When it was taking place, Baker maintains, she was usually too thrilled by the successes she was enjoying to spend much time brooding over what Gibbs (or other singers) might have been doing. "I wasn't bitter, I was really excited," she says of her predominant mood back then. "I figured I was lucky; my records did fairly well. I figured there's enough money in the world for everybody. There's no way you can make it all. And I'm not going to hurt anyone in trying, 'Well, this is all mine.' That's stupid, I think."

By June 1955 the magazine *Our World* was reporting Baker was getting $1,000 a week for personal appearances. As she explained the appeal of her music to the magazine, "Blues, everybody wants it. And when you add rhythm, there's nothing better." The magazine summarized her appeal succinctly in one photo caption: "Her unusual style takes drag out of traditional blues numbers." In April 1956 *Ebony* reported that Baker made $75,000 a year. It quoted her as saying, "I can't understand it. I used to make $15 a night singing the same stuff I'm doing today." "Throwing herself into every performance," the magazine noted, "she belts out blues with tremendous energy, using sexy gestures and daring body movements that create a unique emotional experience for listeners." She told *Ebony* that her goal was to move audiences the way Bessie Smith had, an interesting comment in that many young fans who bought her records probably had no idea who Bessie Smith (billed during the twenties as the "Empress of the Blues") had been.

At this point in her career, Baker was frequently referred to in the press as a rock 'n' roll singer. To most Americans, rock 'n' roll was some new kind of youth-oriented music that presumably had been invented by the likes of such public idols as Elvis Presley and Bill Haley and the Comets. All Baker knew was that she had been singing just the way she felt—music called rhythm and blues—since well before Alan Freed popularized the term rock 'n' roll in the early fifties. In fact, she had been singing professionally even before the term *rhythm and blues* came along; initially, she thought of herself simply as singer of blues—like her aunt or, for that matter, Bessie Smith. When she became passionately declamatory onstage, rousing audiences to excitement, she recalled a black performing style that long predated the creation of the phrase *rock 'n' roll.*

If people wanted to call Baker a rock 'n' roll singer, that was all right with her. She wasn't overly worried about labels. She was making far more money than she had ever made in her life, and she trusted her producers at Atlantic with knowing how best to market her. Her long-range goal, though, was to be thought of simply as a singer, capable of singing the best songs in the best clubs. And she knew that songs like "Tweedlee Dee," "Tra La La," and "Jim Dandy" were not the equals of, say, "Body and Soul" and "Stormy Weather." Baker's "full-throated, vibrant belting with a sexy tease"—as *Billboard* once described her singing—could work well with a wide variety of material. Atlantic head Ahmet Ertegun thought of Baker as a jazz singer who was capable of handling anything from classic blues to ballads. Unlike a number of other commercially successful singers on the rock 'n' roll scene, Baker was an artist in whom Ertegun could and did really believe. However, as much as he and his brother and partner Neshui and fellow producer Jerry Wexler loved jazz and blues, they knew what records would sell best to the increasingly teen-dominated record-buying public, and they kept the bottom line in mind. They sought—sometimes more successfully than others—to meet the needs of both art and commerce.

In the fifties, American teens had more money to spend than ever before, and more and more radio stations and record stores were catering to their tastes. Disc jockeys wanted numbers that grabbed listeners quickly and had energy, a good beat, and a bit of that blues flavoring that seemed to be popular. The records had to last no more than two to three minutes to leave plenty of room on radio shows for disc jockeys' chatter and the all-important commercials. Simpler music went over better with younger listeners. As far as Atlantic was concerned, if that meant giving Baker some slight but catchy novelties to record, so be it. The Erteguns and Wexler didn't feel that they could afford to record only music that they believed to be of the highest quality, not if the goal was to produce hits. And there was no doubt about it, from 1955 into the early sixties, Atlantic and LaVern Baker were producing hits.

Baker no longer sings many of the songs she recorded then. They weren't all numbers of lasting value, and the themes of some would be too juvenile to work well for her now. But it is worthwhile to consider her hits. She followed "Tweedlee Dee," which reached number four on the R&B charts and fourteen on the pop charts, with a sing-along bit of frippery called "Bop-Ting-a-Ling," which made the R&B charts for eleven weeks beginning in May 1955, peaking at number three. Its flip side, "That's All I Need," reached number nine on the R&B charts. On such numbers, with their hokey background vocals and casually thrown-together lyrics, Baker, rough-edged and urgent, is a lot better than the material. She brings strength and guts to songs that wouldn't be worth remembering except for her having recorded them. Ahmet Ertegun and Jerry Wexler, who coproduced most of Baker's recordings, saw to it she was backed well. Among the sidemen who played on Baker sessions were fervent tenor saxists such as Sam "The Man" Taylor and King Curtis, who periodically got to take solos, and pianist Hank Jones, drummers Panama Francis and Connie Kay, bassists Lloyd Trotman and Milt Hinton, guitarists Mickey Baker, Al Caiola, and Bucky Pizzarelli, trumpeters Harry "Sweets" Edison, Taft Jordan, and Shad Collins, and trombonist Urbie Green. Howard Biggs, Jesse Stone, and Ray Ellis were among those who arranged for her.

Baker's lush, melodic rendition of "Play It Fair" made the R&B charts for sixteen weeks beginning in October 1955, peaking at number two. In March 1956 she scored modest successes with both a richly sung "My Happiness Forever" (four weeks on the R&B charts, reaching the number thirteen spot) and its flip side—about as insipid a number as she was ever asked to record (a little birdy's reminding her to wake up bright and early)—"Get Up, Get Up (You Sleepyhead)," which had one week on the charts, reaching the number fifteen spot. In September 1956, she came through with "Still" (seven weeks on the R&B charts, peaking at number four) and its flip side, the Latin-tinged "I Can't Love You Enough" (ten weeks on the R&B charts, peaking at seven). Significantly, both also made the pop charts, "Still" reaching number ninety-seven and "I Can't Love You Enough" reaching number twenty-two.

The phenomenal popularity of "Jim Dandy" (written by Lincoln Chase but inspired by a number that black minstrels had sung more than a hundred years before) surprised Baker and others. It reached number one on the R&B charts and number seventeen on the pop charts.[9] Baker had recorded "Jim Dandy" long before its December 1956 release, but Wexler had thought it so trivial, lacking in any soul, that he had persuaded Ahmet Ertegun not to release it for quite a while—and even then, only as the "B" side to "Tra La La." The melody line had no more substance than an advertising jingle, and there wasn't much more to the lyrics than repeating "Jim Dandy to the rescue," with an occasional "Go, Jim Dandy" thrown in. The song was as simple, rhythmic, and repetitive—and appealing—as "Bo Diddley," a smash hit of the year before.

"Jim Dandy" was every bit as trivial and sing-songy as Wexler had thought, but it was also a tune that stayed in listeners' minds. The various elements of the neatly turned arrangement, from the background vocal accents and bass parts to the exhilarating Sam "The Man" Taylor sax solo, all fit together perfectly. "Tra La La," the side of the record expected to prove more popular, was on and off the charts in a flash despite the exposure it received from being sung by a sensational-looking Baker in Alan Freed's movie *Rock, Rock, Rock* (1956), which featured Chuck Berry, Frankie Lymon and the Teenagers, and others.

Predictably, a follow-up to "Jim Dandy" was quickly rushed out: "Jim Dandy Got Married." Although writer Lincoln Chase made it as close to the original as possible in melody and lyrics, it did not sell as well as the original. It had six weeks on the R&B charts beginning in May 1956, peaking at number seven, and was number seventy-six on the pop charts. "Humpty Dumpty Heart," benefiting from the exposure Baker gave it by singing it in the film *Mr. Rock and Roll* (1957) made the pop charts for seven weeks in September of that year, peaking at seventy-one, but did not make the R&B charts at all. "It's So Fine" brought Baker back to the R&B charts for four weeks beginning in October 1958, the song peaked at number twenty-four.

Although most of the recordings Baker made during these years are fun to listen to—and her vibrant, self-assured voice is always a treat—her abilities were often not being used to best advantage; she's too big a talent for the material. You listen to a lively but contrived number like "Whipper Snapper," which Jerry Leiber and Mike Stoller wrote for her in 1957, and can almost imagine the songwriters thinking, "The less demanding we make this, the more listeners we can hook with it." Baker sings about a "young whippersnapper" who's a "juke-box jitterbug"—no substance here, just simple, slang-filled lines for the young "juke-box jitterbugs" who would hopefully spend dimes on the record. The songwriters were pandering to youth, and Baker was capable doing a lot more.

Although Baker had originally made her mark with numbers that had catchy, rhythmic beats, she scored the biggest commercial success of her career with a ballad in waltz time, "I Cried a Tear," which was enhanced by fine King Curtis tenor sax work. It made the R&B charts for nineteen weeks beginning in December 1958, peaking at number two, and the pop charts for six weeks, peaking at number twenty-one. Baker was now twenty-nine; in the youth-oriented world of rock 'n' roll—where callow teen singers, most of them here-today-gone-tomorrow, were turning out hit records—she was an experienced show-biz veteran. It was gratifying to her that she could score such a success singing a ballad in waltz time (even if it had a bit of a beat to stay contemporary).

The more versatile a performer she was, the more likely it appeared that she would eventually realize her goal of gaining acceptance as an all-around entertainer—not just a "rock 'n' roll singer." Her goal, her dream, since the days she had played the Club DeLisa, had been to some day play the most prestigious clubs and lounges. There was an entertainment world bigger than the fields of rhythm and blues or rock 'n' roll, and she wanted to crack it. Sammy Davis Jr. was part of that bigger world. Dinah Washington was moving into it by re-cording smooth, lushly orchestrated ballads rather than gutsier rhythm and blues numbers. As talented as Baker's relative Memphis Minnie had been, she had never made it into that world. At her peak, Memphis Minnie was the most frequently recorded female blues sing-er in the country. Between 1935 and 1942 she averaged a new re-lease almost every month—no one else in that period had gotten that kind of exposure—for which she had typically received only $12.50 a side. She received no recording artist's royalties, although she did receive composer's royalties for originals she recorded; her yearly in-come typically came to several hundred dollars. Memphis Minnie continued recording and performing, albeit for smaller record labels and in smaller clubs—a hard life—into the 1950s, until her husband's health and then her own began to fail. The business, as Baker knew, could eat a performer up.

Baker wanted to rise as high as she could in the entertainment business, without limitations. She didn't want to feel boxed in, sing-ing only certain kinds of songs and only for young audiences. There were a lot of great old standards on which she would have loved to have been permitted to try her hand. In the meantime, she was re-cording all sorts of contemporary material, some quite good (because she was doing so well on the charts, she was being offered top new songs that in earlier years would have been offered to Ruth Brown first), some quite insubstantial. Her producers suggested the songs for her to record.

Although Baker occasionally wrote or co-wrote songs she recorded—"That's All I Need" was a collaboration with Lincoln Chase and Howard Biggs and "How Often" was her own number—most of her numbers were written by everyone from a Tin Pan Alley veteran like Sam Coslow to such younger songwriters as Neil Sedaka, Doc Pomus, and Leiber and Stoller. In contrast to such R&B singer-songwriters as Charles Brown, Floyd Dixon, and Jimmy Witherspoon, Baker's own songs were not a key part of her repertoire. Her producers sensed which songs would click for her. "I Waited Too Long"—a strong, teen romance-type number coauthored by Neil Sedaka and Howard Greenfield that was about having waited too long to tell a man how she felt toward him—brought Baker to the R&B charts for twelve weeks, beginning in May 1959 and peaking at number five. It reached number thirty-three on the pop charts. She sang the song with authority, interjecting a gospel feeling. Her highly emotional style fit this torchy material well; her pronounced vibrato, which seemed a bit too throbbing on "I Cried a Tear," worked on "I Waited Too Long." (Sedaka recorded the song, too, but his version did not become a hit.)

In August 1959 Baker had hits with both "So High So Low," which reached number twelve on the R&B charts and fifty-two on the pop charts, and "If You Love Me," which reached number seventy-nine on the pop charts but did not appear on the R&B charts. In December 1959 her recording of "Tiny Tim" reached number eighteen on the R&B charts and sixty-three on the pop charts. There was perhaps no better indicator of Baker's popularity than the fact that Atlantic could release an album titled simply *LaVern*. You knew you'd made it when you were identifiable by a first name. Albums by rhythm and blues or rock 'n' roll performers were far from plentiful during the late fifties; only artists who were big-sellers had them. The business was primarily oriented toward singles, which more young buyers could afford; popular teen music shows like Dick Clark's kept track of which singles—never albums—were selling. Atlantic was a leader among independent labels in getting into the business of producing albums.

Surely the most unusual Baker album—and very different from anything any other "rock 'n' roll singers" were recording during the fifties—was the well-received 1958 Atlantic release, produced by Neshui Ertegun, *LaVern Baker Sings Bessie Smith*. Baker sang a dozen numbers, mostly from the twenties, that were associated with Smith, including "Young Woman's Blues," "I Ain't Gonna Play No Second Fiddle," "On Revival Day," "Baby Doll," "After You've Gone," "Money Blues," "Preaching the Blues," "Back Water Blues," "There'll Be a Hot Time in the Old Town Tonight," "Empty Bed Blues," "Nobody Knows You

When You're Down and Out," and "Gimme a Pigfoot (and a Bottle of Beer)." She received first-rate jazz accompaniment from the likes of trumpeter and former Count Basie Band star Buck Clayton (who later recalled being impressed, between takes at the recording studio, by Baker's uninhibited command of salty language), trombonist Vic Dickenson, and guitarist Danny Barker (who had vivid memories of seeing Smith perform years before), with arrangements crafted by Ernie Wilkins, Phil Moore, and Nat Pierce. It's a pity Baker couldn't have made more recordings with such stellar jazz backing.

The album was one LaVern Baker recording that white pop singers like Georgia Gibbs would never be able to cover convincingly. Whether or not one believed that Baker measured up to the memory of Bessie Smith ("the world's greatest blues singer" was a nearly impossible act for anyone to follow), there was no denying that she could relate to Smith's material, and she sang it with spirit, fire, and soul. Baker had sometimes sounded like an old-time blues shouter on her own rock 'n' roll singles; letting her take a stab at classic blues was a perfectly reasonable step. If she wanted to stretch out a little on a song—her pop singles had often run around two and a half minutes— she finally had the chance: "Nobody Knows You" ran to nearly four minutes, "Back Water Blues" to four and a half minutes, and "Empty Bed Blues" was nearly five minutes. Those recordings were longer than would have been optimum for them to get radio play; disc jockeys emphatically preferred shorter sides. Baker and Atlantic deserve credit for putting artistic, rather than commercial, considerations first on the project and aiming for adult, not teen, ears.

The album was a mixed success. I like the brash energy Baker brought to the songs (and she had some great material to work with) and the sexuality her throaty voice projected. I respect her, too, for approaching all of the songs in a fresh manner; she had enough self-assurance to put the emphases where *she* wanted to rather than following Smith's stylistic lead the way most singers of Smith's material would be inclined to do. Although Baker should be credited with originality, her interpretations lacked the majesty and dignity of Smith's. Nor did these songs fit her quite as well as they had fit Smith. Baker carried off some numbers quite successfully, but at times she brazenly pushed through the songs, trying to get by more on verve, sass, and gumption rather than carefully and thoughtfully shaping lines for maximum impact.

The album enjoyed good sales both in the late fifties when it was originally released and in the late eighties when it was rereleased to favorable critical reception. *LaVern Baker Sings Bessie Smith* proved there was much more to Baker than was being captured on youth-oriented commercial hits like "Tweedlee Dee." She further demonstrated her versatility by recording an album for Atlantic that consisted entirely of religious music.

Meanwhile Baker kept turning out singles, the range of which broadened gradually. She had success reviving a few oldies that seemed well suited to her. Baker's wonderfully moving version of the durable "Shake a Hand" (a number-one R&B hit in 1953 for Faye Adams, singing with trumpeter Joe Morris, who'd written the number, and his orchestra, it would subsequently also be a hit for Ruth Brown in 1962 and Jackie Wilson and Linda Hopkins in 1963) put Baker on the R&B charts for four weeks, beginning in March 1960 and peaking at number thirteen. She sang the number with a heartfelt church feeling. Baker's version of "Wheel of Fortune," a number one pop hit for Kay Starr in 1952, put her on the pop charts—although it did not make the R&B charts—for four weeks, beginning in May 1960 and peaking at number eighty-three; its flip side, "Shadows of Love," rose just as high. Baker's recording of "Bumble Bee" again put her on the pop charts, but not the R&B charts, for eleven weeks, beginning in November 1960 and peaking at sixty-five.

Baker reached way back to the repertoire of the "Mother of the Blues," Ma Rainey, for the classic "See See Rider." Many young listeners must have assumed—as I did at the time—that it was a new song. Her single of "See See Rider" landed her on the R&B charts for eight weeks beginning in December 1962. It reached number nine on the R&B charts and number thirty-four on the pop charts. Atlantic put out a LaVern Baker album also called *See See Rider*.

One memorable Baker number, "Saved," had a fervent, revival meeting-type feel and was well-suited for Baker's enthusiastic style. Although it sounded like an old song, it wasn't. "Saved," by Leiber and Stoller, put her on the R&B charts for five weeks beginning in May 1961, peaking at number seventeen on the R&B charts and reaching as high as thirty-seven on the pop charts. The romantic "Fly Me to the Moon (in Other Words)" made the charts in 1962 as a bossa nova instrumental by Joe Harnell and his orchestra. Baker's 1965 recording of the song, which has since become a standard, was its first vocal rendition to become a hit. Her recording kept her on the R&B charts for five weeks, beginning in February 1965, and reached number eighty-four on the pop charts, the same height subsequently reached a few months later by Tony Bennett's recording, the other hit vocal version of the number that year. The success of "Fly Me to the Moon" raises the question of what Baker could have done had she been given more opportunities to record material of that type and quality.

Baker occasionally recorded duets, too. "How Often," a nice recording that didn't sell very well, was with a not-yet-well-known Ben E. King of the Drifters in 1960 (a year before King made his own first hit records, "Spanish Harlem" and "Stand by Me"); "You're the Boss" was with Jimmy Ricks, who had been lead singer of the Ravens. It made the pop charts but not the R&B charts for three weeks beginning in February 1961, peaking at eighty-one. "Think Twice," which Baker recorded with Jackie Wilson for Brunswick after leaving Atlantic, made the R&B charts for three weeks in February 1966, reaching number thirty-seven (ninety-three on the pop charts). That was Baker's final appearance on the charts. In all, twenty-one of her recordings made the R&B charts, twenty the pop charts.

* * *

Baker made the pop charts much more often than any of the other artists profiled in this book. Several factors account for this success. Her career peaked later than those of the other artists, at a time when black performers had greater opportunities for commercial success. She didn't score her first hit until 1955, and she continued to be quite popular well into the sixties. By 1955 the careers of Charles Brown, Ruth Brown, Little Jimmy Scott, Floyd Dixon, and Jimmy Witherspoon all seemed to have crested. They all were still working—and in some cases would have eventual comebacks—but they had all been more popular, based on number of *Billboard* R&B chart hits, during the late forties or early fifties. (Ruth Brown was still turning out hits and would do so into the early sixties, but not with the frequency or impact of earlier years.) One factor in Baker's success was that as the fifties wore on, it became easier for black performers to gain access to radio and television, which helped boost record sales. Although opportunities for blacks were certainly not as good as they would be during the sixties, seventies, and eighties (Baker recalls that in the late fifties black performers seemed to appear last on many television shows), at least Baker was receiving television exposure. In addition, more and more radio stations were playing records of black R&B performers in the late fifties than had been the case in earlier years. The color line was breaking down in the entertainment industry just as it was breaking down in American society in general. Crossover hits—R&B hits that also turned up on the pop charts—became more common during the late fifties than they had been during the early part of the decade.

These points noted, however, the fact remains that Baker was an exceptionally flexible, versatile, well-rounded performer who—regardless of whether opportunities for black performers were expanding in the late fifties—had the potential of appealing to a broader range of people than most of the other singers profiled in this book. She was a striking performer who could effectively handle many different types of songs: fast blues, slow blues, torch songs, graceful ballads—you name it.

Little Jimmy Scott's slow, highly stylized, jazz-inflected, emotionally wrought way of singing would always be something of a specialized taste; mainstream audiences would prefer singing that was more conventional and familiar. When inspired, Jimmy Witherspoon could sing pure blues better—more movingly—than anyone else profiled in this book. But his sheer mastery of one idiom came at a cost; he has never been nearly as effective a singer of ordinary ballads as of blues. Nor has he ever had any interest in singing commercial rock 'n' roll songs he doesn't believe in. He would not have touched songs like "Get Up, Get Up (You Sleepyhead)" or "Whipper Snapper," which Baker recorded. Rather than simply seek out likely hits or play down to younger audiences, he has maintained his artistic integrity. Blues balladeer Charles Brown was the greatest exponent of a particular laid-back "club blues" singing style, which he developed during the forties and which Floyd Dixon and others used effectively. But he wasn't as appealing on jump blues as on slower numbers (Dixon was more at home on jump blues than Brown was) and couldn't get into the louder, wilder rock 'n' roll that developed later in the fifties and sixties at all.

In terms of versatility, only Ruth Brown, who has recorded widely varied types of material, came close to Baker. And even Brown was notably better on some types of songs than others. Give her strong, gutsy numbers she could sock home like "Mama, He Treats Your Daughter Mean" or "Five-Ten-Fifteen Hours"—simple, sturdy songs with a beat that could bear the weight when she'd put everything she had into them—and no one could touch her. She could also sing certain slower songs (often tinged with self-pity) to perfection, too, such as "I Can See Everybody's Baby," "Have a Good Time," and "Why Me," but Brown's forte lay in numbers that, particularly in live performances, gave her the chance to let out all the stops.

Being able to handle all different types of songs rather well—from classic blues, to beautiful ballads, to the most trivial rock 'n' roll ditties for teenagers (even injecting those songs with some soul and sass)—had a lot to do with Baker's widespread appeal. She could scat-sing with a naturalness and ease that would put a lot of self-defined "jazz singers" to shame and inflect a standard like "It Had to Be You" with just enough blues feeling to make it intriguingly her own. Baker could offer something for everybody. And the fact that she made a dynamite appearance added to her appeal, whether in stage shows or on TV or film.

Television played a bigger role in Baker's career than in the careers of other performers discussed in this book. Blacks garnered more television exposure as the years went by, and many American homes had television sets by the middle and late fifties, when Baker's career was strongest. "I did the tour with Alan Freed and that's what opened the door for that," she explains. In addition to her association with Freed, Baker made many appearances on rapidly rising television host Dick Clark's shows, too. "And we did a lot of local disc jockey type shows—they were here today and gone tomorrow," she recalls. She moved up to more important, prime-time network television programs, as well. In 1956, for example, Ed Sullivan asked Harlem disc jockey Dr. Jive (Tommy Smalls) to organize a fifteen-minute R&B segment for his top-rated show, and he chose LaVern Baker, Bo Diddley, Willis "Gator Tail" Jackson, and the Five Keys. "My first big TV show was Ed Sullivan," Baker recalls. "I was on Ed Sullivan quite a bit. And I did the life of Harold Arlen—a 'Du Pont Show of the Month,' but I can't remember what year it was. I did a TV show with Andy Williams when he first started [around 1958]. I did Barbara McNair, that talk show she used to have."

The main thrust of her work, of course, remained in personal appearances—one-nighters throughout the country and occasionally outside of the country as well. In January 1957, for example, Baker went with Bill Haley and his Comets and Joe Turner on an Australian tour. Later that year, she was criss-crossing the United States on an eighty-day tour in what was being billed as the "Biggest Show of Stars for 1957." It lived up to that billing, too, offering in one show Fats Domino, Chuck Berry, LaVern Baker, Clyde McPhatter, Frankie Lymon, the Drifters, Paul Anka, the Crickets, the Bobbettes, the Spaniels, Johnnie and Joe, and the Everly Brothers. There were some substitutions in various parts of the country—Eddie Cochran, for example, played on western dates only—and in several cities of the Deep South, due to Jim Crow laws prohibiting blacks and whites from appearing onstage together, the white performers could not appear.

Yet the fact that in 1957 the biggest package show being offered to bookers nationally was racially integrated was a major change. The R&B package tours of earlier years had traditionally been all black.

Now, changing social conditions as well as the broadening of interest in the music allowed promoters to offer racially integrated tours. Baker was among those who helped pioneer such changes. Old barriers were coming down. At an all-star show at the Brooklyn Paramount Theater with Bill Haley and his Comets and the Four Step Brothers, Baker could sing duets with her old friend Johnnie Ray, who was headlining the bill. Duets between a white male singer and a black female singer—particularly a sexy black singer—wouldn't have been programmed a few years earlier. The show, *Ebony* noted, grossed a whopping $148,000 in a week.

At one of Baker's Apollo Theatre bookings she shared the bill with the Impalas, a recently formed vocal group (best remembered for "I Ran All the Way Home") that was racially integrated—still another sign of changing times. More commonly at Apollo appearances, of course, she shared bills with performers who were black, ranging from jazz tenor sax great Illinois Jacquet, to blues singer Little Willie John, to pop balladeer Johnny Mathis.

She remembers vividly how extraordinarily busy she was kept—she came to feel that she was being worked harder than her body could take—and the additional stress she periodically experienced on the road because of racial prejudice. "I was doing mostly one-nighters, and I never had no time off. Because if I wasn't with Irvin Feld, I was with Henry Wynne; if I wasn't with him, we were with Alan Freed," she says, naming organizers and presenters of touring shows.

Audiences in the South were separated by race. "Some of them had the blacks upstairs, whites downstairs; some of them had a rope in the middle—white on one side, black on the other side. Some places we had to do two shows: white first show, black second show. It was just like that. But we didn't go in there to change anything; we went in there to do our job, make people happy, and leave. And this was the reason of our success; no one interfered with anything. No one complained—even though we didn't like it. But what are we going to do? It wasn't our town. And so many of our white fans wanted to come to us and they couldn't. And with the Everly Brothers, I saw a [black] girl actually cry one night because the police wouldn't let her across the ropes; she just wanted an autograph."

They had no choice but to accept Jim Crow customs in the South. "If we were leaving town, sometimes we had two buses. And we used to send all the white acts to get us a sandwich because we couldn't go into the restaurants," she recalls, briefly laughing at the notion—a laugh that covers her pain. "Yeah, sure. And then when we got into our [black] section, we had to do the same thing for the white performers. It was just the times. Water fountains for whites only. And I'd say, 'Where do I drink water?' And sometimes the reply was nice and sometimes it wasn't. So we all started buying our own little ice chests. We kept ice and drinks so we wouldn't have to go through this. And in the real bad cities at that time, we never stayed overnight. We pulled right out. We kept on going.

"A lot of cities, they didn't want us at the time. Once, I remember, I was on a tour with Nat King Cole, and they were rioting against the show—they didn't want us there. In Montgomery. About two days before we were supposed to come, Mr. Feld had canceled the show. He said, 'I'm not taking the kids into that.' But we got a telegram from the sheriff and the government saying, 'You bring the show in. They will be protected.' So they called out the National Guard. So they stood arm-in-arm, linked, right across the stage. No one could get near us. That was a Nat King Cole show, with Erskine Hawkins's band—Della Reese was the vocalist then with Erskine Hawkins—and a comedian, the original Drifters, and myself. And we were out for fifty one-nighters. But that was the only place we worked where we had an incident."

Was that during the fight over school integration?

"I don't know. We don't have no idea what was going on at the time. We were nervous anyway," Baker says. "Our main concern was, 'Let's do the show and get the heck out of here.' But there were a lot of nights—I'm not going to say I wasn't afraid; you were afraid. Because a lot of nights, the girls, we sat cramped because there was no place for us to go to the restroom. We refused to stop the bus anywhere until we got to a city," she remembers. Everyone tried to make the best of things.

"We didn't mind the hotel situation, as long as the bed was clean," Baker maintains. "We didn't mind where we had to live because that was just for one night. Sometimes we stayed on the bus rather than check into the hotels. The places that they put us. This was all they had. And the managers, they felt bad as heck. But what can they do? They can't change it. So we stayed on the bus. A lot of times, everybody would stay on the bus. We formed a pact together, all of us. *Everybody.* We were a show; we didn't consider ourselves part of anything or any individual. We were one. So if we [the black performers] couldn't stay, then nobody stayed. I know one night we did back-to-back eight-hundred-mile trips. We did eight hundred miles, we did a show, we got back on the bus and did another eight hundred miles. Because we did not want to stay in that town. Everybody. We left."

* * *

Eventually, it all got to be too much for Baker: the ceaseless traveling, the sense of never having a chance to catch up on needed rest,
the singing of the same hit songs over and over again. No matter
how hard she tried to convince herself that such matters didn't bother
her, the stress of being told in one southern town after another that
she had to go "across the tracks" to eat and sleep, or knowing that
she could face hassles at any time over things as basic as being able
to use a bathroom, took its toll. She wonders how well some of today's highly paid young black entertainers who've been spared such
hardships would have coped with what she and other R&B performers of the fifties went through routinely. Yes, Baker was making a good
living, but maybe not quite as good as her publicity suggested. (One
1957 newspaper squib claimed she was spending $4,000 a year on
her poodle. "I used to have one of the greatest press agents in the
world," she recalls, "a former New York newspaperman. He kept my
press going all the time.") But what was the point of making money
if you were too worn out to enjoy it and putting your health at risk?

She wanted to get off of the rock 'n' roll treadmill. Instead of doing one-night stands as part of big rock 'n' roll package shows, she
wanted to play more selective bookings as a featured attraction in
fancier clubs. Ray Charles, who used to tour the same sort of places
she did, was getting into more prestigious venues, and she felt the
time had come to try to do likewise. She invested money in devel-
oping a night-club act—new routines, new arrangements, new
gowns—and made a bid, finally, for the supper-club market.

"A reformed rock 'n' roll singer," is how Arthur Gelb of *The New
York Times* opted to describe LaVern Baker on May 29, 1961, when
she made her "first major night-club appearance," appearing with
Louis Armstrong at New York's prestigious Basin Street East. Gelb
noted that Baker was concentrating "on jazz and blues. She is vivid
and expert in both areas. A solidly built young woman with an arti-
choke coiffure, a skin-tight dress and eyes asparkle with wicked humor, she has a big, self-confident voice, a relaxed but flawless sense
of rhythm and a commanding stage presence."

Although Armstrong was the headliner of the show, which also
included the gifted song stylist Julie Wilson, Gelb felt that duets by
Armstrong and Baker provided "the best part of the evening's entertainment." Their exuberant good humor on "That's My Desire," a
number Armstrong had for many years sung with the recently de-

ceased Velma Middleton, Gelb found particularly infectious. (Baker
still loves to sing that number as a remembrance of Armstrong, sometimes throwing in a well-turned Armstrong imitation for a few lines.)
In Baker's solo turn, Gelb noted, she didn't sing the rock 'n' roll numbers that had put her on the pop charts. She sang oldies like "After
You've Gone," which she said she associated with Bessie Smith, "Yes
Sir, That's My Baby," and "Bill Bailey Won't You Please Come Home"
(with parody lyrics about Nikita Khrushchev and Fidel Castro).

Gelb quoted Baker as saying, "Singing for an adult audience in a
sophisticated club is what I've always wanted to do. But there was a
lot of money in rock 'n' roll and it was hard to break away. My decision to quit came when I realized that the continual one-night stands
in theaters and auditoriums across the country finally started being
detrimental to my health." She said that she had offers to work clubs
in Los Angeles, Chicago, Miami, and Las Vegas; Joe Glaser, who booked
Armstrong, was now booking her. Gelb also wrote that he believed that
Baker would be a natural for a Broadway musical based on the life of
Bessie Smith, a project that had been talked about for years.

The laudatory *Times* piece obviously meant a great deal to Baker;
nearly thirty years after it had been printed she retained a copy of
it—laminated to a piece of wood to form a plaque—in her dressing
room. Gazing at the review, Baker remarks with a touch of wistful-
ness, "That was when I decided to get out of rock 'n' roll." But making the move proved more difficult than she had hoped. Glaser was
able to get her some bookings on her own in top venues, but rees-
tablishing her image with a public that now had her pegged as a rock
'n' roller was another matter.

She explains, "Like Las Vegas, Miami—these places that you struggle to get in when you're a rock 'n' roll star—at that time, they were
not accepting rock 'n' roll artists. All of the big rooms in Vegas at
the time were like that; Sinatra here and this one there. You had to
have an act, you had to do ballads. So I *got* a nightclub act, and I
worked these rooms. And it was so confusing because you give up
everything and you pay for a big act, and you go in and try to do
your act—all new songs, which take you a long time to prepare—and
then somebody hollers out, 'Sing "Jim Dandy"!' Oh, you get so angry! And I wouldn't do it, either. I was just mad. I knew my bosses
got mad at me, but they didn't know how I felt. Here I'd been trying for fifteen years to work this room and I finally get it. I could
never get it up until then because I was a rock 'n' roll artist. And I'd
developed an act—I had songs especially written for me, special
monologues and stuff, and I had 'Suppertime' from Ethel Waters, and

'Stormy Weather' and my show from Basin Street East from Louis Armstrong."

She was not able to reposition herself. Audiences would let her sing some of the songs she wanted to sing but most wanted to hear her past hits. To the public, she was "the 'Tweedlee Dee' girl." It hardly mattered if, as Ahmet Ertegun aptly said to writer John Milward, "The fact that LaVern is mainly remembered for what was a novelty song, 'Tweedlee Dee,' puts the wrong emphasis on her real qualities as a singer."[10] The general public was not going to change its perception of her. If she wanted to work, she had better give the public what it expected.

After leaving Atlantic Records in 1964, Baker signed with Brunswick/Decca. She made some recordings she was happy with (she was particularly glad to get to record duets with the dynamic Jackie Wilson), but by the mid-sixties her time in the spotlight had largely passed. Just as Baker had once overtaken Brown in popularity, so did younger singers come along to overtake Baker. By the late sixties Aretha Franklin, twelve years younger than Baker, had become Atlantic's queen, turning out strongly sung hits such as "(You Make Me Feel Like) A Natural Woman" and "Baby I Love You" that helped define "soul" and made Baker's brand of R&B sound like it belonged to an earlier era. Opportunities for black artists, generally, had significantly improved since Baker had entered show business. By 1968 six of the nation's top ten recording artists (as ranked in Joel Whitburn's *Pop Singles Annual,* using *Billboard* pop chart data) were black. Marvin Gaye was ranked number one for the year; Aretha Franklin, number two; James Brown, number three; Otis Redding, number five; Dionne Warwick, number six; and Tammi Terrell, number nine. By contrast, in 1955, the year Baker had her first chart hit, only one of the top ten artists had been black: Nat King Cole. Baker was pleased to see the progress and know she had been part of it. Although her records were no longer selling the way they once had, she continued touring heavily. She always connected well with a live audience.

In the meantime, her second marriage, to comedian Slappy White, was falling apart. Baker doesn't like to say much about White or about her personal life in general, but she does credit him with having helped her become a more well-rounded entertainer. Recognizing her naturally witty bent and flair for establishing a rapport with an audience, he had written patter for her act, lines she'd deliver for a laugh to enliven her club appearances. After they separated, she not only continued using the lines he'd written for her, but she also appropriated—and made good use of—gag lines she'd heard *him* use countless times in his act.

* * *

Baker particularly loved playing for servicemen and increasingly performed for them. They didn't seem to care whether she currently had
a record on the charts; they always made her feel appreciated. To servicemen stationed abroad, she realized that she represented a welcome touch of home. She notes, "Hey, these guys they had in some
of these place I went, they hadn't seen shows or heard anything from
home for months. I went through all the military bases in Europe,
and I never had any trouble. I've been all over the world—by myself." In 1970 she went to Vietnam. "Those bases I played up there—
Cam Ran Bay, An Khe—I went to all these things by myself. Somebody wrote me up and said I did USO shows, but I've never done a
USO show in my life. I was nervous while I was in Vietnam. I had to
carry two I.D. cards all the time—one to enter the American base and
one to show the Vietnamese that I was non-active, just a citizen. But
it was an experience; I really did enjoy it. And I've found that if you
treat people like you want to be treated, nobody will bother you—
no one's going to just walk up and deliberately shoot you or deliberately touch you for no reason at all."

   While in Vietnam, Baker, whose stamina had been weakened over
the years, became seriously ill. Her heart was enlarged and a lung was
collapsing. She tries to make light of her suffering: "Oh well, I got
hurt a little bit internally—or eternally," she says with a laugh, trying to minimize what she went through. "My lungs and all that stuff,
while working in Vietnam. And from Vietnam, I went back to Thai-
land, and then to Hong Kong to sing at the Playboy Club. And on
the closing night there, I was very, very ill, so they rushed me to the
hospital in Hong Kong, and it was discovered that I had this, that,
and so forth and so on, and it was very dangerous to travel at the
time. As a matter of fact, they pulled my health card and my pass-
port until I was able to travel. Well, I got this coming out of Vietnam. I'm OK now. I'm on the medication for the rest of life, that's
all. High blood pressure and enlarged heart. As long as I stay on my
medication as it's supposed to be, I'm OK," she says. She realized that
her body could no longer tolerate the strain of the constant travel
she endured for twenty years. "Since I had my illness, the doctors
have explained to everyone: if I go to sleep, leave me alone, let me
sleep. Because my body needs it. And my heart and my pressure and
stuff is maintaining cool. I have to be careful of that."

   While in the hospital in Hong Kong in 1970 she determined to slow
her pace, although she had no intention of giving up show business

altogether. "My doctor suggested that I go to a warmer climate. And my agent said, 'I'll let you go to the Philippines' because he's also married to a Filipino, and she wanted to go home anyway. He said, 'Do you want to work the Intercontinental Hotel? I've got you booked there for ten days. Then if you want to rest or whatever, you could stay at my house until you want to do something.' So we did this."

She had no idea when she arrived in the Philippines that she was going to make that country her home for the next twenty years. "I went in the Intercontinental Hotel for what was supposed to be two weeks, and I stayed eleven. And then I started working the bases—Clark Air Force Base, Wallace Communication Base, Subic—doing one-night runs: two shows, sometimes three shows, and they usually would bring you back." She found that she could do all the touring she'd want without ever leaving the Philippines. By the time she'd stayed there through a rainy season she felt that she'd begun putting down roots. Even the exceptional flooding of 1972 didn't stop her from getting to bases and performing. "It rained just like you see in the Bible—forty days and forty nights without stopping. I was with three or four Australian kids; we had the same agent. And we all got terribly wet, we went up on two bonga boats, one bus, and a truck. Everything was flooded, even the rice paddies—everything. We finally got there—the assistant manager saw us on the back of a truck, and he threw us all in his car and rushed us to the base, and they gave us the big tablecloths so we could get dry—it was so cold—and hot tea and hot chocolate and stuff. So we gave a good show, we made it. But then we couldn't get out, so different people on the base put us up at their homes. So we were stuck there for about a week or so. Then I got offered a job and I decided to stay in the Philippines. My health was one of the reasons I stayed, and personal things here in the States is the second one. So I just stayed. As good a place as any. It was a good move. And with the military—at least I got a different audience every night.

"I work at the Marine Staff NCO [noncommissioned officers'] Club. But it's the number one club of the Seventh Fleet—the best marine NCO club there is. Guys come from all over, and they say, 'Hey, this is the best club we've ever been in.' I'm the entertainment director there. I work in the office from Monday to Thursday and then Friday and Saturday, I'm in the club." She says she *is* working there—present tense—because when she signed a six-month contract to appear in *Black and Blue* in 1990 she did not formally resign from her job in the Philippines but merely took a leave so she'd have the option to return. (She's chosen, of course, to stay in the United States.)

LaVern Baker, setting "souls on fire" in the early 1950s. (Author's collection; courtesy of the Institute of Jazz Studies)

An early 1990s reunion of LaVern Baker and Floyd Dixon in Hollywood. (Author's collection; courtesy of Right Time Productions)

A mid-fifties gathering of three of Atlantic's three top recording artists and two of the men who directed the company. From left to right: Jerry Wexler, Ruth Brown, Clyde McPhatter, LaVern Baker, and Ahmet Ertegun. Brown was the company's top female vocal star of the first half of the fifties; in the second half of the decade, Baker supplanted her. (Author's collection; courtesy of Ruth Brown)

"A show stopper anywhere—the gal who put the rhythm in the blues," the slogan read. Baker's 1954 recording of the catchy "Tweedlee Dee" (misspelled on this promotional flyer of the period) was one of her biggest pop hits. But "Tomorrow Night," recorded at the same session, displayed better the strength and sensuality she could so masterfully project. (Courtesy of La-Vern Baker)

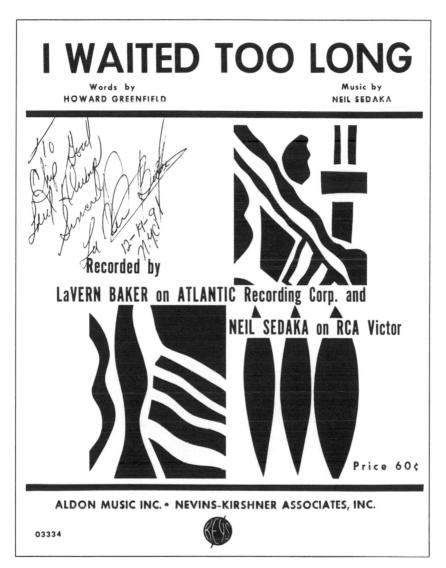

The sheet music for Baker's 1959 hit "I Waited Too Long" (written by Neil Sedaka), autographed by Baker for the author in 1991. (Author's collection; courtesy of Brian Gari)

Baker, looking like a million in one of the fabulous costumes designed by Claudio Segovia and Hector Orezzoli for the Broadway musical production *Black and Blue,* 1990. (Author's collection; courtesy of Marilynn LeVine)

In Medoc, France, in 1991, Baker enjoys a get-together with jazz great Buck Clayton, who had played trumpet on her acclaimed *LaVern Baker Sings Bessie Smith* album thirty-three years earlier. Baker's sassy style scored as well with European concert audiences as with American ones. (Author's collection; photo by Nancy Miller Elliott)

Following her comeback in *Black and Blue*, Baker played clubs and concerts for several years until health problems including a stroke and the amputation of both legs below the knee forced her to suspend activities for two years. She resumed performing in September 1995. (Author's collection; photo by Nick Elgar; courtesy of Third Floor Media)

From almost the moment she began working in the Philippines she felt needed by the troops arriving for rest and recuperation. "There were so many of our boys coming back from Vietnam and believe me they were just uptight. Believe me. And they needed someone to sit and talk to. Dance with. They had gone through so much. I just opened up my heart and I started enjoying it. Even now, after Marines finish their training, sometimes they fly over and get R&R over in our place. And they're so excited, they'll clap to anything. They're just so happy to be entertained. And when they see somebody from home, they don't care what color you are; they're just happy to see you and they're very appreciative. And this means a lot to me, too. They really like you there."

Baker hadn't made a record since the late sixties. The longer she stayed in the Philippines, the rarer and rarer it became for any of the arriving young soldiers to associate her name with her hits of the fifties and early sixties; they were becoming ancient history. She didn't sing her old songs; she simply sang whatever she thought the soldiers might like to hear. "Very seldom would I sing 'Tweedlee Dee' and 'I Cried a Tear.' One guy asked me for 'See See Rider' and the band never heard of it. They told him, 'She don't sing that.' I just don't do it. We do some oldies but goodies, some of the stuff that they're doing today; we try to please everybody. Because you've got a mixed audience. Filipinos, their love is Latin music. So we do cha-cha, merengue. We do blues *a little*, funky rock 'n' roll, we do hard rock, we do everything. And you got the shit-kicking crowd, we have to do country and western. We have to do everything in that club. It's a hard club to work. I like the slow country and western. Look what Ray Charles did. You can take a country and western song and sing it any way you want to. But take a fast song nowadays, it's either fast or six-eight; there are only three ways of making it go. And I like Neil Diamond. I love him. Of course he's not a rhythm and blues man, but I just like him anyway. I like the texture in his voice. It's not a big voice, but it makes you notice. And that's what's important."

She hired other singers to work at the club; if they didn't click, she knew she could step in to liven up show. It may not have been the big time—indeed, she had dropped off the face of the earth as far as many performers in the United States knew—but Baker is proud to have stayed in show business rather than having had to scrub floors or perform other manual labor. She feels that she can hold her head high.

"I don't earn a big salary. I couldn't live off of what I make in the Philippines in the United States. But I live very well-off for there. And it's nice. The Filipinos are nice to me." Baker learned the native language, Tagalog. She bristles when she thinks of one reporter who wrote that she left show business in the United States to work in the Philippines at "an ordinary job," noting, "Now I'm sure that he [the reporter] can't speak Tagalog—that's no ordinary job, baby! I'm dealing with all Filipinos. The only Americans I've got are my bosses, my peers. Everybody else there, all the staff, everything is all Filipinos."

She has also reared four children: her natural daughter, an adopted daughter, and the boy and girl for whom she serves as guardian. "They were left with me by a guy who said he'd be back to get them but never came back. You can't put two kids out in the street," she reflects. "God's been good to me. I haven't wanted for anything for the children, and they've grown to love me."

*　*　*

Meanwhile, in the 1985–86 season the original production of *Black and Blue* was a great hit in Paris. Its principals included singers Ruth Brown, Linda Hopkins, Sandra Reaves-Philips, and Jimmy "Preacher" Robins. (The latter two were not in the show when it opened on Broadway in January 1989.) At the time of the Paris production, Claudio Segovia and Hector Orezzoli, who conceived and directed the show, began looking for Baker for possible inclusion in the Broadway production. Their assistant and press representative Marilynn LeVine recalls on this afternoon in June 1990, "I fished LaVern out in 1986 and found her. She was incognito in Manila. We thought she was with CIA, she was so hard to find."

"I was hiding," Baker interjects.

No one in the business seemed to know exactly where Baker was, LeVine says. They'd heard a rumor that she had moved to the Philippines. "I said, 'Where would she be working in the Philippine Islands for twenty years?' LeVine remembers. "And then somebody said something about the U.S. government, so I figured she must be on a base. I got on the phone and I called every officers' club in the Philippine Islands, asking if LaVern Baker was there. Finally, I got an answer: 'She's not here, she'll be in at 3.' I almost fell over. Meanwhile, Hector was planning a trip to Japan to look at the theaters for the tour of *Tango Argentino*. And he said, 'Well, I'll go to the Philippines.'"

"This man Hector, he flew all the way to the Philippines to see me—in March of 1987," Baker remembers. "I was so surprised. I said, 'What are you doing here?' He said, 'I come to see you.' I said, 'Well come on.' I took him inside the base, I sat him down at the table. I kept him there for about an hour, bought him two bottles of wine while I did my work. I sat and talked and I told him, well at that particular time I wasn't really ready to come back to the United States to do nothing. Maybe a concert or two and then back. Because I explained to him I got my two kids and two more that I'm their legal guardian, so that makes a total of four. In other words, I cannot work there if I have worry here [she points to her head]—you understand what I mean?"

Hector Orezzoli asked her to sing some blues—any of the old Bessie Smith numbers she had recorded in 1958, to give him an idea of how she would be for *Black and Blue* if she were to join the company. He pleaded that he'd traveled half way around the world to see and hear her, but she told him simply that she was sorry that she was not going to able to comply. "He asked me to sing something from the Bessie Smith album," she explains. "I don't do it. I can't. Because the Filipinos don't know any of it. They never even heard of it. Basic songs that they've copied off records, they know—standards. But it's hard for a Filipino band to play the blues unless they have the charts right in front of them. If you walk up on a stage here and tell the guys, 'Hey, baby, give me blues in A flat,' they'll say, 'Hey, right on.' Even in *Black and Blue*, you've got all ex-jazz and blues musicians in this band, and I could say, 'Hey baby, give me blues in D minor'—without any charts you can do it. You can't do that with a Filipino band. So I just never sang the blues. I had many people ask me to sing the blues—many, many, many. And I just—I never have the charts.'"

The producers finally accepted the fact that Baker was not going to be a part of *Black and Blue* when it opened on Broadway, but she stayed in their thoughts. In 1988 Baker accepted an invitation from Ahmet Ertegun and flew back to the United States to sing at Atlantic Records' gala fortieth anniversary celebration at Madison Square Garden. Television audiences could see her reprise her hits "Tweedlee Dee" and "Jim Dandy." "I didn't even know what they were flying me here for," she insists. "Ahmet called me and said, 'Can you come for my fortieth anniversary?' And I said, 'Sure I'll come. I'll just see if my boss will let me off.' So they did, and it was very nice." She got to see old friends she hadn't seen in many years like Ruth Brown, who "told me then that she would like me to come back." Baker displayed enough pizzazz in her singing to receive subsequent invitations to record songs used on the soundtracks of the films *Shag* and *Dick Tracy*. Not bad for a woman who hadn't made a record in some twenty years. But then it was back to her regular job at the Subic Bay base.

In November 1989 Baker was among the honorees selected to receive the first annual Career Achievement Awards from the Rhythm and Blues Foundation. However, unlike such fellow honorees as Ruth Brown, Charles Brown, and Little Jimmy Scott, she did not make the trip to Washington, D.C. to receive the award in person. The foundation had to send it to her in the Philippines.

In the meantime, the producers of *Black and Blue* kept pursuing Baker. The show had opened in New York and was doing well, and they wanted her as a replacement for Ruth Brown when Brown left. They wanted a performer who not only sang well, but—like costars Brown and Linda Hopkins—who also "carried a history" as LeVine puts it. Baker was still playing hard to get. "I said I have to make sure everything is running the way that I want it to run. Then I came back this year [1990] and performed at the Lonestar Roadhouse. The producers came up there to see me," she recalls.

*   *   *

I can't forget Baker's appearance at the Lonestar Roadhouse. Even before she came onstage, the night had the feeling of "an event." The audience packing the house was well aware that this was Baker's first New York club booking in more than twenty years, and it was uncertain when, if ever, she might appear in New York again.

"God bless America. It's nice to be back home, even if it is for a short time," she told us. She spoke of entertaining U.S. servicemen in the Philippines, saying she was able to work there with "pride, and grow old gracefully." Dressed in a seductive red outfit, she looked svelte. She went into "Tweedlee Dee" with aplomb. There was nothing tentative about her performance, no hint of uncertainty about her acceptance although such thoughts may well have been in the back of her mind. Accompanying her were a trombone, a trumpet, a sax, a guitar, a piano, and Hammond B-3 organ as well as two male backup singers.

Her richly timbered voice was resonant. She introduced "the late, great, immortal W. C. Handy's 'St. Louis Blues.'" Her very stance as she spoke was both sexy and assertive. She sang the song briskly with a rock n' roll beat, much as she had recorded it in the fifties, an almost ecstatic expression coming across her face. At intervals the backup singers piped in, somewhat irrelevantly, the words "St. Louis, St. Louis."

She then reprised an old hit, "Bumble Bee." The rendition was short, like listening to a 45 rpm single done live, and she didn't seem to get into the song. She also did another of her old hits, "See See Rider," in an equally professional but perfunctory fashion. Ruth

Brown, to whom she was often compared in her heyday, frequently opens up her old hits when she sings them; she knows when to let a soloist who's on a roll keep playing and when to sing extra choruses, gradually building to maximum impact. Her sense of involvement in her material is almost always strong. Baker wasn't finding as much in her old hits as Brown finds in hers. One reason, no doubt, was that Baker hadn't been performing them regularly for many years. Brown's act has evolved over time, and she is accompanied by a working band that's been exploring her songs with her for years. Considering that Baker hadn't been working with this band or singing the songs regularly—the show had been put together just for this engagement in New York and another in Washington, D.C.—she was doing an impressive job.

At the conclusion of one song Baker told the audience "thank you" in Tagalog. From the audience, she introduced bandleader Paul Schaffer (from television's "The David Letterman Show"), mentioning that they had worked together at the Atlantic Records fortieth anniversary celebration. She also introduced Charles Brown, who was sitting at another table, saying to him softly, "When you get past thirty-five, everything is now a spot that hurts, isn't it Charles?" "Yeah," Brown affirmed. She told the audience, "I don't drink anymore and I don't smoke." With just the right timing she added, "Two out of three isn't bad." When the audience laughed, she quipped, "That's a dirty crowd in here tonight."

She swung smartly into "Jim Dandy." She had decided, it appeared, to do most of her old hits. While she was singing "Jim Dandy to the rescue—go, Jim Dandy," an aging dancer who had toured with her in her youth stood, began waving his arms to the beat and moving in place, and finally danced a bit across the stage. She told us that he had danced behind her in shows nearly thirty-five years earlier; he *was* Jim Dandy. However, midway through the number he suddenly fell; it was an awkward, uncomfortable moment. With great tenderness, Baker spoke to him, "Did you fall down, honey? It's all right. Everybody falls down once in a while." Then she added, honestly, "I told you when you get old, you can't do it no more."

She went on with her act, talking informally with the audience like she was among old friends, and to a considerable extent she was that night. At one table an older black man was waving one of her albums from the late fifties. Looking around the audience, I spotted, before night's end, Little Jimmy Scott, Carrie Smith, and Ruth Brown.

"You know how to make an old lady feel good," Baker told the audience. "It feels good tonight." Referring to herself as being old seemed curious. There was certainly nothing old about the way Baker looked, sounded, or moved as she sang. At one point she shook herself like a belly dancer in a way that seemed wholly natural and sexual. She may have been unaware of her movements; a few days later she told me she'd been annoyed by one reviewer who'd suggested that she'd moved like a shake dancer. She'd never done anything of the sort, she insisted. Of course she had—and the reviewer had not meant to be critical.

One longtime fan requested that she sing "That Lucky Old Sun." She responded that she hadn't rehearsed it and the band wouldn't be able to do it, but she sang it effectively nonetheless with the organist following her. She sang "I Cried a Tear," then brought it all home with "Saved." As she declaimed rhythmically—and emphatically—about how she used to smoke, drink, and dance the hoochy-coochy but now was "saved" she was dazzling. She danced a bit to the music, spontaneously. It seemed as if she had intentionally been holding back on some earlier numbers, perhaps saving her energy. Perhaps the audience's obvious affection had prompted her to give more. They were clearly sharing in her enthusiasm now. At the show's close she commented, as if in response to her zestily appreciative reception, "I'll think about coming back."

Her energy and sexiness made me think of Tina Turner, although I enjoyed Baker more. Some of the flash didn't last; that is to say, Baker's performance didn't have the lasting impact that a performance of Ruth Brown's would. Still, it was a snappily paced, highly professional set, particularly impressive when one considered that Baker had put the act together on short notice.

Having seen Baker on other occasions since her performance at the Lonestar Roadhouse, I realize that she wasn't demonstrating her talent fully on that night. Since she has had the chance to get back into the swing of things and she and her musicians have become comfortable with her act, Baker is singing with more panache. Even though her voice has less body than in her youth, she is capable of creating about as much impact. Compare her 1991 Rhino recording of "Play It Fair" with her 1955 Atlantic recording of the song. She seems to be pulling more from herself on the new recording, which is at least as effective as the original.

The performance Baker gave at the Lonestar, after an absence from American scene of more than twenty years, should have left no doubts in the minds of the producers of *Black and Blue*—or anyone else who came to see her—that she was still in good shape. Before returning to the Philippines, Baker met with the producers and a deal was clinched. She would succeed Ruth Brown in *Black and Blue*.

* * *

What made Baker finally decide to do *Black and Blue?*

In her dressing room, twenty-four days after returning from the Philippines, she responds, "Well, number one—let's not lie—was the salary. If I decide to return to the United States for good, I'll have to get my kids out of the Philippines. I would like to set up things for them here. One of my kids, I left her birthright still Filipino—that's her citizenship—so I'll have to go do a lot of details to get her out, and this takes money. And I have her in college now—her second year, she's a med tech. And my baby will be graduating from grammar school. This is her last year; she'll be in high school next year. These are my own two. Now I have the other two, my two guardians, the little girl, she just graduated from high school but I have her in a vocational school now until I get back, and the little-bitty boy—he's in grade three, but I have someone set up to take care of these two kids if I leave. And they will continue their education. When they were left with me, the girl was about thirteen, because she's seventeen now. And the little boy was in nursery. I just told my housekeeper—she's raised my kids—'Well, what are we going to do?' She said, 'Well, ma'm, we'll keep them.' Now the little girl is going on eighteen; she'll be old enough to stand on her own."

Baker, as it turned out, picked a good time to leave the Philippines. Intensifying civil unrest—attempts to overthrow the government and guerrilla activity—was making life for Americans who lived there much harder. How did she feel about that? "Sure you're scared and you're nervous, but you mind your own business. They said, 'All civilians stay out of the way.' The few that got killed got killed because they did not listen. They let civilians go. They didn't bother anybody. They said, 'Everybody stay out of the way.' If you go up there and then you get shot, you can't get mad at anybody. For my last two months over there, before I came here, my wash-girl did all my shopping for me except for things I could buy on the base itself. I didn't go shopping anymore. She would do all my running around outside. And, of course, my kids, because they're Filipino citizens, can get around much better than I can. Since those last two shootings of the two young Americans, there's been a lot of tension on both sides there. They don't bother women and children—theirs or ours—but you may accidentally get in the line of fire. This is what they're worried about. The Peace Corps has left because of the threats. And a lot of times you don't know who it is, things happen. They'll just shoot somebody and blame it on somebody. Nobody really knows. So we don't talk about it—we're right there, but we just don't talk about it because it's not very pleasant to discuss. But I feel so sorry for the young guys because they're restricted to the base and they want to get out the gate."

*   *   *

On June 4, 1990, after seventeen hours in the air and a four-hour layover, Baker arrived in New York from the Philippines. In just twenty-one days she'd be opening in *Black and Blue*. There was no time for her to get over jet lag; the producers plunged her almost immediately into activities that would have taxed the resources of a woman half her age. LeVine comments, "She's remarkable because she had an extraordinarily short period compared to what everybody else in the cast had. Part of that had to be taken up with making sure the costumes were right. And doing a stage show is not the same as playing a club or even a concert. You have to find your spotlights, you have to move just within a certain range, and sometimes you don't see the musicians—you hear them but you don't see them. She started rehearsing like the day after she arrived here. We got her an apartment fast."

Did Baker find it harder performing on the Broadway stage than in a club?

"The only thing that's different is the many costume changes. But otherwise, it's no different. Because in a nightclub, you're dog tired when you come off a full set," Baker says. "It really is the same. Even in the clubs, in one set I used to change into different gowns while the band played—just to show off the different dresses although they weren't as elaborate as these gowns are. These costumes are fantastic. When I sing 'Body and Soul' the dress I've got on is very, very heavy and I can't move. Really. It's all beaded—the cape, the dress and all. So you just stand in one place. And when I sing 'If I Can't Sell It,' I can't move around either. I can't move around a lot in this show. Believe me, that takes some getting used to! That 'Body and Soul' gown, it's close to two hundred pounds. You can't hang it. It has to be in a basket."

"It's not two hundred pounds. It's about forty-five or fifty," interjects LeVine.

"It's two hundred as far as I'm concerned," Baker says, settling the matter.

She continues, "Everybody in the cast has been fine to me. Well, most of everybody here I've worked with before. Carrie Smith's the only one I didn't know. I've known Linda Hopkins many years. We used to work together, back in 1949, 1952—Linda and I, we go way back. We worked together at the Flame Show Bar in Detroit and at the old Baby Grand in Harlem—Nipsey [Russell] used to be there. Oh, many, many places we worked together. We used to do a few one-nighters together. And a lot of the musicians I've worked with—Jerome Richardson was on my Bessie Smith album. And there's my man Heywood [Henry], who used to be with Erskine Hawkins's band; we used to travel on the tours. And later he was with Reuben Philips's big band at the Apollo. And guitarist Billy Butler, we used to work together. And the drummer, Grady Tate. Oh hell, practically everybody in the band I've worked with, here and there, occasionally. And [tap dancer] Bunny Briggs—we worked together. All the theaters, Bunny worked at."

Baker sought to put something of her own stamp on the role although her freedom was limited. "I worked with Sy Johnson, the arranger—he's very nice—for two weeks every day, four to five hours a day, until it was time for me to go into the show. And we're still working. Because he sits out there. And if I mess up, he'll call me up: 'OK, rehearse tomorrow.' Sy and I and the owners of the show got together, and we're making a few minor changes so that I can feel like I'm doing myself instead of the other actress that was here. When Sy said, 'Do you sing "Body and Soul"?' I said, 'I haven't sung this song in maybe fifteen-twenty years.' Well, that beautiful arrangement on 'Body and Soul' has been changed just a bit because I wanted it to be for my voice. And singing 'Body and Soul,' I've put in a little, just a teeny bit of gospel. It's like, you're a cook, you don't make it salty—you just add enough to make it taste good. And that's what I did."

Although Baker had recorded "St. Louis Blues" in the fifties, the arrangement she used then was too fast and rock 'n' roll-oriented to have worked for *Black and Blue*. Not surprisingly, the producers had her keep the older-style arrangement devised for Ruth Brown and sing the song at a stately tempo. Also not surprisingly, Baker did not sound as effective as Brown had. She seemed reined-in using the arrangement custom-tailored for Brown. It's a pity that she could not have been given more freedom to express herself and still retain an appropriate period feel. In club performances since the show has closed she's belted out "St. Louis Blues" far more effectively, hitting some unexpected higher notes, calliope-style, along the way. She introduces her rendition of "St. Louis Blues" on *LaVern Baker: Live in Hollywood '91* with the comment that people told her how to sing it when she first recorded it and when she did it on Broadway, but *now* she's going to do it *her* way.

Baker felt very comfortable being onstage with old friend Linda Hopkins. "Linda and I do 'Ain't Nobody's Business.' And it's a lot of fun. In the show I'm very pissed that she's got on my dress, so I'm making faces behind her. Linda don't see me doing this behind her. When she looks around at me, I'm just going like this [she smiles innocently]. But behind her I'm really socking it to her. And the audience sees I'm making all ugly faces behind her because she's got on my dress. So Hector was happy with that. He said, 'Keep it in, it's good!' And it's getting better every day, I'll say that. And Linda laughs at me. Because I do things. And others in the cast have already told us, 'Don't you two start on the stage. Because we'll start laughing and we can't stop. And the audience will start laughing. And then that's it. The band will start laughing.' So we don't really look at each other in the face too much on stage. I don't look at her and she don't look at me." But Baker couldn't contain herself the night that sixty-five-year-old Hopkins's dentures fell out.

Seeing Baker several days after she'd taken over the role, I missed the dramatic tension in this number that had existed between Brown and Hopkins, who had bristled with competiveness toward one another both on and off the stage. Although amiable, the interplay between Baker and Hopkins seemed less exciting. Baker sang the lyrics to "If I Can't Sell It (I'll Keep Sitting on It)" a bit differently than Brown had, singing "I refuse to give it away" at one point and "I'm certainly not going to give it away" at another rather than the earthier, more direct, and, to my ears, more effective "I ain't about to give it away."

"Body and Soul" was the one number on which Baker outshone Brown. She sang that ballad with more grace and sensitivity, enhancing it with a slight gospel inflection and making an asset of the tonal beauty of her youthful-sounding voice. Overall, though, her performance in *Black and Blue* did not create as powerful an impression as Brown's had. She sang well—she's in fine voice—but without Brown's high-pressure impact and commanding presence and without, for that matter, the thrilling quality Baker had displayed on her best early recordings, for example, "Soul on Fire." She seemed a subdued, although she was admittedly not quite up to her full strength. Doing *Black and Blue* is taking every bit of her energy. "The jet lag thing is still with me," she says. "I had a rough trip coming in this time. Because of the problems in the Philippines, I had to go the long way around because quite a few of our airlines are refusing to go into

the Philippines now. When I get home from the theater, I am physically and mentally exhausted. Some nights I just sit up—just like I'm
sitting now, fully dressed—and I go to sleep. I'm just tired. I watch
TV for about five minutes. My first two nights in the show, I was very
nervous. The first day I was very tired, because it was a full dress rehearsal and then I went on the same night, so between the nerves
and—mental and physical, I was pretty well worn out when I got
home, just completely exhausted. My throat was sore and tired. The
next night, my throat still wasn't up to par. But by the night after
that, it was great. So far so good." She'll give it all that she's got.

As Brown had, Baker has been receiving invitations to do concerts
and club appearances on her nights off. Unlike Brown, however, she's
not accepting them. "I have a lot of offers, but it's very hard to do.
You're working here six days a week. And I feel that I should keep
myself in good condition for this show. I just turned down several
big offers; there's just so much money you can make," Baker says.
She also has too many memories of being burned by promoters in
the old days to become overly enthusiastic over promised high pay
for gigs. "Sometimes they tell you you've got one show and you get
there and you've got to do two. If you want your money, you've got
to do the second show. And then the money isn't what they say. I
feel like I'm being taken advantage of, and I don't like it. So I just
turned them all down.

"I *would* like to record again," she says. It would be great to hear
her still-youthful-sounding voice on numbers of her choice.[11] She
notes that she already has been offered a recording deal but she
passed on it. "I told them, 'Well, let me check with Atlantic first.'
Because Ahmet Ertegun has first choice with me as far as I'm concerned. Ahmet and I go way back. And Atlantic's been very good to
me. I've had some bad times between 'Nam and getting up on my
feet again, and never ever have I been refused by Atlantic for anything. And with Atlantic, I didn't burn any bridges like the other acts
have done," she notes in an obvious allusion to Ruth Brown. "And
Ahmet told the people who wanted to record me, 'No, you can't get
her. I still want her.' So I will probably do something with Atlantic—
once I get relaxed here."

Once I get relaxed here. You sense a touch of pathos in that line.
It's more than just a question of getting relaxed. These days, she has
to guard her energy and conserve it. She's drawing hard upon her
reserves to do as much as she is doing, but she doesn't feel that the
difficulties a performer may be experiencing are the audience's business. A professional simply goes on and does the show. "When I walk

into a night club, whatever's been bothering me or how angry I am—when I walk in front of the audience, I leave that outside. My job is to entertain them, not to make them irritable. But a lot of people carry it on the stage with them, and you can't do this." She's proud that she's been able to stay in the business as long as she has, proud she's still able to be "Miss Baker," as she puts it, and hold her head high. She's also happy that she's recently been inducted into the Friars Club; her membership symbolizes a long-desired full-fledged acceptance into the entertainment establishment.

Baker's goals for the future now are surprisingly modest. She doesn't seem to have Ruth Brown's burning ambition, nor does she seem to have a clear vision of the songs she'd like to sing and record. Brown can give you lists of them; her main worry is that she won't have time to meet all of her goals. In a surprisingly mild voice—there isn't the force of confidence that is often in Brown's voice—Baker, who has been voted into the Rock 'n' Roll Hall of Fame since returning to the United States, describes how she hopes to get work in oldies revival packages.

"The adults, they remember us—they were our teenagers back then. I have suggested to some of the big promoters to get together a big touring rock 'n' roll show like we used to do. A package deal of the same artists. We could call it something like 'Those Were the Days' or 'Here They Are Again.' Some of us are deceased. But you've still got Fats Domino. You've still got some of the Coasters. You still have the Drifters. I don't know whether Paul Anka would go again or not, but Paul Anka's still around. The Everly Brothers are still existing. Bill Doggett is alive still. Some of us who are still here could get together and make up a package. Don't space the bookings too far apart in distance because we can't do it like we used to, but, with a big bus, within a range of two hundred miles would be fair—nowadays with the highways being as nice as they are. We could make this, say, in four and a half hours. This isn't bad. The buses are very comfortable now."

She talks as if she would be primarily of interest to people of her generation who would enjoy seeing once again stars from their youth. I'm surprised to hear her sell herself short, for she is, after Ruth Brown, as valuable an interpreter of classic R&B songs as exists. I suggest that a new young audience might well rediscover her, too. Baker agrees that young audiences can be reached along with the fifty-and-older crowd. The hardest to reach, she notes astutely, are middle-aged listeners. "The kids are more accessible than those in middle," she says. "*They're* the hard ones to reach with whatever you do—believe that! They're set in their ways, they don't want to go back for anything. And you have to be very, very strong if you're working for them."

Well, LaVern Baker comes on pretty strong in all of her gigs, I suggest gently.

"Yeah," she allows. "I close my eyes and do what I got to do, you know."

6

 JIMMY WITHERSPOON

"How long blues?"

Jimmy Witherspoon had only to sing the first two words—"One day"—before being greeted by some applause and calls of "Yeah!" and "Sing the song!" The mostly older, black audience filling Brooklyn's BAM Majestic Theater recognized that he was going into his signature number "Ain't Nobody's Business." Forty years earlier, in 1949, his hit recording of it had stayed on the R&B charts for thirty-four weeks—one of the longest runs on the charts for any record. He proceeded to sing that number with a tenderness that gave me the shivers. I mentioned that to Witherspoon afterward and how rare the experience is.

"You know what that is?" he asked me, quietly. "I had a lady in Scotland say the same thing. Since my illness, I've been nominated for two Grammies. Since my radiation treatments. It changed me, into a powerful thing. And I'm grateful for that." The illness to which he's so matter-of-factly referring was a cancer of the throat which, in the early 1980s, almost cost him his life. "It changed you which way?" I asked. "Feeling. Yeah. And I wasn't aware that I was projecting like that until I've had four or five people tell me the same thing. It's a feeling that I've never had before. And nothing worries me any more."

When he was fighting the cancer, he wondered whether—assuming he'd beat it—he'd ever be able to sing again. As it turned out, his voice is deeper but less supple and less resonant than before his illness. It is a voice that shows more wear and tear. He clearly has to work harder to get it do what he wants. For a pop singer, a loss of suppleness and resonance might be enough to end a career. But for a blues singer like Witherspoon, the rougher, more strained sound can be an asset, making songs about hard times seem more authoritative. And the depth of feeling Witherspoon can now reach, when he's inspired, makes him a singer of rare impact.

Although he sang for just thirty minutes at the Majestic—he was one act in a concert lineup that included tenor saxist Wilene Barton and organ players Dayton Selby and Jimmy Smith—he was in particularly good form that day. Starting tentatively, he soon hit his stride. Mixing pathos and humor and pulling from the air lines that he had first heard as a boy—he's one of the few performers who keeps alive numbers of long-gone bluesmen like Doc Clayton and Peetie Wheatstraw—Witherspoon soon made one forget there were any other performers on the bill. I didn't want his set to end. From the audience's reaction, it was clear that he was also reaching others—moving some to appreciative laughter, moving some to tears, and, I suspect, touching off plenty of memories in the process.

"It took me up until last year to really realize what the blues was," he commented afterward. "I've been asked the question for a hundred years. And one day, I was just sitting at home when it came to me: The blues is nothing but personal. It hits everybody different." But he was reluctant to do a full-fledged interview that day because he felt the need to conserve his voice. We made an appointment to talk at length. He promised that he'd take me back, cover things from the beginning—and he did just that.

* * *

"I was singing from about five," recalls Witherspoon, who was born on August 8, 1923, in Gurdon in Clark County, Arkansas. "I sang in church. I still sing in church." As a five-year-old choirboy in the First Baptist Church, he used to sing a hymn called "I'm Going Through" while his mother provided accompaniment on piano. His father, who died when Witherspoon was about six, was also a member of the church choir.

Does he think that being part of the church might be important to being a good blues singer?

"No. Being part of, being born to a great family, that's where it is," he says. "That's where your parents come in. The way your parents raise you and bring you up. You may deviate from it later on in years, but you come back to it."

What did his parents give him that helped?

"They gave me strength, whether it be religion, which is a great part of me still. I'm a religious man. I'm not a fanatic, coming around putting my feelings on people; it's personal—which I feel the blues is," he says. He goes from mentioning religion to mentioning the blues as if they're linked in his mind; they're both quite special to him. "My mother played piano until the day she died. Religious music. No blues has ever been played in my mother's home, up until the day she died."

She didn't approve of the blues? "No, sir!" Witherspoon responds promptly. For the first fifteen years of his professional career she never went into any club to see him perform. Although in time he came to disagree with his mother strongly about the worth of the blues, he maintains an overall respect for her values now. As he puts it, "Whatever brought us through the depression, I can't knock it."

In his youth, he accepted his mother's judgment that there was something "dirty" about the blues. It was to be shunned, a holdover from an ignorant past and favored by lower classes of people. Initially, he thought that black popular singers who sang in a polished "white" style—for example, the Ink Spots—were better than the earthier black blues singers; they were the performers to emulate if one wanted to become a singer. From an early age he considered becoming a singer. He was still in grade school when he won a countywide singing contest performing the mournful "Water Boy."

Now, Witherspoon views the blues as a part of his cultural heritage and a source of great pride. But when he was young, many blacks—low in self-esteem—tried to lose their identity and accepted the cultural values of the dominant white society. They tried to be just like whites, he feels. It took him time to understand fully how that process of accommodation worked and the sacrifices it entailed. The more he listened to blues singers in his youth, the more he responded to the honesty and power in their work. Maybe they weren't making the pop charts, but they had a vitality that many successful but more plastic pop singers lacked. He recalls of his Arkansas youth, "I used to see a lot of blues singers—and didn't realize who I was seeing—on the carnival trucks that would come around to your house, hyping the show. They'd be playing on the back of the truck." He'd also hear plenty of blues records—which weren't being played on radio stations in his area—on jukeboxes.

Blues singers were not just offering "entertainment," he notes. If you paid attention, you could hear commentary at times on social conditions, and in words that might go over the heads of white listeners. Blues singers didn't shy from the truth. And times were tough. "Oh man," Witherspoon says, sadness coloring his voice, "you don't really know. Like, Big Bill Broonzy, he was practically illiterate, he couldn't read or write well. I'm very conscious of social problems that we have, as you can tell. And even way back then, he used to do this tune called 'How Long Will It Take for Me to Become a Man? Will it be real soon, or will it be when I get ninety-three?' Do you know the meaning of that lyric?" Witherspoon explains that the song was a protest over black men being called boy. "And then one of the verses is, 'They said I was uneducated, my clothes was worn and torn. / But now I've got a little education, they call me a boy right on.' And then when he gets to be ninety-three he's going to be called 'Uncle.' Oh man, a lot of good blues singers have done a lot of things that folks don't see." Witherspoon adds that he came to think the world of Broonzy. Although he had mixed feelings about the propriety of the blues as a youth—part of him still accepted his mother's judgments—as he grew older he came increasingly to prefer blues singers to pop singers.

Witherspoon's father was a brakeman for the Missouri Pacific Railroad. One valuable "perk" of his job was entitlement to rail passes, good for free rail transportation for his family anywhere in the country. Even after his father's death, Witherspoon was entitled to the passes until he became twenty-one. When he was no more than sixteen he used a pass to leave Arkansas for good, traveling by train to Los Angeles, where he soon found a job washing dishes for $17 a week at the Owl Drugstore at Eighth and Broadway. He eventually worked his way up to cook. When did he determine that he wanted to sing professionally?

"Oh, that had happened around when I was about fourteen," he says. "And once I got out to California, that inspired me." He wanted to become both a singer and a movie star, the latter goal being realized when he appeared in *Black Godfather* (1974)

Were there performers by whom Witherspoon felt particularly inspired?

"Herb Jeffries was one. The Ink Spots. Joe Turner. Jimmy Rushing. And also Scrappy Blackwell and Leroy Carr. And I was inspired by them because of the way they pronounced their words." He liked the fact that during the thirties those bluesmen pronounced words clearly, "properly," rather than using the "dem, dat, and dose" dialect heard on "Amos 'n' Andy." He felt, and continues to feel as part of his mother's value system, that using non-standard English tended to "bring the race down" and hurt its image.

Witherspoon began singing after-hours—just sitting in—at a popular chicken joint called Lovejoy's at Vernon and Central Avenue in Los Angeles. "I used to sing up there with Art Tatum and Slam Stewart. They didn't know I was a dishwasher—they thought I was a professional singer. I didn't tell them any better," he notes. What was he singing? "Oh, blues. I became a Joe Turner fan then. Because I'd seen him with Duke Ellington at the Mayan Theater in Hollywood in *Jump for Joy* [1941]. And I was always inspired by him. Joe and I became close. We'd run around together. I used to go to his house, right here in Los Angeles, before I was singing professionally—knew his mother, sister, and everything. When I first started singing, he said I was going to be a great blues singer. He said that at the Club Alabam in Los Angeles." Witherspoon also became friends with other jazz and blues performers in the area, such as Red and Arthur Prysock and T-Bone Walker, who used to invite him onstage from the audience (as if spontaneously, although it was prearranged) to sing with him at his performances. "I loved him. Loved him. He did so much for me," Witherspoon says of Walker.

During World War II, Witherspoon became a chief steward and cook—racial discrimination limited positions available to blacks—in the Merchant Marine. One night in 1943, while stationed in Calcutta, India, he chanced to sit in with Teddy Weatherford's big band at the Grand Hotel Winter Garden. Almost forgotten today, Weatherford had moved from New Orleans to Chicago in 1922, where he made a name for himself during the next four years as one of the best jazz pianists in the city, a rival to Earl Hines. Then he went to the Far East, where, for nearly twenty years, he played with or led bands in China, India, and other locales. The groups were sometimes made up of expatriate black American musicians and sometimes included British, Burmese, and others who were foreign-born.

Weatherford's band was playing "Why Don't You Do Right?" written by Kansas Joe McCoy (a former husband and performing partner of Memphis Minnie, LaVern Baker's distant relative), which Lil Green and Peggy Lee had recorded successfully. Witherspoon got well into the spirit of that rueful, laid-back song, and the audience encouraged him to sing more.

He was half drunk that night, depressed, and—like a lot of servicemen—uncertain whether he'd make it back to the United States alive. He sang the blues. It seemed the most natural thing in the world, a way of expressing himself fully. Whatever lingering doubts he may have had about the validity of the blues were washed away in the enthusiastic reception he received from his fellow servicemen that night and on subsequent nights. Weatherford, who knew a good thing when he heard it, had Witherspoon sing with the band for the next two or three weeks. He even got to broadcast on an Armed Forces Radio Service show. Virtually everyone treated him as if he were a professional singer. "And Teddy Weatherford told me," Witherspoon recalls, "when I get back to America, let somebody hear me because I had a good voice."

In 1944, his hitch over, Witherspoon was back in Vallejo, California, where his mother lived. By day he worked in a shipyard. On weekends he sang the blues at a club called the Waterfront, his first real employment as a professional singer. Pianist-bandleader Jay McShann, who led what Witherspoon felt was the greatest blues big band in the world, heard him. Walter Brown (known for his singing of such numbers as "Confessin' the Blues" and "Jumping the Blues"), a member since 1940, had just left the McShann band abruptly. "I sang Joe Turner's 'Wee Baby Blues' and I got the job," Witherspoon recalls.

Singing with McShann's band, which Witherspoon did from 1944 to 1948, was a dream come true. "I sang all blues. When I sang those Walter Brown numbers, I had to sing 'em as close to Brown as I could." He tried to copy not just Brown's way of phrasing but also Brown's nasal sound on Brown's big numbers. "Well, I didn't *have* to," Witherspoon clarifies. "Jay McShann asked me if I could; he never put demands on me. But then after, he said, 'Go for yourself.' That's how I got my style, now that I was back." His style owed more to Joe Turner than to Brown. For example, it is from Turner, he suspects, that he picked up the habit of singing behind the beat. But Turner was more a full-time blues-shouter than Witherspoon. Witherspoon could project his rich, deep baritone with the kind of exuberant spirit Turner did, but he also had a quieter side. He could take a number down low, sing effectively with more restraint than Turner did, and, as time went on, he learned to develop that quieter side more fully.

What was Jay McShann like to work for?

"The greatest man in the world," Witherspoon says simply. "As a matter of fact, we played together in Holland about two or three years ago, and the promoter wanted to know how much I was going to sing. And Jay, who was right behind me, told him, 'You're not going to kill him.' Because it was the first time Jay had seen me since my illness. I said, 'Let McShann handle it, I'm still his singer.' And that's the way we work, even today. Because we still get together from time to time. We're going to be working together at the Montreal Jazz Festival. And back then, I was the only artist with his band that he would take home with him. And I know personal things about him and his family that no one in the world would ever know. That's how close we are, even today. He trusted me and I trusted him. As long as I live, nothing would ever be divulged about his family. He's such a beautiful man. His whole family's beautiful. And he taught me so much.

"Last year I did a tour with [pianist] Junior Mance, and he said, 'You're only the second singer I ever worked with in my life—Dinah

Washington was the other one—who can start a tune in the right key that you're supposed to.' I mean jumping from one key to another—like, I just got through singing one number in one key and I'll go right to a different number in another. And I can do it consistently, singing in all keys. I can just start off humming a tune in the right key. And I think that's from being with Jay McShann. Because he used to see who had the greatest ear as we would ride in the bus. If we'd hear somebody hit something on a pipe outside working, as we'd be driving by, I'd say, 'What key is that, Hootie [McShann]?' And we'd be arguing about the key.

"When I joined him he still had the big band. He had to cut down to a smaller group about a year after I left. Paul Quinichette was in the band on tenor sax. Jesse Price was on the drums. I sang all blues," Witherspoon recalls. (McShann had another singer to handle ballads.) Witherspoon was creating his own blues numbers, too. "Yeah, I was writing some—stealing," he says. He could draw upon numbers he had heard from traveling musicians or on jukeboxes in Arkansas, as well as those sung by other singers on the West Coast. He could pick up things from every blues singer he heard. An extensive body of blues lyrics—traditional lines whose origins were obscure—had been passed down, and singers could adapt it, combine it in new ways, and build upon it.

McShann played a strong, two-handed, boogie-woogie-inflected blues style of piano. His band, which had launched the career of Charlie Parker a few years earlier, had always featured the blues prominently. Although it periodically played dates in New York, Los Angeles, and other major cities coast to coast, it worked primarily in the Midwest and Southwest. The band originated in Kansas City and enjoyed its greatest popularity within traveling distance of that city. It played mostly for black audiences, Witherspoon recalls, although sometimes for whites as well. He remembers one dance in El Paso, Texas, where whites were supposed to dance on one side of the ballroom and blacks on the other, a rope was strung across the ballroom from the middle of the stage to the rear. But the kids tore the rope down before the night was over, and the dance proceeded without problem.

Jim Crow laws and customs meant that life on the road often entailed wearisome hassles. Simply getting a meal late at night, after performing, was frequently difficult. When a restaurant or a hotel's personnel told him they'd serve him a meal or rent him a room only if he came in through the back door, Witherspoon went elsewhere. He also wasn't happy with the way that some black-only hotels in the South—knowing they had a captive market because blacks weren't welcome at other hotels in the area—capitalized on the situation and charged more than they should have. Touring was generally more aggravating in those days than now. All of the indignities—some minor, some not so minor—went into Witherspoon's art. As he puts it, he has lived the blues songs that he sings.

When Witherspoon sings, he gives a first impression of great composure. He is always dressed immaculately and initially seems unruffled. But you can sense powerful emotional currents just below the surface, depths of anger and sorrow that give impact to his best work. He may be keeping his emotions in check, but scratch the surface and they're there. When I mention, for example, that I'd heard that Witherspoon had sung during the forties with Johnny Otis, a white bandleader-singer-drummer-club owner who identified thoroughly with the black community and has long played a prominent role in the West Coast R&B scene, he bristles, "What do you mean, sing with Johnny—that's the shit that makes me mad! I'm the one that discovered, that called Johnny to come here [to California] from Omaha. I will tell you something, and I want you to print this. I have a pet peeve about writers, white interviewers—and I'm not paranoid or being facetious, I'm serious about it—when they mention white artists, they'll say, 'Oh, you played with Robben Ford,' or 'You played with Johnny Otis. I'm the son of a bitch that discovered Robben Ford. I'm the man that discovered Johnny Otis."

I indicate I've intended no slight.

"I feel that way! Blacks are always secondary," he insists. His passion has surfaced suddenly, unexpectedly, like a summer thunderstorm, and it vanishes just as quickly. But the barely suppressed anger over racial injustices that he feels and mentions explicitly in his conversations periodically can sometimes shade his singing.

He didn't sing songs of protest. He sang traditional blues, some mournful, some joyous. But he could express a wealth of feeling and attitudes within his songs, and singing the blues, he notes, left him feeling good. It was a soul-lifting, not a depressing, experience. He has happy memories, too, of camaraderie with other blues singers. After leaving McShann's band in 1948, there were often occasions to get together with the others. "Wynonie Harris—I liked working with him; he taught me a lot," Witherspoon recalls of the man who was billed as "Mr. Blues" (and who provided inspiration for Elvis Presley). "We had blues battles, battles of the blues together, me and Wynonie and Joe Turner—that had to be around about 1948. I wasn't known that much, I hadn't cut 'Ain't Nobody's Business.'"

Challenging one another, the singers pulled line after line from their memories and made up new lines as they went along. Being able to improvise blues lyrics on the spot was part of a true blues-man's craft. One night when Harris and Witherspoon were battling each other, they finally ran out of things to say. Suddenly Joe Turner, who'd been watching them, piped up. Breaking the tension, he ebulliently spun out idiosyncratic lines that had a curiously appealing sound and provided fresh fuel for the fires of their imaginations: "We'll patcha, patcha, patcha all night long / patcha, patcha on the doggone telephone." The lines became part of the repertoires of all of the singers present that night and in time of other singers as well, passing into the oral tradition of the blues.

*   *   *

The number with which Jimmy Witherspoon is most closely associated, a song he has long loved to sing, "Ain't Nobody's Business," was written the year before he was born. Bessie Smith made a classic recording of it on August 11, 1923, just three days after Witherspoon's birth. Conscientious about giving credit where it's due, Witherspoon takes care to point out that recording "Ain't Nobody's Business" was not his idea. Al Patrick, who owned Supreme Records and produced the recording session, "asked me to do that tune," Witherspoon says, adding, "and believe it or not, T-Bone Walker had asked me to record it. He'd heard me sing it before." Witherspoon adds that the masterly piano playing of Jay McShann on the record had a great deal to do with its success. It meant much to him that McShann participated in the session. "When I cut 'Ain't Nobody's Business,' I had left McShann. But he was on that record anyway. That's the friendship and love we have for each other. He just happened to be out here, working. And I asked him, would he record with me? There ain't too many of your former employers who would do that."

Witherspoon's generosity in crediting others should not obscure the reality that it was his singing that made the record. He didn't sing the same lyrics Smith had. He felt free to do his own interpretation of the song, to sing words that best expressed his feelings, the kind of freedom that is very much a part of the authentic blues tradition. In a voice rich with emotion, he gave an extended rendition of the song that Supreme would have to issue on two sides of a 78-rpm single: "Ain't Nobody's Business—Parts One and Two." He made only one take of the song, he notes, "Because I had a fight with the producer—something about the music, about coming back and starting or something. I was mad at that man. McShann said, 'Let's stop right now, 'cause Spoon is mad.' So we only cut it once." Wither-spoon remembers that he recorded the side while feeling a controlled anger, cutting his words off more sharply than he ordinarily would. That edge of anger, he believes, may have helped make the record a hit. "After the session, going back to the hotel, McShann said to me, 'You got a hit, you son of a bitch. Get mad every time you record!'" If some of Witherspoon's listeners thought they could sense an un-defined anger beneath the surface of his performances, that was all right; given the racism of the society, many of them felt anger, too.

Witherspoon's version of "Ain't Nobody's Business" reached the number one spot on the *Billboard* R&B charts and stayed on the charts an astonishing thirty-four weeks, beginning in March 1949. Only one previous record that could be considered R&B had stayed on the charts longer: Cootie Williams's 1944 "Cherry Red Blues" had enjoyed a thirty-nine-week run on *Billboard*'s "Harlem Hit Parade," a precurs-er to the R&B charts. More than thirty years would pass before an-other record would enjoy a longer run than "Ain't Nobody's Busi-ness." (Patti Austin and James Ingram's 1982 "Baby, Come to Me" racked up thirty-eight weeks on *Billboard*'s "Black Singles" chart, a successor to the R&B charts.)

Witherspoon's song was a smash hit in black America. Some thir-ty-five years later, Linda Hopkins would argue with the producers of *Black and Blue* that she wanted to sing the words that Witherspoon—not Bessie Smith—had sung because his was the version of "Ain't Nobody's Business" she remembered. Yet the record did not make the white-dominated pop charts at all and was unknown to most white Americans. Indeed, for all of his success in the R&B field, Witherspoon feels that he was not discovered by white audiences until after his appearance at the 1959 Monterey Jazz Festival.

"Ain't Nobody's Business" was still on the charts when Wither-spoon came through with another hit on the Supreme Records la-bel, a recording of an old Leroy Carr number called "In the Evening When the Sun Goes Down" that Charles Brown had recently revived. Witherspoon's version made the R&B charts for four weeks beginning in September 1949, peaking at number five; Brown's version made the charts for ten weeks beginning in August 1949, peaking at num-ber four. Witherspoon didn't receive a dime in royalties for either of those hits or for any other of his Supreme recordings, a situation that angered him greatly then. Now he looks back with charity, pointing out that although the independent record companies generally did not pay royalties they did record R&B artists whom the bigger com-panies did not record at all, and he credits them for doing that.

When Patrick set up Witherspoon's next recording session, renting time at Radio Recorders studio in Los Angeles, Witherspoon balked, refusing to record unless Patrick paid him the money to which he felt entitled for the hits he'd produced. Witherspoon achieved only a Pyrrhic victory. Patrick had the songwriter who had written numbers for the session but had never recorded previously as a singer perform the numbers, thus launching the career of memorable vocalist Percy Mayfield, who made the R&B charts seven times between 1950 and 1952. Witherspoon still can't listen to Mayfield's chart-topping hit "Please Send Me Someone to Love" without thinking that it was supposed to have been recorded by him.

Witherspoon moved over to the Bihari brothers, quickly scoring with a double-sided hit for their Modern Records label. "No Rollin' Blues" was coupled with "Big Fine Girl," titles that made the R&B charts for ten and eleven weeks, respectively, beginning in December 1949, both reaching as high as number four on the charts. The Biharis compensated him much better than Patrick had, sending him a $1,000 check every month like clockwork for about a year.

Most of the songs he recorded in those days (including "No Rollin' Blues" and "Big Fine Girl") were originals he'd written. Some, such as "Spoon's Blues" and "All That's Good," were variations on his most-requested number, "Ain't Nobody's Business," but none duplicated the popularity of the original. Sometimes he'd reach back and do an oldie such as Bessie Smith's classic "Back Water Blues." At times he would also record an original by others, such as "Real Ugly Woman," which was written for him by two newcomers who would come to his house to demonstrate their songs: Jerry Leiber was still in high school when he met Witherspoon, and Mike Stoller had recently graduated. Witherspoon was the first singer to perform Leiber and Stoller material publicly. He did so in December 1950 at Gene Norman's Blues Jamboree at the Shrine Auditorium.

From 1948 to 1952 he toured with his own bands. He didn't keep permanent bands as did Louis Jordan or Roy Milton, but would take a band out for a few months and then later go out again with a different one. He liked the stimulation of fresh players. He played the Apollo Theatre in New York, the Flame Show Bar in Detroit (where he was almost upstaged by an "unknown" singer at the start of her career, Big Maybelle, whom he found as talented as any he'd ever heard), and the Melody Club in Hollywood. He even recorded with the Trinity Baptist Church choir for Modern. Unlike some performers, however, he never sang religious music in clubs; that would have struck him as sacrilegious.

He recorded for Crown around 1951 and for Federal in 1952 and 1953. Some of the same musicians who recorded with Floyd Dixon, such as tenor saxist Maxwell Davis and guitarist Tiny Webb, turn up on Witherspoon's records from this period. In April 1952 he found himself back on the R&B charts for two weeks when Modern released a live recording of one of his 1950 concert performances, "The Wind Is Blowing," which reached number seven on the R&B bestsellers chart.

Witherspoon was living high, though: two cars, a valet, and a fine home in Los Angeles. But reversals came with an unexpected swiftness. A manager absconded with close to $40,000, and he had family troubles, too. Shifts in public tastes meant his records were no longer selling as well as they had. Vocal groups were popular, and then singers who emphasized rhythm more than blues. Although the growing popularity of rock 'n' roll initially looked like it would work in his favor, new heroes and new sounds came along, and he eventually found himself nearly swamped in their wake. Rock 'n' roll was born from R&B; Witherspoon originally considered the term *rock 'n' roll* as simply a new name for rhythm and blues, created when whites began performing the music. As rock 'n' roll became increasingly commercialized, pre-digested, and aimed at young teen buyers, however, he saw it going in a direction he didn't want to take. He didn't like the idea of performing commercialized music in which he didn't believe just to pander to young audiences.

For five or six years, Witherspoon's career slowed markedly. At one point he even had to declare bankruptcy; he was barely making enough to get by. It wasn't as if he wasn't working. He managed to find gigs and record deals throughout the fifties, although without much visibility. In 1954–56 and again in 1959 he recorded for Chess; in 1956, for Atlantic (with Wilbur DeParis's New Orleans Band) and Rip Records; in 1957, for RCA Victor (with Kansas City jazz-blues stalwarts Jesse Stone and Jay McShann); and in 1959 for Vee-Jay Records.

The ascendancy of Elvis Presley and rock 'n' roll not only curtailed Witherspoon's career, but also those of Charles Brown, Amos Milburn, Roy Milton, Wynonie Harris, and Roy Brown. "Elvis Presley came on the scene. And he knocked *all* black artists out," Witherspoon notes, adding, "but he also helped us because he kept the music alive. A positive and a negative thing." In Texas, Witherspoon remembers, before Presley became popular, rednecks tried to force R&B off the air, fearful that their children would somehow be ruined by the crude yet irresistible black music.

Witherspoon was delighted when he saw Presley break through in

1955 and get his first national exposure on Tommy and Jimmy Dorsey's "Stage Show" prime-time NBC television program. Here was a white artist, with the apparent endorsement of the establishment—the Dorseys, NBC, and RCA—performing black music. He guessed, correctly, that Presley's success would squelch those trying to get R&B off the air. "How could you fight NBC and RCA Victor and Elvis Presley?" he asks. Witherspoon knew, if most white American teens did not, the origin of Presley's style—and Presley also knew. Teens might have thought that "Good Rockin' Tonight" was a brand new "Presley song." Witherspoon—who loved to sing that particular song himself—certainly knew better. He had appreciated—as had Presley—the recordings of it made on small R&B labels by his friends Roy Brown (in 1947) and Wynonie Harris (in 1948).

For a while, Witherspoon thought that Presley's success might help open doors for him, too, but it didn't work out that way. "I was still recording, but with small labels," he notes. How could he compete with heavily hyped rock 'n' rollers? For a period, he recalls, he was bitter about the situation. Presley quickly moved on to the "Ed Sullivan Show"; Witherspoon was glad to receive a little Los Angeles radio exposure on the "Johnny Otis Show." He felt—correctly—that his talent would have been an asset to any top television variety show or supper club, but those doors were closed. If you were black and sang the blues, options were limited; big-time bookers treated you as if you were lower class.

How well were his records selling? He never really knew. Witherspoon received no royalties on any recordings he made during those years. Companies could say that although they'd pressed a lot of records, many had been returned from stores unsold; artists had no way of knowing whether they were being told the truth. The smaller record companies always seemed to be "poormouthing." If they were exploiting artists, though, Witherspoon doesn't believe it was a matter of white owners trying to exploit blacks; the record companies treated all the artists he knew, white or black, the same way. The small companies probably didn't make large profits; they released many singles—priced at as little as 59 or 69 cents apiece—which probably didn't sell well. Witherspoon recorded *Singin' the Blues*, which was a good album, for Rip Records in 1956, but the company folded soon afterward. In 1958 another small company, World Pacific Records, resurrected the album and rereleased it on their label.

Singin' the Blues helped spur interest in him in some quarters of the jazz community, and the organizers of the 1959 Monterey Jazz Festival decided they wanted to include Witherspoon in the festival.

This rare photo, taken in California around 1939, shows Jimmy Witherspoon, at left, with a very young Don Cherry (center) and Cherry's father and sister. Witherspoon was living with the Cherry family at the time. Don Cherry would grow up to become a noted jazz trumpeter, recording often with Ornette Coleman. (Author's collection; courtesy of Jimmy Witherspoon)

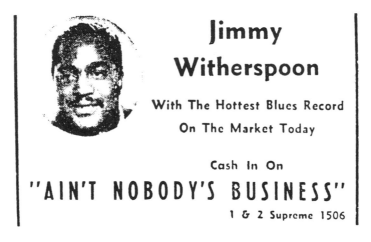
Supreme wasn't lying when it claimed, in this 1949 trade-publication ad that Witherspoon's version of "Ain't Nobody's Business" (with Jay McShann on piano) "was the hottest blues record on the market today." The record enjoyed a whopping thirty-four-week run on the *Billboard* R&B charts. Thirty-three years would pass before another record would surpass that run. (Author's collection.)

Witherspoon with his frequent accompanist Bross Townsend. Townsend works with many singers, as well as with leading trios of his own. But Witherspoon brings out the best in him, eliciting deeply felt jazz and blues playing. Townsend, who went completely blind not long after this photo was taken in 1991, plays by ear. (Photo by Chip Deffaa)

Jimmy Witherspoon with Joe Franklin, a New York City radio and television host for more than four decades. (Photo by Chip Deffaa)

Jimmy Witherspoon. (Author's collection; courtesy of Abby Hoffer)

Jimmy Witherspoon with longtime manager Abby Hoffer. (Photo by Chip Deffaa)

Jimmy Witherspoon, accompanied by Bross Townsend, at Fat Tuesday's in New York, 1994. (Photo by Chip Deffaa)

They couldn't locate him, however. He had dropped out of sight. By the time they found him—singing and playing bass with Charles Brown at a Newport, Kentucky, gambling casino—it was too late to add his name to the festival publicity and programs. But they said that they would include him if he could get to Monterey, which he did.

It was late when he arrived. People were already leaving, having been satiated with music from an all-star aggregation that included Ben Webster, Coleman Hawkins, Roy Eldridge, Gerry Mulligan, Earl Hines, and Woody Herman. Then Jimmy Lyons announced a surprise guest: Jimmy Witherspoon. Some who'd begun walking out returned and sat down. Witherspoon, accompanied by those jazz all-stars, wowed the crowd. Although he'd honed his craft over fifteen years of performing, he was to many of the listeners that night a "new artist."

His appearance at Monterey proved a turning point in his career. If he sang especially well that night, it wasn't just because he was accompanied and inspired by masterly players who had a real understanding of jazz and blues, it was also because there was someone special in the audience. "The Monterey Jazz Festival," he recalls, "that was the night my mother was there. They finally got my mother to come to hear me. My mother had never heard me sing the blues before that night. And that's the only performance of mine she ever went to—because they didn't have no whisky there! She'd heard me sing in church, and on television."

Witherspoon sang his heart out at Monterey. He established himself, with both fans and first-rate jazz musicians, as a true star. His triumphant appearance—a live recording of which was released by HiFijazz Records—brought him back into the spotlight. He received more—and better-paying—gigs. *Down Beat* caught his act at the Renaissance in Hollywood and reported he sang such numbers as "Good Rockin' Tonight," "When I Been Drinkin,'" and "Ain't Nobody's Business" and that "Spoon's singing is innately musical. . . . His voice can bellow on occasion; conversely it can become almost caressingly gentle with a ballad such as 'Gee Baby, Ain't I Good to You.' The feeling pours out like molasses from a keg. There lies half hidden in Spoon's voice, moreover, an elusive quality of pathos, a touching thing that impels close attention from the listener."[1]

He takes pride in the fact that when he went to see top jazz musicians, including Miles Davis and Dizzy Gillespie, people exceedingly particular about which singers perform with them, he'd be invited to sing. Because he has worked with so many major jazz players through the years, I can't help asking whether any musicians are especially high on his list. "Oh, Ben Webster was my number one. Yeah, we were together for three years after the Monterey Festival. We didn't take no job without each other. He was great," Witherspoon says. He did gigs with Webster in 1960, 1961, and 1962. He also gigged with others, of course, notably Gerry Mulligan (with whom he recorded, too) and Coleman Hawkins. He toured Europe with trumpeter Buck Clayton in 1961, a tour that yielded both a Belgian jazz film short (*Buck Clayton and His All-Stars*) and an album (*Olympia Concert* on Inner City Records).

He returned to sing at Monterey every year through 1963. In 1961 Witherspoon sang at Carnegie Hall and at the Newport Jazz Festival. That same year, he won the *Down Beat* International Critics' Poll's New Star Award as best new male vocalist. That Witherspoon, who had been singing with a distinguished bandleader as far back as 1944 and had recorded one of the most successful R&B sides of all time in 1949, could be pronounced a "new star" in 1961 is a telling remind-er of the realities of racial divisions in this country. To many white Americans he *was* new.

He was finding happiness in his personal life as well. In 1962 he married Diane, his second marriage. He was also recording frequent-ly; HiFijazz even let him record some religious music with a full choir. Bigger labels sought him out. He recorded for both Reprise and Co-lumbia during the early sixties. Some producers thought they could make him more commercially popular by trying different material. *Down Beat* panned one such attempt, a Reprise album called *'Spoon*. Pete Welding noted, "He's trying to go the ballad route, since that's been commercially successful for Ray Charles. But Witherspoon is not a good balladeer. The very qualities that mark his blues preaching with such driving authority seem to work against him when he sings ballads. All the way through this dismal collection he has troubles with pitch and intonation. . . . His plodding work throughout this collection has a strained, tentative, amateurish note to it. It's really unfair to Witherspoon, for in his metier—the blues—he's peerless."[2]

When he returned to the older-style blues material he did best for a Reprise album called, appropriately, *Roots*, the same reviewer praised the effort:

> With this strong, persuasive set, Witherspoon takes his place alongside his mentors, for this is easily the finest realization of his powerful blues singing on LP.
>
> In the past few years, Witherspoon's singing has taken on an increasing authority and a relaxed ease that are beautifully cap-

tured on this recording. These qualities have tempered and directed the others—the big, full sound, passionate drive, and sin-
uous thrust—that have always characterized his singing from the
day he joined the Jay McShann Band. . . .

Today, Witherspoon is one of the most gripping, emotionally satisfying blues shouters around, his voice huskily attractive
and resilient enough to move in whatever direction his mature
musicianship directs it. And he is using it much more sensitively
these days, employing insinuation and understatement where
before he would have relied almost wholly on overwhelming
power. Listen in particular to his delightful behind-the-beat
phrasing, drawing out words and phrases to the last possible
moment and then snapping off a resolution in a forceful dem-
onstration of tension and release.[3]

In 1963 Witherspoon toured with Count Basie and his orchestra
(including a trip to Japan) and made appearances on public television's "Jazz Casual" with Ralph Gleason and on the syndicated "Steve
Allen Show"; the following year, he appeared on Canadian television's
"Quest." He also appeared periodically at prisons to entertain inmates
throughout the sixties.

In 1963 and 1964 he recorded for Prestige, and "You're Next," one
of his Prestige recordings, happened to make *Billboard*'s pop charts
for a week (reaching the number ninety-eight spot on March 6, 1965).
During 1965 Witherspoon appeared—among the rock 'n' rollers aiming to please America's teeny-boppers—on the pop-rock television
variety shows "Hollywood A Go Go," "Shivaree," and "Shindig" although he was more comfortable sharing stages with such jazz greats
as Ben Webster and Count Basie or with master bluesmen, artists he
considers his peers.

"You notice the way I dress?" he asks. "That comes from working
with people like Coleman Hawkins, Sweets Edison, Ben Webster, and
Count Basie, and being around these men. These are men of distinction, these are men of class, and it rubbed off on me. I remember
Ben Webster said, ''Spoon, buy one good suit and let the bargains
alone.' And that's what I do." He wants to project a sharp image. "I
don't have to overdo it; it's just there."

Unlike many singers, Witherspoon, a musician himself, is always
generous in giving solo space to other musicians who work with him.
"There's no ego trip," he says. "You know, there are singers that musicians won't work with. I'm just the opposite, because I make the
musicians so much of Jimmy Witherspoon. [Pianist] Bross Townsend

plays with all kinds of singers. But they say he never sounded as good as he sounds with Jimmy Witherspoon. Do you know why? Because we enjoy ourselves. I give 'em that freedom." He'll sing a bit, then point to a musician and say, "Take some," knowing that the musician's virtuosity enhances his work. He's not afraid of sharing the spotlight, and he can appreciate good musicians more than average singers seem to.

Who are some of Witherspoon's favorite singers? "You got Lowell Fulson," he notes. "And this is going to really shock you. One of my favorite blues singers is Albert King. That big son of a bitch can sing! And he's one of the greatest blues guitarists living today.[4] I was on a show with he, Bobby 'Blue' Bland, who's another favorite singer, and then B. B. King." It's interesting that Witherspoon has named pure blues singers—no pop or rock artists. Although he's shared bills with all kinds of performers, including those who do pop and rock, his heart lies in the blues tradition.

In 1965 Witherspoon won England's *Melody Maker* magazine poll as top blues singer. Over the next few years, he recorded for Verve, BluesWay, and Prestige, with accompaniment by such distinguished modern jazz players as Bill Watrous, Kenny Burrell, Pepper Adams, and blues guitar master T-Bone Walker. He guested on Bill Cosby's first NBC-TV comedy series during the 1969–70 season. "He's done a lot for me," Witherspoon says of Cosby. "He's done a lot for a lot of blues and jazz. He don't want to be known for it, but he's helped a lot of people."

During the late sixties Witherspoon appeared at such leading jazz clubs as New York's Village Gate and the Village Vanguard and toured U.S. military clubs in Japan. He played Harlem's famed Apollo Theatre in an all-star blues show with Muddy Waters, B. B. King, and others. Although the participants loved doing the show—the master bluesmen brought out the best in one other—less-than-hoped-for box office receipts convinced the Apollo management that the black community no longer supported the blues. The supposition was that younger blacks associated the blues with an earlier era that they didn't remember nostalgically.

Ironically, as black interest waned in the sixties and seventies, the blues were being discovered by young white audiences. The "British invasion" of popular music during the mid-sixties—the sudden dominance on American pop charts of British groups to the exclusion of seemingly everyone else, including American black artists—helped revive interest. Many of the British musicians had been inspired by older black American blues and rhythm and blues artists. When they acknowledged that influence in interviews or sometimes shared bills with the older black performers, they helped refocus attention on the older styles. Singers ranging from Little Richard and Fats Domino to Big Joe Turner and Jimmy Witherspoon eventually benefited from the popularity of blues-based British rock bands and were booked in Great Britain and the United States as performers of the roots of contemporary music.

Eric Burdon, lead singer of the Animals, was a prime mover in spurring the popularity of blues-based rock. Witherspoon believes Burdon deserves a great credit for his role in reviving interest in black music and for the sincere interest he's long had in black musicians. In 1964 Burdon's hoarse, gutsy vocal on "House of the Rising Sun"— one of the first British hits to top American charts following the emergence of the Beatles—enthralled American youths who had no idea that Burdon's potent style of singing was derived from that of older American black blues performers. The song—which many young Americans probably assumed was "new" and an "Animals song" (others no doubt imagined it had originated with Bob Dylan, who had also recorded it)—was an adaptation of a traditional number that black blues-folk singer-guitarist Josh White, who was born in 1915, and others had long performed. The song is about a house of prostitution in New Orleans, something American disc jockeys apparently found more acceptable if sung about by a white British singer than by a black American one. Burdon's singing paved the way for the Rolling Stones and other immensely popular blues-based groups. Many of his fans soon learned about his admiration for black blues and R&B performers, including Joe Turner and Jimmy Witherspoon. After leaving the Animals, Burdon sang with a band called War, most of which was black, before going out on his own.

In 1971 Burdon had Witherspoon tour with him, providing exposure to many younger rock and blues concert-goers who otherwise would never have known of Witherspoon. They also recorded together on an album called *Guilty!* on MGM Records, and Burdon helped Witherspoon to set up his own company, Spoon Productions, within Burdon's Far Out Productions. Spoon Productions put out recordings not just by Witherspoon but by others, notably Robben Ford, a young guitarist Witherspoon had discovered who went on to work during the seventies with former Beatle George Harrison before going on his own (all the while under contract to Witherspoon).

Witherspoon's paths increasingly intersected with those of rock and pop musicians. How did he feel about sometimes being packaged with rock musicians? "Well, I had to survive. That's surviving, you understand what I mean? I went along with it, but I wasn't contented or happy. I did it well enough to get my point over, to get the money for the survival of my family. So I leave it alone. I don't knock it." Some of the young rock musicians "learned from me, which I'm proud of. I'm proud of that." Did any of them ever acknowledge him publicly the way he might have liked? "No. No. Even Eric Burdon. And you know, I'm the godfather of his son. He was on the "Today Show" one day. I called him up and said, 'You're a jive son of a bitch. Here you are coast to coast, and you wouldn't even mention my name. You're a phony mother. And I taught you how to say Lawd! You cats were saying "Lord, lord, lord."' [Witherspoon pronounces the word *lord* with a exaggeratedly proper, almost British inflection, and laughs.] At least he could have mentioned my name."

One of the odd—at least from Witherspoon's perspective—developments of the blues resurgence was that the more primitive a bluesman seemed to be, the more popular he was. It was a plus to be—or appear to be—older and uneducated, which would presumably put you much closer to the roots of the music than younger, more urbane artists. Thus Witherspoon's appeal with the younger generation of blues fans was not as broad as singer-guitarist John Lee Hooker's, six years Witherspoon's senior. Hooker was a son of Clarksdale, Missouri, sharecroppers, hadn't had much schooling, and talked, sang, and played in a much more rough-hewn manner than Witherspoon. For new blues enthusiasts, a blues singer considerably more "refined" than Witherspoon, such as Charles Brown, would be beyond the pale altogether.

For Witherspoon, projecting emotions was paramount, but concern for form and musicality was also important. If Witherspoon was singing a twelve-bar blues, it would *be* a twelve-bar blues. Hooker might choose to sing twelve bars or he might choose to sing ten bars (or some other number)—a liberty that a bluesman primarily interested in accompanying himself on guitar can take but that makes working with other musicians problematic. Witherspoon was interested in structure—how he got into a tune, how he'd make it build, and how he'd get out of it. He was concerned with keeping good time and singing in tune—values he shared more with the master jazz and blues instrumentalists who often accompanied him than with itinerant Mississippi Delta-type bluesmen. He always wanted to sing as well as he possibly could—a desire that prompted him, in middle age, to take vocal lessons.

In 1971, when Witherspoon was touring and recording with Burdon, John Lee Hooker was touring and recording (and making the pop charts) with Canned Heat, a blues-based American rock band whose lead singer, Bob Hite, had been collecting blues and R&B 78s since his early teens (by 1971 he owned some seventy thousand). Witherspoon liked Hooker personally and hardly begrudged him his success. But Witherspoon didn't consider Hooker's lack of education and unlettered sound an asset, remarking instead, "That's his problem."

Witherspoon was bemused to note that some new, young blues fans who were white presumed those singers who spoke and sang in a stereotypical downhome black dialect to be more authentic than others, an idea that reflected a romanticization of poverty and ignorance. Even when Witherspoon was a boy, there were some acknowledged blues masters such as Leroy Carr who did not use that kind of so-called Black English. "I don't dig Taj Mahal for that [using dialect] because he's an intellectual who's gone to school," he says, "and he's bringing blacks down, black history. And I don't appreciate that at all. I told him that on a television show.[5] All blacks wasn't raised on a farm. But most of the writers about the music say, 'Oh, you've got to be from Georgia, you've got to be illiterate, you've got to be poor.' Bullshit! I don't understand why they think that way. Blacks have been in poverty all their life. They've been on the back burner. That's why they want to come on the front burner. It has nothing to do with their records."

Witherspoon is sensitive about the issue of what style of singing is to be considered most authentically black. His kind of blues singing, he knows, was too black by establishment standards for him to have received the kind of major mainstream television exposure that he would have liked when he first made the R&B charts in 1949 and 1950. He would have loved nothing better than to have been a full-scale star, known to all Americans. Still, he plugged away through the years, doing what he did best and hoping audiences would find him. Recording for bigger labels during the sixties and seventies, then for the independents with which he had started, he received better distribution—and, consequently, chances for wider exposure—than he had in the early years.

In 1974 he recorded an album in Great Britain for Capitol Records. The album was produced by Mike Vernon and called *Love Is a Five-Letter Word*. Its title song, released as a single, made the *Billboard* R&B charts for fourteen weeks, beginning in January 1975 and peaking at thirty-one. For two weeks in March 1975 the album made *Billboard*'s pop charts—the only Witherspoon album ever to do so—and reached a position of 176. Witherspoon, quite happily, made money on that album, but it pained him to discover that KGFJ, a black station in Los Angeles, where he lived, wouldn't play it until he pressured them. They said that it sounded too much like white music for them.

He received plenty of other radio exposure throughout the seventies, however. In 1972 the "Jimmy Witherspoon Show" debuted on KMET-FM in Los Angeles and soon went into syndication. He played blues and R&B records of both past and present and chatted with guest artists. Witherspoon not only informed many listeners about the history of the music, but he also found that he learned a lot himself from doing the show. "That was great," he says of the experience. He recalls, "Me and Dr. Demento, we had the top shows for those three hours [in Los Angeles]. I followed him. I caused a lot of confusion there one night. I broke a record of John Mayall [the "Father of British Blues"]. He didn't show up. I waited until about thirty seconds before I got off the air. I said he couldn't disappoint my listeners like that. 'Who do you think you are, John Mayall?!' Wham! Broke it! Physically cracked it! On the air. And then, later on, I started making an announcement: 'John Mayall, wherever you are, let's do a battle of the blues and give the donation to the retarded children's foundation, which I think you should belong to.' [He laughs at the recollection.] Yes I did! Finally one night, guess who walked in—John Mayall, because we were friends, you know. He said, 'Man, I've got to come get this off my shoulder.' I said, 'You better come up here.' It was all over then. I was determined to get him up there. And I was trying to test my listeners, too, to see the reaction."

Witherspoon has always loved getting together with other blues singers; they share a sense of community. He remained close to Joe Turner in particular, recording an album with Turner just a few months before Turner's death in 1985, visiting Turner at the hospital within two days of Turner's death, and dedicating his first album after that, *Midnight Lady Called the Blues* (Muse), for which Dr. John and Doc Pomus supplied the songs, to Turner.

Throughout the seventies Witherspoon's career seemed to be moving on an upward curve. Besides making return visits to the Monterey Jazz Festival and to jazz clubs that had long booked him, he worked Playboy Clubs for the first time although he wasn't always happy with the audiences, appeared on Johnny Carson's "Tonight Show" and on NBC's "Midnight Special," and landed a starring role in the film *Black Godfather*. "I loved it, I loved it," he says of making the movie. How did he get the part? "A guy who had been a fan of mine for years in Chicago, a writer-producer, a black guy—he never forgot me." He would love to do more movies—he'd particularly love to sing in films—but feels that blacks are still given second-class treatment in Hollywood.

Disc jockey Anthony Navarro and writer Frank Joseph interviewed Witherspoon on Navarro's blues show on WYEP-FM in Pittsburgh in 1976. Their transcribed interview became a *Living Blues* magazine cover story (July-August 1977), helping boost interest in Witherspoon among blues aficionados. To Navarro and Joseph, Witherspoon expressed his belief that an audience for the blues could be found anywhere in the United States if promoters would do their jobs.

He was receiving more invitations to work than he could accept; he even refused some out of racial pride. "I don't even do benefits no more," he explains. "When they call me, I say, 'What time will I go on?' 'Three o'clock in the morning.' I say, 'I don't do black prime-time television.' And I'm serious about it. I have speak up about it. I don't do a benefit—I don't give a damn who it's for—if they don't put me on the prime time like the top white artists. I've never been an Uncle Tom. And that has hurt me. It has hurt me in my business. Definitely. It has closed doors."

The seventies also found him working more frequently than ever overseas. He made appearances in Japan and the Far East in 1973, in England in 1974, in Germany in 1976, in Switzerland in 1976, and in France in 1980, where he recorded an album, *Jimmy Witherspoon Sings the Blues with Panama Francis and the Savoy Sultans,* that was released in Europe by Black and Blue Records and in the United States by Muse Records. But he disputes the often-expressed notion that Europe is more appreciative of jazz and blues than America. "You interview other black blues singers or other artists who don't have the name that I have, and when they go over there it's like a new thing for them, because they can't work in the places here in America. But America's the greatest place in the world for Jimmy Witherspoon. That's financially, feeling, and everything else."

Witherspoon has far more money these days than he did early in his career, he notes, and he's a better singer than he was then. "Oh yes. Yes, yes—Lord, yes," he says, the cadence of his affirmation sounding like a song. From the mid-seventies on, he received royalties for recordings, something that had rarely happened to him before. He reckons that he had recorded some five hundred songs by that point. He was also receiving awards which, he felt, were really belated acknowledgments of a lifetime of accomplishments. He was glad to receive, for example, an NAACP Image Award in 1975 and an *Ebony* magazine Hall of Fame Award in 1977. He also says, "I'm happy the Black American Cinema Society gave me the Billie Holiday Phoenix Award. It's for achievement—just an award for my contributions. That is heavy. This award is so gorgeous—a phoenix statue."

As Witherspoon entered the eighties, the future looked as full of promise as it ever had during his career. But while touring England in 1981, on one of what had become his annual trips abroad, he realized that he was not well. The symptoms weren't obvious and he didn't grasp their seriousness, but he went to a doctor, complaining of an earache and a spot on his throat that was uncomfortable. "The doctor diagnosed it right away," Witherspoon says of the life-threatening cancer of the epiglottis—that flap of tissue in the throat that covers the opening of the windpipe when one swallows. "They went in and did a biopsy. The doctor said if I hadn't been a singer, they wouldn't have detected it that early. That's how people get caught—because they're not aware of it; they think it's just a sore throat or something, from talking or just getting hoarse. But because I'm a singer, I was more aware than someone else might be."

Did he fear that he would die?

"Well, that's hard to answer. You have faith. The first time, the first day, I was afraid. The second day, it didn't bother me." Everyone seemed to think that if he succeeded in beating the cancer he'd never be able to sing again. He kept the seriousness of his condition to himself. In the United States, his mother had no idea that his life was in jeopardy, and he had no idea that her health was failing. "I was in the hospital in England when my mother died. She never knew I was sick," he notes. His doctors were not certain that his cancer had been detected in time; it was out of the question for him to interrupt treatment and return to the United States for his mother's funeral. In retrospect, he supposes that was a blessing. "By not being able to go to the funeral because I was taking treatments, I didn't view the body and have that morbid memory. It's better that way. It's better to remember them as they were."

Witherspoon's regimen of care continued. "I had twenty-eight radiation treatments on my throat—twenty-eight straight working days," he recalls. And then he had a slow period of rest and recovery to build his strength before he could know where things stood. In time, it was apparent that the threat to his life was over. He decided he wasn't going to accept the notion that he'd never sing again. His voice was different than it had been before the cancer. It was somewhat hoarse and well worn—perhaps an octave has been added to his lower register—and his control over it seemed less secure than it had been. But Witherspoon was determined and worked at

regaining as much use of his voice as he could. Six months after being treated for the cancer, he performed a benefit performance for
the hospital.

Resuming his career, Witherspoon found that his fans accepted his
new voice. At times, your heart would go out to him because of the
difficulty he seemed to have making his voice do what he wanted it
to do. And yet, curiously, he was at least as compelling a performer
as he had been in earlier years. Although Witherspoon had been capable of very good work from the beginning of his recording career,
he also made his share of records that had the casual sound of a man
who knew he could sing well without half trying and perhaps didn't
always feel the need to try too hard. Now he had to strain for results, which added drama. He had to pace himself, too, and parcel
out phrases with greater deliberateness and restraint, saving the occasional upward rise into a brief, raw-edged shout for when it would
count most. The ability to distill emotion and offer it at peak moments and in intensely concentrated forms had always been a major
part of Witherspoon's appeal, as, for example, on his moving performance of "Ain't Nobody's Business" at the 1959 Monterey Jazz Festival and available on the highly recommended Fantasy CD *The 'Spoon
Concerts*. This ability now took on even greater importance. His brush
with death may have shaken him, may have humbled him, and may
have left him with less voice, but it also left him with even more
emotional colorations with which to work when he sings. He is able
to express vulnerability as well as strength.

John S. Wilson wrote of Witherspoon in *The New York Times* on
May 10, 1987, "He is fighting a throat problem that leaves his voice
less rich, less resonant and free than it once was. But the effort gives
his performances a sense of involvement that can be unusually
strong, even with a restricted voice." Peter Watrous of the *Times* observed aptly on December 10, 1989, that Witherspoon "more than
makes up for" range limitations "by pushing his notes carefully until they bleed emotion."

When Witherspoon tells an audience something like (as he said
at one Highlights in Jazz concert) "I'm the luckiest man in the world
. . . to be working with Harold Ashby," he isn't just expressing gratitude at being able to work with a distinguished tenor saxist. He is
grateful to be able to work at all and grateful to be alive. It is a quality that infuses his work with a little something extra. The effects of
the cancer as well as the natural changes that occur because of aging may have left Witherspoon with a much less reliable voice than
he once had. It often takes him several numbers to "get the rust"

out of his pipes, and there are nights when singing seems to be exceedingly difficult for him.[6] Yet at his best he is as moving as any singer working today. No one can sing a slow blues better, and his repertoire encompasses a wealth of blues and R&B history.

"Like that 'Big-Leg Woman,' I sang the other day—that's actually Peetie Wheatstraw," he notes. "That's from my home; I heard that when I was a boy. I'd hear the blues on records . . . at the juke joints, we called them. In Glasgow, Scotland not long ago—that was the first time I ever sang it. It just came to me. And when I sang it, a lady called me a chauvinistic bastard!" She didn't take the song, he feels, in the spirit that was intended. The blues don't always transplant well when offered to people of different cultures. Some of the song's lyrics are "Big-leg woman, keep your dresses down. / You got something make a bulldog love a hound." Sometimes, singing such a blues in a club setting, Witherspoon will fix his eyes on a woman in the audience, as if addressing his remarks just to her. "Little-leg woman, you got something good," he'll croon innocently before zinging in with the capper he learned in his youth—"If you don't believe me, ask all my friends in the neighborhood."

In the blues, the antagonism is captured as well as the attraction that exists between the sexes. Singing an old Saunders King blues, Witherspoon will tell of having done more for his woman than the good Lord ever did, repeating that line earnestly while the audience wonders just what he'd done for her. Then he explains that he'd bought her some hair when the good Lord hadn't given her any. There's a brief pause before the audience seems to catch on and begins to laugh.

Shifting moods, he'll swing easily through Amos Milburn's rhythmic 1953 hit "One Scotch, One Bourbon, One Beer." He'll recall the late Jimmy Reed with a couple of Reed's early-sixties numbers, singing feistily of that "Big Boss Man" who ain't so big, just tall, and bringing just the right touch of nervous tension to "Bright Lights, Big City." He'll sing new songs he's written, too, and old ones he's reworked. Those who know Witherspoon's story can sometimes hear bits of autobiography in his words. He'll sing his version of "When I Been Drinkin'," an old Bill Broonzy favorite, and throw in a line about wanting a woman "who digs 'Ain't Nobody's Business.'" He'll ease through "Nobody Knows You When You're Down and Out." Bessie Smith may have sung of buying her friends bootleg whisky when times were good; he sings of buying his friends "whisky, grass, and wine." She may have sung in a general way of having fallen on hard times; he specifies, "In 1954, I began to fall so low." It's not just a song, it's his story that Witherspoon sings. And when he vows that if he ever gets his hands on a dollar again "I'm going to squeeze that mother 'til the eagle grins," there's nothing old-hat about the song. It speaks to us now.

He sings simply, directly, and—always—sincerely. He's a less stylized performer than Charles Brown, Little Jimmy Scott, or Ruth Brown. And he's a walking library of the blues, a summation of a long line of blues and rhythm and blues artists, all the more to be valued now because today's up-and-coming singers aren't carrying on this heritage.

What are Jimmy Witherspoon's goals at this point?

"Just to be healthy," he says. "And enjoy life."

Suggestions for
Further Listening and Reading

One problem with recommending recordings (particularly compilations of reissued sides) in a book is that they can go in and out of print so quickly that a discography may well be partially obsolete by the time the book is published. Throughout this book, noteworthy original R&B recordings (which in most cases were initially issued as 78 rpm or 45 rpm singles) have been mentioned. Reissues of some are likely to remain available even if specific albums or CDs listed in this section (all of which were available during the period this book was being written) do go out of print, because companies in the United States and abroad periodically compile new collections of older recordings.

Records issued by larger labels such as Atlantic and Fantasy can be found in (or quickly ordered by) most well-stocked stores. Where possible, I will list addresses of U.S.-based record companies to make the ordering process easier. Mail-order sellers of hard-to-find and out-of-print recordings regularly advertise in music publications such as *Living Blues, Goldmine, Down Beat,* and *Jazz Times.* For example, Stackhouse/Rooster Blues Records (232 Sunflower Ave., Clarksdale, MS 38614; telephone 601-627-2209) sells records by mail, both U.S. and hard-to-find import labels, and specializes in blues and R&B, and the Institute of Jazz Studies (in the Dana Library at Rutgers University, 185 University Ave., Newark, NJ 07102; telephone 201-648-5595) will, for a fee, make copies for research purposes of out-of-print recordings from their extensive collection of jazz, blues, and rhythm and blues recordings.

Ruth Brown

Ruth Brown: Miss Rhythm, Greatest Hits and More (Atlantic 7-82061-2), a deluxe 1989 double-CD reissue compilation—a "must have" for any serious R&B collector—gathers many of Brown's strongest performances (including her original versions of "Mama, He Treats Your Daughter Mean," "Five-Ten-Fifteen Hours," "Teardrops from My Eyes," and "Have a Good Time"), along with some forgettable ones—a generous forty selections in all made from 1949 to 1960 (Atlantic Records, 75 Rockefeller Plaza, New York, NY 10019). Additional performances from this period are included on a hard-to-find European import, *Ruth Brown and Her Rhythmakers: Sweet Baby of Mine* (Route 66, KIX 16). This is not nearly as strong a set as the Atlantic collection, but offers some rewards nonetheless, such as "Rain Is a Bringdown" and "Am I Making the Same Mistake Again?" It's worth noting that eleven of the sixteen recordings in this set are not duplicated in the Atlantic set. However, only those who prefer complete works are likely to want to try to get hold of a copy of Charly Records' 1984 *Ruth Brown* album (Charly CRB 1069), because only three of the sixteen selections on it are not duplicated on the Atlantic set (which boasts better sound quality)—and only one of those three, in my judgment, is significant: the exciting (or frantic, depending on your tastes) "Hello Little Boy" from 1953, sung at the fastest tempo of any recording Brown ever made (Charly Records, 155-166 Ilderton Road, London, SE15 1NT, England). *Ruth Brown: Help a Good Girl Go Bad* (DCC Jazz, DJZ-602) is a recent reissue of 1964 recordings originally made for Mainstream (DCC Compact Classics, 8300 Tampa Ave., Northridge, CA 91324), including the old Nellie Lutcher hit "He's a Real Gone Guy," a moving rendition of "Porgy," and "On the Good Ship Lollipop," sung sincerely as a slow ballad.

Ruth Brown with the Thad Jones/Mel Lewis Orchestra: Fine Brown Frame (Capitol Jazz CDP 0777 7 81200 2 5), a strong 1968 set, includes a reprise of one of her early successes, "Be Anything (but Be Mine)," the blues classic "Trouble in Mind," a playful "Yes Sir, That's My Baby," and a surprisingly effective reinterpretation of Al Jolson's "Sonny Boy."

If you can find a copy, *Ruth Brown: Gospel Time* (Lection Records 839315-2), presented Brown in a gospel vein (recorded 1963).

For samples of Brown since her rediscovery in the mid-eighties (all readily available) check out *Ruth Brown: Have a Good Time* (Fantasy F-9661-2), which includes impressive live 1988 performances of such oldies as "Have a Good Time" and "Teardrops from My Eyes," along with songs she's added to her repertoire in more recent years, notably "Always on My Mind," with backing provided by her regular touring band (and no touring band gives a singer better support) under the direction of Bobby Forrester (Fantasy Records, Tenth and Parker, Berkeley, CA 94710). Her Grammy-winning 1989 studio recording *Ruth Brown: Blues on Broadway* (Fantasy F-9662-2) includes excellent renditions of songs she sang in *Black and Blue*, "St. Louis Blues" and "If I Can't Sell It, I'll Keep Sittin' on It," along with a memorable "Nobody Knows You When You're Down and Out" with backing from Britt Woodman, Spanky Davis, Hank Crawford, and other fine jazz musicians. The original Broadway cast recording *Black and Blue* (DRG CDSBL 19001) includes Linda Hopkins and Carrie Smith as well as Brown (all three share vocal duties on "I'm a Woman" and "Black and Blue"). Brown's voice is recorded better on this album than on the Fantasy albums—the warmth of her tones are captured better—but her performances of "St. Louis Blues" and "If I Can't Sell It, I'll Keep Sittin' on It" don't pack the punch of her performances of those same numbers on *Blues on Broadway* (DRG Records, 130 W. 57th St., New York, NY 10019).

The strength and spirit of Brown's current work is particularly well captured on *Ruth Brown: Fine and Mellow* (Fantasy FCD-9663-2), which includes her versions (recorded in 1991) of such R&B oldies as "It's Just a Matter of Time," "I'll Be Satisfied," and "Knock Me a Kiss." The high point is "A World I Never Made," a powerful, from-the-guts performance that has a depth not on her early recordings.

Ruth Brown: The Songs of My Life (Fantasy FCD-9665-2), recorded in 1993, is not (as the title might seem to imply) a collection of the songs that made Brown famous, but rather of assorted ballads and torch songs she likes, with relaxed jazz backgrounds. (It's a pity they couldn't have included one rousing up-tempo number for variety.) Brown's masterly, bittersweet rendition of Alec Wilder's "While We're Young" is emotionally nourishing; she's sharing wisdom acquired over a far-from-easy life. Other numbers include "It Could Happen to You" (which she sang at her first Apollo Theatre appearance), the wartime favorite "I'll Be Seeing You," and Eric Clapton's "Tears in Heaven" (which she has taken to singing in her club appearances in recent years and delivers with great impact). All of these are reminders that in recent years she's become a more subtle interpreter of ballads—she says she finds herself paying attention to the meaning of lyrics now more than ever—than she was on her early recordings and was in performances even just a few years earlier.

An appealing 1993 performance by Ruth Brown of "Have Yourself a

Merry Little Christmas" is included in *Christmas Songs* (Milestone MCD-9211-2), a 1993 compilation (both new recordings and reissues) performed by Anita O'Day, Coleman Hawkins, Chet Baker, and others.

Atlantic Blues: Vocalists (Atlantic 81696) is an overview of blues recordings by Atlantic artists from 1949 to 1982. The CD version of this collection includes one Ruth Brown performance "Rain Is a Bringdown" (1949), which she wrote (and which features strong piano support from Amos Milburn); the long-playing album version of this collection includes a second number performed and written by Brown that is not on the CD version: "R. B. Blues" (1950). The collection is recommended because it includes performances by twenty artists, including Brown, LaVern Baker, Jimmy Witherspoon, Joe Turner, Wynonie Harris, Sippie Wallace, Percy Mayfield, Esther Phillips, Aretha Franklin, and others, helpful in setting in context the performances of artists discussed in this book.

Brown bootleg albums from all sources (including, most recently, Czechoslovakia) turn up fairly often in stores.

Compelling live footage of Brown singing "Have a Good Time" during the fifties at Harlem's famed Apollo Theatre is included in the recommended videotape *The Ladies Sing the Blues,* which also includes performances by Bessie Smith, Billie Holiday, Sister Rosetta Tharpe, Dinah Washington, and other greats (V.I.E.W. video number 1313 [V.I.E.W. Video, 34 E. 23rd St., New York, NY 10010]).

Brown not only narrates the readily available 1993 videotape *Blues Alive* (BMG Video 72333-80005-3), but she is also seen performing "If I Can't Sell It" (although it's unfortunate that the producers have cut off her introductory lines, making the double-entendre song more of a single-entendre song). This video also includes recent live club performances by Willie Dixon, Albert Collins, and Charles Brown (singing his classic "Drifting Blues").

Little Jimmy Scott

Little Jimmy Scott's original hit 1950 recording of "Everybody's Somebody's Fool," as well as another number he recorded with the Lionel Hampton Band, "I Wish I Knew," are included in the two-album set *The Best of Lionel Hampton* (MCA Records, MCAC-4075E) (UNI Distribution Corp., 70 Universal City Plaza, Universal City, CA 91608).

In 1991 Fantasy Records released (in CD form) on its Specialty label previously unreleased live 1951 recordings of *Little Jimmy Scott and the Paul Cayten Band: Regal Records—Live in New Orleans* (Specialty SPCD 2170-2). Although audio fidelity is far from recording-studio standards and the band sounds a bit ragged, the set provides a rare, fascinating "you are there" feel of a night at a black theater some four decades ago. The announcer's patter, the highly enthusiastic audience responses, and some heated tenor sax work from Sam Butera all add to the atmosphere. Scott sings "Everybody's Somebody's Fool," "All of Me" (taken at a faster tempo than he'd choose now), and "Anytime, Any Place, Anywhere," and you can feel the impact he has upon listeners. The band also does a couple of instrumentals.

Little Jimmy Scott: Very Truly Yours (Savoy Jazz SV-0239) includes "Imagination," "When Did You Leave Heaven," "The Show Goes On," "Everybody Needs Somebody," and other studio recordings from the fifties, when Scott's voice was in excellent shape. Budd Johnson, Mundell Lowe, and Charles Mingus are among the musicians accompanying him. The Savoy Jazz label is part of Denon Records, 135 W. 50th St., Suite 915, New York, NY 10020.

Additional sides from this period were included in the following two long-playing albums, which went out of print as this book was in preparation. You may find copies in some stores; it is likely that the recordings will eventually be reissued on CDs. *Little Jimmy Scott: All Over Again* (Savoy Jazz SJL 1155) includes "I'm Afraid the Masquerade Is Over," "Everybody's Somebody's Fool," and "Sometimes I Feel Like a Motherless Child." A weaker collection is *Little Jimmy Scott: Can't We Begin Again?* (Savoy Jazz SJL-1183), 1975 recordings with pianist Ace Carter and strings, including "Close Your Eyes," "You've Changed," "The Way We Were," and "When I Fall in Love."

After Scott's rediscovery in the mid-eighties and before he received a major-label record deal in 1991, Scott satisfied requests he received from fans for recordings by offering casually produced cassettes on his own label, "J's Way Jazz." On *Jimmy Scott and the Jazz Expressions: Doesn't Love Mean More?* from 1990 and recommended only for those who want his complete work, Scott, backed by local musicians, sings some of his own songs (J's Way Records, PO Box 668, East Orange, NJ 07019.)

In late 1991 Scott signed a five-album contract with Warner Brothers Records, which has helped bring him to the attention of a lot more people. Warner has been willing to spend the money needed to record and promote Scott properly. His first release under the contract, *Jimmy Scott: All the Way* (Sire/Warner Bros./Blue Horizon 9 26955-2), issued in 1992, was not only his first new release in nearly twenty years but also the most fully realized album he'd ever done. It hardly matters that, in his late sixties, Scott's emotionally charged voice doesn't soar quite as high as it once did, nor that his vibrato has broadened. The all-ballads collection (featuring such numbers as "Someone to Watch Over Me," "I'm Getting Sentimental Over You," and "Every Time We Say Goodbye") is sad, wise, and strangely moving. Scott tugs melodies in directions you don't expect them to go, while world-class jazz artists like Kenny Barron and David "Fathead" Newman (arranged by such pros as Johnny Mandel, Dale Oehler, and John Clayton) provide the first-class backing he rarely received in his youth (Sire Records/Warner Brothers Records, 3300 Warner Blvd., Burbank, CA 91510). This recommended CD was produced by Tommy Lipuma, one of the top names in the field.

Jimmy Scott: Dream (Sire/Warner Bros./Blue Horizon 45629), a 1994 release, features such numbers as "I Cried for You," "Talk of the Town," and "Laughing on the Outside"—all of which are particularly well suited for him. The album's executive producer knows Scott's repertoire almost as well as Scott does—he's Jimmy McDonough, the caring music journalist who was so devoted a Scott fan that he once used his earnings from an article about Scott to finance recording a Scott demo. This is a small-group session, with jazz pianist Junior Mance, bassist Ron Carter, vibes player Milt Jackson, and others providing tasteful but spare backing. Overall the CD is not as successful as the previous one (*All the Way*); the lusher instrumentation on the previous CD helped mask the natural signs of age—the occasional waver, the cutback in tonal richness—in Scott's voice. But Scott remains a touching vocalist nonetheless.

Jimmy Scott: Lost and Found (Rhino/Atlantic and Atco Masters Series R2 71059), a 1993 release, gathers four sides from the 1969 album *The Source*, which was quickly withdrawn for legal reasons, and five sides from a never-released 1972 album. Sides like "Day by Day" and "Unchained Melody" from 1969 capture the great tonal beauty of Scott's voice when it was at (or very near to) its peak and are essential to any Scott collection. He seems to relate well to the lyrics of such numbers as "Sometimes I Feel Like a Motherless Child" and "Exodus." This is a welcome compilation of recordings Scott never expected to hear again. The master tapes for the 1972 session were believed to have been lost or destroyed by Atlantic at the time of my interviews with Scott; a copy subsequently turned up in producer Joel Dorn's home.

Lou Reed: Magic and Loss (Sire/Warner Bros. CD 26662), a 1991 CD by rock singer-guitarist-songwriter Lou Reed, features a touch of "the legendary Little Jimmy Scott," as the album credits read, on one cut, "Power and Glory: The Situation." Reed is the primary vocalist, but Scott adds haunting, heartfelt responses ("I wanted all of it, not some

of it") in the background. The album is a reminder of Reed's appreciation for Scott and also of their joint appreciation for the late songwriter Doc Pomus, who was a source of inspiration for the recording.

Perhaps there's no surer sign of Scott's rediscovery than his inclusion as a guest star (along with such younger pop recording artists
as Deborah Harry and Mavis Staples) on the 1994 release *Jazz Passengers in Love* (High Street Records 72902 103282). Scott's sole cut,
"Imitation of a Kiss," doesn't catch him in the very best of voice,
but it's fascinating nonetheless to hear him tackle thought-provok-
ing new material, and he sounds good with the open, free backing
provided by Roy Nathanson and Curtis Fowlkes's Jazz Passengers (a
staple of New York's Knitting Factory club). The musicians, all young
enough to be Scott's children, pride themselves on being risk-takers,
and Scott seems right at home. High Street Records is a part of
Windham Hill Records (75 Willow Rd., Menlow Park, CA 94025).

Scott is represented by one cut ("I Wish I Knew" from his Lionel
Hampton days) on the CD *The Legendary Big Band Singers* (1994, Decca
Jazz/GRP GRD-642), a hip compilation of thirties', forties', and early
fifties' recordings that focuses primarily on black big-band vocalists
including Pha Terrell ("Until the Real Thing Comes Along"), Ella
Johnson ("Since I Fell for You"), Dinah Washington ("Blow Top
Blues"), and Walter Brown ("Hootie Blues"), all of whom were mentioned as influences by one or another of the artists discussed in this
book.

Scott has also recorded numbers for the soundtracks of the films
A Rage in Harlem and *Street of Dreams*. Those seeking complete sets
of his work may want to seek out the home video versions of those
films or soundtrack recordings.

Charles Brown

Charles Brown: All My Life (Bullseye Blues/Rounder Records CD BB
9501) includes 1990 recordings of "When the Sun Comes Out," "Nobody Knows the Trouble I've Seen," and "Fool's Paradise," as well as
duets with Ruth Brown ("Tell Me Who") and Dr. John ("A Virus Called
the Blues") (Bullseye Blues/Rounder Records, One Camp St., Cam-
bridge, MA 02140). This excellent release was nominated for a Grammy Award and was chosen, in *Down Beat's* International Critics' Poll,
as the best blues album of the year.

Bonnie Raitt, a strong booster of classic R&B, makes two guest appearances on the 1992 release *Charles Brown: Someone to Love* (Bullseye Blues/Rounder Records CD BB 9514), singing a duet with Brown

on the title track and providing exceptionally sympathetic slide-gui-
tar accompaniment for him on "Every Little Bit Hurts." Brown switch-
es from piano to organ for the closing track, "I Don't Want to Get
Adjusted."

Charles Brown: Just a Lucky So and So (Bullseye Blues/Rounder
Records CD BB 9521), a 1994 release, mixes new material with fresh
versions of such old Brown favorites as "Driftin' Blues" (winningly
done, with some nice riffing by the band), "Black Night," and "I Fell
in Quicksand." What makes this album distinctive—and gives it more
variety than most—is its effective use of a full big band and strings
on selected cuts.

Charles Brown: These Blues (Verve 523 022-2), another 1994 release,
may find wider distribution than the previous CDs because Verve is
a much bigger company than Rounder, but it's not as highly recommended. There's less variety in terms of both repertoire and instrumentation in this CD than on the other, better-produced CDs. Ron
Levy, producer of Brown's Bullseye Blues/Rounder recordings, deserves
recognition for his contributions. But one standout cut—a nearly sev-
en-and-a-half-minute version of "I Did My Best for You" in which
Brown's piano playing gradually gains intensity—is a significant addition to Brown's recorded legacy.

The Legend, Charles Brown: Blues and Other Love Songs (Muse MCD
5466), a 1992 release, features appealing performances of "Do You Want
Me?" "I Put Myself Together," and a particularly strong "Who's Beating
My Time?" (just Brown on piano and vocal and no additional musicians on that number; on most other cuts he's backed by three or four
musicians). The rightness of Brown's choice of notes as a pianist is easier to savor on this album than on many others. There's a fair amount
of his piano, and few other instruments obscure his playing.

Charles Brown: One More for the Road (Alligator AL 4771) includes
"I Cried Last Night," "Cottage for Sale," "Travelin' Blues," and "One
for My Baby" (Alligator Records, Box 60234, Chicago, IL 60660). This
1989 release is a slightly changed rerelease of the album of the same
name issued in 1986 by a now-defunct label, Blue Side (BLC 60007-
4). Either version of the album, which played an important role in
spurring Brown's comeback, is a good introduction to latter-day
Brown. Nine of the eleven selections are the same on both the Alligator and Blue Side version of the album; each version contains two
selections not available on the other. For example, "Get Yourself Another Fool," included on the Blue Side album, which I prefer sightly,
was replaced by "I Stepped in Quicksand" on the Alligator version.

Mosaic Records, which does first-rate work in all aspects of the reissue field, from audio quality to annotation, issued *The Complete Aladdin Recordings of Charles Brown* in 1994. (Mosaic Records are available only by mail order from 35 Melrose Place, Stamford, CT 06902; telephone 203-327-7111.) This highly recommended set, gathering ninety-seven songs recorded between 1945 and 1956, includes not only the original recordings of most of Brown's hits (reason enough to buy it) but also such rarities as a previously unreleased 1945 first-take of "Drifting Blues" (the variant opening line has him walking and drifting rather than drifting and drifting as on the often-imitated hit version) and intriguing experiments at placing Brown in different instrumental settings. For example, lush strings are heard on "The Message" and "All My Life" (1951), and an infectiously rocking New Orleans band, with such stalwarts of the New Orleans scene as saxist Lee Allen, bassist Frank Fields, and drummer Earl Palmer, are on previously unissued recordings of "Knock Me a Kiss" and "There Is No Greater Love" (1956).

A much less expensive alternative to the Mosaic boxed set is *Driftin' Blues: The Best of Charles Brown* (Aladdin/EMI Blues Series CDP-7-97989-2, available from Capitol Records, Hollywood and Vine Streets, Hollywood, CA 90028). This widely distributed CD from 1992 includes twenty of Brown's most popular recordings from 1945 through 1956, including the original versions of "Driftin' Blues," "Trouble Blues," "Black Night," and "Fool's Paradise."

Not to be confused with *Driftin' Blues: The Best of Charles Brown* is the similarly titled *Charles Brown: Driftin' Blues* (DCC Jazz, DJZ-603). This collection of 1963 recordings (originally released on the Mainstream label) ranges from a fine remake of Brown's classic "Driftin' Blues" to such early R&B favorites as "Since I Fell for You" and "So Long" to such then-contemporary numbers as "Go Away Little Girl" and "Days of Wine and Roses." The more contemporary material doesn't always suit Brown well, though; overall, the set is far from Brown's strongest.

The out-of-print European-import LP *Charles Brown: Sunny Road* (Route 66, KIX 5) offers a good cross-section of recordings spanning 1945 to 1960, ranging from early hits of Brown's with Johnny Moore's Three Blazers to later New Orleans sessions.

In addition to the original recording of the title number of *Charles Brown: Please Come Home for Christmas* (King KC-15019X), which was Brown's last chart hit in 1960, this sixteen-track Christmas collection with guest-star organist Bill Doggett includes "Merry Christmas Baby" (a remake of the hit Brown first recorded with Johnny Moore's Three Blazers), "The Christmas Song," "Christmas in Heaven," "I'll Be Home for Christmas," and more. The collection, originally marketed by King in 1960 and marketed in subsequent years by Gusto Records, is out of print, but Bullseye Blues/Rounder Records met the need for a Charles Brown Christmas album by recording and releasing in 1994 *Charles Brown's Cool Christmas Blues* (Bullseye Blues CD BB 9561), a stronger collection. There are new versions of "Merry Christmas Baby," "Please Come Home for Christmas," and "Christmas in Heaven," as well as other Christmas favorites Brown had never recorded. All are infused with his laid-back blues feeling. His striking piano interjections—now sparse and spidery, now lush and florid—give "Silent Night" in particular fresh life.

Just one Charles Brown recording is among the fifty gathered in the two-CD boxed set *The Swing Time Records Story: R&B, Blues and Gospel 1946–1952* ("B&O Blues," 1948), an anthology that is highly recommended. It includes work by Jimmy Witherspoon and Floyd Dixon and a representative sampling of the sounds of the era. Featured are such artists as Ray Charles, Lowell Fulson, Percy Mayfield, Johnny Otis, and others. Just how strongly Charles Brown influenced young Ray Charles is apparent on such Charles cuts as "Lonely Boy" (1950), in which he initates Brown's laid-back, somewhat exaggerated vocal style, and a Charles original called "I'm Wondering and Wondering" (1952) that is modeled on Brown's "Drifting Blues." The set is available from Capricorn Records, 120 30th Avenue North, Nashville, TN 37203.

Recommended primarily for those who wish complete sets of Brown's work is *Keys to the Crescent City* (Rounder CD 2087), a 1991 release that includes three selections by Brown (one, "Nobody Knows the Trouble I've Seen," is also on the CD *All My Life*) and three or four selections apiece by New Orleans pianists and vocalists Eddie Bo, Willie Tee, and Art Neville. One nice thing about these particular recordings is that Brown is unaccompanied by other musicians, making his piano easy to hear clearly.

Floyd Dixon

Currently in production (as of mid-1995) is an as yet untitled new CD by Floyd Dixon. Expected to be released in 1996, it will be Dixon's first widely available new studio recording in many years—a long-overdue representation of his latterday work, with backing by his usual musicians, guitarist Port Barlow and the Full House Band (Alligator Records, Box 60234, Chicago, IL 60660).

The most readily available Dixon reissue set is *Floyd Dixon: Mar-*

shall Texas Is My Home (Specialty/Fantasy Records SPCD-7011-2). This 1991 compact disc compilation of recordings made between 1953 and 1957 includes "Hard Living Alone," "Hey Bartender," "Ooh-eee! Ooh-eee!" and previously unissued versions of numbers including "Call Operator 210" and "Reap What You Sow," with knowledgeable annotation by producer Billy Vera.

Floyd Dixon with Port Barlow and the Full House—Live at the Monterey Jazz Festival, a 1992 cassette available from Right Time Productions (382 North Lemon Ave., Walnut, CA 91789; telephone 909-594-1841) captures a joyfully exuberant latter-day Dixon.

Three LPs provide a good introduction to Dixon's work—a broader overview than on any other albums. Although the manufacturer, Route 66, has stopped pressing them—and they have not, as of this writing, been made available in compact disc form—copies can still be found in some stores. The easiest way to purchase them (and virtually all other Dixon recordings), however, is by mail order from Right Time Productions (which acquired a supply of them before the manufacturer discontinued them). Right Time Productions not only distributes Dixon recordings, but also Dixon tee shirts, buttons, information on forthcoming Dixon recordings and bookings, and fan-club membership. *Floyd Dixon: Opportunity Blues* (Route 66, KIX-1) consists of 1949 through 1961 recordings—some with Johnny Moore's Three Blazers, some with Eddie Williams and his Brown Buddies, and still others with miscellaneous backing—including such hits as "Dallas Blues," "Broken Hearted," and "Telephone Blues," as well as exuberant 1951 live concert recordings of "Too Much Jelly Roll" and "Baby, Let's Go Down to the Woods." *Floyd Dixon: Houston Jump* (Route 66, KIX-11) consists of 1947 through 1960 recordings, including "Mississippi Blues," "Girl Fifteen," "Sad Journey," and "Tight Skirts." *Floyd Dixon: Empty Stocking Blues* (Route 66, KIX-27) consists of 1947 through 1953 recordings, including "Hard Living Alone," "Red Cherries," "Do I Love You?" featuring a particularly fine sample of Oscar Moore's sensitive guitar work, and two rare gospel sides,"Precious Lord" and "Milky White Way."

Available either from Right Time Productions or from the recording company, Cottontail Music West (PO Box 191041, Los Angeles, CA 90019; telephone 213-731-5548) are an LP capturing Dixon in the mid-eighties, *Hitsville Look Out—Here's Mr. Magnificent* (most notable for the spirited title blues number, which conveys some of his sincere, unpretentious, and firmly held religious beliefs, and a rollicking instrumental version of "Dr. Kildare," which lets him stretch out as a pianist) and Dixon's latest recording, a 1994 compact disc release called *Floyd Dixon: Mr. Magnificent Hits Again*. It's hard to imagine anyone not responding to the ebullience Dixon projects on the latter on new studio recordings of "Hey Bartender" and "Wine, Wine, Wine." A live performance of "Operator 210," taken from his guest appearance on Billy Vera's radio show, has considerable character, too. But his performance of "Boogie Bear Woman" has been cut off awkwardly, unprofessionally at the end; Dixon should be recording with a bigger label that would give him more caring production.

Atlantic Blues: Piano (Atlantic 81694) is a noteworthy, easily obtainable 1986 compilation recommended even though only two of its twenty-three recordings ("Hey Bartender" and "Floyd's Blues," both from 1954) are by Dixon because it helps put him in context. Sides from artists include Ray Charles, Amos Milburn, Texas Johnny Brown, Jay McShann, Vann "Piano Man" Walls, and Champion Jack Dupree, players who helped inspire Dixon, Charles Brown, and others discussed in this book.

The two-CD boxed set *The Swing Time Records Story: R&B, Blues and Gospel 1946–1952* includes Floyd Dixon singing and playing his own "Mississippi Blues" (1947), as well as Eddie Williams and his Brown Buddies (with Floyd Dixon) doing "Saturday Night Fish Fry" (1947 or 1948).

A five-CD boxed set released in 1994, *The Specialty Story, 1944–1964* (5SPCD-4412-2), includes one recording by Dixon, "Hard Living Alone" (1953), along with those of assorted other R&B and early rock 'n' roll performers such as Roy Milton, Percy Mayfield, Smokey Hogg, Lloyd Price, and Little Richard.

LaVern Baker

LaVern Baker: Soul on Fire—The Best of LaVern Baker (Atlantic 82311) is an essential 1991 compact disc compilation of twenty Baker recordings from her peak years of popularity (1953–62), including such smash commercial hits as "Jim Dandy" and "Tweedlee Dee," along with others that didn't sell as well but are often stronger artistically, such as the first-rate "Soul on Fire," "Tomorrow Night," and "Shake a Hand."

Baker's surprisingly youthful, unblemished voice was well recorded on her first studio album in more than twenty years, *Woke Up This Morning* (Disques Swing 8433), made in 1991 and featuring such numbers as "Why Don't You Do Right?" "Body and Soul," "That's My Desire," and "Trouble in Mind" (available from DRG Records, Inc., 130 West 57th St., New York, NY 10019).

Her warmth and sly humor were captured more vividly on a re-laxed live recording made that same year, *LaVern Baker: Live in Hollywood '91* (Rhino R2-70565). Here are stirring performances of old favorites ranging from "Tweedlee Dee" and "Jim Dandy" (nostalgic fun, although the numbers may be on the juvenile side, it's good to hear them again) to others that draw more feeling from her, including "Tomorrow Night," "Play It Fair," "Tennessee Waltz," "Shake a Hand," "Saved," and "Slow Rollin' Mama," a double-entendre number in a pseudo-twenties' "dirty blues" vein that Doc Pomus coauthored and that she sang in *Dick Tracy*. The album, which includes representative samples of Baker's playful bantering with the audience between numbers, provides an excellent feel for her latter-day work. Accompanied by a polished (if unimaginative) R&B septet and two backup singers, she proved that after all those years away from the scene she still had it (available from Rhino Records, 10635 Santa Monica Blvd., Los Angeles, CA 90025-4900).

LaVern Baker Sings Bessie Smith (Atlantic 7-90980-1), reissued in 1989, includes "Gimme a Pigfoot," "On Revival Day," "Empty Bed Blues," and other numbers Smith sang in the twenties and thirties. Baker recorded them in 1958 sessions with such jazz musicians as Buck Clayton, Vic Dickenson, Urbie Green, Danny Barker, and Jerome Richardson. One of the strongest performances from the album, "Gimme a Pigfoot," may also be found on *Atlantic Blues: Vocalists* (Atlantic 81696).

Useful for context-setting is a three-CD boxed set *The OKeh Rhythm-and-Blues Story, 1949–1952* (Epic/OKeh/Legacy 48912), with samples of various R&B artists such as Big Maybelle, Larry Darnell, and Hadda Brooks. The set also includes one performance by LaVern Baker—although she is not billed as such. You can hear her full-voiced 1951 rendition of "I Want a Lavender Cadillac" ("and I want it now," she insists), which is credited on the back cover (as on the original recording) to "Maurice King and his Wolverines with Bea Baker (vocal)."

Baker has also recorded numbers for the soundtracks of such films as *Dick Tracy* and *A Rage in Harlem*, which are on home video.

Jimmy Witherspoon

The 'Spoon Concerts (Fantasy FCD-24701-2), an important Witherspoon CD, gathers fifteen selections from two different HiFijazz albums that introduced Witherspoon to white audiences, including live recordings from his acclaimed "comeback" appearance at the 1959 Monterey Jazz Festival. (Gene Lees described Witherspoon, in a con-

temporary *Down Beat* account, as having dominated that festival.) The
set offers "Ain't Nobody's Business," "When I Been Drinkin'," and
other Witherspoon favorites, with accompaniment by such jazz stars
as Ben Webster, Coleman Hawkins, Woody Herman, and Roy Eldridge.

Jimmy Witherspoon: Spoon's Life (Evidence ECD 26044-2), a 1980
set recorded with excellent Chicago blues band backing (featuring
Magic Sam-protégé Johnny Dollar on guitar and George Smith on
harmonica) is a satisfying sampling of mature Witherspoon. This is
a relaxed, slow-tempo set, and he sounds fully comfortable with his
backing. He's in good voice, singing such numbers as T-Bone Walker's "Cold, Cold Feeling," Willie Nelson's "Night Life," and his own
"Big-Leg Woman," "Bags under My Eyes," and "Did You Ever?" The
set is worth ordering directly from Evidence Music, a leading pur-
veyer of blues reissues, at 1100 E. Hector Street, Suite 392, Consho-
hocken, PA 19428.

Jimmy Witherspoon: Spoon so Easy—the Chess Years (Chess/MCA
Records, Chess 93003), a compact disc issued in 1990, is the first compilation of Witherspoon's Chess recordings (from 1954 through 1956
and 1960), including a previously unreleased version of "Ain't Nobody's
Business," along with titles Floyd Dixon wrote for Witherspoon.

Jimmy Witherspoon: Spoonful o' Blues (Kent Records KLC2005), a
rather casual-sounding set, includes renditions of "Jelly Jelly," "Boogie-Woogie Woman," "Stormy Monday," and "Come Home Baby"
(Kent Music, 1100 Glendon Ave., Los Angeles, CA 90024).

Evenin' Blues (Fantasy/Original Blues Classics OBC-511; previously released as Prestige 7300) consists of 1963 recordings, remastered
and reissued in 1987, including "Money's Getting Cheaper," "Good
Rockin'," and "Kansas City," with accompaniment by T-Bone Walker, Clifford Scott, and others. Additional Witherspoon selections from
that period may be found on a 1990 reissue, *Baby, Baby, Baby* (Fanta-
sy/Original Blues Classics OBC-527; previously released as Prestige
7290). On a Big Joe Turner album featuring Jimmy Witherspoon,
Patcha, Patcha All Night Long (Pablo 2310-913, distributed by Fantasy Records), Witherspoon may be heard singing with one of his original idols and inspirations.

*Jimmy Witherspoon Sings the Blues with Panama Francis and the Sa-
voy Sultans* (Muse MR 5288) (recorded in Paris in 1980 and originally released in Europe by Disques Black and Blue) includes "Sometimes
I Feel Like a Motherless Child," "Boogie-Woogie (I May Be Wrong),"
"Good Morning Blues," and a Witherspoon original, "Rain Keeps Falling Down," with valuable contributions from soloists such as trumpeter Irvin Stokes and saxist Bobby Smith (Muse Records, 160 W. 71st

St., New York, NY 10023). This is an unusual Witherspoon album in that most of the numbers are associated with Jimmy Rushing, making the album sound almost like a tribute to Rushing. At times, Witherspoon's enunciation of words echoes Rushing's.

Jimmy Witherspoon: Midnight Lady Called the Blues (Muse MCD 5327), is a 1986 CD consisting of all new songs written by Dr. John and Doc Pomus, with accompaniment from such talented players as David "Fathead" Newman, Hank Crawford, Dr. John, and others.

Jimmy Witherspoon: Rockin' L.A. (Fantasy F-9660) is a highly uneven 1988 live set that finds Witherspoon (accompanied by a combo including Teddy Edwards on sax and Gerald Wiggins on piano) for the most part not in very good voice. It includes a few niceties such as "You Got Me Running," "Big Boss Man," and a medley with "Careless Love" and "One Scotch, One Bourbon, One Beer," but it's painfully uncomfortable to listen to Witherspoon struggle through "Sweet Lotus Blossom."

A much better sampling of Witherspoon's work from roughly the same period may be found on *Jimmy Witherspoon Live at Condon's, New York* (RTV CD-21037), with Bross Townsend's group. This 1991 CD is not without flaws. The sound quality is lackluster and Witherspoon is not in his best voice, although he's certainly in better voice than on *Rockin' L.A.* But the choice of material (including "Trouble in Mind," "Ain't Nobody's Business," "Gee Baby, Ain't I Good to You," and "Don't You Miss Your Baby?") is superb, and the live performance flows more naturally than the studio set. Witherspoon's at home with every one of these timeless songs. He has an intuitive knowledge of when to lag behind the beat or squeeze a syllable until it begins to squeal, when to declaim a word with particular force, or fill out a line with a soft-voiced, descending "oooh-oooh-oooh." And the intangible qualities—conviction and understanding of what these songs are about—are apparent (RTV Communications Group, Inc., PO Box 290007, Fort Lauderdale, FL 33329).

Live—Jimmy Witherspoon and Robben Ford (Avenue Jazz/Rhino R2 71262) is a 1993 reissue of a 1976 set in which Witherspoon is backed by guitarist Ford and three other musicians and sings such favorites as "Past Forty Blues," "No Rollin' Blues," and "S-K Blues."

The appealingly full voice of young Jimmy Witherspoon is featured on five of the fifty recordings gathered in the two-CD boxed set of assorted artists, *The Swing Time Records Story: R&B, Blues and Gospel 1946–1952* (Capricorn Records, 120 30th Avenue North, Nashville, TN 37203). The set includes Witherspoon's original 1947 recordings for the Supreme label of the hits "In the Evening When the Sun Goes

Down" and "Ain't Nobody's Business" (with some wonderful Jay McShann piano) although, oddly, only part one of the latter recording is included. "Ain't Nobody's Business"—Witherspoon's biggest hit—was originally issued with parts one and two on two sides of a 78.

Harder to find than some of the previous recordings but well worth looking for is *Jimmy Witherspoon: Ain't Nobody's Business* (Drive DE2-41006). This 1994 reissue of early recordings captures Witherspoon exuberantly shouting the blues in strong voice (some of Big Joe Turner's influence is in his phrasing), with irresistible jump-blues band backing. Whether taking the blues slow ("Sweet Lovin' Baby") or fast ("New Orleans Woman"), he's highly engaging (available from Drive Archive, 10351 Santa Monica Blvd., Suite 404, Los Angeles, CA 90025).

Two fine selections by Witherspoon may be found in *Atlantic Blues: Vocalists* (Atlantic 81696): "Trouble in Mind" and "In the Evening When the Sun Goes Down." These are the only numbers currently in print from a 1956 album, *New Orleans Blues,* in which Witherspoon was backed by a seven-piece traditional New Orleans-style band with trumpeter Sidney DeParis, trombonist Wilbur DeParis, clarinetist Omer Simeon, and others. It is to be hoped that the rest of the recordings Witherspoon made with this unique backing will be reissued.

Samplings of Witherspoon with McShann (someone should record them together again; they fit perfectly and love working with one another) are on two out-of-print albums: *Hey Mr. Landlord: Jimmy Witherspoon with Jay McShann* (Route 66, KIX 31) and *Goin' to Kansas City Blues: Jimmy Witherspoon with the Jay McShann Big Band* (RCA An1-1-1048[e]).

Witherspoon recorded one album of religious music in his career, *Feelin' the Spirit.* In particularly attractive voice and singing such numbers as "Sometimes I Feel Like a Motherless Child," "Nobody Knows the Trouble I've Seen," and "The Time Has Come," Witherspoon is effecting, although the impact of his sincere efforts is sometimes undercut by the slick white background vocals. Although the original long-playing album is long out of print, a CD entitled *Jimmy Witherspoon: Feelin' the Spirit* (Laserlight Digital 17-033) was released in 1994 by LaserLight Digital (part of Delta Music Inc., 2500 Broadway Ave., Suite 380, Santa Monica, CA 90404). This curious reissue includes the ten numbers Witherspoon recorded for the original LP and two concluding numbers sung by a singer who is unidentified. Nothing on the cover or in the liner notes, however, indicates that two of the twelve recordings on the CD are not by Witherspoon. Even stranger, LaserLight Digital also released a companion CD in 1994, *Jimmy Witherspoon: Amazing Grace,* ostensibly more of his recordings of religious music, and Witherspoon is not heard on that CD at all. The twelve cuts are by the same unidentified (and undistinguished) singer who sings on the last two cuts of *Jimmy Witherspoon: Feelin' the Spirit,* and he sounds nothing like Witherspoon. The songs are ones Witherspoon has never recorded, he told me on December 28, 1994, expressing anger that a record company would use his name and picture on the cover of a CD of someone else's work.

A warmly recommended videotape *The Buck Clayton All-Stars,* released in 1993 by Shanachie (call 201-579-7763), includes two excellent performances by Witherspoon (who's shamefully underdocumented on film): his classic "Ain't Nobody's Business" and "Roll 'Em Pete," performed with the renowned Count Basie alumni Buck Clayton, Earle Warren, and Buddy Tate, who were reunited for a 1961 European tour (available from Shanachie Productions, 37 East Clinton St., Newton, NJ 07860).

R&B Anthologies

Record companies are forever repackaging collections of early R&B recordings, and it's worth checking local stores to see which such collections may be available. One widely distributed, well-annotated series is particularly recommended as providing a broad rhythm and blues overview. *Atlantic Rhythm and Blues* encompasses 186 recordings made between 1947 and 1974 and may be purchased either as a boxed collection of fourteen LPs or cassettes or as individual volumes (seven separate CDs, double-LP, or double-cassette sets). Volume one (1947–52) includes Ruth Brown, Joe Turner, Willis Jackson, Ray Charles, and so on. Volume two (1952–55) includes Ruth Brown, LaVern Baker, Clyde McPhatter and the Drifters, and more. Volume three (1955–58) includes Ruth Brown, Chuck Willis, Ivory Joe Hunter, the Drifters, and more. Volume four (1958–62) includes LaVern Baker, Ben E. King, the Coasters, Ray Charles, and more. Volume five (1962–66) includes LaVern Baker, Sam and Dave, Percy Sledge, and more. Volumes six (1966–69, including Aretha Franklin, Brook Benton, and others) and seven (including Roberta Flack, Aretha Franklin, and others) are outside of the focus of this book.

Highly recommended is *The R&B Box: Thirty Years of Rhythm and Blues* (Rhino R2 71806). This 1994 compilation gathers 108 sides by 108 different artists who recorded for diverse labels between 1943 and 1972. There is Ruth Brown ("Mama"), LaVern Baker ("Tweedlee Dee"),

Charles Brown ("Drifting Blues"), as well as Mabel Scott (with Charles Brown providing piano accompaniment on "Elevator Boogie"), Nellie Lutcher, Percy Mayfield, Johnny Otis, Fats Domino, Louis Jordan, The Ravens, Amos Milburn, and many others (Rhino Records, 10635 Santa Monica Blvd., Los Angeles, CA 90025-4900.)

An appealing assortment of rhythm and blues recordings may be found on *The RCA Victor Blues and Rhythm Revue* (RCA 6279-1-R). Here are lively, stylistically diverse sides by artists who include a post–Charles Brown edition of Johnny Moore's Three Blazers, Lucky Millinder and his orchestra featuring vocalist Anisteen Allen, Lil Green, Little Richard, and others (MG, 1133 Avenue of the Americas, New York, NY 10036).

Magazines that may interest readers include *Living Blues* magazine, a bimonthly covering blues and R&B (from the Center for the Study of Southern Culture, Hill Hall, Room 301, University of Mississippi, University, MS 38677); *Blues and Rhythm: The Gospel Truth,* a British magazine published ten times a year and covering blues, R&B, and gospel music (13 Ingleborough Drive, Morley, Leeds, LS27 9DT England); *Juke Blues,* a British quarterly covering blues and R&B (represented in the United States by Dick Shurman, 3S 321 Winfield Rd., Warrenville, IL 60555; its British address is PO Box 148, London W9 1DY, England); and *Jefferson* from the Scandinavian Blues Association, a quarterly covering blues, R&B, and related styles of music from rock 'n' roll to gospel (Scandinavian Blues Association, Zetterlunds v 90B, 186 51 Vallentuna, Sweden).

Notes

Although most of the information in this book has been obtained from interviews (which I tape-recorded and transcribed) with the artists, the clippings files of the Institute of Jazz Studies at Rutgers University in Newark, New Jersey, have been valuable sources of newspaper and magazine reviews and articles from publications as varied as the *New York Times, Down Beat, Our World,* and *Jet,* as well as press releases and miscellaneous other items helpful in reconstructing artists' careers. Additional background information is from clippings in the library of the New York *Post* and also the Library of the Performing Arts at Lincoln Center, a division of the New York Public Library.

Introduction

Transcriptions of quotations by participants at the Rhythm and Blues Foundation's awards presentation are from my tape-recording of that day's proceedings (November 10, 1989). Information on the foundation was provided by Howell Begle and Suzan Jenkins. Sources for historic data in this chapter concerning the rise of R&B are Ward, Stokes and Tucker, *Rock of Ages* (the statistics on the amount of airplay devoted to different genres in 1953 came from page 85 of that book) and Shaw, *Honkers and Shouters.*

1. Shurman and O'Neal, "'People Like Me,'" 20.
2. Jerry Wexler, liner notes to the 1987 album *The RCA Victor Blues and Rhythm Revue* (RCA Victor 6279-1-R).
3. Brisbane, "Charles Brown," 12.

Chapter 1: Ruth Brown: "Nobody knows you. . . ."

Portions of this material originally appeared in a profile of Brown that I wrote for *Living Blues* (July–August 1990) and in notes I wrote for the CDs *Ruth Brown: Miss Rhythm, Greatest Hits and More* (for which I interviewed Herb Abramson, Nipsey Russell, and Jerry Wexler) and *Ruth Brown: Blues on Broadway.* I interviewed Brown on March 14, 1988, at the office of publicist Henry

Luhrman in New York City and in my car while driving her home afterward; on June 13, 1989, at a recording session at RCA studios in New York City; on July 5 and August 5, 1989, in Brown's dressing room at Broadway's Minskoff Theater and at a nearby restaurant; and February 21, 1990, in her dressing room. She has also provided me with updates into 1995 at a variety of subsequent meetings. Carrie Smith provided helpful insights during a May 8, 1990, interview, and Alan Eichler's input, in various conversations, is also appreciated.

Shaw's interview with Brown in *Honkers and Shouters* was a valuable additional source of information but not of quotations. Feather, "Ruth Brown's Battle Royal," was helpful for clarifying the royalties issue. The conscientious liner notes by Peter Grendysa for the album *Ruth Brown and Her Rhythmakers: Sweet Baby of Mine* were also a boon. I learned additional details from an unsigned feature, "Miss Rhythm," from Lee Hildebrand's liner notes to *Ruth Brown: Have a Good Time,* and from Brown's public radio shows and her guest shots on television talk shows ranging from Joe Franklin's to Johnny Carson's. I'm grateful to Bob Porter for allowing me to hear some out-of-print Brown recordings, including some takes that have never been released, that I could not have found elsewhere, and to the Institute of Jazz Studies for letting me tape copies of other out-of-print recordings.

1. The "Tree of Hope" was a polished tree stump that amateurs traditionally touched for luck, the remnants of a Harlem tree that had stood before the Lafayette Theater and served as a meeting spot for performers who might pass on job tips.

2. Herb Abramson to author, August 3, 1989.

3. Herb Abramson to author, August 3, 1989.

4. Herb Abramson to author, August 3, 1989.

5. At the 1994 Rhythm and Blues Foundation Awards ceremony, Little Richard acknowledged Ruth Brown's influence, explaining that his familiar way of squealing "Lu-cille" came directly from hearing the way she'd squeal a word like "ma-ma."

6. Nipsey Russell to author, August 15, 1989.

7. Jerry Wexler to author, August 2, 1989.

8. Nipsey Russell to author, August 15, 1989.

9. Ed Castleberry, who used to date Brown and was one of the important early black R&B disc jockeys (at WEDR in Birmingham and other stations), recalled (on September 2, 1994) that he realized how popular Ruth Brown was becoming when he found imitators getting work using her billing. They would perform her dynamic numbers in little clubs for fans who didn't know precisely what she looked like. Once Castleberry went to check on one spurious "Ruth Brown" and found the person to be a man in drag.

10. Herb Abramson to author, August 3, 1989.

11. Herb Abramson to author, August 3, 1989.

12. Herb Abramson to author, August 3, 1989.

13. Herb Abramson to author, August 3, 1989.

14. Jesse Stone to author, August 19, 1989.

15. Herb Abramson to author, August 3, 1989.

16. Jerry Wexler to author, August 2, 1989.

17. Begle, "I Smell a Rat," 5.

18. Begle, "I Smell a Rat," 5.

19. For full details on reforms that have been achieved concerning the payment of royalties to R&B performers, see "A Note on the Rhythm and Blues Foundation."

20. Brown had a clear sense of her worth, according to her co-star and friend Carrie Smith. In Deffaa, *Traditionalists and Revivalists in Jazz,* Smith recalled (281) how Brown objected strenuously to *Black and Blue*'s producers when the advertisements that appeared on the sides of New York buses showed attractive young dancers from the show rather than Brown and her costars. The young dancers hadn't been born when Brown had begun paying her dues as a performer in one-nighters across the segregated South. "I rode in the *back* of the bus so these young performers can ride on the *side!*" she reminded the producers.

Chapter 2: Little Jimmy Scott: "Like a motherless child. . . ."

I interviewed Scott at his home in East Orange, New Jersey, on November 21, 1989, and at his home and also while riding into New York City and back on November 22 and December 6, 1989. I learned more from Scott from interviews at his home on November 4, 1991, and during a radio interview by Jon Sanders and myself on WFDU-FM, in Teaneck, New Jersey, on November 8, 1991, and received further updates in occasional chats into 1995. McDonough's extraordinarily thorough and insightful "For Whatever the Reason" was immensely valuable in helping me not only to understand Scott but also to know which questions to ask.

I gained further information from Michael Cuscuna's fine liner notes to Scott's Savoy albums, Billy Vera's liner notes to Scott's Specialty album, and Joel Dorn's liner notes to Scott's Rhino-Atlantic CD, as well as Romero, "Jimmy Scott" and assorted additional pieces by Doc Pomus, Nathan Heard, and others, copies of which I found at the Institute of Jazz Studies. Reig and Berger's *Reminiscing in Tempo* provided useful information on the world of rhythm and blues record producing in general, and Reig's work with Scott in particular.

1. Foxx died on October 11, 1991.

2. Whitburn, *Joel Whitburn's Top R&B Singles 1942–1988,* a standard reference, erroneously credits the vocal to one of Hampton's female vocalists, Irma Curry.

3. Reig and Berger, *Reminiscing in Tempo,* 12.

4. Pomus, "The World of Doc Pomus."

5. Heard, "Remembrances of Little Jimmy Scott." A copy of this highly valuable article was found in the Institute of Jazz Studies clippings file; the publication indicated that the article was derived from a videotape documentary that had been made in 1987, *The Ballad of Little Jimmy Scott.*

6. Heard, "Remembrances of Little Jimmy Scott."

7. Shaw, *Honkers and Shouters*, 358.

8. Joel Dorn, from his liner notes for the CD *Jimmy Scott: Lost and Found*.

9. Ibid.

10. One happy result of Scott's comeback is that numbers from both the 1969 and 1972 Atlantic sessions have been made available on a Rhino-Atlantic CD *Jimmy Scott: Lost and Found* (1993); in addition, an agreement was worked out (thanks to the efforts of Howell Begle) whereby Scott would receive royalty payments for sales from this reissue.

11. Since this chapter was completed, Scott and Earlene Rogers have separated.

Chapter 3: Charles Brown: "I'm driftin' and driftin'. . . ."

I interviewed Brown by telephone on July 13, 1990, with a follow-up in person at S.O.B.'s Club in New York City on February 21, 1991. Alan Eichler and Kathleen Barlow, among others, have helped apprise me of Brown's activities. Valuable printed sources of information (but not direct quotations) were Mazzolini, "Living Blues Interview: Charles Brown," Shaw, *Honkers and Shouters*, and Tosches, *Unsung Heroes of Rock 'n' Roll*.

Also helpful in providing background information were Jerry Wexler's appreciative liner notes to Brown's CD *All My Life* and Harris, *Blues Who's Who*. Although the focus of Shurman and O'Neal, "'People Like Me,'" was naturally on Dixon, it also included useful information on Brown.

Steve Karas, publicity director for the now-defunct Blue Side record label (a division of Upside Records, Inc.) and Joan Myers of Myers Media supplied copies of many articles and reviews relating to Brown. Among the recent ones are two particularly comprehensive and deserving of note: Brisbane, "Charles Brown" and Mark Humphrey's liner notes for *The Complete Aladdin Recordings of Charles Brown*, released by Mosaic Records in 1994. Both provide valuable information, especially concerning his early years.

1. Charles Brown's birth date is usually reported as September 13, 1922; however, his being born in 1920 (Harris, *Blues Who's Who*) would seem more consistent with the fact that he graduated from college in 1942.

2. Schiffman, *Harlem Heyday*, 209.

3. Charles, *Brother Ray*, 45.

4. Shurman and O'Neal, "'People Like Me,'" 20.

5. Harris, *Blues Who's Who*, 76.

6. Brown, "When I Was a Teen-Ager" (a photocopied clipping, without a page number, in the Rutgers Institute of Jazz Studies files).

7. Jerry Wexler, liner notes for the CD *Charles Brown: All My Life*.

8. The publicity department for the Blue Side record label supplied photocopies of reviews of Charles Brown's work cited in this paragraph: Anthony DeCurtis, undated clipping syndicated in the *Los Angeles Times* newspaper network; "KZ," in *The Gavin Report*, February 13, 1987; Don Palmer, *Music*

and Sound Output (February 1987); Ken Tucker, *Philadelphia Inquirer,* February 15, 1987; Jill Pearlman, "Best of the Arts" (n.d., n.p.); Robert Christgau, *Village Voice,* June 10, 1987; and Peter Keepnews, "Jazz Blue Notes," *Billboard,* May 16, 1987.

9. Morse, "For Charles Brown and Bonnie Raitt," B1.

10. Myers Media supplied photocopics of articles cited in this paragraph: Sheila Rogers, "Random Notes," *Rolling Stone,* September 20, 1990, and Alan di Perna, "Jazzin' the Blues with Charles Brown," *Musician* (April 1991): 80.

Chapter 4: Floyd Dixon: "Hard living alone. . . ."

I interviewed Dixon at his home in Los Angeles and at a nearby restaurant on February 14, 1991, with subsequent questions answered by mail and further updates (into 1995) provided by his manager, Kathleen Barlow. Barlow (who also was present, occasionally contributing comments, when I interviewed Dixon) has been exceptionally helpful in providing discographical data, background information, recordings, and photographs that otherwise would have been almost impossible to obtain. I learned a great deal, too, from Billy Vera's lengthy on-air interview with Dixon at KCRW-FM, Santa Monica, California (October 20, 1990), a tape of which was supplied by Barlow. Highly valuable sources of information (but not quotations of Dixon) were Mazzolini, "Living Blues Interview: Floyd Dixon" and a sidebar, Shurman and O'Neal, "'People Like Me.'" Harris, in *Blues Who's Who,* provided additional details on Dixon's career, which has not received the degree of documentation that it should.

1. Shaw, *Honkers and Shouters,* 231.

2. Mazzolini, "Living Blues Interview: Floyd Dixon," 14.

3. Mazzolini, "Living Blues Interview: Floyd Dixon," 14.

4. Jonas Bernholm, liner notes to the album *Floyd Dixon: Empty Stocking Blues.*

5. Jonas Bernhold, liner notes to the album *Floyd Dixon: Empty Stocking Blues.*

6. Norris, "Dave Alexander," 18; Harris, *Blues Who's Who,* 154.

7. It was a matter of considerable satisfaction to Dixon when the Rhythm and Blues Foundation presented him with its Pioneer Award in 1993. The recognition by his peers—not to mention the highly welcome cash grant— helped soothe memories of past injustices.

Chapter 5: LaVern Baker: "Where ya been so long?"

I interviewed Baker on March 2, 1990, in the office of Myers Media in New York City, and on June 29, 1990, in Baker's dressing room at Broadway's Minskoff Theater. I asked follow-up questions on December 19, 1991, at a New York restaurant. Marilynn LeVine, publicist for *Black and Blue,* was present for part of the second interview and also helped fill in details. I've learned further details, and have received updates on Baker, from Alan Eichler (who worked for a while as her manager), Ruth Brown, and Suzan Jenkins.

Among many articles about Baker, I found Milward, "Everything's Just Jim Dandy," and McGarvey, "Tweedle Dee!" particularly valuable. I learned things, too, from Robins, "Lavern Baker Back in Town," from "The Tweedlee-Dee Girl," and from "Tweedlee Dee Girl," as well as from Tosches's liner notes for *LaVern Baker: Soul on Fire—The Best of LaVern Baker*. Buddy Morrow provided me with information regarding the practice of covering records in an interview on December 5, 1990. In *Cry*, Whiteside offers valuable information on Baker's relationship with Ray, as well as on the rhythm and blues scene generally.

I owe extra thanks to Robert Pruter, who provided articles and shared generously of his knowledge of Baker's career and the musical scene in her home city of Chicago. The chapter is much stronger thanks to his considerable expertise regarding R&B.

1. LaVere, "Memphis Minnie," 5.

2. The quotes from disc jockey Al Benson, *The Pittsburgh Courier*'s Phil Waddell, and bandleader Maurice King appear in promotional material (from either 1952 or early 1953, because it says that Baker records exclusively for King Records and is booked exclusively by the Gale Agency) found in the Rutgers Institute of Jazz Studies files.

3. Jackie Wilson was another R&B star who got his start at the Flame Show Bar (a few years after Baker and Ray) and cited Jolson as an influence. The influence was readily discernible in his phrasing as well as in his showmanship. He once recorded a whole album in tribute to Jolson.

4. Promotional material (from either 1952 or early 1953, because it says that Baker records exclusively for King Records and is booked exclusively by the Gale Agency) found in the Rutgers Institute of Jazz Studies files.

5. This is not to imply that all who have voiced concerns over the content of songs were racists or prudes, although a number were. Rhythm and blues songs typically had a more positive, accepting, and healthier attitude toward sex than traditional Tin Pan Alley songs. Part of their appeal to white teens growing up during the sexually repressive fifties was their implicit message that sex should be treated more naturally than the establishment maintained. I don't find anything threatening in 1950s' R&B songs; society's sexual mores needed to be loosened. I do agree with those who argue that a number of songs since then have gone too far, encouraging an unhealthy trivialization of sex and contributing to problems like the spread of sexually transmitted diseases.

6. Marc Jennings quoted in Ward, Stokes, and Tucker, *Rock of Ages*, 105.

7. Bob Shad to Arnold Shaw, quoted in Hemming and Hajdu, *Discovering Great Singers of Classic Pop*, 192.

8. "The Tweedlee-Dee Girl," *Our World*, June 1955, 47–48; "Tweedlee Dee Girl," *Ebony*, April 1956, 106, Rutgers Institute of Jazz Studies files.

9. The song, of course, became a staple of her live appearances. The dancer

in the number told me in 1994 that Baker was viewed by everyone who toured with her as a strong, street-smart woman. He said that she carried a razor blade concealed in a cork, which she'd reportedly put to highly effective use when one man had tried to take unwanted sexual liberties.

10. Milward, "Everything's Just Jim Dandy," 62.

11. She has recently recorded CDs for Rhino Records and DRG Records.

Chapter 6: Jimmy Witherspoon: "How long blues?"

Portions of this material originally appeared in a profile of Witherspoon I wrote for *Living Blues* (September–October 1990). Witherspoon and I spoke briefly backstage at the B.A.M. Majestic Theater in Brooklyn on May 28, 1989. The bulk of the interview was subsequently conducted by telephone on May 30, 1989, with some follow-up conversation on September 10, 1991, at Condon's, a club in New York City, and at other club appearances since then, up through 1994, with additional updates provided by Witherspoon's manager, Abby Hoffer. Valuable sources of information (but not quotations) were: Norvarro and Joseph, "Living Blues Interview: Jimmy Witherspoon" and Hess, "Living Blues Interview: Jimmy Witherspoon"; the interview with Witherspoon in Dance, *The World of Count Basie*, and the interview with Brown in Shaw, *Honkers and Shouters*. I learned additional details from Oliver, *Blues off the Record*; Welding, "Spoon, an Informal Portrait"; Welding, "Jimmy Witherspoon"; Feather, "Blindfold Test"; and Harris, *Blues Who's Who*.

1. Tynan, "Caught in the Act," 61.

2. Welding, "Jimmy Witherspoon," 44.

3. Welding, "Jimmy Witherspoon," 31.

4. Albert King died on December 21, 1992.

5. I don't agree with Witherspoon that performers such as Taj Mahal are necessarily "bringing down" blacks by using a down-home manner of speaking. At least since the seventies, a number of linguists have acknowledged the legitimacy of black dialect as a variant form of English, emphasizing its grammatical consistency and dispelling the notion that blacks employing it are simply "making mistakes." I can also appreciate Witherspoon's desire, by dressing sharply and using language well, to offer a more urbane and sophisticated image and yet not loose touch with the honesty of the blues.

6. I once saw Witherspoon stop a performance because he was so dissatisfied with the sound of his voice that night. He handed the club owner one of his tapes and suggested the club play that for listeners instead. Generally, however, he says that singing is easier for him today than in his youth.

Bibliography

Albertson, Chris. *Bessie*. New York: Stein and Day, 1985.

Balliett, Whitney. *American Musicians: Fifty-six Portraits in Jazz*. New York: Oxford University Press, 1986.

Basie, Count (as told to Albert Murray). *Good Morning Blues: The Autobiography of Count Basie*. New York: Random House, 1985.

Begle, Howell. "I Smell a Rat: Royalty Practices of Classic R&B Recording Companies." *Rhythm and Blues Foundation News* 4 (October 1994): 5–7.

Berry, Jason, Jonathan Foose, and Tad Jones. *Up from the Cradle of Jazz: New Orleans Music since World War II*. Athens: University of Georgia Press, 1986.

Bogle, Donald. *Blacks in American Films and Television: An Encyclopedia*. New York: Garland Publishing, 1988.

Brisbane, John Anthony. "Charles Brown." *Living Blues* 25 (November-December 1994): 10–29.

Bruyninckx, Walter. *Sixty Years of Recorded Jazz, 1917–1977*. Mechelen, Belgium: n.p., 1978.

Case, Brian, and Stan Britt. *The Harmony Illustrated Encyclopedia of Jazz*. 3d ed. Revised and updated by Chrissie Murray. New York: Harmony Books, 1987.

Charles, Ray, and David Ritz. *Brother Ray: Ray Charles' Own Story*. New York: Dial Press, 1978.

Charters, Samuel B. *The Blues Makers*. New York: Da Capo Press, 1991.

———. *The Legacy of the Blues: Arts and Lives of Twelve Great Bluesmen*. New York: Da Capo Press, 1977.

Chilton, John. *Who's Who of Jazz*. 4th ed. New York: Da Capo Press, 1985.

Clayton, Buck, and Nancy Miller Elliott. *Buck Clayton's Jazz World*. New York: Oxford University Press, 1987.

Collier, James Lincoln. *Duke Ellington*. New York: Oxford University Press, 1987.

Cook, Bruce. *Listen to the Blues*. New York: Charles Scribner's Sons, 1973.

Dance, Helen Oakley. *Stormy Monday: The T-Bone Walker Story*. New York: Da Capo Press, 1990.

Dance, Stanley. *The World of Count Basie*. New York: Charles Scribner's Sons, 1980.

———. *The World of Duke Ellington*. New York: Charles Scribner's Sons, 1970.

———. *The World of Swing*. New York: Charles Scribner's Sons, 1974.

Dannen, Frederic. *Hit Men: Power Brokers and Fast Money Inside the Music Business*. New York: Random House, 1991.

Deffaa, Chip. "The Blues Is Nothing but Personal: Jimmy Witherspoon." *Living Blues* 21 (September-October 1990): 17–19.

———. "I'll Come Back Someday: The Grand Reemergence of Ruth Brown." *Living Blues* 21 (July-August 1990): 14–17.

———. *Swing Legacy*. Metuchen: Scarecrow Press and the Institute of Jazz Studies, Rutgers University, 1989.

———. *Traditionalists and Revivalists in Jazz*. Metuchen: Scarecrow Press and the Institute of Jazz Studies, Rutgers University, 1993.

———. *Voices of the Jazz Age: Profiles of Eight Vintage Jazzmen*. Urbana: University of Illinois Press, 1990.

Dixon, Robert M. W., and John Godrich. *Recording the Blues*. New York: Stein and Day, 1970.

Eberly, Philip K. *Music in the Air*. New York: Hastings House, 1982.

Ellington, Duke. *Music Is My Mistress*. Garden City: Doubleday, 1973.

Ely, Melvin Patrick. *The Adventures of Amos 'n' Andy: A Social History of an American Phenomenon*. New York: Free Press, 1991.

Feather, Leonard. "Blindfold Test." *Down Beat*, May 25, 1972, 27.

———. *The Encyclopedia of Jazz*. New York: Da Capo Press, 1985.

———. *The Encyclopedia of Jazz in the Sixties*. New York: Da Capo Press, 1986.

———. *From Satchmo to Miles*. Briarcliff Manor: Stein and Day, 1972.

———. "Ruth Brown's Battle Royal." *Los Angeles Times,* July 3, 1988.

Feather, Leonard, and Ira Gitler. *The Encyclopedia of Jazz in the Seventies*. New York: Da Capo Press, 1987.

Ferris, William. *Blues from the Delta*. Garden City: Doubleday, 1978.

Fox, Ted. *Showtime at the Apollo*. New York: Holt, Rinehart and Winston, 1983.

Friedwald, Will. *Jazz Singing: America's Great Voices from Bessie Smith to Bebop and Beyond*. New York: Charles Scribner's Sons, 1990.

Garland, Phyl. *The Sound of Soul*. New York: Pocket Books, 1971.

Gart, Galen, and Roy C. Ames. *Duke/Peacock Records: An Illustrated History with Discography*. Milford, N.H.: Big Nickel Publications, 1990.

George, Nelson. *The Death of Rhythm and Blues*. New York: E. P. Dutton, 1989.

Giddins, Gary. *Satchmo*. New York: Doubleday, 1988.

Gillett, Charlie. *Making Tracks: Atlantic Records and the Growth of a Multi-Billion-Dollar Industry*. New York: E. P. Dutton, 1975.

Gitler, Ira. *Swing to Bop*. New York: Oxford University Press, 1985.

Godrich, John, and Robert M. W. Dixon, comp. *Blues and Gospel Records, 1902–1942*. London: Storyville Publications, 1969.

Gottfried, Martin. *In Person: The Great Entertainers*. New York: Harry N. Abrams, 1985.

Gottlieb, William P. *The Golden Age of Jazz*. New York: Da Capo Press, 1979.

Gourse, Leslie. *Every Day: The Story of Joe Williams*. London: Quartet Books, 1985.

———. *Louis' Children: American Jazz Singers*. New York: Quill, 1984.

———. *Unforgettable: The Life and Mystique of Nat King Cole*. New York: St. Martin's Press, 1991.

Govenar, Alan, and Benny Joseph. *The Early Years of Rhythm and Blues: Focus on Houston*. Houston: Rice University Press, 1990.

Green, Abel, and Joe Laurie, Jr. *Show Biz: From Vaude to Video*. New York: Henry Holt, 1951.

Groia, Philip. *They All Sang on the Corner: New York City's R&B Vocal Groups of the 1950s*. Setauket, N.Y.: Edmond Publishing, 1974.

Guralnick, Peter. *Feel Like Going Home: Portraits in Blues and Rock 'n' Roll*. New York: Outerbridge and Dienstfrey, 1971.

———. *Searching for Robert Johnson*. New York: E. P. Dutton, 1989.

———. *Sweet Soul Music: Rhythm and Blues and the Southern Dream of Freedom*. New York: Harper and Row, 1986.

Hampton, Lionel, with James Haskins. Discography by Vincent Pelote. *Hamp: An Autobiography*. New York: Warner, 1989.

Harris, Sheldon. *Blues Who's Who: A Biographical Dictionary of Blues Singers*. New York: Da Capo Press, 1987.

Haskins, Jim. *The Cotton Club*. New York: New American Library, 1984.

Heard, Nathan C. "Remembrances of Little Jimmy Scott in Newark in the 1950s." *Blue Newark Culture*. 1990.

Hemming, Roy, and David Hajdu. *Discovering Great Singers of Classic Pop*. New York: Newmarket Press, 1991.

Hess, Norbert. "Living Blues Interview: Jimmy Witherspoon. Part 2." *Living Blues*, no. 33 (July-August 1977): 21–24.

Hinkley, David. "This Baker Still Cooks." *New York Daily News*, December 24, 1992, 25.

Holiday, Billie, with William Dufty. *Lady Sings the Blues*. New York: Lancer Books, 1969.

Jaeger, Barbara. "Twenty Years Later, the Lady's Still Singing the Blues." *The Record* [Hackensack, N.J.], December 24, 1992, C1, C5.

Jones, Le Roi. *Black Music*. New York: William Morrow, 1967.

———. *Blues People: Negro Music in White America*. New York: William Morrow, 1963.

Keepnews, Orrin, and Bill Grauer, Jr. *A Pictorial History of Jazz*. New York: Bonanza Books, 1966.

Kernfeld, Barry, ed. *The New Grove Dictionary of Jazz*. New York: Grove's Dictionaries of Music, 1988.

Larkin, Philip. *All What Jazz?* New York: Farrar Straus Giroux, 1985.

LaVere, Steve. "Memphis Minnie." *Living Blues*, no. 14 (Autumn 1973): 5.

Lax, Roger, and Frederick Smith. *The Great Song Thesaurus*. New York: Oxford University Press, 1984.

Ledbitter, Mike, and Neil Slaven. *Blues Records, January 1943 to December 1966*. London: Hanover Books, 1968.

Lissauer, Robert. *Lissauer's Encyclopedia of Popular Music in America, 1888 to the Present*. New York: Paragon House, 1991.

Mazzolini. Tom. *"Living Blues* Interview: Charles Brown." *Living Blues,* no. 27 (May-June 1976): 19–27.

———. *"Living Blues* Interview: Floyd Dixon." *Living Blues,* no. 23 (September-October 1975): 14–20.

Merrill, Hugh. *The Blues Route.* New York: William Morrow, 1990.

McDonough, Jimmy. "For Whatever the Reason: All the Way with Jimmy Scott." *Village Voice* (Winter 1988): 16–24.

McGarvey, Seamus. "Tweedle Dee! It's LaVern Baker!" *Now Dig This* (October 1992).

Milward, John. "Everything's Just Jim Dandy." *Los Angeles Times,* April 14, 1991, 3, 62–63 ["Calendar" section].

"Miss Rhythm." *Our World* (January 1954): 16–19.

Monaco, James, and the editors of Baseline, Inc. *The Encyclopedia of Film.* New York: Perigee Books, 1991.

Morgenstern, Dan (text), and Ole Brask (photographs). *Jazz People.* New York: Harry N. Abrams, 1976.

Morse, Steve. "For Charles Brown and Bonnie Raitt a Legendary Past Is Present Again." *Boston Sunday Globe,* July 22, 1990.

Murray, Albert. *Stomping the Blues.* New York: McGraw-Hill, 1976.

Navarro, Anthony, and Frank Joseph. *"Living Blues* Interviw: Jimmy Witherspoon. Part I." *Living Blues,* no. 33 (July-August 1977): 15–21.

Neff, Robert, and Anthony Connor. *Blues.* Boston: David R. Godine, 1975.

Nite, Norm N. *Rock On: The Illustrated Encyclopedia of Rock 'n' Roll: The Solid Gold Years.* New York: Thomas Y. Crowell, 1974.

Nite, Norm N., with Ralph M. Newman. *Rock On: The Illustrated Encyclopedia of Rock 'n' Roll: The Modern Years, 1964–Present.* New York: Thomas Y. Crowell, 1978.

Norris, John. "Dave Alexander." *Coda,* no. 144 (January-February 1976): 18.

Oliver, Paul. *Blues off the Record: Thirty Years of Blues Commentary.* New York: Hippocrene Books, 1984.

———. *Conversations with the Blues.* New York: Horizon Press, 1965.

———. *The Meaning of the Blues.* New York: Collier Books, 1966.

———. *Screening the Blues.* London: Cassell, 1968.

———. *The Story of the Blues.* Philadelphia: Chilton, 1969.

Oliver, Paul, Max Harrison, and William Bolcom. *The New Grove Gospel, Blues and Jazz.* New York: W. W. Norton, 1986.

Palmer, Robert. *Deep Blues.* New York: Viking, 1981.

Pearson, Nathan W., Jr. *Goin' to Kansas City.* Urbana: University of Illinois Press, 1987.

Pleasants, Henry. *The Great American Popular Singers.* New York: Simon and Schuster, 1974.

Pomus, Doc. "The World of Doc Pomus: `Cookie's Caravan' with DJ Bill Cook." [Source unknown.] In the Institute of Jazz Studies, Rutgers University, Newark, N.J.

Propes, Steve. *Those Oldies but Goodies: A Guide to Fifties' Record Collecting.* New York: Collier Books, 1973.

Pruter, Robert. *Chicago Soul.* Urbana: University of Illinois Press, 1991.

Ramsey, Frederick, Jr. *Been Here and Gone.* New Brunswick: Rutgers University Press, 1969.

Ramsey, Frederick, Jr., and Charles Edward Smith, eds. *Jazzmen.* New York: Limelight Editions, 1985.

Reig, Teddy, with Edward M. Berger. *Reminiscing in Tempo: The Life and Times of a Jazz Hustler.* Metuchen: Scarecrow Press and the Institute of Jazz Studies, Rutgers University, 1990.

Robins, Wayne. "LaVern Baker Back in Town." *Newsday,* February 23, 1990.

Romero, Michele. "Jimmy Scott: His Break Came at Sixty Five." *Entertainment Weekly,* June 24–July 1, 1994, 68.

Rust, Brian. *Jazz Records, 1897–1942.* Chigwell, England: Storyville Publications, 1982.

Sackheim, Eric, comp. *The Blues Line: A Collection of Blues Lyrics from Leadbelly to Muddy Waters.* New York: Schirmer Books, 1975.

Sanjek, Russell. *From Print to Plastic: Publishing and Promoting America's Popular Music (1900–1980).* New York: Institute for Studies in American Music, Conservatory of Music, Brooklyn College of the City University of New York, 1983.

Schiffman, Jack. *Harlem Heyday.* Buffalo: Prometheus Books, 1984.

Schuller, Gunther. *The Swing Era.* New York: Oxford University Press, 1989.

Shaw, Arnold. *Black Popular Music in America.* New York: Schirmer Books, 1986.

———. *52nd Street: The Street of Jazz.* New York: Da Capo Press, 1977.

———. *Honkers and Shouters: The Golden Years of Rhythm and Blues.* New York: Collier Books, 1978.

———. *The Rockin' Fifties: The Decade That Transformed the Pop Music Scene.* New York: Hawthorn Books, 1974.

———. *The World of Soul: Black America's Contribution to the Pop Music Scene.* New York: Cowles, 1970.

Shirley, Kay, ed. Annotated by Frank Driggs. *The Book of the Blues.* New York: Leeds Music, 1963.

Shurman, Dick, and Jim O'Neal. "'People Like Me': Floyd Dixon on Record." *Living Blues,* no. 23 (September-October 1975): 20–21.

Simon, George T. *The Big Bands.* New York: Schirmer Books, 1981.

———. *Simon Says: The Sights and Sounds of the Swing Era, 1935–1955.* New York: Galahad Books, 1971.

Southern, Eileen. *The Music of Black Americans: A History.* New York: W. W. Norton, 1971.

Stambler, Irwin. *The Encyclopedia of Pop, Rock and Soul.* New York: St. Martin's Press, 1974.

Stearns, Marshall. *The Story of Jazz.* New York: Mentor Books, 1958.

Stearns, Marshall, and Jean Stearns. *Jazz Dance.* New York: Schirmer Books, 1968.

Stewart-Baxter, Derrick. *Ma Rainey and the Classic Blues Singers.* New York: Stein and Day, 1970.

Stokes, W. Royal. *The Jazz Scene: An Informal History from New Orleans to 1990.* New York: Oxford University Press, 1991.

Titon, Jeff Todd. *Early Downhome Blues: A Musical and Cultural Analyis.* Urbana: University of Illinois Press, 1979.

Tosches, Nick. *Unsung Heroes of Rock 'n' Roll: The Birth of Rock in the Wild Years Before Elvis.* New York: Harmony Books, 1991.

"The Tweedlee-Dee Girl." *Our World* (June 1955): 47–48.

"The Tweedlee Dee Girl." *Ebony* 14 (April 1956): 106–8.

Tynan, John. "Caught in the Act: Jimmy Witherspoon–Paul Horn Qunitet." *Down Beat,* November 26, 1959, 61.

Welding, Pete. "Jimmy Witherspoon." *Down Beat,* December 7, 1961, 44.

———. "Jimmy Witherspoon." *Down Beat,* January 3, 1963, 31.

Ward, Ed, Geoffrey Stokes, and Ken Tucker. *Rock of Ages: The Rolling Stone History of Rock and Roll.* Englewood Cliffs: Prentice-Hall, 1986.

Welding, Pete. "Jimmy Witherspoon: There'll Always Be the Blues." *Down Beat,* July 13, 1967.

———. "'Spoon, an Informal Portrait." *Down Beat,* November 22, 1962, 22–23.

Wexler, Jerry, and David Ritz. *Rhythm and the Blues: A Life in American Music.* New York: Alfred A. Knopf, 1993.

Whitburn, Joel. *Pop Memories, 1890–1954.* Menomonee Falls, Wis.: Record Research, 1986.

———. *Pop Singles Annual, 1955–1990.* Menomonee Falls, Wis.: Record Research, 1991.

———. *Top Pop Albums, 1955–1985.* Menomonee Falls, Wis.: Record Research, 1985.

———. *Top Pop Singles, 1955–1986.* Menomonee Falls, Wis.: Record Research, 1987.

———. *Top R&B Singles, 1942–1988.* Menomonee Falls, Wis.: Record Research, 1988.

Whitcomb, Ian. *After the Ball: Pop Music from Rag to Rock.* Baltimore: Penguin Books, 1974.

———. *Rock Odyssey: A Musician's Chronicle of the Sixties.* Garden City: Doubleday, 1983.

Whiteside, Jonny. *Cry: The Johnnie Ray Story.* New York: Barricade Books, 1994.

Wiener, Jon. *Come Together: John Lennon in His Time.* Urbana: University of Illinois Press, 1991.

Index

Easely, Bill, 60
East West record label, 123
Ebb record label, 164
Ebony magazine, 34, 186, 197
Ebony magazine Hall of Fame Award, 238
Eckstine, Billy: big band of, 33; gigs with
    Ruth Brown, 36, 44, 51; influence on
    Charles Brown, 108; influence on Lit-
    tle Jimmy Scott, 80; popularity of, 116,
    119; singing of "Drifting Blues" by,
    112; success of, 163
Eddie Williams and His Brown Buddies,
    149, 253, 254
Edison, Harry "Sweets," 188, 232
"Ed Sullivan Show" (television show),
    196, 229
Edwards, Teddy, 257
Eichler, Alan, 179
Eisenhower, Dwight D., 10
Eldridge, Roy, 230, 256
electric blues music, 128
"Elevator Boogie," 121, 260
Ellington, Duke, 27, 116, 184, 220; band
    of, 26, 108
Ellis, Perry, 22
Ellis, Ray, 188
"Embraceable You," 108, 109
"Empty Bed Blues," 191, 192, 255
"Empty Stocking Blues" (Floyd Dixon,
    Mark Hurley, and Johnny Moore), 154
Epic/OKeh/Legacy record label, 255
Ertegun, Ahmet: assistance to LaVern
    Baker, 12; comments on Ruth Brown,
    24; contract offer to Floyd Dixon by,
    160; "discovery" of Ruth Brown by,
    27–28; and fortieth anniversary cele-
    bration for Atlantic Records, 206; gold
    disc presented to Ruth Brown by, 43;
    musical taste of, 42; recordings by La-
    Vern Baker produced by, 187, 188,
    201, 214; and royalty payments, 57,
    58, signing of Ruth Brown by, 29;
    songs by, 35, 181. *See also* Atlantic
    Records
Ertegun, Neshui, 97, 187, 191
Ervin, Frankie, 118
Evans, Jimmy, 85
Evenin' Blues (Jimmy Witherspoon), 256
The Everly Brothers, 196, 197, 215
"Everybody Needs Somebody" (Fred

Mendelsohn, Rose Marie McCoy, and
    Howard Biggs), 87, 247
"Everybody's Somebody's Fool," 82, 89,
    91, 95, 98, 246, 247
"Every Little Bit Hurts," 250
"Every Time It Rains, I Think of You," 57
"Every Time We Say Goodbye," 248
Evidence Music, 256
"Evil Gal Blues," 26
Exclusive Records, 115, 121
"Exodus," 248

Fabian, 45
Faddis, Jon, 99
Falling in Love Is Wonderful (Little Jimmy
    Scott), 96
Fantasy Records: recordings by Floyd
    Dixon for, 170, 253; recordings by Jim-
    my Witherspoon for, 240, 255, 256,
    257; recordings by Little Jimmy Scott
    on, 246–47; recordings by Ruth Brown
    for, 16, 63, 65, 244–45
Far Out Productions, 234
Fat Tuesday's (New York City), 13
Federal Artists (talent agency), 117
Federal record label, 40, 228
Feelin' the Spirit (Jimmy Witherspoon),
    258
Feinstein, Michael, 62
Feld, Irvin, 197, 198
Festival of the Arts (University of Chica-
    go, 1976), 168
"Fever," 13
Fields, Dorothy, 48
Fields, Frank, 251
First Baptist Church (Gurdon, Ark.), 218
Fischer, William, 97
Fisher, Carl, 66
Fisher, Eddie, 38
Fishman, Ed, 117
Fitzgerald, Ella: at the Apollo Theatre,
    25; influence on Charles Brown, 108;
    influence on LaVern Baker, 175; in-
    fluence on Little Jimmy Scott, 80; in-
    fluence on Ruth Brown, 23, 33, 68
The Five Keys, 46, 124, 196
"Five-Ten-Fifteen Hours," 33–34, 38, 57,
    63, 67, 195, 244
"Five-Ten-Fifteen Minutes" (Rudy
    Toombs), 34

Books in the Series Music in American Life

Only a Miner: Studies in Recorded Coal-Mining Songs
Archie Green

Great Day Coming: Folk Music and the American Left
R. Serge Denisoff

John Philip Sousa: A Descriptive Catalog of His Works
Paul E. Bierley

The Hell-Bound Train: A Cowboy Songbook   *Glenn Ohrlin*

Oh, Didn't He Ramble: The Life Story of Lee Collins, as
Told to Mary Collins   *Edited by Frank J. Gillis and
John W. Miner*

American Labor Songs of the Nineteenth Century
Philip S. Foner

Stars of Country Music: Uncle Dave Macon to Johnny
Rodriguez   *Edited by Bill C. Malone and Judith McCulloh*

Git Along, Little Dogies: Songs and Songmakers of the
American West   *John I. White*

A Texas-Mexican *Cancionero:* Folksongs of the Lower
Border   *Américo Paredes*

San Antonio Rose: The Life and Music of Bob Wills
Charles R. Townsend

Early Downhome Blues: A Musical and Cultural Analysis
Jeff Todd Titon

An Ives Celebration: Papers and Panels of the Charles Ives
Centennial Festival-Conference
Edited by H. Wiley Hitchcock and Vivian Perlis

Sinful Tunes and Spirituals: Black Folk Music to the Civil
War   *Dena J. Epstein*

Joe Scott, the Woodsman-Songmaker   *Edward D. Ives*

Jimmie Rodgers: The Life and Times of America's Blue
Yodeler   *Nolan Porterfield*

Early American Music Engraving and Printing: A History
of Music Publishing in America from 1787 to 1825, with
Commentary on Earlier and Later Practices
Richard J. Wolfe

Sing a Sad Song: The Life of Hank Williams
Roger M. Williams

Long Steel Rail: The Railroad in American Folksong
Norm Cohen

Resources of American Music History: A Directory of Source Materials from Colonial Times to World War II   *D. W. Krummel, Jean Geil, Doris J. Dyen, and Deane L. Root*

Tenement Songs: The Popular Music of the Jewish Immigrants   *Mark Slobin*

Ozark Folksongs   *Vance Randolph; edited and abridged by Norm Cohen*

Oscar Sonneck and American Music   *Edited by William Lichtenwanger*

Bluegrass Breakdown: The Making of the Old Southern Sound   *Robert Cantwell*

Bluegrass: A History   *Neil V. Rosenberg*

Music at the White House: A History of the American Spirit   *Elise K. Kirk*

Red River Blues: The Blues Tradition in the Southeast   *Bruce Bastin*

Good Friends and Bad Enemies: Robert Winslow Gordon and the Study of American Folksong   *Debora Kodish*

Fiddlin' Georgia Crazy: Fiddlin' John Carson, His Real World, and the World of His Songs   *Gene Wiggins*

America's Music: From the Pilgrims to the Present Revised Third Edition   *Gilbert Chase*

Secular Music in Colonial Annapolis: The Tuesday Club, 1745–56   *John Barry Talley*

Bibliographical Handbook of American Music   *D. W. Krummel*

Goin' to Kansas City   *Nathan W. Pearson, Jr.*

"Susanna," "Jeanie," and "The Old Folks at Home": The Songs of Stephen C. Foster from His Time to Ours Second Edition   *William W. Austin*

Songprints: The Musical Experience of Five Shoshone Women   *Judith Vander*

"Happy in the Service of the Lord": Afro-American Gospel Quartets in Memphis   *Kip Lornell*

Paul Hindemith in the United States   *Luther Noss*

"My Song Is My Weapon": People's Songs, American Communism, and the Politics of Culture, 1930–50   *Robbie Lieberman*

Chosen Voices: The Story of the American Cantorate   *Mark Slobin*